The Army of Frederick the Great

The Army of Frederick the Great

CHRISTOPHER DUFFY

HIPPOCRENE
BOOKS, INC.

Hippocrene Books, Inc.
171 Madison Avenue,
New York, N.Y. 10016

Library of Congress Catalog Card Number 74-80439
ISBN 0-88254-277-X

Contents

HISTORIC ARMIES AND NAVIES

GENERAL EDITOR: *Christopher Duffy*

in preparation

The Army of the Second Empire   *Richard Holmes*
The D-Day Armies   *E. Belfield*
The Indian Army   *I. A. Heathcote*
The Jacobite Army of the '45   *Count Nikolai Tolstoy*
Maria Theresa's Army   *Christopher Duffy*
Nelson's Navy   *Michael Orr*

Illustrations

Line Drawings

Maps

Diagrams

Cartographical drawings by Peter Leath
Line drawings by the author

Introduction

On the morning of 5 November 1757 King Frederick II of Prussia and his army of 22,000 men faced a host of more than 40,000 French and Germans near the little village of Rossbach. By the time his work was done Frederick had swept the enemy from the field and rendered 10,000 of their troops *hors de combat*, losing just 548 of his own men in the process.

Here was a very potent military machine indeed. It was more. It was one of the most powerful forces at work in the shaping of modern Europe. Frederick's conquests and victories brought Prussia into the ranks of the first powers of Europe, and set Prussia (though Frederick had never foreseen it) on the path of aggression that was going to lead to the temporary unification of a Prussianised Germany, and so to the ruin and partition of 1945.

It was in response to the Prussian threat that Frederick's opponent, the gracious Maria Theresa of Austria, set to work to remodel the Habsburg empire into a unitary state. The France of Louis XV, less fortunate, lost moral and financial credit in the fight against Prussia, rendering the task of reform all the more difficult in the last decades of the *ancien régime*. Europe as a whole was mightily impressed with what Frederick had done, and soldiers concluded that his secret resided in a perfection of drill, turn-out and discipline – the 'spit and polish' ethos which has moulded armies until the present day.

It is an interesting exercise to take apart the mechanism of the Frederician army and examine the components in some detail, remembering all the time that the machine was propelled by human effort. The memoirs and journals of the time bring back to life the experiences (some of them quite appalling) of the rank-and-file, and present the Prussian officer as a more complicated and, on the whole, a more sympathetic creature than the popular stereotype. Students of military psychology will find here some object lessons in what may be accomplished by an army that is held on its course by fear and constraint rather than 'inner leadership'.

The angular and snuff-bedaubed figure of Frederick is never far distant. We must resist the temptation to load his crooked back with all the ills of Prussian militarism, and yet Old Fritz remains one of those few people who show themselves to be ever less appealing upon closer acquaintance. If not an early exponent of 'Hun frightfulness', he was certainly capable of carrying out his frightful business in a Hunnish kind of way.

C. D.

CAESAR CROSSED THE RUBICON AND TOOK
ROME. DID HE DO IT ALL BY HIMSELF?

Bertolt Brecht

1

The Land, the Age, the Man

The Hohenzollerns: there was something peculiarly acquisitive about the family from the beginning. It drew its very name from the activities of its earliest recorded ancestors, a line of rapacious barons who exacted tolls (*Zollern*) from people travelling through the Swabian hills.

Early in the fifteenth century one of the Hohenzollerns, a certain Friedrich, was canny enough to advance a loan to the hard-up Elector of Brandenburg, who was casting about for money to finance his bid to be chosen Emperor of Germany. The gamble paid off for both parties. Not only did the candidature succeed, but the grateful new Emperor rewarded Friedrich by appointing him Elector of Brandenburg in his place.

Thus the family was transplanted from its home in south-west Germany to the inhospitable north-east, where the Mark ('borderland') of Brandenburg stretched between the lower reaches of the Elbe and the Oder in a dreary plain of pinewoods, marsh and sandy levels.

The new masters of Brandenburg battered the local nobility into submission, then embarked on a policy of peaceful accretion, gradually gathering in one after another of the small territories which were grouped around the original core of the Mark. In 1618 the elector was lucky enough to inherit the extensive province of East Prussia, which was separated from the main body of the Hohenzollern states by the Polish territory of West Prussia.

The Hohenzollerns also turned their ambitions towards the area of the lower Rhine, where in 1666 they were confirmed as the rightful owners of the territories of Cleves, Mark and Ravensburg. And so by the second half of the seventeenth century the Hohenzollerns owned three inconveniently separated chunks of land – the Brandenburg heartland in the middle, the territory of East Prussia eastwards along the Baltic coast, and finally Prussian Westphalia, which was stranded in western Germany.

The Hohenzollern territories were therefore badly articulated even by the standards obtaining in the 'Germany' of that time, which was a geographical expression covering a chaos of independent duchies, principalities and cities that were grouped together under the nominal authority of the Emperor. This office was usually held by the reigning head of the Austrian house of Habsburg. Furthermore, the Hohenzollern lands in many ways lagged behind the social and economic development of the rest of Germany. The writ of ancient Rome had never run as far east as the Elbe, let alone the Oder, and in more modern times the subjects of the Hohenzollerns were numbered among the last of the European peoples to fall under the warming, civilising influence which radiated from the court of the French 'Sun King' Louis XIV. The population was a mixture of German colonists and Slavonic tribesmen, and the aristocrats an impoverished and ignorant squirearchy, again flavoured with a dash of the Slavonic and more specifically the Polish. 'Though these families became thoroughly Germanised in habit and outlook, the censorious might claim to see the marks of a distinctive origin in a haughtiness that was crude beyond the average and in their occasional tendency to wild extravagance.'[1] Polish blood was the origin of all those Prussian names ending in '-ske' or '-schke'.

While the aristocrats of western Germany began to find attractive opportunities for exercising their talents in the capacity of lawyers, administrators or businessmen, the 'Prussian' squirearchy remained fundamentally agricultural, generation upon generation of *Junkers* who spurred on their serf-like peasantry to ever greater efforts to cultivate those remote and sandy estates. This was a natural officer class, which was accustomed to enforcing its will with fist, stick and tongue, and which was all the more conscious of its authority from its closeness to its underlings in manners and blood. An eighteenth-century Austrian officer wrote: 'I respect the poor country nobility. It is this class which makes the composition of the Prussian army so excellent.'[2]

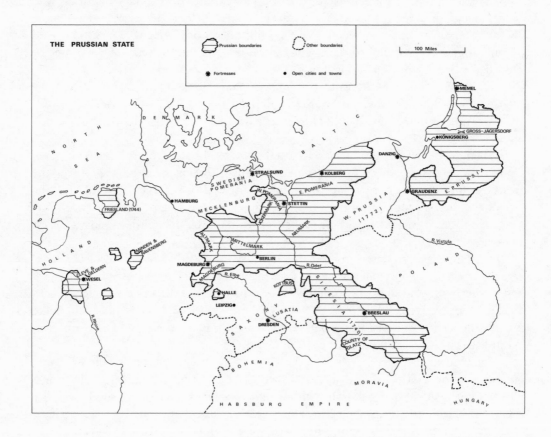

The Reformation too played a role in the subjugation of the north German peasantry. The Church (and to some extent the Almighty Himself) was deprived of independent authority, and the sovereign was able to channel all the subjects' devotion through himself.

The further direction of the Hohenzollern policies was profoundly influenced by the work of Frederick William, 'The Great Elector', who ruled from 1640 to 1688. Frederick William was enraged by the sight of those armies of Swedes and Imperialists which had tramped backwards and forwards over the unresisting soil of Brandenburg during the destructive Thirty Years War, and he conceived the ambition of building his patrimony into one of the premier military powers of Europe. He was sure that this was the only way he could deter his neighbours from treating his scattered and impoverished domains in the same cavalier fashion as in the past.

The penalties were heavy. Since Brandenburg-Prussia owned nothing like the resources of powers like France or Austria, the Great Elector had to direct all the energies and values of his state towards military ends. He broke the power of the *Stände* (noble assemblies), he reorganised the finances and he began to colonise and reclaim the waste-lands – all with the ultimate military purpose. Even the most pacifically minded of his counsellors of state might find himself transmuted overnight into the ferocious-sounding *Kriegsrat* (councillor of war).

The prowess of the new Brandenburg army was displayed in a spectacular manner when the Great Elector beat the Swedes in the open field at Fehrbellin (18 June 1675), and Frederick William left his heirs the legacy of a smallish but excellent force of 18,000 men.

Under the Great Elector's immediate successor the state of Brandenburg-Prussia lived through a quarter-century of bewigged, bejewelled magnificence, not at all in keeping with the spartan singlemindedness that later German historians attributed to the House of Hohenzollern. Still, the gentleman in question, the Elector Frederick, had some important achievements to his credit. He persuaded the Emperor to raise him in 1701 to the authority of King of Prussia (or more pedantically King in Prussia, ie East Prussia), and he encouraged young officers like Prince Leopold of Anhalt-Dessau to reform the army on the best modern lines. King Frederick departed this life in characteristic style in 1713. He was consigned to the tomb amid scenes of baroque extravagance, leaving behind heavy debts, a sumptuous collection of jewellery, a wealth of ornamental court functionaries – and an efficient army of 40,000 troops.

As if deliberately breaking with his late father's style of life King Frederick William I (1713–40) cultivated to an extreme those highly prized 'Prussian' qualities of directness, hard work and plain living. He despised all learning beyond the level of the bare literacy that was needed to master his military regulations. He transformed the royal parks of Berlin and Potsdam into parade grounds, and the dark and poky rooms of the palaces reverberated with the endless *slam, slam, slam* of the platoon fire of the troops who were exercising outside, a sound occasionally broken by a distinctive crash and tinkle when one of the ramrods was fired away by accident and came flying through the windows.

In his creative work for the Prussian army Frederick William's achievement far surpassed the activity of his more famous son, Frederick the Great. Stout, bad-tempered Frederick William was the man who regularised the recruiting of the army at home and abroad, who cemented the peculiar bond between the King of Prussia and his officer corps, who set up the first Prussian hussars, who created the Prussian armaments industry and devised the patterns of the muskets and swords that Prussian soldiers were to carry for most of the remainder of the century. An event of great symbolic importance was the *Stilbruch* (break in style) of 1718, when Frederick William deliberately drew back from the manners, fashions and outlook of Frenchified Europe, and invented a sober and distinctively Prussian style of military dress.

Foreign craftsmen and colonists were encouraged to come to Brandenburg-Prussia in their thousands, which helped to develop the resources of the old Hohenzollern state,

Frederick the Great wearing the full regimentals of the First Battalion of the Garde (before 1752). Blue coat with red cuffs and turnbacks and silver rococo brandenbourgs, yellow waist-coat and breeches, hat embroidered in silver and edged with white plumage. He usually wore the much simpler Interims Uniform and in 1721 Frederick William gained full international recognition of his rights over a conquest he had recently made from the Swedes, namely Western Pomerania with the fortress-port of Stettin. This territory was a particularly useful acquisition, for it formed an integral strategic unit with the central Brandenburg heartland (Brandenburg and Eastern Pomerania), and the tough and simple-minded Pomeranians got on very well indeed with their new Prussian masters.

Not only did Frederick William increase the resources of the state in absolute terms, but he augmented the proportion of the revenues which went on military expenditure. Between 1713 and 1732 he devoted between 4 and 5 million thalers each year to his army, and put aside only 1 million per annum to cover all the other costs. By 1740, therefore, Prussia owned the very respectable total of 83,000 troops, which gave Frederick William the fourth largest army in Europe, even though his lands stood at tenth in order of size and only thirteenth in population.

Despite all these warlike preparations, the foreigners could never bring themselves to take Frederick William entirely seriously. To begin with, the man was so transparent and so dutiful that no one could imagine that he would employ his powerful army for any purpose except the common good of the Empire. Thus in 1734 Frederick William sent a contingent of troops to take part in the Emperor's war against the French on the Rhine. There was little glory to be had in this particular confrontation, for the overall commander was the Austrian veteran Prince Eugene of Savoy, 'an honourable relic of olden times', who made no serious attempt to disturb the French in their siege of Philippsburg. All the same it was gratifying when Eugene reported that 'the Prussian troops are the best of the German forces. The rest are pretty well useless'.[3]

Then again there was the unmistakably clownlike aspect of Frederick William's character, as expressed in the daily buffoonery of his 'Tobacco Parliament' and above all in his grotesque obsession with physical size. He judged units and individual officers more by their stature than any other criterion, and he lavished an extravagant attention upon his almost 3,000-strong regiment of giant grenadiers. The smallest of these military freaks measured over six feet in height, while some of the more highly prized specimens came near to attaining an altitude of eight feet.

Odder still was Frederick William's brutal treatment of his family, and above all his barbarity towards his eldest surviving son Crown Prince Frederick, who was born in 1712. Frederick was sensitive, intelligent and slightly built, and under the influence of his mother and his beloved elder sister Wilhelmine the young man's interests turned more and more to the language and arts of France. All of this was calculated to draw down the anger and scorn of the old king. Frederick William subjected his son to endless indignities in the circle of the royal family and the boon companions of the Tobacco Parliament, and even in the presence of foreign dignitaries he did not hesitate to push and pull that drooping figure about and belabour it with his cane.

Crown Prince Frederick made his first direct acquaintance with the manners of the wider world in 1728, when the king took him on a visit to Dresden, the glittering centre of the joint state of Saxony-Poland. Here Frederick was drawn into some complicated intrigues involving a naked lady, a scheming Polish countess and two sets of curtains, and before long his scandalised father had to haul him back home – a paler, wiser and much more excited youth than the one who had set out just one month earlier.

Following a final series of affronts, in 1730 the Crown Prince made an incompetent attempt to escape to freedom in France. He was detected, escorted back under arrest and confined in the stronghold of Küstrin to await court martial as a deserter. For a time the governments of Europe held their breath, wondering whether Frederick William would actually steel himself to kill his own son. In the event the king contented himself with having Frederick's chief accomplice, Lieutenant v. Katte, beheaded in the yard beneath the prince's prison window.

Over the following years Frederick gradually worked his way back into his father's graces. In 1732 he contracted a loveless marriage with Princess Elizabeth of Brunswick-Wolfenbüttel, which gave him at least a degree of independence, and in the same year he was appointed *Chef* (colonel proprietor) of a regiment at Ruppin. Frederick's confidence and physical strength grew as he learnt to enjoy his first detached command, and the bearing and drill of his regiment of Kronprinz began to draw one or two favourable comments from the lips of the old king. Frederick displayed considerable coolness under fire in the Philippsburg campaign of 1734, which advanced the reconciliation still further, and two years later he was allowed to set up a little court of his own at Rheinsberg, near Ruppin.

At Rheinsberg Frederick delighted in the company of officers who had impressed him by their professionalism or their support in the last few harrowing years, veterans like Leopold of Anhalt-Dessau and General Schwerin, as well as his young near-contemporaries Hans v. Winterfeldt and Captain de la Motte Fouqué. It was therefore as a well-formed soldier that Frederick came to the throne of Prussia upon the death of the old king in 1740.

So much for what we may term the 'vertical' influences upon the young Frederick, the inheritance of his Brandenburg-Prussian past. What of the temper of the times, the 'horizontal' context? Here we have to enlist the support of two crude but useful concepts – those of Enlightened Absolutism and Limited War.

Enlightened Absolutism remains the best shorthand label we have for the style of kingship of Frederick and some of his contemporaries. By the 1740s the old mercantile and militarist drive of the reforming monarchies of the seventeenth century was being transmuted into something wider – a notion of rational stewardship according to which the sovereign was guided by the light of Reason to arrange affairs for the greatest good of his subjects. The activity of such a Philosopher King was characterised by a tolerance of religious opinions, reforms in education and law, the rationalisation of the state administration and the raising of the condition of the peasants. The enlightened absolutist was flattered by the attention of men of wit and learning, though he was usually sensible enough not to take their opinions too seriously: in their turn people like Voltaire were drawn to such a sympathetic monarch, believing that it was better to be ruled by a single lion than by a thousand rats of their own kind. Frederick indeed came close to being considered the archetypal enlightened absolutist. His wars were dismissed as a distressing aberration, and the whole of 'enlightened' Europe admired his abhorrence of idleness and superstition, and the way in which he filled out the ranks of his army with mercenaries, leaving the native peasants and craftsmen to get on with their work undisturbed.

The very powers of the enlightened absolutist helped to abate in some degree the inevitable horrors of war. A complete master in his own house, he was largely free of the deadweight of public opinion, and consequently was at perfect liberty to make or break alliances and wage or terminate wars as best suited the needs of his state. However jealous he was of his rights and territories, he was still prepared to look upon the other sovereigns as his 'brothers' and 'sisters' in a closed community of European nations. Catherine of Russia was physically sick when she heard that Louis of France had been executed by his own subjects.

History had shown that the undue preponderance of any one monarchy encouraged the other powers to unite in a chain of hostile alliances, which helped to restore the equilibrium. Even a serious war did not really threaten to disturb the harmony of Europe, for until the 1750s the rival sovereigns knew that when peace came they would merely have to settle the account in the loose change of frontier provinces, Italian duchies or distant colonies. In one sense the Seven Years War (1756–63) offered an exception to the norm, for the state of Brandenburg-Prussia was fighting for its survival, yet even here Frederick's enemies were ready to 'pull their punches' to a surprising degree, doing nothing to close off Frederick's access to Poland, with its resources of grain, remounts, cattle and recruits. In fact the Emperor Francis Stephen was known to have made a thriving personal business of sending supplies to the Prussian army, his public opponent. In 1748 the same gentleman required the British fleet to blockade Genoa, while simultaneously lodging a protest against the British action in his capacity as Grand Duke of Tuscany.

This was an age of aristocratic values, another influence which militated against the vulgar passion of national hatred. French culture and the French language reigned supreme in what Gibbon called 'The Republic of Europe', and the cosmopolitan nobleman of the day cultivated a code of chivalry which emphasised that he owned more in common with the aristocrat of other states than with his own countrymen of common birth. In time of peace the professional soldier could pass from one king's service to another with no stain upon his honour, while even a state of hostilities was considered to be no more than a partial and temporary hindrance to social intercourse.

There were further ways in which these languid, uncaring aristocrats helped to limit the totality of war. In some countries, notably France, they claimed exemption from taxes by right of birth, which drastically reduced the revenues of the state. Furthermore, by their near-monopoly of the officer class they barred the promotion of many an able and energetic *roturier*. Frederick himself excluded all but selected bourgeois from commissioned rank in the field arms.

Thus the sovereign was able to wage war with only a proportion of the material and human resources of his realm, despite his supremacy in all other matters of policy. Rather more creditably there were public men and jurists who recoiled from the horrors which Europe had experienced in the Thirty Years War (1618–48): they wished to hold the civilians at a distance from the scene of war, and let the armies and the kings continue with their rough sports at the minimum inconvenience to the community.

To a greater or lesser extent the educated aristocrat embraced the philosophy of rationalism, which was the cheerful assumption that sheer brainpower was ultimately capable of providing an aesthetically satisfying explanation for everything that was dark and confused. The passions were mistrusted, and form and elegance dominated literature and the arts. There was much in the physical world that was being illuminated by the torches of mechanics and chemistry, and since the calculations of the military engineers had already arrived at a code of siegecraft and fortification, it was natural to ask whether the whole of warfare might not be susceptible to rational analysis of the same kind. Thus the Marshal de Saxe and other people began to look upon battles as messy departures from a well-ordered norm of scientific manoeuvres. We find a characteristic expression in the Saxon *Dienstreglement* of 1752: 'A battle is at once the most important and most dangerous operation of war . . . A great general shows his mastery by attaining the object of his campaign by sagacious and sure manoeuvres, without incurring any risk.' A 'scientific' commander could get the better of the enemy by cutting their lines of communication and dominating the resources of the countryside by his light troops (the Austrians were especially good at this), and he might borrow a leaf from Vegetius and encourage the foe to depart by way of a 'Golden Bridge' he had built for their convenience.

An eighteenth-century commander could find a multitude of reasons and opportunities for evading battle. The army of the time was an indivisible block composed of dozens of regiments. It could be moved over the theatre of war only with excruciating difficulty, and several hours might pass before it could shake itself out from order of march to line of battle, all of which afforded a timid enemy plenty of time to make good his escape. In the eighteenth century a consummated battle therefore represented a seduction rather than a rape.

Once locked in combat the armies proceeded to massacre one another by exchanging cannon shot and volleys of musketry at point-blank range. The experience was invariably distressing for the commanders. What upset them was not so much a humanitarian regard for the soldiers as the knowledge that every casualty represented the loss of something like a three years' investment in rations and the drill-master's time.

To some extent Frederick had to break out of the constraints which held back his contemporaries. In 1740 he snatched the Austrian province of Silesia, trusting that he would be able to enjoy his stolen goods undisturbed. He badly underestimated the resilience of the Austrians, which was why he had to fight through a couple of very dangerous campaigns in 1745 and put up a struggle for outright survival in the Seven Years War.

Thus Frederick had to seek out decisive battles as a matter of principle, for he could not afford a kind of war which allowed his enemies the leisure to bring their superior forces to bear on him. Nobody else of the time made his troops march harder: no one else made a habit of prolonging his campaigns so late into the winter 'closed season' or resuming them quite so early in the spring. Frederick burnt out his mercenary troops in the early campaigns of the Seven Years War, and he had to rely on native soldiers who fought with patriotic 'enthusiasm', which was the least typical of eighteenth-century emotions. And yet, when it was all over, Frederick showed himself so much the man of his time that one of the first things he did was to fill his army up again with foreigners.

Such humanity as Frederick showed to his enemies came close to the marxist definition of the code of aristocratic chivalry, namely an expression of a selfish instinct for class preservation. He displayed precious little mercy for the common soldiers, if they happened to be Saxons or Russians, while his bombardment of Dresden in 1760 rivalled some of the worst barbarities that the Thirty Years War had to show: the notorious destruction of Magdeburg in 1631 at least owned the saving grace of having been a kind of horrible accident.

Thus Frederick of Prussia against his background and his environment. We have seen that after a singularly unpromising start he began to prove himself a fitting heir to the Great Elector and Frederick William I. As a man of the eighteenth century he approached the ideal of the Enlightened Absolutist, though he could scarcely be termed a typical practitioner of Limited War: perhaps his habits of mind were too extreme, or perhaps he ruled a state which was not fundamentally European.

The soldiers of Frederick's time did not have the inclination to try to fit Old Fritz into any such pompous categories. They were aware before anything else of the 'peculiar magic' which 'resided in Frederick's voice, when he wished to win mens' hearts, and that look in his great eyes which inspired fear and trembling whenever he became angry'.[4]

They saw a man who stood about five feet eight inches tall, allowing for the pronounced stoop. The eyes were blue and compelling and the forehead was broad, though the strong nose and the incipient jowels became thinned out with advancing years.

Frederick wore his clothes 'as long a decency will permit; and indeed, sometimes longer'.[5] He appeared in a plain and shabby officer's coat of Prussian blue with red collar and cuffs, or, less commonly, in the elaborate regimentals of the First Battalion of the Garde. The lapels were usually buttoned across (for his spare frame felt the cold keenly), and the whole front, together with the tatty star of the Black Eagle, the cuffs, hands and face were disgustingly daubed and stained with Spanish snuff. He wore a simple sword, and the knot that was wound about the hilt was the one common to the officer corps, of black shot through with silver. The sash was worn outside his coat – a departure from fashion that was dictated by his desire to hide the peculiarity of his shape, with his wide hips and hollow back.

The riding boots were badly creased around the ankles, and Frederick refused to be parted from an especially highly regarded pair of breeches which survived until at least the 1770s, assuming an ever darker hue of black, and becoming increasingly worn from the saddle and the scrabbling of the paws of his whippets.

Frederick clung so faithfully to such ancient garments not just out of meanness, but because 'he still wanted to appear exactly as he had done on the fields of Lobositz, Rossbach, Leuthen and Kunersdorf'.[6] The whole effect was calculated to accentuate the closeness of the bond which united him with his army – a connection that one of his veterans compared with the union of a Scottish chieftain and his clan.[7]

In other lands the armed forces were state institutions which stood under the administration of a special department, but in Frederick's Prussia the army was a private organisation at the immediate disposal of the king. In wartime Frederick pitched his tent in the middle of the camp, and rose as early as four in the morning to tour the regiments and make a start on dealing with the scores or even hundreds of items of correspondence which came to his notice every day. 'His quarters are quite quiet without any noise or hurly-burly,' wrote an Englishman. 'Everything moves like clockwork, and no wonder, as he directs it all himself.'[8]

In time of peace Frederick attached great importance to seeing the army go through its paces in the annual reviews and manoeuvres:

There is a lot of truth in the proverb which says that the horse prospers under the eye of his master. The military (by which I mean the officers) wish to be led on by sentiments of ambition, and nothing inspires this feeling more than the sight of the sovereign and the princes setting an example . . . A general laxness would set in if the regiments were not assembled and exercised frequently in the presence of the master.[9]

Frederick saw to the running of the First Battalion of the Garde as narrowly as any full-time commandant, yet he found the time to make himself acquainted with the character and career of the majority of the officers of his army. He signed all commissions in person, and he admitted very few eyes other than his own to the secrets of the Army List, which remained in manuscript until he sanctioned a restricted publication in 1784.

The choice of a new regimental *Chef* was a matter of real moment. In 1752, for instance, he made a point of summoning the new proprietor of regiment no 32 to dine with him. After the meal he walked up and down with the recipient, General v. Uchlander, and delivered a little sermon:

'Now listen here, my good Uchlander, I am giving you a good and brave regiment. But it is up to you whether it remains a good and brave regiment. The men will degenerate unless they are kept under control. You must be very attentive on that point. Do not allow the officers to get away with too much, otherwise they will run wild.'[10]

Frederick's officers accepted his well-known quirks of character in the same un-thinking way that a family learns to live with the oddities of a father. He disliked fat men, he distrusted any officer who bore a Polish name, and he abhorred the sight of a muff. One day he happened to catch sight of one of these items on a table, and promptly threw the offending object into the fire. Too late he found out that the muff belonged to a member of the suite of the Russian envoy, a person he was very anxious not to offend.

Frederick did not have the unthinking bravery of famous heroes of the past like Condé. In fact his conduct at Mollwitz and Lobositz probably verged on the cowardly. Yet this was the same man who had horses shot from under him on six battlefields, and who twice (at Kolin and Kunersdorf) showed signs of wanting to take on the enemy single-handed. There was certainly nothing timid about Frederick's horsemanship. He rode with a very short stirrup (by the standards of the time) and habitually tore about the battlefield and the scenes of reviews at a gallop, leaving his suite jolting along behind. The French officer Guibert saw him at a review in 1773 and exclaimed that he looked like a centaur.

Frederick was coldly indifferent to the fate of his troops in the mass, and he was capable of showing the most unkingly vindictiveness towards individuals. At the same time he could never accustom himself to the sight of suffering. He left the scenes of the battles as soon as he reasonably could, and he made no secret of his aversion to blood sports – in notable contrast to the Habsburgs of Austria who delighted in the organised slaughter of the *parforce Jagd*. The undoubtedly humane Field-Marshal v. Schwerin signed far more death warrants than did the king, who admitted his weakness in this respect to foreign visitors. Even the ordinary field punishments had to be staged well out of the royal sight.

Frederick's dealings with men of intellect were marred by his compulsion to meddle in what was best left alone, and by his preference for the second-hand and the second-rate. In 1773, the same year in which Frederick declared his contempt for German literature, there appeared Goethe's *Leiden des Jungen Werthers*, which inaugurated the cult of romantic sensibility in Central Europe, and Berlin saw its first production of that expres-sion of the 'Prussian spirit', Lessing's play *Minna von Barnhelm*. In just the same way Frederick made his native military engineers undergo repeated indignities, while he lent a ready ear to any foreign charlatan who came to him with a new system of fortification.

The town and palaces of Potsdam were the epitome of Frederick's reign. They stood on a closely guarded peninsula that was formed by the windings of the Havel. An anonymous account from 1753 states:

> All reasonable people who know this place stay there the shortest time they can. Few moments pass without some offence to defency. Five battalions are stationed there in garrison, and they never leave the locality. You see hardly anyone else but soldiers, who are encouraged in their licentious behaviour. There are no women save a few wives of officers and soldiers, who scarcely dare to leave their quarters. Insult and rape are seldom punished.[11]

The wide and straight streets were immensely impressive at first sight, but then you began to notice the plaster falling away from the badly mortared bricks, the soldiers' breeches draped from corinthian pilasters, and the demigods and beer advertisements that competed for space on the peeling walls. Sometimes there seemed to be more bad statues lining the roofs than there were passers-by in the streets below. The long royal palace of Sans Souci appeared to sag in the middle (because Frederick had interfered with Knobelsdorff's designs) and the building and its terraces were set amid an arid landscape of dusty trees and sandy alleys.

The Prince de Ligne, an Austrian connoisseur, remarked that at Potsdam Frederick had the chance of doing something fresh and interesting, but instead 'he believed that he could bend Nature to his will by the force of his intellect, in the same way as he attained his victories, and managed war, politics, population, finances and industries. But Nature has a way of laughing at heroes. She prefers a Somerset farmer'.[12]

2

The Officer Corps

It is only natural to begin our tour of the Prussian army by calling in on its corps of officers, for as a national phenomenon they represented something as bizarre and distinctive as the duck-billed platypus or the pyramids of Gizeh.

The social contract

The kings of Prussia demanded some very hard things of their officer class: a total commitment to the profession of arms from early adolescence, a narrowly circumscribed mental and physical environment, the strong possibility of an early and painful death or, failing that, the prospect of an impoverished old age. In return the Prussian officer enjoyed a prestige higher than that of his counterpart in any other king's service.

Frederick William I was the man who more than any other was responsible for creating the peculiar ethos of the Prussian officer corps. Whereas other kings arrayed themselves in brocades, lace and silk, Frederick William was content to wear the same kind of uniform as was owned by the other officers, thus enabling the lowliest subaltern to claim that he carried 'the king's coat' (*Königs Rock*).

Frederick too was at pains to strengthen the sense of caste solidarity which existed between the king and all his officers. He granted interviews to his subalterns on the same basis as to his field-marshals, and he was quick to reprimand the commander who treated his subordinates with anything less than the full dignity due to Prussian officers. One of the people who ran foul of him was General v. Rebentisch, who had come from the Austrian army, where they ordered things differently. Rebentisch tyrannised his officers mercilessly, and after a particularly painful scene involving one of his lieutenants Frederick wrote to him on 23 December 1743 'to make it clear once and for all that in the Prussian service the custom has always been, and must always remain, for a commander to refrain from addressing an officer in insulting words, or treating him in an unseemly way, regardless of the provocation . . . Such behaviour is contrary to the honour of the Prussian service, whatever the usage obtaining in other armies'.[1]

The native-born Prussian generals and colonels scarcely needed reminding of what they owed to their underlings. They might subject an idle ensign or lieutenant to a blistering rebuke, but they would scarcely put him to such an indignity as waiting attendance behind a chair at table, or holding a horse's head while his superior heaved himself into the saddle. An insult to one of the caste was considered an insult to all.

The Minister Tettau held an assembly one day at Königsberg in 1764. A young ensign happened to be looking for something behind a curtain, which aroused the displeasure of the minister's wife, who saw that his powdered hair was marking the curtains. She asked him: 'What are you looking for? Your hat and sword?' At this the provincial Inspector took such offence that he stalked out. All the other officers followed him.[2]

The officer gained his privileged position not just by noble birth but in virtue of his noble manner of life. Here too Frederick followed the lead given by his father, who had forbidden his officers to engage in trade or other demeaning occupations (in Part IX of the *Reglement* of 1726).

All the same Frederick could not entirely quell the entrepreneurial spirit. Cavalry officers still engaged in some profitable horse-trading when they obtained remounts for their regiments, and Colonel Schätzel, the commandant of the Garde du Corps, managed to carry on such a prosperous money-changing business that the Jews of Potsdam had to complain to the king about the unfair competition.

The mere civilian was made clearly aware of his place. A Saxon officer visited the Silesian manoeuvres of 1785 and recorded his astonishment at seeing the

> conduct of the Minister v. Hoym (who seemed to me a fairly important personage, virtually the viceroy of Silesia). During the period of the manoeuvres he had to put up in a peasant's house, and then, when the *Parole* [password] was given out at head-quarters, he stood at some distance, neatly dressed and bare-headed, sedulously making way for every officer. When the sun became unendurable he went and stood in the shade of a stable door behind the guards. It appears to me that every ensign and cornet considers he is as important as a minister of state.[3]

Count v. Schwerin, nephew of the famous field-marshal, became so irked at the frustrations of civilian life that he abandoned his successful career as a diplomat and a man of letters and instead embraced the profession of arms as an ensign. He ended up as a major-general.

Frederick ordained that 'the officers must not be permitted to go about with common folk and townspeople. On the contrary they must seek the company of the higher officers and such of their comrades as behave themselves well and are fired with ambition'.[4] Regulations such as these sound forbidding enough, yet they did not in any sense permit military society to crush the civilian. The Frederician officer did not behave like his Portuguese contemporary, who had the right to gatecrash any private civilian function, or even show the arrogance of the Prusso-German officer of the later nineteenth century.

It was the job and entitlement of the useful, hardworking bourgeoisie to produce taxes and the materials of war with the least possible interference from the military. Frederick's inclination, indeed, was to favour the civilian side whenever the two estates came into dispute: 'Nobody, from commander to the lowliest drummer, shall presume to oppress the townspeople. Officers or NCOs who behave in this way will be immediately placed under arrest and punished. If it is a private who is responsible, he must be beaten with sticks.'[5] When a regiment had any complaint to make against the citizens of a town, it was expected to address itself in the first instance to the burgomaster, who would look into the case by civilian procedures.

Saldern at Magdeburg, Lossow at Goldap and Schwerin and Bernd v. Diringshofen at Frankfurt-am-Oder were all generals who took an interest in the local life and liked to stand on good social terms with their civilians. As usual the irrepressible cavalry commander Seydlitz refused to conform to any norm. He rebuked any officers who took a short

(above left) *Hans Karl v. Winterfeldt, éminence grise of the Prussian army in the middle 1750s, wearing the uniform of the Infantry Regiment no 1;* (above right) *Kurt Christoph v. Schwerin, wearing the uniform of Infantry Regiment no 24, with the star of the Black Eagle and the sprig of oak leaves;* (below left) *Johann v. Lehwaldt, wearing the uniform of Infantry Regiment no 14. On the left lapel he carries the royal portrait set in brilliants – a sign of his almost viceregal authority in East Prussia;* (below right) *Duke Ferdinand of Brunswick, commander of the army of British and German auxiliaries in western Germany in the Seven Years War. He wears a Prussian coat, with the Order of the Garter and British waistcoat and sword* cut by riding across fields of growing crops, yet he allowed himself to be irritated beyond reason by the burgomaster of Ohlau, who ensconced himself in pipe and nightcap in a window opposite Seydlitz's quarters, thus disturbing the cavalryman at his own meditations. Seydlitz finally got rid of the nuisance by discharging a pistol through the burgomaster's window.

In theory at least the Prussian military caste was a closed circle of nobles. Frederick admired the bravery and loyalty of his aristocrats, and he considered himself to be under an obligation to prevent the bourgeoisie from buying estates. 'If the commoners were allowed to own land,' he wrote, 'they would open their way to every kind of employment. Most of them have a common turn of mind and make bad officers – you cannot use them anywhere.'[6] However, corps like the hussars, the free battalions, the engineers and the gunners occupied a low place on the social scale, and as such they were held to be the proper place for the commoner officer.

Frederick praised his father's selectivity when he 'weeded out from the officers of every regiment such people whose conduct or birth did not accord with the gentlemanly standards of their profession. Ever since then the sensibility of the officers has permitted them to number among their comrades only men of unimpeachable character'.[7] Frederick himself instituted a similar purge when he rooted out many of the bourgeois officers who had won commissions during the crisis of the Seven Years War.

The process showed Frederick at his most cruel. One of the men who had the best title to Frederick's gratitude was the *Kämmerprasident* v. Domhardt, who had somehow contrived to send money and recruits from East Prussia when it was under Russian occupation, and yet when the king detected Domhardt's only son in the hussar regiment of Zieten (where he ought to have been safe enough) he hauled this good young officer out and told him 'now you can be a clerk, like your father!'[8] This kind of operation was often accompanied by a tug with Frederick's famous crutch-stick.

By the time of Frederick's death in 1786 the bourgeois officers numbered only one-tenth of the total of 7,000. The disproportion became even more severe with the higher ranks, for among the majors and senior officers there were just 22 bourgeois to set against 689 nobles.

However, the system of noble exclusiveness never operated with complete rigidity, even outside the technical arms. Among the lowly born generals were counted people like Konstantin Salenmon, a Jew, the Württemberg bourgeois Wunsch, the deserving Tobias Kümpel (the son of a drummer), and the bastard Mayer who had no idea at all who his father might have been. From time to time bourgeois officers were put in charge over some of the most prestigious field regiments, as witness the cases of General v. Rohdich, the *Chef* of the Grenadier-Garde-Bataillon, who was the son of a Feldwebel, or the preacher's son General v. Stolpen, who commanded infantry regiment no 1.

Dozens of deserving military men were raised to the nobility when they convinced Frederick that they had shown qualities worthy of a gentleman. A celebrated case was that of David Krauel, a fifty-year-old musketeer of the regiment of Braunschweig-Bevern who was the first soldier to storm into the Ziskaberg fortification at Prague on 12 September 1744. He was rewarded by being elevated to the nobility under the style of 'Krauel v. Ziskaberg'.

The definition of 'nobility' was itself looser in Prussia than in most other states. Frederick could never have tolerated the state of affairs which developed in the last years of the army of the *ancien régime* in France, where the authorities insisted on proof of complete 'quarters' of patented nobility. There were many Prussian military dynasties which could not have survived the test: whole villages in Pomerania had assumed the name of their feudal masters (rather like Scottish and Irish clansmen, or negro slaves in North America), while as late as 1708 the clergyman grandfather of Friedrich v. Steuben was able to insert himself into the nobility by quietly slipping a 'von' in front of his name.

What mattered to Frederick was not so much that blue blood coursed through the veins of his officers, as the fact that he must be the one man with authority to determine exactly in what 'nobility' consisted. Thus the Prussian military aristocrats were never driven to such extremes of reaction as their French counterparts in the 1770s and 1780s, who feared that they were about to be swamped by the prosperous bourgeoisie. In fact Frederick 'preferred poor officers to any other kind, considering that they were the most conscientious and the most devoted to his service'.[9]

Officer recruitment

Something like one-third of eighteenth-century Prussian officers were trained for their profession in the Berlin Cadet Corps.

From 1717, the date of the Corps' foundation, until the death of Frederick William in 1740 a total of 1,400 cadets passed through the establishment, and of these 39 ultimately became generals. During Frederick's reign the Corps trained 2,987 cadets, 41 of whom became generals.

The Cadet Corps accepted the new intakes at about the age of thirteen (though as low as ten in the Seven Years War), and processed them at the hands of officers, NCOs and civilian professors until they were deemed fit for the army about three years later. The pupils were put up on the Friedrichstrasse in 'an old building built in the form of a circus, which had once been used for fights between wild beasts. The halls of study, the dining rooms and the sleeping chambers were arranged in the interior'.[10] The place could accommodate almost 400 cadets at a time.

Frederick William used to fill the place in a characteristic style, by having lists drawn up of young noblemen, then choosing certain of their number and dragging them off to the cadet house under armed escort. The treatment of the unfortunates in the Corps was correspondingly harsh, though the king tried to persuade their parents that he was giving their sons a useful and healthy education.

Very soon after his accession Frederick ordained that the 'Feldwebels must no longer behave towards the cadets in a coarse or boorish manner. They must be treated like noblemen and future officers, not like farm labourers'.[11] At the same time he placed a greater emphasis on academic instruction. The most famous member of the faculty during the Frederician period was the poet K. W. Ramler, who served on the staff for forty-one years (being, like most military academics, unemployable in the outside world), and retained the affection of his charges long after they left the Corps.

However, most of the good intentions were vitiated by the mismanagement of the aged governor, Colonel F. A. v. Wulffen, who was 'weak and almost childish'.[12] The little staff of officers and NCOs failed to keep order among their charges, and the more powerfully built cadets terrorised their feebler comrades, some of whom actually died of exposure after being drenched under the pumps in the depths of winter. One of the cadets who came there early in 1758 remembers how, one night,

a swarm of these ruffians broke into the room where my brother and I lived. They chose as their victim a cadet called B—, who had attracted their ire, and they mistreated him badly. Fearing that we were about to undergo the same fate we seized the muskets standing behind our beds, which had fixed bayonets. We levelled them in front of us in the firm resolve to skewer the first one who so much as dared to lay a hand on us. Then they came to our bed. They saw that we were ready to defend ourselves and heard us say that we would not hesitate to use our bayonets if we were not left in peace. At this they tried to pretend the whole thing was a joke, and assured us that they never intended us any harm. After that they made themselves scarce.[13]

In 1759, however, the Cadet Corps entered a new and prosperous period with the appointment of Major-General J. J. v. Buddenbrock as the new governor:

It did not take a man like him much effort to re-establish discipline and order among the cadets . . . Formerly the cadets had to sleep two by two in itchy feather beds, but now each was given his own bed complete with mattress, pillow, cover and linen. Now the meals were really good, healthy and ample. The instructional arrangements were also changed, the cadets being placed in classes according to their abilities. The general himself frequently visited the teaching periods. He directed the methods of instruction and he inquired after the diligence of the cadets. He praised the industrious cadets and invited them to his table, but heaped censure and scorn upon their idle comrades.[14]

After Buddenbrock had put the Corps in order, he founded junior cadet schools at Stolp in Pomerania (1769) and Kulm in West Prussia (1776), so as to make sure that the entrants to the senior branch already owned the rudiments of an education. Buddenbrock left one last memorial of his distinguished governorship in the form of a new cadet house in Berlin, which was opened in 1778.

The better pupils of the Cadet Corps vied with one another for the honour of being numbered among the twelve whom Frederick sent every year from 1765 to attend the Académie des Nobles. Here they lived in considerable luxury, and studied a wide variety of subjects alongside the sons of rich noblemen with the object of fitting themselves for a high career in the army or the diplomatic service.

The other able cadets were sometimes allowed the privilege of choosing their own regiments. More frequently, however, the cadet and his regiment were matched by what can be best described as a kind of 'marriage market', in which the cadet sought to impress his prospective colonel by his ambition, his qualifications or his influential connections. Such dealings were usually carried on at the winter quarters of the regiments (in wartime), or in the Lustgarten in Berlin.

The remainder of the officer corps was made up from a variety of sources. The least painful and most promising path of entry was probably by way of the corps of royal pages, many of whom were launched on a promising military career.

In addition the colonel of nearly every regiment took on young officers and officer aspirants in what was virtually the capacity of private pages. Such was the case with Christian v. Prittwitz, who entered the regiment of Bevern at the age of fifteen simply on the strength of a remote family connection with an adjutant to the *Chef*. He wrote afterwards that he came to the military life with no other preparation except some gifts from his mother – a nightshirt, a sleeping bag, some bed linen and a monthly allowance.

Foreign-born officers had formed a significant element in the Brandenburg-Prussian armies ever since the Great Elector and Frederick I had welcomed large numbers of persecuted Huguenots from the France of Louis XIV. The children of these refugees were represented in Frederick's army by such commanders as the lieutenant-generals Hautcharmoy and Pennavaire, both of whom were veterans of the War of the Spanish Succession, as well as by a host of junior officers like Frederick's friend La Motte Fouqué.

From the German states came people like Schwerin (Mecklenburg), Kyau and Georg Konrad v. d. Goltz (Saxony), and Wunsch, Phull and Massenbach (Württemberg). The Austrian service provided a large crop of aggrieved commanders, among whom were numbered Karl zu Wied, the accomplished staff officer Schmettau, the ill-fated and tyrannical Rebentisch, and the hussar general Werner who pursued a vendetta against his former comrade the Austrian general Nádasti. The 'Prussian' lieutenant-colonel v. Gemmingen commanded one of the better grenadier battalions at Kolin, and found himself pitted against his own father, who was serving with the Austrians on the same day as a lieutenant-general.

Distant Russia paid its tribute to the prestige of the Prussian arms in the shape of Manstein, Finck and Keith. More exotic still were specimens like Major 'Ludwig v. Steinmann', who was actually a Turk, or Frederick's elegant and fatuous favourite Rupert Scipio v. Lentulus, who came from Switzerland by way of Austria and claimed descent from a family of ancient Rome.

Altogether foreign lands provided over one-sixth (54 out of 317) of the generals who commanded the Prussian armies in the vital years between 1740 and 1763. At a lower level the proportion of foreign officers varied greatly from one regiment to another, although generally speaking we find high concentrations of foreigners in the new fusilier regiments, as well as in some other regiments towards the end of Frederick's reign, when he recruited many officers from the Empire to replace the weeded-out bourgeois.

The ranks and their responsibilities

The aspiring officer was usually expected to make his way to the regimental *Standort* (station) by his own devices. The products of the Cadet Corps had some inkling of what was expected of them, but the young people who came straight from home entered a totally unfamiliar world. The sixteen-year-old Jakob v. Lemcke was luckier than most, for his uncle Colonel v. Pritz was commandant of his chosen regiment of Alt-Anhalt (no 3) when he arrived at Potsdam in 1754. The colonel received him graciously, and

> scarcely had he gone when Feldwebel Höber came up with the regimental tailor. No longer was I the boy, who was not regarded as fully grown-up: on the contrary they made me so many compliments that I became somewhat uneasy. The tailor and the shoemaker proceeded to take my measurements. Then came the barber, who cut and dressed my hair, and the valet who brought my linen. Meanwhile two servants laid the table, where I was expected to sit alone and get through more than eight

courses. Two other servants stood behind my chair and awaited my orders. In short my circumstances had changed so rapidly that I hardly knew what I was at.[15]

Immediately afterwards the inexperienced *Junkers* were placed among the rank and file. Christian v. Prittwitz tells that in the regiment of Bevern he and his younger brother were issued with the lightest weapons, 'but I was nowhere near as big or as strong as my brother, even though I was the senior, and since the drill was very rapid and long it often happened that my bayonet sank towards the earth when we were ordered to level our muskets. However my seniors were tolerant enough not to reprimand me'.[16]

Before he could be recognised in the full status of NCO our *Junker* had to stand four watches – one every four days. At the first watch the private soldiers appeared and claimed a gift of bread and brandy, at which the senior private would give a *Hoch!* for the Herr Baron. The company NCOs came to the second watch for beer and tobacco, but the Feldwebel reserved his visit for the third watch, when he was supposed to be presented with a glass of wine and a piece of curled tobacco on a tin plate.

Senior or better-connected entrants were taken on straight away at the rank of *Freikorporal* (*Standartenjunker* in the cuirassiers, *Fahnenjunker* in the dragoons and hussars). The free corporal was expected to have a full mastery of drill and the day-to-day routine of regimental life, and he was given the special responsibility of bearing the company colours. When on duty he had the status of an NCO, but in 1763, in the general tightening-up which took place after the Seven Years War, Frederick warned the regimental commanders to tell their free corporals that they were being altogether too familiar with the 'ordinary' NCOs and men, whereas they ought to cultivate the company of the officers.

From free corporal the young man advanced to ensign (*Fähnrich*), a strange intermediate rank which offered many of the burdens but few of the privileges of a full officer, apart from an entitlement to free lodging in the garrison town and the services of a batman. Another consolation was the fact that when the battalion was drawn up in line his place was in the rear of the platoon: a veteran complained that 'the frivolous ensigns treated manoeuvres like a kind of military promenade. They strolled carelessly behind the ranks without ever having to use their brains'.[17]

According to our informant Prittwitz, the transformation to the fully commissioned rank of lieutenant (*Lieutenant*; the spelling *Leutnant* was not introduced until 1899) was nothing short of miraculous. He writes that he was given a coat of fine cloth (even if it was second-hand and displayed a sinister bullet hole), he wore riding boots instead of constricting gaiters, he revelled in his small water-tight tent, and he much appreciated the convenience of being able to travel on horseback and load his effects on to a pack-horse.[18]

Just as the free corporal actually carried the colour for the nominal ensign, so the lieutenant ran most of the routine affairs of the company for its commander, the captain. According to the generosity of their captain, the lieutenants received a greater or lesser bonus on top of their pay, which by itself was quite inadequate. In the infantry the first lieutenant received 13 thalers 18 groschen per month, and the second lieutenant and the ensign 11 thalers. Out of these sums 3 or 4 thalers were automatically deducted for the 'free clothing', which left the subaltern with precious little to pay for his other needs, when bad food for a month cost at least 4 thalers, and a pair of boots might set him back 6 or 7.

After years of demanding and underpaid service the more fortunate of the first lieutenants might hope to become captain (*Hauptmann* in the infantry, *Rittmeister* in the cavalry, company *Chef* in the artillery), and as such the holder of one of the most significant ranks in the Prussian military hierarchy.

With any contrivance the infantry captain in the earlier part of Frederick's reign could make himself 3,000 thalers per year, while the *Rittmeister* was usually in a position to acquire still more. They found themselves in this happy situation because they were appointed as the middlemen between the state on the one hand, and the company sub-alterns, NCOs and private soldiers on the other. Every year they took in considerable sums that were supposed to cover the costs of the soldiers' pay, the company administration, the maintenance of weapons and uniforms, and the supply of the smaller items of clothing (*Klein-Bekleidungsstücken*) – stock, shirt, gaiters, knee straps, shoes and the like. However, in peacetime the native soldiers were sent away on leave for the greater part of the year, and *der Alte* was entitled to keep for himself such pay as was due to them for that period, as well as to ask them to pay for their *Klein-Bekleidungsstücken* out of their own pockets.

In theory the captain was bound to employ this huge windfall to pay for recruiting soldiers for his company in foreign parts, but he found little difficulty in retaining most of the money for himself. After the Seven Years War Frederick introduced a general recruiting for the army as a whole, and limited the company recruiting (and the captain's income with it). All the same, the Prussian captain was better off than most of his counterparts in foreign armies. Hence the position of captain remained the goal of every subaltern's ambitions, and, as Mirabeau remarked, 'you would scarcely believe just how much this prospect binds people to the Prussian service'.[19]

There were many other practices which tell us that the fundamental administrative unit of the Prussian army remained the old mercenary band, under its new guise of the company. The weapons of the unit were considered to be the commander's stock-in-trade, for which he demanded 800 thalers when a new captain took over in his place. Likewise the senior officers clung to their companies, regardless of the altitude of their rank. The colonel commandant retained the second company in order of seniority as the Com-mander's Company, while his *Chef* (who was usually a general, as well as being the colonel of the regiment), remained the proprietor of the first, or *Leib* company. Each of these companies was entrusted for its actual running to a staff captain (*Stabskapitän*), who was an unfortunate lieutenant who received only a lieutenant's pay.

No commander was ever so grand as to forget his connection with his company. At a spring review in 1786 a French officer expressed his surprise at seeing the 'generals dis-mounted at the head of their companies, spontoon in hand'.[20] King Frederick himself retained a company in the First Battalion of the Garde, and required a daily report on its condition.

The next three rungs up the hierarchy were more purely functional ones, being con-cerned with the day-to-day direction of the regiment. The major (*Major*, pronounced with the stress on the second syllable) had the primary important responsibility of com-manding the battalion (two to each regiment), which was the lowest tactical 'brick' of the army's order of battle.

Frederick was in the habit of creating great quantities of majors, so as to have a reserve of officers at hand for detached duties, and the regiment might well have more majors on its books than the two that were strictly necessary for leading the battalions.

The regiment as a whole was commanded by the most senior regimental 'staff officer', who might be a colonel, or a lieutenant-colonel (who were rather rare birds), or simply one of the majors.

The commander answered for the running of the regiment to the *Chef* (colonel-in-chief, or proprietor), who 'owned' the regiment in much the same way as the captains held the individual companies. The *Chef* was the man who more than any other was responsible for giving the regiment its distinctive character. As early as 1729 Leopold of Anhalt-Dessau had numbered off the regiments according to the order of their foundation in his famous *Dessauer Stammliste*, but the *Chefs* managed to put up a successful resistance to these cold mathematical designations for nearly eighty years more. 'Everything in the history of a regiment was living and personified. The regiment harboured the names of all its officers as examples of praiseworthy or reprehensible conduct.'[21]

The relationship of *Chef* and regiment was more than just a spiritual one. The canny proprietor was careful to siphon off a proportion of the expenses of the regiment as a whole (*Regiments Unkosten*) for his own profit. Then again he was deeply involved in the process of military administration, for this was a period of 'regimental' armies, by which we mean that the king or his immediate deputies ran the army in direct association with the heads of the scores of component regiments. Thus on 1 January of every year the *Chef* had to send to Frederick a list of his officers, detailing the 'conduct of every officer, whether good or bad'.[22] In the process the *Chef* invariably revealed something of himself. Zieten wrote characteristically of one of his lieutenants that he was 'no boozer, though when he does get drunk he gets very drunk indeed'.[23]

It was clues like this which helped Frederick to determine which people owned the qualities he demanded of his generals.

The hierarchy of field officers ran as follows: major-general (*Generalmajor*, of whom there were twenty-three in 1740), lieutenant-general (*Generallieutenant*, thirteen in 1740), general of infantry and general of cavalry (*General der Infanterie*, *General der Kavallerie*, two in 1740), and field-marshal (*Feldmarschall*, five in 1740).

The major-general commanded a brigade of two or three regiments, or the equivalent in grenadier battalions. His function was a demanding and unglamorous one which corresponded closely with that of the senior first lieutenant in the regimental hierarchy. He was responsible for the alignment and movements of his brigade in battle, and for making sure that it moved speedily and in the right direction on the march.

Every now and then he was chosen by rotation to become 'major-general of the day', responsible for the security of the whole army. As such he had to tour the outposts before daylight, and collect information to bring to the king when he made his report later in the morning.

The lieutenant-general was entitled to be addressed as *Exzellenz*, a privilege which emphasised his superiority over the mere *Generals*. His command usually comprised two brigades (four to six regiments), which was large enough to permit him to exercise a decisive influence on the course of a battle. Above him stood the full general of infantry or cavalry, who was responsible for managing an entire wing or line of the order of battle.

In peacetime the general exercised no command other than his own regiment. On campaign he knew the sphere of his responsibilities from the 'orders of battle', formalised plans of the army which were worked out periodically.

With lieutenant-general and full general we have reached the summit of the hierarchy proper. Frederick had no great use for the rank of field-marshal, and he allowed the office to die out completely by the end of his reign. Economy must have been at the root of one of his objections, for every field-marshal cost him 20,000 thalers a year. Another probably harks back to the time of his first campaign in 1740, when he found that three of his field-marshals (Borcke, Roeder and Katte) were unfit for active service, leaving him with only two (Leopold of Anhalt-Dessau and the newly promoted Schwerin) who were any good. Most important of all was the fact that the real job of a field-marshal was supposed to be to command an independent army: Schwerin and Keith did this work efficiently enough in the first campaigns of the Seven Years War, but after they were killed off Frederick found that his own brother Prince Henry was content to soldier on in their stead with the rank of full general. Hence there came into existence a promotion block which prevented deserving commanders like Bevern, Fouqué, Seydlitz and Zieten from ever becoming field-marshals.

Frederick in fact was doing far too little to train generals for independent command. During the Seven Years War he was in the habit of sending peremptory orders to generals in distant theatres (as often as not stampeding them into some unsuitable action) and he informed generals only of their specific tasks, giving them no idea at all of the general plan of operations. After the war the generals were only too thankful to return to the humdrum routine of their own regiments and arm of service.

If Frederick's army was heavily officered at the regimental level, the senior commanders were much more thinly spread, and they had to make their way by conspicuous merit. It was the very challenge of the Prussian service, not its easy promotion, which attracted so many princes and dukes from Protestant Germany. Among the lists of generals who served in the period 1740–60 we encounter eight princes of Anhalt (one reigning), five dukes of Brunswick (one reigning), three princes of Hesse, two dukes of Holstein and two dukes of Württemberg. A characteristic member of this tribe was Duke Friedrich of Württemberg (1732–97), who was an enterprising lieutenant-general of cavalry in the middle of the Seven Years War and was often given command of detachments, being 'brave, humane, alert and vigilant in procuring intelligence'.[24]

There were lesser princes of the royal house of Brandenburg in plenty, of whom Margrave Friedrich was killed at Mollwitz and Margrave Friedrich Wilhelm at the siege of Prague in 1744. All three of Frederick's younger brothers served as generals, namely the unfortunate Prince Augustus William, Prince Henry, and the brave but untalented Prince Ferdinand. Frederick's own brother-in-law Friedrich Franz of Brunswick was beheaded by a cannot shot at Hochkirch. The diarist Lehndorff wrote that 'what distinguishes our army from all others is that our princes are soldiers themselves, and put up with the same hardships as the private soldier . . .', moreover 'it is very useful for a king to have princes at hand to whom he can give the command of his armies: when anyone else is entrusted with the command, a spirit of jealousy sets in among the generals'.[25]

Promotion

In the first half of his reign Frederick could promise his army plenty of 'bloody wars' if not many 'sickly seasons'. Consequently the rate of promotion was gratifyingly brisk. The able officer could expect to spend four to eight years as a captain, four to six as a major, one or two as a lieutenant-colonel, and five or six as a colonel – a state of affairs which produced subalterns in their twenties, captains in their thirties, majors and lieutenant-colonels in their forties, and colonels and major-generals by the early fifties. There were not many individuals left like the forty-four-year-old lieutenant who appears in a list of the regiment of Kleist in 1740. Favoured individuals were whisked up the scale of promotion, the unspeakable Wilhelmi Anhalt making colonel from second lieutenant in five years. More deservingly Seydlitz was major-general at thirty-six, while the poor and uncouth Hülsen rapidly advanced to major-general after sticking fifteen years at ensign.

Frederick often exercised his undoubted privilege to make or break officers as the mood took him. In 1765 he pleased old Zieten by appointing the infant son of his second marriage as a cornet in the hussars at the age of nine days: conversely there were many fat and slow-witted officers who were unfortunate enough to attract the royal ire at one of the reviews, and found themselves consigned to the garrison regiments as a result. In the normal course of things, however, the promotion of an officer was effected by a royal *Cabinets-Ordre* upon the recommendation of the *Chef* or commandant. Similarly most field officers lived in the expectation that they would advance up the scale of the military hierarchy by the inexorable working of the system of seniority. Even during the hurly-burly of the Seven Years War there were generals who resented the favour shown to individuals like Finck, and in the following decades Frederick gradually bowed before the pressure of the traditionalists. By the end of the reign foreign observers noted that with the exception of the royal adjutants (who could be advanced out of turn up to the rank of major), promotion in the Prussian army proceeded by strict seniority.

Rewards and punishments

Frederick's delight in the whimsical and arbitrary was evident in every aspect of his relationship with his officer corps.

To reward men who pleased him the king had two 'official' decorations in his gift – the Order *Pour le Mérite* and the Order of the Black Eagle (*Schwarzer Adler*). The *Pour le Mérite* was founded by Frederick in June 1740 as a more specifically military decoration to supplement the somewhat devalued Order *de la Générosité*. The elegant blue enamelled maltese cross of the new award was bestowed in fair profusion upon fortunate lieutenants and captains: perhaps they had distinguished themselves on the battlefield, perhaps they had put forward a well-reasoned memorandum or a useful invention (like Lieutenant v. Freytag's conical touch hole), or perhaps they had merely presented a smartly turned out company at a review. Veritable fistfuls of the *Pour le Mérite* were showered upon regiments which brought off some particularly spectacular feat of arms. The officers of the regiment of Meyerinck collected fifteen crosses for their day's work at Leuthen, and on occasion the entire corps of a regiment's captains and majors might emerge with the coveted decoration (the regiment of Kleist for Lobositz, the regiment of Prince Ferdinand for Liegnitz). Other officers, equally deserving, lived out their days without the consolation of the award, as witness the cases of Lieutenant-General Salenmon, the defender of Wittenberg in the Seven Years War, or Lieutenant-General v. Finckenstein who served loyally for fifty-eight years.

Upon advancing to the rank of lieutenant-general it was customary for the newly promoted officer to receive the large, embroidered silver star of the senior award, the Black Eagle, and hand back the *Pour le Mérite*. Altogether ninety-eight generals (in addition to the royal princes) received the decoration in Frederick's reign. Here too there were some notable exceptions to the norm. Seydlitz was awarded the Black Eagle while only a very new major-general, for his brilliance at Rossbach, while Lieutenant-General Wunsch received no decoration at all, even though he was reckoned the most able commander to have emerged from the free battalions.

Sometimes Frederick felt inspired to strike a special medal after a particularly glorious action, and distribute it among the officers most directly concerned. Such was the case after the obstinate defence of Kolberg, and the battles of Mollwitz, Leuthen and Torgau. In honour of the Bayreuth Dragoons, who charged with such devastating effect at Hohenfriedberg, he bestowed coats of arms upon General v. Gessler and Major v. Chazot, and drew up a 'diploma of honour' upon which he entered the names of all the officers of the regiment.

Frederick was no less generous when he bestowed recognition of a more tangible kind. To Winterfeldt, his *éminence grise*, he awarded the estate of Göden in East Friesland – which that shrewd gentleman promptly sold for 40,000 thalers, using the proceeds to buy three estates which were more conveniently situated for him in Silesia. Major-General v. Driesen put up a good performance with his cuirassiers at the Berlin review of 1754, and was pleasantly surprised to find himself loaded with a present of 2,000 thalers, a yearly pension of a further 1,000, and the income from a post in the civil administration of East Prussia.

The more idealistic among the officers might find themselves amply rewarded by a mere gesture of royal consideration, such as the one which Frederick showed to the wounded Colonel Forcade after the campaign of 1745 when, seeing him leaning against a window during a long audience at Potsdam, he carried up a chair with his own hands and begged him to sit down. Indeed there were generals like Zieten and Ferdinand of Brunswick who did not recommend a single officer for an award during the Seven Years War, because they held that heroism ought to be a commonplace duty among Prussian officers.

Towards the end of his reign Frederick celebrated the memory of Seydlitz, Winterfeldt, Keith and Schwerin in a unique way when he had their statues set up in the Wilhelmsplatz. This was at a time when it was the custom to hide away representations of near-contemporary figures in arsenals or private galleries.

Frederick's resourcefulness and ingenuity were no less evident when he wished to chastise some wretch who had crossed his path. His anger might break out on any occasion, though the season of the spring reviews was always dangerous, and the time of the giving of the *Parole* on the watch parade was the most perilous of all.

An officer was just as likely to draw down the king's anger over some trifle, like owning a name that was difficult to pronounce, as because he was responsible for some spectacular disaster in drill. In these circumstances it was wise to pay the closest attention to Frederick's choice of his mode of address, for this gave a reasonably accurate clue as to the state of the royal temper. It was a bad sign if he called you *Monsieur!* and even worse was to come if he used the German pronunciation *Musjeh!* or addressed you as *Herr!*

Frederick drew freely on his wide range of punishments, and (contrary to an important principle of man-management) he did not hesitate to humiliate officers in front of their inferiors. An officer might consider himself fairly lucky if he was merely marched off parade under escort and placed under a brief *Stubenarrest* in the officers' guardroom (in Berlin it was the *Weisser Saal* of a building on the Hacke'scher Markt). 'Fortress arrest' was usually a longer-term punishment, though one that was much less onerous or disgraceful than real imprisonment. Simple cashiering was a drastic but clean punishment which Frederick often meted out on the spot by telling the individual that he could 'go to the devil'. More heinous offenders were 'cashiered with disgrace' (*infam kassiert*). The officer deserter was hanged in effigy, and his portrait was left nailed to the scaffold until it fell down in the course of time.

There was hardly a single one of Frederick's commanders who did not have to endure a longer or shorter period of disgrace. At various times he showed his deep dissatisfaction with Saldern, Schwerin, Zieten and the outspoken Seydlitz, and he broke the careers of the Intendant Retzow and of his own brother Prince Augustus William.

Was Frederick acting out of pure caprice? The son of the unfortunate Retzow believed that Frederick's manifest injustices proceeded from the fact that he 'wanted everyone to believe that he had accomplished all his deeds without the help of anybody else'.[26] At the same time we cannot rule out the possibility that Frederick simply held that it was bad in principle for any officers or families to think that they could be sure of the royal favour. Perhaps that was why he was so unwilling to help any young officers who were recommended to him by his generals. 'His suspicions in this respect went so far that whenever two candidates for promotion were suggested to him, and there was no particular reason to prefer one or the other, he liked to choose the one whose name led him to expect that he had no close connection with any ministers or generals.'[27]

Further training

As regards the schooling of his officers Frederick's immediate concern was to make sure that the whole of the army attained a uniformly high degree of proficiency in basic drill and tactics. There was a constant stream of traffic to and from Berlin as infantry officers from the provinces came to see the crack Potsdam battalions put through their paces, while selected Garde officers went out to the country to keep the remoter regiments up to the mark.

Similarly a large number of cavalry officers were ordered to Potsdam and the large exercises in Pomerania to see how the cavalry *Reglement* of 1743 ought to be put into practice. The Gensd'armes (cuirassiers), the Bayreuth Dragoons and the Zieten Hussars were held up by Frederick as fine practitioners of their respective kinds of cavalry service. In particular a great deal was expected of the officers of the Garde du Corps (cuirassiers), who had 'the reputation of being so well-informed that they could discuss military affairs with any general without the slightest embarrassment'.[28]

Before the Seven Years War Lieutenant-General v. Schmettau happened to speak to Frederick about the lack of proper training among the generals. The king was in full agreement, and he commented that by the time a man had reached general's rank he was often beyond help. As a result of this conversation Frederick decided to enlarge his suite to include twelve promising young adjutants, mostly chosen from likely-looking officers who came to his attention at reviews. In the fullness of time they were released to make way for others and take up what was supposed to be a promising career.

These adjutants spent their time working under Frederick's eye on the making of surveys, the marking out of camps, the fortification of villages and hills, the calculation of columns of march, and the sounding out of rivers and swamps. Unfortunately, as Frederick admitted, 'the progress of these young officers is retarded by their extreme frivolity and their inclination to debauchery'.[29] There was the case of the young officer from a Pomeranian regiment who repeatedly betrayed his earlier promise. In a last attempt to strike a spark Frederick asked him to prepare the plan of an impregnable position. A few days later the Pomeranian handed in the sketch of a swamp in the middle of which was an island held by troops.

> 'Now just listen, my son,' said Frederick, 'with your troops in this position I could cannonade them from every side.'
> 'With respect, Your Majesty, the swamp is so broad that no cannon shot can carry over it.'
> 'Yes, yes! but do you have enough provisions on the island?'
> 'For at least twenty years, Your Majesty.'
> 'Well, I just have to wait until the swamp is frozen over.'
> 'With respect, Your Majesty, the swamp never freezes over.'
> 'But how on earth did you get on to the island? And how are you going to leave again?'[30]

The officer remained silent, and Frederick sent him back to his regiment – one of many who went the same way.

The Duke of Bevern used to engage professors to lecture his young officers on mathematics and geometry, and paid foreign-speaking private soldiers to hold classes in their native languages. Such enterprise was very rare, and the officer corps in most regiments was sunk in such hoggish ignorance that in 1763 Frederick ordered the engineers to provide staff for five district schools (at Wesel, Magdeburg, Berlin, Breslau and Königsberg) where they were to instruct selected young officers from the field regiments during the four winter months from November to February. Frederick was inspired by the example of the military schools of ancient Greece, and as always he laid great stress on the elements of fortification and topography, for 'terrain for the military man is the same as the chess board for the player who wants to deploy and move his pawns, knights and elephants in the most effective way'.[31]

The commentator Berenhorst complained that the system certainly turned out some good staff officers, but that at the regimental level the products acted like 'little masters' who were of less use in ordinary duties than the 'outright idiots'.[32]

Frederick advised the *Chefs* in their turn to encourage their more ambitious officers by opening regimental libraries (even the unbookish Seydlitz assembled one of them), and he tried to draw out the talents of military men of all ranks by requiring them to submit reports and memoranda on a variety of topics.

Over the course of the years Frederick drew up a number of papers for the more particular instruction of the higher generals. With the help of his secretary Eichel he completed two important memoranda on 14 August 1748, namely an *Instruction* for the major-generals of the infantry and a counterpart for the major-generals of horse. The two *Instructions* were printed and circulated under the greatest secrecy, every lieutenant-general receiving both sets but the major-generals only the one appropriate to their arm.

A complete edition fell into the hands of the Austrians when Fouqué was captured at Landeshut in 1760.

A similar fate befell another memorandum, which Frederick had originally drawn up for his own satisfaction and then circulated to the generals in 1753 under the title of *Die General Principia vom Kriege*. The commanders were laid under the most stringent orders concerning the safekeeping of the document, but in spite of these precautions Major General v. Czettritz and his copy were captured at Cossdorf in 1760, and translations were shortly afterwards published in several languages.

Partly on account of some changes in the art of war, and also no doubt because of the loss of security, Frederick up-dated the *General Principia* in the form of the *Eléments de Castramétie et de Tactique*, a paper which was distributed among the generals in 1771.

These general memoranda were backed up by detailed prescriptions which were sent to the inspectors, selected categories of generals and regimental commanders. Many individual generals or fortress commandants also received special instructions which were tailor-made to their requirements.

As was the case with the rest of Frederick's educational work, the result turned out to be strangely incommensurate with all the effort which had gone into it. The trouble was that Frederick did not like to reveal to his generals the working of the army as a whole. On campaign the commanders found that the king allowed them precious little initiative (see p. 34), while in peacetime the infantry and cavalry exercised together only during the autumn manoeuvres and on the third day of the spring reviews. Even the *General Principia* were concerned with the command of a detachment rather than of the main army. Thus the Frederician general gradually lost the inclination (if he ever had it) to think comprehensively and independently.

Uniforms

Frederick retained the simplified range of uniforms which had been introduced by his father, namely coats of Prussian blue for the officers and men of the infantry, and coats of straw or white for the cuirassiers and dragoons (sky blue for the dragoons from 1745).

The distinction between officer and man was most pronounced among the infantry, where the officers invariably wore three-cornered hats (as opposed to the brass-fronted cap of the NCOs and men of the grenadiers and fusiliers). The hair was carefully dressed and powdered, and extended down the back in the long military pig-tail. Officers with thinning hair used to douse their heads with essence of bergamot (which gave senior Prussian commanders a powerful scent like oranges), while bald-pated gentlemen had to treat themselves to an expensive wig. The stock (neck-cloth) was white, in contrast with the red or black of the private soldiers.

The infantry officer's coat was of fine dark blue cloth, as supplied by the better Berlin textile firms to the royal *Lagerhaus*. The waist was elegantly tailored, and the generous skirt hung in folds, except when it was fastened back for riding. The lapels, cuffs and the collar (if any) were made of velvet, coloured according to the individual regiment, and the coat was liberally adorned with the characteristically Prussian *Brandenbourgs* or *Schleifen* – rococo cartouches or bars of finely-worked gold or silver thread. The *Brandenbourgs* were usually carried in three pairs of two each down each lapel, with a further pair on the coat front just below the lapel. Other *Brandenbourgs* were sometimes sewn on the sleeves above the cuffs, down the pocket edges, and on either side of the parting of the coat tails. In some regiments a little tassel swung from the end of each of the *Brandenbourgs*. Film-goers will be familiar with the design of one of the characteristic Frederician *Brandenbourgs* from the collar patches of twentieth-century German generals, which were copied in 1900 from the uniform of regiment no 26.

The coats of the officers of the new fusilier regiments were somewhat less gaudy, but in comparison the hats were decorated with broad bands of gold or silver braid.

Infantry officers (but not the officers of the fusiliers, *Jägers* or cavalry) wore a moon-shaped gorget of silver suspended about the neck. The gorget was an ornamental survival of the neck-piece of the medieval suit of armour, and it was still thick enough to turn a musket bullet.

Around his waist the infantry officer wore a thick sash of black cloth and silver thread. It lay immediately on top of the waistcoat, and it was turned over in a broad knot just in front of the left hip. The sash was seldom worn off duty.

The otherwise insignificant sword-knot (*Portepee*) was regarded in the Prussian army as the most important sign of the officer's authority. A strip of cloth which terminated in an ornamental tassel, it was normally wound about the guard of the sword hilt.

The clumsiest item of the infantry officer's equipment was undoubtedly the spontoon, which was a steel-headed pike about eight feet long. On campaign it was usually carried by a servant, for it was unwieldy and liable to catch in branches.

The diminutive *Junkers* were expected to shoulder a still heavier weapon, the mis-named *Kurzgewehr* (half-pike) of the NCOs, which was ten feet long. In February 1755 Frederick distributed an extra-long model among the *Junkers* and NCOs and some of the men of the third rank, with the idea of supplementing the 'cold steel' effect of the bayonet of the infantry muskets. According to a subaltern of the First Battalion of the Garde, 'when the soldiers level their muskets the NCOs are supposed to lower their half-pikes. But these weapons are at once too short and too heavy towards the blade, so that the NCOs do not have the strength to make proper use of them'.[33] Frederick therefore had to shorten the *Kurzgewehr* to its original length, and take the weapon away from the men of the third rank.

The spontoon and the *Kurzgewehr* looked very well on parade, and they were not without their uses in actual combat: with the help of his little pike the officer or NCO could skewer a fleeing soldier (as the regulations permitted), or he could beat down the musket barrels of troops who were firing too high, or he could level the weapon along the small of the mens' backs and push them towards the enemy. In the action at Korbitz in 1759 an NCO contrived to catch an Austrian major of cuirassiers with the hook of his *Kurzgewehr* and drag him from the saddle.

Among the smaller variations in dress we may mention that in cold weather officers sometimes buttoned the lapels of their coats across their chests, or put on greatcoats or cloaks of dark blue. Even the pedantic Saldern sometimes permitted himself the liberty of sporting breeches of serviceable black at the Potsdam manoeuvres, instead of the 'regula-tion' white or straw. Riding boots were of course worn instead of gaiters by generals, adjutants, senior regimental officers and all other folk whose function required them to go into action on horseback.

One of the most striking features of the Prussian service was the virtual absence of any visible differentiation of rank within the officer corps. The general wore exactly the same uniform as the subaltern, with the sole distinction of the hat plume which was introduced in 1742. Here we have an outward manifestation of the sense of corporate unity of the body of officers, and an impressive contrast with the glitter of the French and Austrian generals of the same period.

The vicissitudes of fortune

In all our talk about organisation and uniforms it is easy to forget that the main business of the officer was fighting, and that once the army was launched upon a war he could count himself fairly lucky to emerge alive. Thus in 1759 A. D. Ortmann could congratulate an officer friend on having survived to date with a mighty cut across his head and a bullet wound in the body[34] – he was supposed to be one of the lucky ones.

In proportion the field officers suffered at least as heavily as their subordinates, for this was a period when generals shared the physical dangers of the battlefield to the full. Thirty-three generals (including two field-marshals) were killed in the first four years of the Seven Years War alone.

In a bitterly fought battle a Prussian officer might stand in some peril of his life immediately after he had the misfortune to fall into the hands of the enemy. As a general rule, however, he was merely relieved of his money, watch, sash and gorget, as the custom decreed, and sent back under escort to some secure place in the enemy hands, where he waited in reasonable comfort until the next exchange of prisoners.

The Austrians reaped an exceptionally fine crop of officer prisoners in 1759 and 1760, with the capture of the two entire corps of Finck and Fouqué, and the surprise of the fortress of Glatz. Most of them ended up on parole in the pretty Danubian town of Krems, in Lower Austria. The local people turned out to be friendly enough, and the chief hardship for the Prussians lay in making the trek to the inn of the Weisser Ochs at the village of Dürnstein, where the thirsty northerners discovered a stock of beer that 'tasted very well, but was so strong and heady that it often happened that one or other of the officers had to be carried back to his quarters, being incapable of getting there on his own two feet'.[35]

Unfortunately tempers were already fraying rather badly. Not only did the awkward General Fouqué antagonise his Austrian captors, which launched a series of reprisals and counter-reprisals, but the Austrians and Russians became more and more obstinate at the cartel negotiations, as they began to appreciate that Frederick was running out of officers. The Russian exchanges ceased entirely in 1759, the Austrian in 1760.

Such were some of the specific dangers and hardships of the service. The Prussian officers preferred them – and the crushing boredom of garrison life – to the obscurity and poverty which faced them if they chose to retire. They knew only too well that Frederick had reserved only the most inadequate resources to help his aged officers (about 25,000 thalers in the *Domanenkasse*, forty captaincies worth 500 thalers each, prebendary incomes in every cathedral, and some pensions at the expense of the Silesian abbeys), and that he was capricious and miserly in the way he dispensed his bounty. One of the more fortunate commanders, for instance, might receive an annual pension of up to 3,000 thalers, though it took an energetic personal intervention by Seydlitz to secure so much as 1,000 for the aged and helpless Major General v. Bredow.

Frederick eked out his funds by resorting to some more or less pernicious expedients. A good many veterans were found jobs in the administration of the excise and the tobacco monopoly, where they became objects of pity and scorn for the serving officers.[36] Likewise three grades of postmastership were set aside for aged officers, though the veterans did their work so badly that Frederick was at last compelled to turn over their actual functions to civilian postmasters and pay the old incompetents their pensions direct from the funds of the *General Postamt*. Frederick granted fortress governorships to a number of senior officers who could not be fitted in anywhere else – a circumstance which had disastrous effects when the fortresses came under siege by the French in 1806.

All of this left many people totally unprovided for, and in any case the officers knew that they would have to brave Frederick's sarcasm and anger when they sought permission to retire. To make such a request in wartime was to invite public disgrace.

Even the temporary respite of leave was granted rarely and grudgingly. From 1763 the *Chef* and regimental commandant were denied authority to let an officer go for more than a single day, without royal authority, and the sentries at town gates were placed under standing instructions to take the name of every officer who passed by. One can only admire the bravery of Major v. Sparr of the Bayreuth Dragoons who asked the king for leave in 1744. Frederick replied that he 'ought to die of shame – a young and healthy man who asks to go on leave during a campaign'.[37]

It was hardly surprising that Frederick bequeathed to his successors an aged, inward-looking and self-seeking officer corps. The future Field-Marshal v. Knesebeck wrote that when he entered the regiment of Kalckstein (no 20) in 1783 he found that the captains were mostly 'aged, portly gentlemen, who had eventually attained a very prosperous income after much endurance and hardship, and were now bent on getting what enjoyment they could out of life, a life which up to now had offered them nothing but toil . . . The regimental staff officers were frequently older still, and there were very few of them who were still capable of riding after some fashion, and did not have to hang on to the pommel of their saddles in order to stay on horseback'.[38]

Manners, mores and ideals

Writing at the outbreak of the War of the Bavarian Succession in 1778, a Prussian rejoiced in what seemed to be the spartan spirit of the young officers:

> Just now it did my patriotic heart good when I caught sight of a laden pack-horse. There was a tent, a leathern stool, a small table, a mattress and a chest with the necessities of life – such were the items with which our young hero (perhaps a very wealthy man) must be content . . . They say that at the mobilisation various subalterns had to leave behind or sell luxuries to the value of six hundred, eight hundred or even one thousand thalers – tapestries, carpets, sofas, large mirrors, gilded furniture, soft and magnificent beds, warm dressing gowns . . . All of these are things he must now learn to live without.[39]

By modern standards the allowance was by no means ungenerous. In the field it was the custom in the earlier part of Frederick's reign for the subalterns to sleep together in an oval-shaped tent, one section of which was carried by each member of the tent

Kameradschaft on his pack-horse. During the Seven Years War, however, the lieutenants became entitled to small individual tents of the kind that was seen by our friend with the patriotic heart. The captain's tent was a rather magnificent affair, which owned a separate sleeping compartment beneath its capacious oval roof. Some degree of privacy was certainly desirable, for many of the company's affairs were conducted immediately outside.

All of this helped to load down the regiment with an astonishing quantity of baggage. The horse and baggage allowance of 1740 (an allegedly severe one) permitted the colonel no less than 2 baggage carts, 6 pack-animals and 4 riding horses, with the lower ranks less in proportion. Thus the regiment was encumbered with 13 carts, 50 pack-horses or donkeys and 49 riding horses – and all in addition to the normal regimental baggage (counting the complement at 1 colonel, 1 lieutenant-colonel, 2 majors, 6 captains and 32 lieutenants). The use of tin vessels was prescribed instead of those of silver, for the sake of lightness, though at least one officer contrived to take a harpsichord.

The king took on himself the cost of providing the officers' horses. In the Silesian Wars Frederick merely advanced the necessary money and left it to the officers to make the purchase themselves, which caused a good deal of inconvenience when so many officers wanted to buy horses at the outset of campaigns. In the 1750s, therefore, he began the practice or buying or enrolling horses by the thousand, and distributing them among the regiments *en masse* when the army marched to war. The arrival of the horses invariably caused much excitement among the subalterns. It was recorded during the mobilisation of 1778 that 'unless you saw the sight you would have no idea how the ensigns spent the whole day riding around flat out . . . some of them went so far as to render their horses totally lame, which compelled them to make the next march on foot'.[40]

The officer was sometimes permitted as a favour to retain a soldier of his regiment as a servant, failing which he hired civilian servants and clad them in a livery at his own expense. A particularly resourceful first lieutenant in the regiment of Krockow tells us that when he went to war in 1778 he took along a married soldier and his wife as servants, together with a groom who fed and attended his three horses, and a fifteen-year-old running footman 'who had to dress my hair and carry my spontoon and overcoat on the march. He was also responsible for bearing my canteen, which contained everything necessary for the making of coffee'.[41]

Even the less well-off subaltern did not fare too badly in the field, provided he had a captain who followed the Prussian custom of inviting the ensigns and lieutenants to dine at his table. In 1758 a British observer noted that 'by this means the young officers are constantly under the eye of their superiors, have no pretence for absenting themselves, and have nothing to attend to but their duty; whilst quarrels, caballing and all other inconveniences of too many young men messing together are avoided, of which I have myself seen many bad effects in other armies'.[42]

At the siege of Schweidnitz in 1762, when provisions were exceptionally short, the young subaltern J. G. Scheffner was lucky enough to hitch up with two majors 'who relieved me of all anxiety for my food, except when I went on watch, my lunch invariably consisting of beef and rice, and my supper of a soup made of ration bread sweetened with honey'.[43] Even grand personages like regimental *Chefs* were also not averse to seeing their subalterns at table from time to time. Christian v. Prittwitz remembered how on such occasions the Duke of Bevern delighted in comic stories, 'at which he would laugh out loud, setting his whole vast bulk in motion'.[44]

Strangely enough, there were some ways in which the service of the king of Prussia was less onerous than that of other sovereigns. The Prussian officer was not subjected to such unnecessary inconveniences as getting up every morning to see how the drummers beat reveille, as happened in some foreign armies. He was not expected to have his hair cut every month, and he was not ruined by frequent and costly changes in the style of his uniform. In fact the Frederician officer succeeded in establishing a very necessary distinction between the time he spent on duty and whatever was left over for leisure.

Whereas in the mornings everything was promptitude, obedience and exactness, an entirely different creature emerged in the afternoons. 'As soon as duty was over, the ensign was every bit as free as the lieutenant-general. We knew nothing of that absurd and subservient sense of ceremonial that still obtains in the Austrian army, according to which the second lieutenant may not sit down as long as the first lieutenant is still standing'.[45]

That civilised institution, the officers' mess, was introduced to Prussia only after King Frederick William III saw how the British army managed its affairs in 1814. In Frederick's time the off-duty subalterns crowded together in their smoke-filled guard-rooms (*Wachtstuben*) or whatever inns or coffee houses were to be found nearby. From Carl v. Hülsen we learn how the *Junkers* of the regiment of Below diverted themselves at Königsberg in the early 1750s:

> Not far from the NCOs' quarters there was a coffee house which owned a billiard table. I heard a lot of talk about this game, but I had no idea how it was played. One day I went there with another *Junker* when we were off duty. We took instruction from the landlord, and this game made such an impression on me that I was able to master the principles at once, and in the evening I won a ducat from an English merchant . . . Unfortunately gaming at dice was very fashionable at the time, and whatever I won at billiards I proceeded to lose with the dice.[46]

At a higher level the senior officers of the Berlin garrison used to take off their boots at the close of the morning's work, then have their hair dressed *à outrance* with powder and curls, don silk stockings and a shirt with flowing lace cuffs, seek out their best uniform, and finally place the hat under the arm and go forth into polite society. To Mirabeau the performance seemed 'a quite extraordinary metamorphosis'.[47]

The officers of the Gensd'armes, the First Battalion of the Garde and other fashionable regiments at Berlin danced constant attendance at the functions of the carnival season which lasted from December to February – a round of official assemblies, plays and *redoutes*, as well as magnificent private parties. The Marquis de Toulongeon reported towards the end of the reign: 'We are very much in error concerning the frugality and extreme simplicity which are supposed to prevail among the Prussian generals.' He cited the case of General Möllendorff who dwelt in a 'magnificent house which is furnished with great elegance. He owns an army of servants and is hospitable in the extreme, laying out every day a table of thirty places for the officers of the garrison. Prittwitz and others also live in high style'.[48]

Given the basic similarity of uniforms within the officer corps, it sometimes happened that at such a social gathering an inexperienced young subaltern might treat an important superior with too much familiarity. The senior officer usually took such a gaffe with equanimity, 'convinced that the younger man, as soon as he became aware of his mistake, would immediately behave himself once more in a suitable manner'.[49]

In settings of a more formal kind Frederick was anxious to keep the younger officers in their place, but even he was willing to allow a subaltern to demand an apology from a senior officer if he felt that he had been insulted. The king merely stipulated that the young man should bottle up his resentment for as long as he was actually on duty.

As for the relations between officer and man, Frederick told the regimental commanders in 1763 that they 'must be very careful to prevent the *Junkers* from mixing so much with the private soldiers, apart from what is necessary for the service. Such company will always leave its mark on these young people when they reach higher rank'.[50]

The officer certainly kept a narrow watch on the character and moods of his men, but it was only to be warned in good time if they were likely to desert. To have shared the life of the NCOs and men as a comrade would have been considered as 'a kind of abuse of familiarity'.[51]

By no means all of the spare-time activities of the Prussian officer corps were as elegant as the diversions of Möllendorff and his kind. A large proportion of the officers were inveterate gamblers. Drunkenness, strangely enough, presented no great problem until the Prussians first made the acquaintance of drinkable wine in the Rhine war of the middle 1730s. The boozing flared up again whenever the army made an incursion into Austrian territory and came across a good source of Bohemian or Hungarian wine. Winterfeldt and Seydlitz were well known as heavy drinkers.

The results of the drinking were interesting and unpredictable. In 1758 Second Lieutenant v. Lemcke took offence at being turned out of his lodging by the landlord, Dr Küntzel:

> The same evening [writes Lemcke], I betook myself to the Italiener-Keller at Malibernow and had a little too much to drink, whereupon I recalled that I had promised Dr Küntzel that I would break his windows for him. I went along to his house and saw some stones outside, though my head was swimming so badly that I was unable to pick them up. But the sentry came up from the nearby Thomas Gate and asked: 'What are you looking for, lieutenant?'
>
> I replied: 'Stones, I want to break that lad's windows.'
>
> 'Ah well! We'll get some then!'
>
> He laid down his musket, brought up even more stones than I needed, and joined in so industriously in the window-smashing that soon there was not a pane intact on the ground floor and the first storey.[52]

The authorities punished Lemcke with a short period of detention.

It would have been surprising if a good many of the officers had not succumbed to the coarser pleasures of the great cities in this, one of the most blatantly sexual societies of the time. In Berlin the public prostitutes were 'more numerous than in any town in Europe in proportion to the number of inhabitants. They appear openly at the windows in the daytime, beckon to passengers as they walk in the streets, and ply for employment in any way they please, without disturbance from the magistrate'.[53] Indeed the Bloody Finger and other Berlin establishments became so much a part of city life that some of the officers used to drop in for a smoke and a chat, without any intention of sampling the wares that were on offer.

An old regimental *Feldscher* told the serious-minded *Junker* Saldern (the future general) that mortality was exceptionally heavy in the First Silesian War because so many officers were riddled with venereal infection and succumbed to the slightest flesh wound. He therefore advised him: 'Spare your powder for the service, for your future wife and for your old age!'[54] Saldern followed the counsel, with spectacular results in all three directions.

Most notorious among the libertines was General v. Seydlitz, the great cavalryman, who learnt his wild ways during the time he spent as page to the crazy Margrave of Brandenburg-Schwedt. He made a slow recovery from his wound at Rossbach because he had caught the pox in Silesia from the 'society of a lady of high birth but lowly conduct'.[55] It was the same story after the battle of Kunersdorf.

Seydlitz made a disastrous marriage in 1760, which only strengthened his dislike of all social contact save promiscuous womanising. In 1772, already afflicted by a stroke, he commissioned an officer to bring back two of his favourite Circassian girls from a horse-buying expedition to Turkey. The officer returned with the ladies, and the consequences for Seydlitz were literally fatal.

Seydlitz was lucky to have married at all, for the king was a famous woman-hater and believed that marriage was an unnecessary distraction from military duties. Among most regiments the married officers amounted to between one-sixth and one-seventh of the total, while the Bayreuth Dragoons went to war in 1778 with an entire corps of seventy-four unmarried officers.

In peacetime the wives of the officers lived with their husbands in quarters in the garrison towns, and they were supposed to stay there alone in time of war, being forbidden to travel with the regiments on campaign. Officers' wives, being the most formidable of creatures, were not the people to be put off by royal regulations. In 1758 the wife of General v. Tresckow, the commandant of Neisse, managed to browbeat the Austrians into letting her through to the fortress while it was under siege. Two years later Lehndorff was surprised to discover the wife of Lieutenant-Colonel v. Pannwitz abroad in the camp near Stralsund: he recalled how she used to shine in Berlin society, and how 'at that time she would have feared to damage her beauty if she had exposed herself to the slightest hardship. But now she is perfectly content with her present situation: she has put up with two other ladies in a house in a miserable village, and every day she goes half a league to dine with her husband in a tent, where they are surrounded by all the smell of the cavalry horses'.[56]

A widowed officer's wife could place her young children in the officers' department (founded 1 February 1744) of the Potsdam Military Orphanage (*Militärwaisenhaus*), though she herself was in danger of being left without any provision at all. The widows' pension fund was established only on 1 April 1776, and it was filled entirely by voluntary contributions from officers who wished to put aside something for their wives.

What with all the drinking, gambling and whoring – not to mention the ordinary tensions attendant upon the Prussian service – even the most inoffensive officer was liable to be caught up in a quarrel with an obstreperous comrade. The implications were potentially lethal, for duels at that time were serious affairs which had little in common with the repulsive artificiality of the nineteenth-century student *Schlager* bout. A typically bloody set-to was staged in August 1762 when Lieutenant-General v. Platen and the quarrelsome Major-General v. Meier hacked each other about messily in the head. General v. Hülsen stepped in to break up the fight and received a stab in the arm for his pains.

Sometimes the formalities were dispensed with altogether. Thus in January 1746

Major v. Chazot of the Bayreuth Dragoons found himself fighting for his life against Bronikowsky, an officer whom he had once had occasion to reprimand. Chazot was able to draw his sword before he could come to serious harm, and

> now the battle took a more favourable turn, and with one of my cuts I slashed the eguillettes from his uniform, so that they were scattered around the room in shreds. Since he was bigger than I was, and considered himself the more powerful, my real aim was to disarm him.
>
> I drove him across the room as far as the stove, where I intended to snatch his sword, but I lost my footing and the major dealt me a blow in the right arm which bit to the bone. The pain of my wound increased my violence, and I was unlucky enough to give him a cut which split his skull. He collapsed on the floor just in front of the door where he had first attacked me.[57]

His antagonist died of the wound, and Chazot was sentenced to one year's fortress arrest in Spandau, of which he served only a few weeks.

Duelling had been prohibited in Brandenburg-Prussia by laws of 1652 and 1685, and again in draconian style by an edict of Frederick William's dating from 1713. Yet even that fierce old disciplinarian was willing to concede that an officer might be justified in fighting a duel in extreme circumstances. Frederick had to concede the same point, though he held in principle that the duel was a barbaric custom that arose from a mistaken sense of honour.

All this time the officers persisted in ostracising any comrade who shrank from a duel. They chafed against the prohibitions, and their feeling ran solidly against the 'courts of honour' which Frederick proposed in a draft code of civil law in 1785. The king died in the following year and the project was never put into effect.

It is doubtful whether Frederick was any more successful in curbing the other manifestations of the officers' wildness. In January 1741 he proclaimed that he had no intention of promoting any officer who was known as a gambler or a drunkard, an announcement which produced a salutary but short-lived shock. He had to renew his prohibitions at the close of the Seven Years War, and again at the end of the War of the Bavarian Succession.

While the reprobates attracted most of the attention, a significant number of senior officers set an example of quiet and sober conduct. There was Schmettau, who had the reputation of being 'one of the best-living and most pious generals in Frederick's army',[58] there was the almost Victorian figure of Saldern, and there was the emotional hussar general Belling who had the alarming habit of conducting fervent hymn sessions in the immediate presence of the enemy. Schwerin, Stille, Fouqué, Zieten, Moller, Kahlden and the like were known as commanders who combined 'the soldier's profession with true Christianity'.[59]

Frederick's table at Potsdam was the scene of many odd juxtapositions of Frenchified wits and sceptics on the one hand, and conventionally minded Prussian generals on the other. Saldern and Schmettau put up what defence they could of their old-fashioned beliefs, though innocents like the honest and ignorant Pomeranian general Lettow were lost amid the flying epigrams.

Away from the royal salons we do not expect to find anything resembling a genuine intellectual life in the body of the Prussian army, and it is a remarkable testimony to the resilience of the human spirit that such a phenomenon managed to survive and even flourish.

Certainly the discouragements were extreme. In the majority of regiments the tone was set by the crudities of the *Wachtstube* and loud-mouthed, ignorant young officers of the kind who were to disgust Gneisenau in later years. Frederick actually found it necessary in 1751 to order all free corporals to learn the rudiments of writing, so that they could at least compose a passable military report. At a higher level Prince Moritz of Dessau excelled in total illiteracy even over General v. Ramin, who 'really belonged in the age of the Huns and Vandals'.[60] This is not to suggest that many other commanders did not have a shaky grasp of letters. There was one old general who caused some confusion when he recommended a young relative to Frederick as being 'very cowardly' (*sehr feig*) when he really meant to write that he was 'very capable' (*sehr fähig*). Another warrior went to a bookshop to buy some maps and became very angry at an assistant who enquired: 'Does the general want local maps or general maps?' 'What a question to ask! I'm a general, so I must have general maps!'[61]

Frederick's own influence on published writing was strongly negative. Captain Marquart, an able topographical engineer, fell mortally ill and asked Frederick for permission to publish a treatise entitled *Coup d'Oeil Militaire*, which he composed in the winter of 1759. The king merely replied that he would be better employed in staking out camps. The case was typical. Probably the only important work of military technology to be published with royal approval was Tempelhoff's *Bombardier Prussien* of 1781, which was a scientific investigation of ballistics. Tempelhoff had already put forward a more down-to-earth treatise on the tactics of infantry and artillery, but the king had rejected it as being unsuitable for publication – in other words, too useful.

Fortunately, perhaps, Frederick expressed little or no interest in the coming-together of a particularly significant group of literary men in the later 1750s. One of the leading lights was the highly cultivated officer Ewald Christian v. Kleist (1715–59), who had studied law and mathematics in his youth and was known as the author of a pretty poem celebrating the beauties of spring ('Frühling', 1749). He was moved by the first campaigns of the Seven Years War to compose his 'Ode an die preussische Armee' (7 May 1757), which in turn inspired his correspondent, the civilian Johann Wilhelm Gleim, to embark on his famous series of *Kriegslieder*. As if feeling the approach of his own death, Kleist turned in his last work (the epic poem *Cissides und Paches*, 1759) to the subject of two young Thessalians who fell in battle against the Athenians. He himself was mortally wounded at Kunersdorf shortly afterwards.

The 'German Horace' K. W. Ramler (see p. 28) published a collected edition of Kleist's works in 1760, and another friend, Gotthold Ephraim Lessing, made the fallen officer the model for 'Major v. Tellheim' in his play *Minna von Barnhelm* (written 1763). Lessing had a further contact with the officer corps in his capacity as secretary to the redoubtable General v. Tauentzien from 1760 to 1764.

Other intellectually minded officers found congenial conversation in the company of people like Prince Henry, General v. Retzow, General v. Kalckreuth, the French philosopher Maupertuis (President of the Berlin Academy), and the generals Hautcharmoy, Fouqué and other members of the Huguenot colony. Field-Marshal Keith was acquainted with eleven languages, while his elder brother George Keith the Earl Marshal of Scotland was known as the protector of Rousseau, and lived from 1766 to 1778 in a convenient

The intellectual officer. Ewald Christian v. Kleist at his writing desk

house at the entrance to Sans Souci where he encouraged officers in their reading of foreign literature.

Elsewhere in the army, amid all the philistinism, there was an unpretentious minority which was well acquainted with polite literature,[62] as well as a larger element of the naturally intelligent and curious. Thus the hussar general Daniel v. Lossow possessed only the sketchiest education, but after the Seven Years War he made it his business to pursue a serious study of military history, mathematics and French, and he frequently invited the philosopher Kant to dine at his table at Goldap.

In the second half of the century an increasing number of junior officers fell under the spell of a Werther-like wistful melancholy. In the Seven Years War the idealistic young J. G. Scheffner became an officer in the unlikely setting of the regiment of Ramin, and he tells us that

> at every opportunity most of my comrades would ride off to the towns as soon as they heard that some ball or gaming session was afoot. I preferred to walk over the open hills for the sake of the view, and I still remember how my comrades laughed at me when, after a strenuous march, I preferred to climb the Landeskron instead of riding to Görlitz, where they promised to show me the most wonderful things . . . While in the camp at Glogau I set about reading Rousseau's newly-published *Nouvelle Héloise*, which pleased me so much that contrary to my usual unpraise-worthy custom I took the trouble to copy out long extracts. Then again during a short stay at Liegnitz the bookseller Siegert lent me the first two volumes of the Wieland translation of Shakespeare. It attracted me powerfully, and I left a glittering evening party in order to spend the whole night reading it.[63]

Likewise in the 1770s the Garde lieutenant Winanko used to wait impatiently for the appearance of Goethe's latest plays, and he corresponded on Ossian, Quixote and other literary matters with three of his fellow-subalterns.

Amid so much diversity there somehow arose a sense of corporate identity among the officers which was seen as specifically Prussian. Frederick and his officers liked to think that they went about affairs in a way that was practical, prompt and clear-headed, while being free from pedantry and any useless ceremonial or servility. Another important ingredient of the style was a 'nobility of conduct and a certain sense of dignity'.[64]

Even the sceptical Kaltenborn and Trenck were willing to bear testimony to the remarkable sense of comradeship of the officer corps, and its devotion to the king.[65] In an odd way the officers were almost proud of Frederick's displays of tyrannical temperament, which drove them together for protection and reassured them that the king really cared how they looked and behaved. An officer in the newly formed uhlan regiment of Natzmer describes how his men reached the royal camp at Strehlen on 20 June 1741 and 'waited for the king on a broad meadow, in holy silence under a brilliant sun. Up he rode, accompanied by Zieten and two other commanders. It was the first time I had seen him . . . My heart was racing wildly, and my eyes filled with tears when I met the gracious greeting that was in the royal gaze. I felt I ought to be falling to my knees'.[66] Other officers, at the first sight of Frederick, talked of being raised to Olympus,[67] or having some inkling of what it must have been that had made Alexander, Scipio and Caesar unbeatable.[68]

An Austrian commander, the Prince de Ligne, wished that his own army had more officers like the young Flemming v. Hagen, who was captured by the Austrians in 1778

(above left) *Prince Henry of Prussia, the king's brother and victor of Freiberg (1762)*; (above right) *Heinrich August de la Motte Fouqué. Harsh but dedicated, and a favourite of the king. He is wearing studio armour. The fortress of Glatz is in the background*; (below left) *Friedrich Christoph v. Saldern, the drillmaster of the late Frederician army*; (below right) *Wichard Joachim v. Möllendorf. Urbane and respected, one of the leaders of Berlin society in the later reign. Below the Black Eagle he is wearing the Stiftskreuz of Havelberg cathedral, from where he drew a prebendary's income* and turned aside some good-natured enquiries about his girl friends with the declaration 'I love nothing more dearly than my sword!'[69]

It was this lack of humour which made the greatest impression on some of the English observers. They encountered a 'pensive attention to duty',[70] a 'staid, serious appearance, exceedingly different from the grave, dissipated, *dégagé* air of the British or French officers'.[71] John Burgoyne carried away the same impression, and concluded that the driving force of the Prussian army resided in the technical proficiency of the lieutenants and NCOs and their principle of unthinking obedience. He believed that the vigour of the army declined 'as the ranks ascend, and other qualifications than those of mere execution become requisite'.[72]

What can the writers and speakers of the time tell us about the motivation of Frederick's army? For the preacher F. E. Boysen, who held forth at Magdeburg in the Seven Years War, loyalty simply proceeded from the ancient obligation to fear God and honour the King. Contemporary writers (J. G. Zimmermann, *Von dem Nationalstolze*, 1758, T. Abbt, *Vom Tode für das Vaterland*, 1761) elaborated on the theme, and held that a loyal people might bask in the reflected glory of a hero–king like Frederick. Two young Königsberg men-of-letters, David Neumann and our friend Scheffner, abandoned their studies and took themselves off to the army clutching the book by Abbt.

Gleim of the grenadier *Kriegslieder* did not feel the need for such a roundabout justification, for he was passionately convinced of the justice of the Prussian cause. He rejected the cosmopolitan outlook as inadequate, writing to Ramler in 1759 that 'the cosmopolitan wants everything to go well with the world. But when the whole world wants everything to go badly with our fatherland, we must of necessity oppose the whole world, until it is brought to a better way of thinking'.[73]

Such a sense of pride did not embrace Germany as a whole, despite all the scorn and hatred which the Prussians worked up against the French in the Seven Years War. Indeed in his *Siegeslied nach der Schlacht bei Rossbach* Gleim delights in the misfortunes of various categories of Germans – the Franconians, crying like cats in a trap, or the soldiers from Cologne who clung to memories of white wine amid all the gushing red blood.

It is difficult to imagine such sentiments coming from the lips of genuine Prussian grenadiers who actually had to fight the enemy, who were fellow-soldiers. All the same there is something more than faintly fanatical about the outlook of the professional officer Kleist, who was less concerned with patriotism as such than with a bleak sense of honour which drove on the warrior to victory or death. His 'Ode an die preussische Armee' revelled in the scene when his 'invincible army' chased after the enemy and drove deep into their skulls with its death-dealing swords:

> *Du eilest ihnen nach und drückst mit schwerem Eisen*
> *Den Tod tief in ihren Schädeln ein . . .*

We are a world removed from the spirit of General James Wolfe, quietly reading Gray's 'Elegy' on the way to his death at Quebec.

It is an unreal Kleist, as personified in Lessing's *Minna von Barnhelm*, who has come down to posterity as the archetype of the Frederician officer. 'Major v. Tellheim', the officer in question, has been dismissed from the army after the Seven Years War, and while preserving a quirky sense of honour is perfectly willing to look back on his military career as a passing phase in the evolution of his character:

I became a soldier from partisanship, rather than any political principles, and because it struck me that it might be good for an honourable man to spend some time getting acquainted with danger and acquiring coolness and resolution. But only the most extreme necessity could have driven me to make a vocation out of this expedient! It was an incidental pursuit, not a trade.

There is little here which calls to mind the Prussian officer of history, who was willing to give life-long service to a king as ungrateful as Frederick.

3

The Men

Recruitment

In the make-up of its rank and file the Prussian army of Frederick's time is best described as a curious amalgam of Territorial Army and Foreign Legion. One element consisted of part-time native troops. Foreign mercenaries made up the other.

The native conscripts were selected by the workings of the Cantonal System, which had been set up by Frederick William I between 1727 and 1735. What the old king did was to assign every regiment a permanent catchment area around its peacetime garrison town (*Standort*), from where it drew its draftees for lifelong service. It was possible for the same districts to be shared for this purpose by regiments of line infantry, garrison infantry and cavalry as well as by companies of artillery, for the physical requirements for each arm were so different.

Frederick gradually extended the system to newly conquered Silesia in the 1740s, and by creating supernumerary cantonists (*Überkompletten*) he raised a reserve of 10,000 additional native troops in time for the Seven Years War.

After the Seven Years War the cantonal administration was brought to full perfection. The name of every duty-bound male was entered on a roll at birth, and as he grew to age he was drawn deeper and deeper into the military machine: he swore an oath immediately after his confirmation ceremony, to remind him of his duty, and he was told that if he escaped abroad he would be declared a deserter and that his parents' property would be confiscated.

Meanwhile the regimental *Chefs* kept themselves up to date on the details of the age, height and appearance of all such young 'disposable men' (those without an exemption), and every year before the spring review a regimental officer and a civilian official jointly selected such recruits as were needed to make up the regiment's annual requirement for native draftees. The term of service was indefinite, so as to make sure that the army got the full benefit from the time it put into training its soldiers.

In terms of the native prowess of their recruits Frederick ranked the regions of his kingdom in something like the following descending order of merit:

Pomerania and Brandenburg
Magdeburg and Halberstadt
Lower Silesia (Lutheran)
Upper Silesia with Glatz (Catholic)
East Prussia (with its treacherous nobility)
Prussian Westphalia (though Minden and Herford were good)
Berlin

At the top of the scale the Baltic plains produced the Pomeranians – direct, reliable, brave and uncomplicated folk who made what Warnery called 'the best infantry in the world'.[1] With troops like his Pomeranians and Märker, said Frederick, he could rout the Devil from Hell.

In Westphalia, at the other extremity, the three Wesel regiments had to be recruited from foreigners, 'because the people of these provinces are flabby and soft, useless as soldiers', while the nobility 'have almost destroyed their reason with wine'.[2] As for the natives of his own capital, Frederick hardly ever took a born Berliner into the Garde, for he 'liked the Berliners almost the least of all his subjects'.[3]

The native element in the Prussian army amounted to 50,000 out of a total of 133,000 troops in 1751, 70,000 out of 160,000 in 1768, and 80,000 out of 190,000 at the time of Frederick's death in 1786.

Frederick so arranged affairs that this drain on manpower caused the least possible inconvenience to his kingdom, which at the end of his reign owned less than five million subjects. First of all there was a large and growing list of exemptions which extended to whole localities such as the cities and towns of Berlin, Potsdam, Brandenburg, the duchy of Cleves and the principality of Meurs, and the flax-growing and politically sensitive mountain areas of Silesia, not to mention a host of 'non-disposable' individuals like businessmen, craftsmen, small landowners, fathers of families, sons of widows, and cooks, gardeners and all other people who had been trained for specific work at the cost of their masters. In any case Frederick believed that many of these folk had little military aptitude.

Secondly the regiments were required to be up to strength only for the few weeks of the spring reviews and the summer exercise season. For something like ten months, therefore, the native troops were free to return home to their families and trades, and the cavalryman actually took his horse back with him to the native farm.

The captain was only too glad to see most of his company disappear on leave, for as long as the men were absent their military pay went straight into his pocket (see p. 32). His only obligation, though it was a strict one, was to keep enough troops with his company to ensure that every man who remained (usually a foreigner) could enjoy three days' rest for every one spent on guard duty.

Even during the stay at the *Standort* reliable troops of all kinds were given permission to pursue civilian trades as *Freiwächter*, provided they remembered to turn up for the church parade every Sunday. The Swiss poet Ulrich Bräker, who is an unfailing source of information on the life of the other ranks, recalls that as he strolled one day beside the Spree he saw that 'hundreds of soldiers were at work loading and unloading merchandise, while the timber yards were full of toiling warriors. Back in the barracks the same kind of thing was going on, with the soldiers pursuing every kind of activity, from fine handiwork to spinning'.[4]

Some of the garrison routine orders read almost like guild regulations. 'All military men who are engaged as masons, carpenters or day-labourers are hereby seriously warned that, in the event of a master punishing a soldier, they must not intervene in the affair or create a mutiny. From now on the soldiers may not take wood from the building sites to their quarters in the evening. Nor may they linger too long over breakfast, for in that way much working time is lost.'[5]

On the whole the Prussian system of native recruiting worked very well. The conscripts laboured under no real sense of grievance, and when they returned home they usually proved to be very good managers of their civilian affairs, 'for you know very well what a high state of discipline and order prevails among our military men'.[6]

The Marquis de Toulongeon noted that the cantonal authorities were careful to select only the best-set-up men, and he remarked that 'all the ordinary companies of fusiliers are good enough to have been fine companies of grenadiers in our own army'.[7] By its association with the reserves of manpower in the canton the regiment became virtually immortal, to use Frederick's phrase, while 'the men of the same regiment all know each other, being drawn from the same province. This makes their life much more agreeable, and creates a comradeship which is most useful on the day of battle'.[8] The action at Domstadtl in 1758 proved how well even a collection of raw cantonists could fight when they were left to their own devices.

Indirectly the cantonal system helped Frederick in his work of consolidating the conquest of Silesia. Bakers, brewers and butchers set up shop around the new Prussian garrisons, which promoted the local economy. Moreover, according to a contemporary report, the returning cantonists set 'the example of refinement in their native villages, thereby contributing towards enlightenment. It often happens that soldiers on leave are the only people in Upper Silesian villages who speak any German or have a civilised appearance'.[9]

The infantry *Reglement* of 1 June 1743 stipulated 'that the captains must spare the men in their cantons as a permanent and sure resource'. This precious reserve of manpower, conserved so carefully over the years, proved to be Prussia's salvation in the crisis of the Seven Years War.

The rest of the troops were foreign cannon fodder, brought into the army to fill out the ranks and be killed off in the first campaigns of a war. Every regiment sent officers and NCOs ranging through Europe and especially the German states, bringing in any man of passable stature who might be persuaded to don the blue coat through inclination, gullibility or misfortune. Bräker says that before the Seven Years War he saw five Prussian recruiting officers simultaneously at work in the Swiss town of Schaffhausen. Bräker ignored the fine offers which accompanied their champagne and burgundy, but he himself was tricked by a lieutenant into travelling all the way to Berlin where, instead of being taken into service as a lackey, he was impressed into the notorious *Donner und Blitzen* regiment of Itzenplitz.

Other men of taste and learning found themselves in the same predicament. The Duke of Bevern encountered no difficulty in obtaining language tutors for his young officers from among the many intelligent foreigners who had fallen on hard times and entered his regiment. One of the privates in his *Leibcompagnie* ultimately left the army and pursued a career in the civil administration, becoming the head of a department in the Breslau treasury. Still more fortunate was the penniless Abbé Bastiani, who came to Prussia as a recruit for the regiment of Tauentzien, and ended up as one of Frederick's wittiest and most valued companions.

Generally speaking, the foreign mercenaries were interesting people, the many Italians and French

whiling away the time partly with comedies, dances and songs, and partly talking about wine, girls and what had happened in the wars. They rarely uttered any noise or complaint when one of their comrades took more than his share of the rations . . . When the company of the soldiers became really repulsive and irksome was when the exercise season was over and the cantonists spent a time in the garrisons. These folk were mostly peasants, miners and other labourers, and their inborn coarseness and rudeness, combined with their high degree of stupid pride and impertinence, all served to render their society distasteful in the extreme.[10]

Foreign recruits of a decidedly less agreeable kind ended up in the regiment of Hessen-Cassel (no 45), which became the repository of all the criminals which the squeamish Landgraf could not steel himself to condemn to death. More dangerous still was the general practice of impressing enemy prisoners of war, especially when, as happened in 1756, they were taken over in entire units.

The cost of recruiting the unreliable foreigners was extremely heavy, in both financial and military terms. Altogether the foreign recruiting cost the state 18,400,000 thalers in Frederick's reign. Moreover the entire army had to be organised and conducted in a way that made sure that the foreigners were always under the eye of an officer. Thus the regular troops could hardly ever be employed as light infantry or independent foragers.

Conditions of service

Bräker describes the first impressions of a recruit in some detail. The first person to confront him at the outset of his military career was a sergeant-major, who came up to him with a uniform coat over his arm, spread the coarse blue cloth on a table, put down a six-groschen piece and pronounced: 'That's for you, sonny! Wait a second and I'll bring you a piece of ration bread.' Bräker now appreciated that he was well on the way to becoming a lifelong soldier of the King of Prussia, and he made his protests to the major of the battalion, 'a mighty great man, with a hero's face and a pair of fiery eyes like stars'. All was in vain.

Next they led me to the quartermaster's stores, where they fitted me up with breeches, shoes and gaiters, and gave me hat, stock and hose. Then I had to go with twenty-odd other recruits to Colonel Lattorff. They conducted us into a hall, which seemed as big as a church, and brought up several badly-holed colours and ordered each of us to take hold of a corner. An adjutant, or whoever he was, read us a whole screed of articles of war and pronounced a few formulae, which the others murmured after him. I kept my mouth shut and fixed my attention elsewhere – I believe I thought about Annie [his girl friend]. Lastly he swung a colour over our heads and dismissed us.[11]

Bräker probably did not remember the last episode of the ceremony, which was when the regimental auditor gave the recruit his *Abrechnungsbuch*, a most holy document which specified all the small items of uniform he had just received.

In peacetime the recruit lived through a full 'recruit year', for most of which he was quartered with a veteran who taught him how to clean his uniform and equipment, how to salute his superiors, and all the rest of the unwritten lore of the Prussian army. On the drill square the recruit was 'at first treated with a degree of gentleness . . . they seem cautious of confounding him at the beginning, or driving him to despair, and take care not to pour all the terrors of their discipline upon his astonished senses at once'. A subaltern then took over the training of the recruits, and 'in the park at Berlin, every morning may be seen the lieutenants of the different regiments exercising with the greatest assiduity, sometimes a single man, at other times three or four together; and now, if the young recruit shows neglect or remissness, his attention is roused by the officer's cane'.[12] As the recruits became proficient, so they were taken from the recruit platoon and incorporated in the main body of the company.

As a general rule the drilling of the raw troops went on for a solid six months of the 'recruit year'. In addition most of the troops who were present in the garrison were drilled on Sundays and on the first, fifth, eleventh, sixteenth, twenty-first and twenty-sixth days of the month. The drill sessions were short (except for the recruits), but they were exacting in the extreme. 'None of the higher commanders ever took into account the exhaustion of the younger men, who might be suffering from tuberculosis and spitting blood, any more than they did of the limping or stiff soldiers of fifty years or so.'[13]

The infantry private received 2 thalers pay every month (the cavalryman usually a little more), which was made over by instalments every five days. From this magnificent sum 12 groschen were deducted for bread (at 2 lb a day, but free in wartime), and 5 groschen 8 pfennigs as *Fleischgeld* (for meat at $1\frac{1}{2}$ lb a week).

The majority of the infantry were billeted upon private householders in the garrison towns. On visiting Potsdam an English traveller was 'not a little surprised . . . to see buff-belts, breeches, and waistcoats, hung to dry from the genteelest-looking houses, till I was informed, that each housekeeper has two or more soldiers quartered in his house, and their apartments are, for the most part, on the first floor, with windows to the street'.[14] One of the soldiers was under orders to collect five groschen per month from each of his comrades, from which he was to keep house and prepare meals on the householder's fire – an arrangement which was supposed to foster comradeship and self-reliance.

In the last decades of the reign more and more troops were put into the barracks that were being run up at Berlin and the other major towns. The chambers contained between twenty-five and thirty beds (two men taking turns to sleep in each bed), and in those crowded halls the air was 'always thick and infected, for the soldiers, like the German peasants, are accustomed to keeping the windows of their rooms shut for at least six months of the year'.[15]

It was Frederick's policy to keep the infantry in the towns, where the troops could be kept together under close supervision, and assembled quickly and quietly in the event of mobilisation. The cavalry, on the other hand, needed ample stabling and plenty of open country for fodder, and so the regiments of horse were scattered among the little villages.

The private's life was compounded of a series of strong impressions: the maddening exactitude of the watch parade, the mind-crushing but mercifully short drills and parades, the appalling punishments, and the blessed solace of the off-duty hours (few for recruits but ample for everyone else) when he was free to pursue his own interests or simply wander about the streets.

Every Sunday all the available troops were called in for one of the high points of the week, the church parade. Prittwitz writes:

We had to march off in files to the church appropriate to our religion. Everyone had to go, whether he wanted to or not. Frequently the service took the form of a communion, and on such occasions I found something extremely elevating and blessed in the silence and reverence which reigned among that mass of warriors.[16]

In turn the training routine of the year revolved around the grand reviews and manoeuvres. Inevitably the impressions were somewhat confused:

The endless fields were covered with soldiers, and there were many thousands of spectators on every side. To begin with there would be two large armies drawn up artistically in order of battle. Then the heavy guns would open up on each other from the flanks, and finally the troops advanced and opened fire, blinding you with smoke and making such a frightful thunder that you could not hear your neighbour.[17]

The troops were less concerned with the beauty of the tactics than with the damage that might be caused to their uniforms, particularly in the muddy season of the autumn manoeuvres, for they were bound to pay for replacements out of their own pockets. 'I took part in three such manoeuvres at Magdeburg,' complained Laukhard, 'and each time my little treasury was exhausted.'[18]

Once the king ordered a mobilisation for war the native cantonists had to tear themselves from their houses and families and return to the colours. That was why the Prussian soldier 'went less willingly to the field than any other'.[19]

To begin with, the foreign soldiers were only too glad when war arrived to break up the round of the peacetime year. But then came those terrible marches:

The heat was so oppressive than one day, the 6th July [1760] 105 Prussians dropped dead in their ranks. Everyone yearned for water, yet the heavily-laden soldiers were not supposed to be allowed to drink it, even though they were dripping with sweat. But once they came across a spring, a stream, a pond or even a puddle, their raging thirst overcame all their other instincts, even the fear of the stick . . . They sprang from the ranks, scooped up the water in their hats, and refreshed themselves regardless of the blows that were raining down on them.[20]

When, however, Frederick allowed his army a little rest, the camp became a mirror image of life in the *Standort*. The tent and its seven-man *Kameradschaft* took the place of the billet in the town, with one man maintaining discipline, while the others saw to the laundry and cooking, or went off to fetch provisions, wood and bedding straw.

Bread and meat were furnished free on campaign, thanks to the overwhelming generosity of the king, but almost everything else had to be bought from the sutler, which put the monied soldier at a great advantage. There was a characteristic scene when the Prussian army sat down to blockade Pirna in September 1756.

Life in the camp went on exactly as in a town. There were swarms of sutlers and butchers, and all day long you could see long streets of stalls where food was being boiled or roasted. You could have everything you wanted, or rather everything you were able to pay for – meat, butter, cheese, bread and every kind of vegetable and fruit. Except for the men on watch duty the troops occupied themselves as the fancy took them, playing skittles, gaming, or strolling in the camp or outside. Only a few individuals crouched idly in their tents.[21]

In every company between five and a dozen soldiers' wives actually accompanied their husbands on campaign. These extremely tough females were added to the regimental strength on the understanding that they would help out with the laundry and the care of the wounded. Unless they were kept under strict control, however, they were apt to engage in fights, plundering expeditions and other kinds of misbehaviour. On the hot morning of the battle of Kolin the enterprising wives of the regiment of Bevern broke into an underground ice-house, and came back bearing chunks of ice which they broke into small fragments and sold at high prices to the sweating soldiery, who stood in ranks in the open field.

Frederick strongly favoured stable marriages for his private soldiers, 'so as to populate the country, and to preserve the stock, which is admirable'.[22] Thus the soldiers and their families formed a significant proportion of the population of the garrison towns. Out of the 100,000 souls who dwelt in Berlin in 1776, there were 17,056 NCOs and men, as well as 5,526 military wives and 6,622 children. The sheer quantity of soldiers and their dependents was itself a powerful factor making for the militarisation of Prussian society.

In peacetime the wives of the foreign soldiers lived with their husbands either in quarters in the town or in the barracks, where they received a small salary in return for cleaning the rooms and making the beds. Their husbands were given an allowance of eight groschen per day, in lieu of victuals, which accounts for the name of *Achtgroschenmänner* that was applied to them by their unmarried comrades.

In time of war the wives who remained in the garrison town were granted bread and a small pension by the state, and they could correspond with their husbands gratis by taking their letters to be stamped with the municipal seal. The return correspondence was stamped with the regimental seal, though all too often the soldiers failed to survive to be able to answer the letters from home. By 1758 two thousand children of dead or destitute soldiers were being raised in the huge Potsdam Military Orphanage – the boys for the military service, and the girls for a variety of fates.

Among the unmarried troops the libertines consorted with the large class of prostitutes, which itself was largely recruited from the daughters of soldiers:

> The girls pursued their affairs mostly on the street or in the taverns. Music, if you can call it that, was played in such soldiers' taverns every day. The standard was appalling, but it was good enough to dance to, or at least to provide the girls with a beat for gambolling around, which sufficed for the taste of these nymphs.[23]

Concubines, if they were healthy, were on occasion allowed to live in the soldiers' rooms.

The Potsdam Military Orphanage was the favourite resort of the grenadiers of the First Battalion of the Garde, and there was a curious custom by which they were permitted to set themselves up in private quarters with the girl of their choice. All that was needed was to obtain a form from the company commander stating 'Grenadier . . . has leave to take . . . to himself as his beloved'. The partners lived together for as long or as short a period as was agreeable to them, and they consigned any children of their liaison to the Orphanage, there perhaps to begin the process again.

Aged private soldiers hung on in their regiments for the same bad reason as the aged officers, namely the bleakness of the prospect of life in the outside world. In the Seven Years War every regiment owned a number of ancient veterans who could scarcely keep up on the march, and the proportion grew still higher during the long peace that followed.

At first we are impressed by the enumeration of the facilities for the invalids (discharged soldiers). The *Reglement* of 1743 stated that when men were forced to leave the army through age or infirmity the regiments were under an obligation to report their names to the king, 'so that they may be taken care of and spared the necessity of begging'. The NCOs and some of the more deserving soldiers were found jobs in the excise or the tobacco monopoly, or settled on waste land as colonists. Others were granted monthly

Invalid and cadets

pensions of one or two thalers from the New Fund, which was set up in 1748. Altogether 600 married invalids were granted rooms with their wives in the Invalid House, a massive building which was sited outside the Oranienburger-Tor in Berlin. Above the gate ran the same inscription that Louis XIV had put up on the Invalides, LAESO ET INVICTI MILITI, and inside the warren of chambers the invalids were supposed to live out their lives in contentment, being uniformed, fed and paid by the state. In fact the house was 'badly kept up, and pervaded by a most unhealthy stench',[24] and the invalids found that they were in danger of starving if they did not go out to work or escape from the place altogether.

The 480 or so invalids of the Garde were undeniably happier. In 1730 Frederick William had given them a pretty village of their own on the Werder island in the Havel.

These arrangements left the great majority of Frederick's invalids quite untouched. Their grateful master took care of them by the simple expedients of expelling the aged foreigner from Prussia and giving the native invalid a licence to beg. Whenever the army assembled for manoeuvres or campaigns the headquarters was invariably besieged by the local military beggars who importuned the king, the generals and the wealthy foreign officers for alms.

The loyal Lossow conceded that the cruel treatment of the invalids represented probably the worst side of Frederick's military system.[25] Kaltenborn is characteristically more forthright, and claimed that ten or a dozen invalids used to wait for Frederick on the road from Sans Souci to Potsdam, hoping that he might throw them a thaler 'rather like you might toss a bone to some dogs that were howling from hunger'. When Frederick was not in such a good mood he would just tell the pages 'Drive the scum away!'[26]

Discipline

'In general the common soldier must fear his officer more than the enemy.' This frank avowal of Frederick's guiding principle of leadership appears both in the *Cavalry Instruction* of 1763 and the *Political Testament* of 1768. The sentiment came straight from ancient Sparta, but Frederick was persuaded to make it his own from what he knew of more recent history, notably the decay of the Dutch army after the death of William III. Self-respect and *esprit de corps* were useful in themselves, but in Frederick's view they were no substitute for the knowledge that the officer's sword and the NCO's spontoon were pointing at your back.

The kind of discipline that Frederick desired was nothing short of 'a blind obedience. This principle of subordination submits the soldier to his officer, the officer to his commander, the colonel to his general and the body of generals as a whole to the commander of the army'.[27]

On 21 June 1749 Frederick issued a circular to the regimental *Chefs* which put at their disposal the complete range of punishments without reference to higher authority.

Blows with sticks and fists already passed without mention, as being part of the normal intercourse between a superior and the men under his command. They were laid on for 'spots of water on the gaiters, badly polished coat buttons, mishandling of the musket, or making a half-turn too early, too late or just without enough snap. Young officers were fond of wielding the stick just to awaken astonishment among the spectators'.[28]

Next in the scale came the various degrees of arrest or imprisonment, and minor

Running the gauntlet

corporal punishments such as chaining to bedsteads, the *Eselsreiten* (riding a sharp-backed wooden horse), and the painful process of *Krummschliessen* by which alternate arms and legs were bound tightly together by leather straps. Incorrigible thieves were branded deep on the hand with an 'S' (for *Spitzbube*, rogue) and turned out of the regiment, while men involved in desertion plots sometimes had their noses and ears cut off in addition to the other punishments that came their way. The worst offenders of all were usually hanged or shot, though at Potsdam in 1755 a private in the Garde who had killed an NCO was broken on the wheel, beginning with the lower limbs 'so as to produce all the greater impression on the others'.[29]

Of all the means of punishment the Prussian authorities were most fond of running the gauntlet (*Gassenlaufen* or *Spiessruthen*), for it was susceptible to almost indefinite repetition according to the severity of the case, and it was a spectacular ceremony which directly involved a great number of men. In this carefully thought-out process the offender was stripped to the waist and made to walk between two ranks of soldiers, each composed of 100 of his comrades, who lashed him with hazel wands soaked in water. A sergeant walked backwards with a *Kurzgewehr* levelled at the man's chest, to curb any inclination to break into a run, while corporals roamed behind the ranks with sticks in their hands and beat any soldier who was not laying on hard enough. All the time the pipes and drums played a merry tune to drown the shrieks. General d'Hullin states that as a punishment the gauntlet was 'so severe that the majority of those who are condemned to undergo thirty-six runs (which are spread over three days) actually die under the blows'.[30]

Because of its lethal potential the holding of the *Gassenlaufen* was a matter for the *Chef* or commandant. It was the stipulated punishment for soldiers who got drunk or argued on duty (*Raisonniren unter dem Gewehr*), but it really came into its own when there was a question of dealing with a deserter. By the articles of war the foreign deserter was liable to twelve 'runs' for his first offence, twenty-four for the second attempt, and thirty-six for the third or for complicity in a desertion plot. The cantonist deserter, being considered as a kind of traitor, underwent thirty-six 'runs' for his first experiment, and (if he survived) he was hanged for a repetition.

Under the salutary influence of Seydlitz the cavalry regiments abandoned corporal punishment almost altogether, although even this enlightened leader bore down heavily on any man who lost his hat or fell from his horse.

As Dr Moore commented, 'the Prussian discipline on a general view is beautiful: in detail it is shocking'.[31]

The NCOs

The tightness of the Prussian service could never have been attained without the participation of a numerous and highly regarded body of NCOs, for these men saw more of the troops than their superiors did, and by words and blows they were able to convey the intentions of the officers in a language that the densest recruit could understand. Thus Frederick placed fourteen NCOs on the establishment of every company, as opposed to the totally inadequate allowance among the Austrians of six.

The ranks ran upwards by the following stages: the lance-corporal (*Gefreiter*) who was a knowing old soldier who assisted the NCOs proper; the corporal; the sergeant; and finally the sergeant-major (*Feldwebel*), a most important personage who saw it as one of his duties to safeguard the interests of his company against the battalion commander.

Frederick selected many of the NCOs in person when he toured the ranks of the army at review, looking for soldiers who had an air of authority and nine or ten years of good service behind them. He wrote that 'they must all be veteran soldiers. I have never allowed a student or a young man, unless a nobleman, to be presented to me for this office. A brave and war-hardened veteran can make himself respected by the common soldiers, whereas a scribbler cannot issue his orders with authority and he lacks the strength to stand up to hardship'.[32] However, Frederick seldom commissioned his NCOs, for he believed that the presence of these men in the officer corps would give rise to embarrassing situations.

The status of the NCOs was conveyed in various ways. 'They encourage them to develop a feeling of honour, and the officers treat them politely. It is true that military discipline demands that they should be liable to punishment by blows with the flat of the sword, but this treatment is meted out very rarely and only in the gravest cases.'[33] Among their distinctive signs of uniform and equipment they possessed a *Kurzgewehr* (or pike or rifled carbine in the grenadiers), a stick, gloves, a black-and-white sword knot, and a braided and cocked hat. The bald NCOs, to their chagrin, had to wear coarse wigs that got sodden in the rain and sat on their pates like cold poultices. More welcome was the pay, which amounted to three thalers per month for the corporal and four for the sergeant, as well as a 6 lb loaf every five days.

The 'officer's-eye view' of the Prussian NCO is presented in Lessing's *Minna von*

Barnhelm in the person of Sergeant-Major Werner, who stuck by his chief through thick and thin, who was so stiff and formal on parade but so good-hearted and friendly off duty. For the opinion of the rank and file we have the testimony of F. C. Laukhard, who compared the generality of NCOs with the Oriental eunuchs, who had to be all politeness and servility to their superiors, but who took out their frustrations on their unfortunate soldiers. In particular Laukhard was fascinated with the character of Zutzel, an NCO with whom he lodged. This gentleman went to church every Sunday and talked a great deal about the love of God,

> but I doubt whether there was any seaman of the East India Company who could curse and swear better than friend Zutzel . . . In addition to these virtues he was, like many of his kind, a confirmed drinker of spirits. He used to go out regularly to buy the drink in person, then consume it at leisure with his wife – who herself would knock back a whole flask and call it 'just a drop'. Nothing was more amusing than to see friend Zutzel when he sat with his sword at his side, his blue cloak wrapped about him, a black fur cap on his head, a pair of spectacles on his nose and a flask of spirits before him. Thus equipped he used to spend his time darning or knitting stockings – two arts of which he had a masterly understanding.[34]

Desertion

A number of escapes were available to the soldier who was the victim of this system of oppression. Bräker writes of a Mecklenburger of his regiment who simply stood outside his billet every evening and addressed imprecations to his officers, the King of Prussia, the city of Berlin and all the race of Brandenburgers. Bräker himself used to gaze from his window at the moon, and transport himself in imagination to Switzerland and his beloved valley of Tockenburg.

In their desperation a number of unfortunates were driven to suicide. French troops were particularly susceptible to this temptation, as were those grenadiers who served in the First Battalion of the Garde under the command of the sadistic Lieutenant-Colonel v. Scheelen (1773–86).

A much greater quantity resorted to the more constructive course of running away, and it is significant that Frederick had to devote the whole of the first article of his *General Principia* to the precautions that must be taken against the evil of desertion.

In peacetime it was literally true to say that one half of the army kept watch on the other. In barracks and billets or on sentry-go the officers made sure that every man of doubtful inclinations was dogged by somebody reliable like a good cantonist: this arrangement demanded a good knowledge of the character of the two soldiers concerned, for if they got on too badly together they made life in the company a misery, whereas if they got on too well they might desert together.

All the comings and goings at the town gates were closely controlled. A characteristic *Parole* order enjoined the sentries of one regiment 'to be especially suspicious of stout women', and told the lance-corporal to question 'any apprentice or workman who is passing out of the gate and has the stature or the air of a soldier'.[35] Patrols and chains of sentries kept watch outside the perimeter in case anybody was tempted to let himself down from the wall.

The enterprising deserter who survived to reach the countryside now discovered that his perils were only beginning. Sooner or later a cannon shot would sound the signal from the walls, and an officer would thunder out of the gate in pursuit on a fast horse that was kept saddled for the purpose. Now that his absence had been reported our deserter was liable to be stopped by every countryman on the road and required to produce his travel pass, or he might run into one of the watches of up to twenty or more men which every village was expected to stake out for forty-eight hours after the first alarm.

This being Frederick's Prussia, everybody was given a powerful incentive to intercept the runaway. Probably the man's NCOs and subalterns were already being called to account for their negligence, not least because the company commander was expected to furnish a substitute at his own cost if the deserter made good his escape. The country-people too were all eagerness, for they were rewarded with 6 or 12 thalers for every deserter they delivered up to the regiment, whereas their village was liable to a fine of 100 thalers if they allowed a deserter to slip through their hands. A foreign visitor was told that 'experience shows that at Berlin out of one hundred men who desert, ninety-eight are brought back'.[36]

Above all the authorities dreaded a 'desertion plot' – a scheme for a mass breakout – and the officers were therefore empowered to break up any group of soldiers with their sticks. The largest and ugliest episode of this kind in peacetime occurred at Halle after the Seven Years War, when 360 impressed Saxons in the regiment of Anhalt-Bernburg tried to escape to the nearby frontier. Unfortunately the plot was betrayed by a talkative girl, and the grenadiers of the regiment were able to contain the escape in an hour-long pitched battle, in the course of which a bullet passed through the Prince of Bernburg's hat. The

The Regiment of Bernburg is restored to favour

man who shot at the prince was broken on the wheel, the sixteen ringleaders were hanged, and the rest were beaten or made to run the gauntlet.

Altogether it was better to wait until the vicissitudes of war brought a reasonable chance of getting away intact. That is not to say that when Frederick was on campaign he did not do his best to convert his army into a mobile prison: he kept close march discipline, with patrols of hussars closing up the flanks and rear of the columns, and he observed special precautions when the troops were marching through woods and villages; in camp he kept the perimeter under watch by sentries and patrols.

All these precautions proved of little avail once the bands of discipline were loosened. Thus at Glatz in 1760 the fortress fell to the Austrian general Loudon simply because the regiment of Quadt went over to the enemy *en masse*.

Truly desertion was the bane of the Prussian army. The regiment of Jung-Braunschweig (no 39) lost 1,650 men from this cause in the Seven Years War, which was the equivalent of its entire complement. In the period 1740–1800 the regiment Garde in Potsdam, the most distinguished and favoured in the whole army, lost 3 officers, 93 NCOs, 32 musicians and 1,525 men by desertion, not to mention the 130 suicides and 29 executions.

Frederick and his soldiers

There is no reason to dissent from General v. Warnery, one of Frederick's own officers, when he claims that the king was in the habit of comparing his soldiers 'to lemons which you squeeze for the juice and then throw away'.[37] Yet repression and exploitation are not the whole story. At one level of communication Frederick got on remarkably well with the soldiers. He rode with the regiments on the march, occasionally dealing blows with his crutch stick, but much more often giving utterance to a cheerful 'Good day to you, lads!' to which the standard replies were 'The same to you, Fritz!' or 'Good day, Fritz!' The Garde allowed itself especially wide liberties, giving vent to loud and critical comments on the ragged state of the king's coat. In camp Frederick permitted the soldiers to stay in their tents while he rode through the streets, and he made the best of the opportunities to snatch a little relaxation. 'Sutlers' tents were often pitched immediately next to his headquarters, and gambling, music and uproar lasted day and night. Just after supper Frederick liked to stroll around the tents alone, enjoying the cheerful turmoil.'[38]

To regiments as a whole Frederick displayed the same range of approval or condemnation that he showed to individual generals or soldiers. A regiment which had behaved badly in action might find itself issued with cloth buttons and deprived of the right to play the grenadier march. In extreme cases it might be struck from the army list altogether, like the hussar regiment of Gersdorff after Maxen. Frederick bore a perpetual grudge against the 'Maxen regiments' as a whole, and the two East Prussian regiments which did badly at Zorndorf and ever afterwards made his 'stomach turn over at the sight of their uniforms'.[39]

By the same token Frederick bestowed a variety of favours upon such regiments as had pleased him or his ancestors. When he saw the Pomeranian regiments of Bevern and Manteuffel he more than once exclaimed: 'These troops have been, and are still, an honour to the House of Brandenburg.'[40] At times the regiment of Forcade was equally high in favour. Prize money sometimes went to regiments that captured enemy colours and artillery, the regiment of Prinz v. Preussen doing particularly well out of the battle of Liegnitz.

However, Frederick was nothing if not consistent in his inconsistency. A single regiment might be held up one year as an example to all the rest, and blasted the next year as the worst in the army. The regiment never knew where it stood until it marched past the king on the first day of the spring review. The regiment knew it was safe if Frederick greeted the *Chef* in a friendly fashion and asked to see him afterwards. If, on the other hand, the king took no notice and simply fixed his telescope on the unit behind, things were sure to go badly with the offending regiment, 'even if every trooper happened to be a Seydlitz or every musketeer a Saldern'.[41]

It would be unhistorical to regard all these goings-on from the point of view of the later twentieth-century civilian. First of all the manners of the time were brutal in the extreme. The contemporary British navy enforced a discipline that was every bit as draconian as the Prussian, and with rather less excuse – after all, it was more difficult to run away from a ship on the high seas than from the King of Prussia's army. Moreover, as General v. Lossow pointed out, in those times 'the common soldier regarded the king as the representative of God, whom he must fear, honour and love. The articles of war expressly stipulated that, regardless of regiment or arm, he had to show the same submissiveness to every officer and NCO'.[42]

Significantly enough, the Prussian deserters who found their way to foreign armies were often critical of the sloppy ways that obtained there, and they actually hankered after the old discipline. In a German free city one of Frederick's former NCOs made a minor mistake in drill, and was called to account by the colonel of the town militia. The NCO stepped in front of the troops and declared in a loud voice: 'Never forget, colonel, that I have served the King of Prussia!'[43] He made a right about turn and stalked back to his place. The colonel did not dare to reply.

4

The Infantry

Organisation

MUSKETEER REGIMENTS

The infantry regiment of Frederick's time was a community of about 1,700 souls, made up of about 50 officers, 160 NCOs, 40 musicians, a dozen medical orderlies, the personnel of the *Unterstab* (clerks, treasurer, almoner, auditor, provost) and some 1,430 rank and file.

The regiment was divided into two battalions of equal strength. By an absurd and illogical arrangement, however, the battalion was broken down into two completely separate kinds of organisation, one of which was administrative and the other tactical.

The administrative organisation of the battalion was one of six companies (five musketeer companies and one grenadier company). The individual company stood under the command of the captain, a first lieutenant, one or two second lieutenants, an ensign and up to sixteen NCOs and *Junkers*. The company establishment proper of rank and file remained at 114 throughout the Silesian Wars and the Seven Years War (thirty-eight files in three ranks). To the total should be added the seven or eight ordinary supernumeraries (*Überkompletten*) and (from 1755) a varying number of additional supernumeraries (*Überüberkompletten, Extraüberkompletten* or *Ausrangirten*). This last category consisted of trained veterans who were released to the canton to serve as a reserve and make way in the company for a corresponding number of young cantonists. A further NCO and up to thirty or forty men were added to the strength of each company according to an 'augmentation' decreed in 1768.

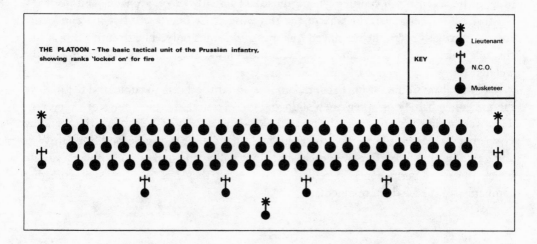

THE PLATOON – The basic tactical unit of the Prussian infantry, showing ranks 'locked on' for fire

KEY
Lieutenant
N.C.O.
Musketeer

The tactical organisation of the battalion (five musketeer companies) comprised four divisions of two platoons each, making eight platoons in all. The transition of the battalion to the tactical organisation was accomplished under the direction of the battalion adjutant, who first closed the companies up, then told off the men into eight platoons, namely six of twenty-four files and two (the sixth and seventh) of twenty-three. While this was in train the battalion commander (a major) assigned the NCOs and officers to their respective divisions – one captain each to the first and third divisions, and one lieutenant each to the second and fourth. Thus in action many men found themselves under the command of an officer whom they scarcely knew.

GRENADIER BATTALIONS

On the field of battle Frederick liked to have at his disposal certain units of especially reliable and aggressive troops. These were made up of picked men who were concentrated in the regiment's two companies of grenadiers. Whenever the army made ready for manoeuvres or war each set of two grenadier companies left its parent regiment and joined with two grenadier companies from another regiment to form a grenadier battalion, which was a force of about 700 officers and men. By a happy chance the administrative and tactical organisations of the grenadier battalion *did* coincide, each company corresponding with a division of two platoons. Still, the divorce between the grenadier battalion and the parent regiment was an inconvenient one, and it hindered the process of repair after (as frequently happened) the grenadier battalion was massacred in battle. Sometimes the grenadiers were kept in the field only by the expedient of uniting several depleted units in 'combined grenadier battalions'.

The individual grenadiers were selected not on account of their size (in fact they tended to be on the small side), but because they were 'reliable and robust men, of mature years and good marchers'.[1] As for their appearance, an old regulation stipulated that 'a grenadier should not have an effeminate aspect. On the contrary he must present a formidable sight, with darkly tanned countenance, black hair and a vigorous moustache: he must not appear too amiable or allow himself to laugh too easily'.[2] Grenadiers were proud above all of their mitre caps – tall, brass-fronted affairs which derived from the time in the seventeenth century when grenadiers actually threw grenades and needed a hat that would not get in the way of the throwing arm. The 'grenadier marches' were another distinctive sign, being played by pipes and drums only. The drummers beat in a characteristic style, striking alternate rhythmical blows on the skin of the drum and the wooden rim.

It was always difficult for Frederick to find suitable officers to command the mass of the grenadier battalions when they suddenly coalesced at the beginning of every war. That was one of the reasons why he created a second category of grenadiers, the Standing Grenadier Battalions. He formed the first two in the course of the Second Silesian War, and an additional four after the peace. They normally consisted of six companies each, which remained permanently together, even though they had the status of grenadier companies of the garrison regiments.

THE GARDE

The grenadiers were splendid fighting soldiers, but in turnout, drill and social prestige they ceded place to the royal Lifeguard of Foot. The kernel of the Garde, the *crème de la crème*, was represented by its thousand-strong First Battalion, which was formed by the

Grenadiers of Infantry Regiment no 27. Blue coat, red cuffs and lapels with yellow snake-like border, white waistcoat and breeches, grenadier cap with brass plate, red top, white rim, red pom-pom with yellow spot. The colour must have belonged to another unit since grenadiers did not have colours of their own

king in June 1740 from the most serviceable men of Frederick William's *Leib-Regiment*. The officers sported white plumes in their hats, and had the fronts of their coats richly embroidered in gold, while the uniforms of the guardsmen were so costly that when, after two years, the guardsmen were issued with new coats, they were able to sell the old coats to the Jews for twenty thalers each.

The troops of the First Battalion were quartered for life in some of the most miserable streets of Potsdam. Their ordinary duties were notoriously light, which was why they were so hated by the rest of the garrison, but nobody could deny that they were magnificent when they were in their element, staging a parade at Potsdam.

> The slow, serious measure of their advance was almost unbroken by drum beat or music. The occasion was profoundly moving. Far distant from any theatrical presentation, it held a dignity all of its own, which overcame every other sentiment through the sheer impressiveness of the spectacle.[3]

The remainder of the Regiment-Garde proper was made up of the Second and Third Battalions. A detached unit, the Grenadier-Garde-Bataillon (infantry regiment no 6) was created in 1740 as a specific commemoration of Frederick William's old Potsdam grenadiers, whose uniforms and weapons it retained intact.

FUSILIER REGIMENTS

The Prussian fusiliers were a lightweight regular infantry, fighting in mass formation like the rest of the line infantry, but drawn principally from newly acquired provinces where the men did not have the loyalty or physical stature of people like the Pomeranians and Brandenburgers. Such at least was the outlook of Frederick. He inherited four rather good regiments of fusiliers, which he promptly converted into regiments of line infantry, and he designated as 'fusiliers' only the sixteen or so regiments which he raised after he had conquered Silesia. Taking account of their small stature, Frederick issued them with short muskets, and gave them scaled-down brass-fronted grenadier hats which made them appear more fearsome in battle. 'The headgear certainly looked impressive enough, when the sun shone on such a battalion of fusiliers and gave them the appearance of a row of fiery palisades. Even as seen from behind the caps had a lively look, thanks to the coloured cloth of the crown.'[4]

GARRISON TROOPS

In Prussia the permanent guard of the fortresses was entrusted to a special category of second-rate troops – the battalions of garrison infantry and the companies of garrison artillery. Frederick took over four such battalions upon his accession, and in the course of the First Silesian War he set up five further battalions and one artillery company to hold the fortresses he had captured from the Austrians. By the end of the reign the garrison infantry numbered twelve battalions, standing under the command of one lieutenant-general and six major-generals.

According to Warnery the garrison battalions were 'as you know . . . made up of invalids or other officers who are too bad to appear in the field. The soldiers are likewise the refuse of the army, and they serve most unwillingly'.[5]

Fusiliers of regiment no 48. Blue coat, red cuffs and turnbacks, and red lapels each with six white brandenbourgs with hanging orange tassels, straw waistcoat and breeches, fusilier cap with brass plate and dark blue top. The cartridge pouch, bread bag and knapsack are clearly drawn, though the water flask was somewhat larger than shown here

In the Seven Years War, however, Frederick ran so short of troops that he had to incorporate garrison battalions in the detached armies on the 'side theatres' facing the *Reichsarmee* and the Russians (Field-Marshal Lehwaldt had 6,000 at the battle of Gross-Jägersdorf in 1757).

The New Garrison Regiments, or Land Regiments, were a further and, if possible, still less battleworthy kind of fortress infantry. There were five of them, and they were raised in the event of war. We may judge their quality from the queen's comments on the garrison regiment of Major-General v. Kraatz which 'guarded' Berlin in April 1745; the men, she said, were 'no longer the veteran troops, but simply whatever peasants could be rounded up from all the neighbouring villages. They make a laughable sight when they mount guard, for they wear their own coats or sometimes just their smocks'.[6]

MILITIA

The militia was a local and temporary body, called into being in the Seven Years War when the eastern provinces were in danger of being invaded by the Russians. These provincial formations were raised between May and August 1757, the object being not so much to stimulate local patriotism as to deprive the enemy of manpower – we are far removed from the spirit of the *Landsturm* of the War of Liberation of 1813–14.

Altogether twelve battalions, ten grenadier companies and some small but rather good units of hussars and *Jägers* were raised in Pomerania, one battalion in East Prussia, and three battalions each in the Neumark, the Kurmark and the district of Magdeburg, making about 17,000 troops in all.

THE FELDJÄGER-CORPS ZU FUSS

The light infantry service demanded men who were nimble and lively, who possessed a good knowledge of fieldcraft and who were intelligent and loyal enough to be trusted to fight in dispersed formation. Like many other sovereigns of the time, Frederick turned for this work to his foresters and gamekeepers, the *Jäger*.

The Prussian foot *Jäger* began life in 1740 as a force of sixty *Guiden*, whose purpose was to protect reconnaissance parties and guide the regular troops through difficult country. They wore a practical uniform of green coat with leather waistcoat and breeches, and they were armed with the characteristic German *Büchse* – a heavy-calibre rifled carbine with a faceted barrel, having an accuracy and a stopping power that were very effective in bringing down a charging boar. While the *Jäger* could pick off enemy infantry at their leisure, they were exceedingly vulnerable to cavalry, for their weapon lacked a bayonet and they had to force the bullet down the rifling by brute strength.

In July 1744 Frederick ordered the establishment to be raised to two companies of 100 men each, a step which marks the emergence of the Prussian *Jäger* as light infantry proper. The strength of the *Jäger* was gradually built up over the course of the Seven Years War, and they entered the fatal year of 1760 as a complete battalion of 800 men. The first of their misfortunes was to pass under the command of Major v. Baader. This individual was so corrupt and incompetent that Seydlitz came up to him on parade and proceeded to break his sword and rip the straps from his shoulders. On 10 October of the same year, under their new commander Major des Granges, the *Jäger* were caught out in

Infanterie Regiment, Mousquetier

Infanterie Regiment, Fusilier

Curaßier Regiment.

Hußaren Regiment.

(above left) *Officer and musketeer of the regiment of Wedell, 1759 (IR no 26). Blue coat, red cuffs and collar, gold (officer) or yellow (musketeer) brandenbourgs, white waistcoat and breeches; (above right) fusilier and officer of the regiment of Grabow, 1759 (IR no 47). Blue coats, lemon yellow cuffs, lapels and collar, white waistcoat and breeches, fusilier cap with lemon yellow top; (below left) officer and trooper of the cuirassier regiment of Baron v. Schönaich, 1759 (CR no 6). Coat (Kollet) and breeches straw, cuffs, sabretache and ornamental borders light brick and red white; (below right) officer and hussar of the Black Hussars, 1759 (HR no 5). Black dolman and pelisse, with white borders and embroidery, red and white barrel sash*

75

the open near Spandau by a force of cossacks and virtually annihilated. The survivors were re-formed into three companies in the following winter, but one company was disbanded again after the peace and the number of men sank to 300.

Three companies were added to the corps in 1773 and a sixth company came into being at the outbreak of the War of the Bavarian Succession. For various reasons (see p. 205) the *Jäger* gave a bad account of themselves in the new war, but Frederick was now bent on creating a large and effective body of light infantry. He gave the *Jäger* the establishment of a full regiment of ten companies in 1784, and in the following year he toyed with the idea of setting up two additional regiments of light infantry, though nothing was done in that direction until after his death.

Thus Frederician Prussia never produced a force of light infantry which was up to dealing with the menace posed by the Austrian Croats, of whom more anon. The greatest obstacle was the lack of native recruits, which in turn derived from the fact that the qualities required by the service of light infantry were not ones that were encouraged under Frederick's régime.

FREE BATTALIONS

Lacking a proper native light infantry, Frederick turned in the Seven Years War to the desperate expedient of raising 'free battalions' – brigand-like mercenary bands that were recruited from the very dregs of mankind.

The approach of the Seven Years War attracted three foreign mercenaries to Prussia, Lieutenant-Colonel le Noble from the Palatinate, Lieutenant-Colonel Mayr from Saxony and Colonel d'Angelelli from Holland, all of whom received permission on 18 August 1756 to raise their own free battalions. Counting the battalion of Kalben, altogether four battalions were available for service at the beginning of the campaign of 1757. More battalions materialised in rapid succession, but a decline in quality was soon evident, the aptly-named battalion of Rapin, for instance, being recruited chiefly from French prisoners taken at Rossbach. By the end of 1758 Frederick was complaining that 'our free battalions are weak and composed of deserters, and it often happens that they do not so much as dare to show themselves in the presence of the enemy'.[7] A further disintegration was evident after November 1759, when the only really able commander of free battalions, General Wunsch, was captured at Maxen.

The individual free battalions distinguished themselves in various unenviable ways. On 6 September 1757 the free battalion of Chossignon contrived to get itself captured intact by the Austrians at the castle of Bautzen. The Etrangers Prusses, another battalion of French desperadoes, broke up on 2 September 1761 when three of the companies shot the commanding major and went over to the *Reichsarmee* with the battalion chest and one cannon. In numerical terms the most successful free bands were those raised by Friedrich Wilhelm v. Kleist ('Green Kleist'), who began work in 1759 and ultimately set up ten squadrons of free hussars, three squadrons of free dragoons and a free battalion of *Jäger* or *Preussische Kroaten*. From the beginning, however, the reputation of Kleist's band was tarnished by its predatory conduct on Prince Henry's raid into Franconia in 1759.

At the end of the Seven Years War Frederick ordered all the free battalions to march to the fortresses – Colonel Bauwer's newly enlisted corps of Hanoverians to Wesel, and the rest to Magdeburg. 'When they approached the glacis of these fortresses they found

Men of the free battalions attending to their business

the garrisons drawn up in order of battle. They were surrounded and made to lay down their arms.'[8] The NCOs and men were pressed into the regiments of the line or formed into garrison regiments, while the officers were discharged (like Lessing's Tellheim) and forced to yield up the uniforms and arms of their companies without compensation.

Undeterred by these experiences, Frederick sanctioned the raising of twelve new free battalions at the time of the War of the Bavarian Succession. Only three of them ever saw action, and they performed as dismally as their spiritual ancestors back in the 1750s.

Apart from a few units which were dressed in green, the free battalions wore blue infantry-type coats with light blue or dark blue facings, hence the nickname of 'Double-Blues' (*Zweimalblauen*). For the sake of mobility they dispensed with tents and kept the rest of their baggage to the minimum. Their artillery was of a light regimental type, and was served by men of their own units. At full strength the size of a free battalion varied between five and seven hundred troops, though in the course of the Seven Years War the complement often sank to one-third or one-quarter of that number.

Uniforms, arms and equipment

Frederick hardly bothered to change the uniforms of any of the regiments he had inherited from his father. As Kaltenborn observed, he 'harboured a distaste for all novelties. Alterations in uniforms and other small formalities were well beneath his dignity'.[9] That was why the French commentator Guibert found such a variety in the colours and cut of the Prussian uniforms, a diversity that was all the more surprising in view of the efforts which the French were making to imitate the supposed uniformity of the Prussian military garb. 'You have no idea of the wise indifference of the King of Prussia to all these externals.'[10]

In the veteran regiments the troops wore stocks (neck-cloths) of red, and sported expensive braid and buttons down their coats. The cost of all the finery bore hard upon the officers, and especially the subalterns, but 'the officers say that both they and the private soldiers find considerable satisfaction in being well dressed'.[11] The simplest uniforms of all belonged to the new regiments of infantry – the fusiliers – which Frederick raised during his own reign.

The infantry hats came in three styles: the tall, brass-fronted mitre cap of the grenadiers; the similar but lower cap of the fusiliers; and the little three-cornered hat of the veteran line regiments. They all had their inconveniences. The three-cornered hat owned a shallow crown and was in perpetual danger of blowing away, while the grenadier and fusilier caps were weighed down heavily by the brass plate in front, which compelled the soldier to jerk his head back every now and then in order to keep the object upright.

The hair hung down at the back in a long military pigtail which reached as far as the hem of the coat: if the man's own hair was unequal to the task he had to make up the length by attaching an artificial tail. The head was powdered, and the hair on either side of the temple was curled into a number of locks. In the regiments of line infantry the right-hand side of the head was lacking in one lock, so as to make room for the three-cornered hat, which was worn with a slight tilt to the right.

It is worth mentioning here that the best-known illustrations of Frederick's army, by the nineteenth-century artist Menzel, invariably show the three-cornered hat with a vertical fore-peak – a feature which obtained only at the end of the reign. The hat of 1740 had a fore-peak with a pronounced forward rake, and that of the Seven Years War was only slightly more abrupt.

The ground colour of the infantry coat was the famous Prussian blue. The cut was decidedly skimpy (for Frederick was anxious to spare cloth), and the hem extended only as far as the middle fingers of an arm held vertically down the side of the leg. Indeed there was very little of the blue cloth to be seen at all, except for the narrow sleeves, the eye being drawn instead to the contrasting lapels, cuffs and turned-back coat tails, which were often of a dull poppy red (*Ponceaurot*).

Towards the end of the reign the coat was cut so narrowly across the chest that the soldier could not button the lapels across the front in cold weather. Moreover, the material was coarse and thin, being designed to last only two years, and the quality got worse as the reign went on. Frederick actually abolished the cloak in 1740, and as Lossow remarked, 'it is surprising how the soldiers were able to conduct long wars without the protection of this garment'.[12] Sometimes the soldiers shared out greatcoats among themselves, like the sentries at Breslau early in 1741, and sometimes they wrapped lengths of fur about their middle – Austrian grenadier caps offered good material for this purpose.

Beneath the coat the soldier wore a waistcoat of white or yellow, then a linen dickey (*Kolleret*) and finally a coarse linen shirt. For parade purposes a false linen cuff was fastened beneath the sleeve of the coat.

The breeches were of coarse wool, and were dyed the same colour as the waistcoat, namely white, yellow or straw.

Frederick stipulated that the gaiters (*Stiefeletten*) 'must not be narrow, but cut fully and broadly. It does not matter if they do not lie smoothly, for gaiters are intended for the comfort of the soldier, and not for show'.[13]

In the first two decades of the reign the material of the gaiters was most commonly of ticking for ordinary service, and linen for parades. After the Seven Years War the ticking was replaced by ordinary cloth, which was more durable. Gaiters were originally coloured white throughout the army, but in 1741 Colonel Fouqué made a levy on the clergy of a Moravian town and used the proceeds to fit out his grenadier battalion with gaiters of serviceable black. Frederick introduced the black gaiter to the whole army for winter wear in 1744, and (except in the First Battalion of the Garde) the white gaiter disappeared altogether after the Seven Years War. The gaiter was closed down the side by a row of little buttons, and secured below the knee by a band. Despite what Frederick had to say about comfort the fit was decidedly tight, and a false calf was sometimes inserted down the back in order to eliminate wrinkles.

The shoes were of good black leather, and made in a characteristically Prussian style with square toes and high heels. Together the shoes and the gaiters served to hide the sweaty horror of the woollen stockings that lay beneath. Many soldiers, indeed, used to cut off the bottom of the stockings altogether, and wrap the feet in strips of cloth which were impregnated in tallow. Not surprisingly the scent of marching soldiers was powerful in the extreme, and on a still day the stench used to hang in the air like an infection for minutes after a regiment had passed.

A broad bandolier of whitened leather was slung over the left shoulder and held the cartridge pouch suspended behind the right hip. The pouch was a large box of thick boiled leather, stained black. It contained a leather bag, which in turn held an inner box or *cartouche*. The *cartouche* was open on top and contained compartments for about eighty cartridges. In 1741 the allowance of cartridges was increased from thirty to sixty. Since, however, there were still a large number of empty compartments left, Frederick recommended that the cartridges should be kept together in the middle holes so as to save the soldier from groping about.

The cartridge itself was a tube of cartridge paper which was stuffed with black powder and held a leaden musket ball at one end. The ball was reckoned at fifteen to the pound (31·3 grammes each). The powder charge weighed under half an ounce (15·6 grammes) until it was increased in 1755 (to 19·53 grammes).

The tin water flask was attached to a narrow strap of white leather which came over the right shoulder. The men of each tent *Kameradschaft* originally took turns in carrying the large field kettle, but from 1748 onwards it was loaded with the tents on the regimental pack-horses.

The knapsack was a bag of untanned calfskin which was worn on the left side of the back, just behind the sword, and it hung from a narrow strip of white leather which was slung over the right shoulder. Deep and commodious, this hold-all contained the spare dickey, shirts, gaiter buttons, breeches, hose, foot bands and flints, as well as such items as gloves, bandage and tourniquet, under-cuffs, hair powder, knife, fork and spoon, salt, mirror, brushes, combs, wax for the shoes and cartridge pouch, buff leather polisher, gaiter hook, screwdriver, gun oil and ramrod worm. As if all this were not enough, three tent pegs were tied to the supporting strap, and a linen bread bag was suspended on its own little strap just below the knapsack.

In the spring of 1744 Frederick carried out some experiments at Potsdam to test the comparative mobility of men with and without their knapsacks. As a result he decreed that 'if time allows, the men must take off their knapsacks and all other impedimenta before every action'.[14]

The sword belt of white leather was buckled around the man's middle and lay immediately on top of the waistcoat. The pattern of the sword survived intact from about 1716, apart from being shortened in 1744 by six inches to two feet. A sword knot was wound round the brass hilt and guard, and the hanging tassel came in a great variety of colours according to the regiment and company. The scabbard was of stout leather, or of wood covered in leather, and it was attached to the left side of the belt at an angle of thirty degrees. Considered as an instrument of war the sword was probably useless, 'but the soldier came to associate this weapon with a certain concept of honour, and he would have considered it shameful to have carried no sword'.[15]

The bayonet was a narrow, triangular-sectioned blade brazed to a metal sleeve which fitted over the muzzle of the musket. Its home was a scabbard which hung on the sword belt near the sword, though after the battle of Mollwitz Frederick insisted that the bayonet must remain fixed to the musket for as long as the soldier was on duty.

In design the Prussian musket was a clumsier and more eccentric version of the typical military flintlock of the day. The pattern had been devised by Liège gunsmiths early in the reign of Frederick William. The barrel was 3 ft $5\frac{1}{2}$ in long (a little less in the fusilier regiments), and the calibre a generous three-quarters of an inch. The lock was crude but substantial.

The stock was elaborately carved. The material was originally walnut, but before the Seven Years War the regiment of Fouqué found that the maple of the county of Glatz made a cheap substitute, which caused Frederick to instruct the manufacturers to turn to the new material. Throughout Frederick's reign the Garde, the Grenadier-Garde-Bataillon and infantry regiment no 3 retained their distinctive musket stocks of light brown. In the other regiments the stocks were lacquered in red or reddish brown until after the Seven Years War, when they were stained black. The sling was made of red Russian leather.

The ramrod was a very solid affair of iron, being a direct descendant of the rammer which Leopold of Anhalt-Dessau had introduced in his regiment in 1698. This gave the Prussian infantry a clear advantage over the Austrians, who retained their fragile wooden ramrods until 1744. The Prussians took another lead in ramrod design thirty years later, when Prince Ferdinand of Brunswick devised his thick 'cylindrical', or rather double-ended version, which was as broad at the bottom as at the top, and saved the musketeer the trouble of having to reverse the ramrod after he had drawn it from its hole beneath the barrel. By 1777 the factory at Spandau had turned out or converted 140,000 muskets incorporating the 'cylindrical' ramrod. The new ramrod was 1 lb heavier than the old model, and in compensation the barrels in the musketeer regiments were sawn down to the length of the muskets of the fusiliers.

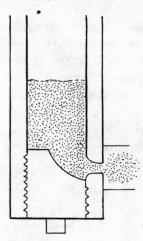

Another time-saving device, the 'conical' touch hole, was adopted on the recommendation of Lieutenant v. Freytag in about 1781. The breech plug and the edges of the touch hole inside the barrel were rounded in such a way as to funnel a portion of the main powder charge out through the touch hole, and so the pan was primed automatically from the inside by the action of ramming the charge down the barrel.

In 1776 the lock received some much-needed protection against rain in the form of a detachable box of red leather, which was open to the rear to allow for the cocking of the hammer and the priming and shutting of the pan. The soldiers exercised with the box in position on several occasions every year, but for the rest of the time the box was worn suspended from the cartridge pouch.

Despite all these gadgets the Prussian musket remained one of the worst in Europe. Firing was a decidedly uncomfortable experience, for the trigger was set too far forward in the guard, the comb of the butt rose so high as to make aiming almost impossible, and, worst of all, the long barrel, the bayonet and the cylindrical ramrod combined to make the weapon muzzle-heavy by three pounds, thereby inducing the soldiers to shoot very low. Guibert saw 'whole battalions, even the battalions of the Garde, which are the most highly trained of all, discharge entire volleys at very short range against platoons of soldiers painted on wood, and still fail to score more than a few hits, and these all in the legs. All the other bullets were fired into the ground'.[16]

In spite of its weight the musket still failed to stand up very well to the exigencies of the service. The maple stock was liable to crack along its narrow neck when the weapon was slammed to the ground during drill, and the iron of the barrel became worn danger-ously thin over the years, what with all the polishing of the exterior and the abrading effect of the heavy ramrod on the inside.

THE MAINTENANCE AND WEARING OF THE INFANTRYMAN'S EQUIPMENT

All told, the Prussian soldier suffered more hardship on account of the livery of his trade than from all the efforts of the enemy. Every time he came off duty he had to polish his musket barrel to mirror brightness with a thick piece of buckskin, as well as rubbing the wood of the stock with preservative paste, oil and wax. The cartridge pouch also demanded frequent attention with wax, to keep it waterproof.

After that our soldier was free to wander about the streets as he pleased – without breeches, perhaps, if that condition took his fancy. Unfortunately the very relaxation of the leisure hours compelled him to prepare himself all the more meticulously when the time came near to appear once more on parade or sentry duty. Up to half an hour had to be allowed for the putting on of the gaiters, the buttons of which were forced into position with a gaiter hook. The hair demanded one hour's attention. The crown and back were smeared with wax and fastened back so tightly by a ribbon that individual hairs were liable to spring out again with an almost audible snap. Finally the head was liberally sprinkled with powder (at an allowance of about 2 lb a month), and the locks at the side were curled up by one of the soldier's comrades or by the company *friseur* at the captain's quarters. The grenadiers had the special obligation of keeping their moustaches stiff and smooth with black wax, and in order to keep the points in pristine condition they used to tie them up with thread before they went to sleep.

On campaign the soldier was conscious above all else of the weight and the constricting power of his equipment. When Ulrich Bräker and his comrades of the regiment of Itzen-plitz set off for the invasion of Saxony in 1756,

> everyone was laden down like a donkey. First of all you were girt about with a sword belt. Then came the cartridge pouch, which hung from one shoulder by a five-inch-wide strap. Over the other shoulder hung the knapsack, full of laundry and the like, as well as the bread bag which was packed with bread and other food. In addition everybody had to carry some item of field equipment: a communal water flask, a kettle, an axe and so forth, all hanging on straps. On top of that you have the musket with yet another strap. Altogether we were bound five times over by straps passing cross-wise over our chests, and to begin with we all believed we were going to suffocate under the load. As if all this were not enough, we were squeezed by our tight uniforms, and the heat was so appalling that I seemed to be walking on hot coals. I opened my shirt to let in a little air, and steam rose up as if from a boiling kettle.[17]

Bräker must have been carrying equipment that weighed in the region of 60 lb.

Tactical formations and evolutions

The first printed outline of the Prussian military service was given by Frederick William I in his infantry regulations of 1714. Another *Reglement* was published in 1726, and on 20

June 1742 Frederick issued an *Instruction* of his own. The new code formed the basis of the *Reglement* of 1743, which was re-published with minor alterations in 1766 and 1773. With all this information at hand it is strange that we have so much difficulty in ascertaining just how the Prussian army fought its battles. On the one hand there were several useful evolutions which were considered too valuable to be revealed to the world at large, and consequently never appeared in print. Conversely there were many practices which figured largely on the drill square or in the recruits' training, but which were seldom employed in combat: among these we may cite the thirty-nine *Handgriffe* of the manual exercise of arms, the four-rank line, the various kinds of squares, the firing by platoons, and the deployment from column of march to a right-angled line of battle.

One of the ascertainable facts is that the line infantry were packed in extremely tight formation. According to the *Reglement* of 1743 the troops were closed up so fast that the right arm of one man was positioned behind the left, musket-carrying, arm of his neighbour to the right. In 1748 this awkward arrangement was abolished in favour of the more reasonable but still crowded interval of elbow-to-elbow, one foot ten inches being allowed for each man's space. The gap between the ranks (rows) varied between two paces and one foot, the closer interval being favoured towards the end of the reign.

Deep formations had been at a premium in the seventeenth century, when the majority of the infantry were still armed with pikes. The effective employment of musketry, however, demanded a thinner formation. The armies responded gradually to the new needs, and Prussia retained a four-rank formation until 29 November 1740, when Frederick ordered all the regiments marching to Silesia to re-form themselves into three ranks. This arrangement was extended to the whole army by an instruction of 20 June 1742. Man-power was so short in the Seven Years War that for a time Frederick had to tease out the length of his line of battle by adopting a two-rank formation. After the emergency Frederick reverted to the sensible compromise of the three-rank line as soon as he could: not only did the rearward ranks enhance the fire-power of the line, but they acted as a reserve to the tall men in the first rank, who invariably intercepted a good many enemy bullets in the course of an action.

The first documentary evidence of a prescribed pace in Frederick's reign dates from 2 May 1747, when a circular recommended a rate of 90–95 steps to the minute at the beginning of an advance, but thereafter only 70 or 75, 'which is quite fast enough'. By the end of Frederick's reign the pace of 28 German inches (nearly 29 English inches) and 75 steps to the minute had acquired the same kind of status as the 'Company pace' of British India, being employed at drill, in the field, on the march, off duty and even in the carrying of loads. 'The measure of this pace is imprinted in the soldier's brain, and his legs have been so accustomed to working at this speed that they seem to act by clockwork.'[18] A quick step of up to 120 paces to the minute was employed in wheeling or in deploying from column to line, when speed was at a premium.

The legs were kept stiff during the march, with the toe sweeping close to the ground rather as in the modern British slow march, though without the check half-way through the stride. As a means of progression it was easy and untiring, and looked like the natural pace of a man 'who is walking deliberately and solemnly towards some objective'.[19]

The musket (with its permanently fixed bayonet) was held as near to the perpendicular as possible, with the barrel facing to the front. The weapon was supported either by jamming the left forearm perpendicularly below the hammer, or extending the left arm

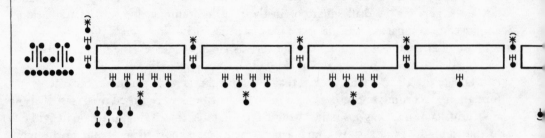

BATTALION OF EIGHT PLATOONS IN ORDER OF BATTLE

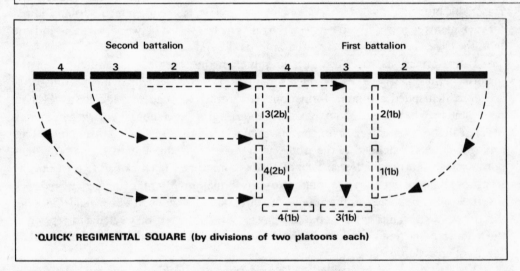

'QUICK' REGIMENTAL SQUARE (by divisions of two platoons each)

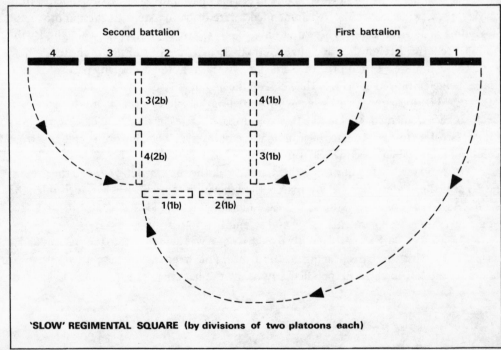

'SLOW' REGIMENTAL SQUARE (by divisions of two platoons each)

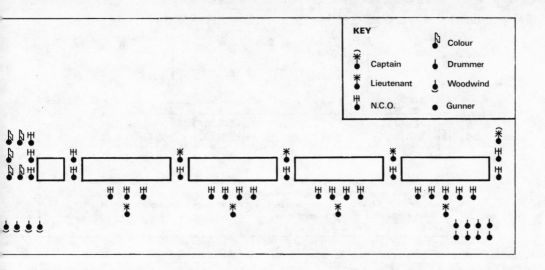

at full length and letting the end of the butt rest in the fingers.

When he was loading his musket on the march the soldier broke into a curious prancing step, bending the knee and setting the heel of one shoe to ground immediately on a line with the toe of the other. The effect was not unlike that of the present American march, though very much shorter and slower. The hideous goose-step was imported (along with some other bad things) from the Russian army in the Napoleonic period.

The basic tactical units of the Prussian army were the battalion (frontage 150–200 paces), the division (40–50 paces) and the platoon (20–25 paces).

On the march the two main lines of the army usually proceeded by column of platoons, that is to say on a frontage of one platoon, with all the other platoons following in succession behind. The platoon column was of two types: the closed column, with the minimum interval between the platoons, and the more common open column in which the interval was the equivalent of a platoon frontage, leaving the platoons with enough room to wheel upon command into a single line.

The wheeling of entire battalions was practiced before the Seven Years War, and it was an operation which could be achieved in about two minutes. After the war Saldern and others learnt how to pivot a battalion about its axis, which made for many a pretty evolution on the parade ground. Rather more useful than these *tours de force* was the advance of successive battalions in staggered formation (*in Staffeln*, *en échelon*), a device which was applied with notable success on the battlefields of Rossbach and Leuthen in 1757.

Military pedants rubbed their hands with glee at the prospect of forming a square, which was the classic formation of infantry against cavalry. There was the 'quick regimental square' (*Geschwindes Karree*) which remained in fashion until 1743, when it was largely supplanted by the 'slow regimental square' (*Langsames Karree*). For smaller units there was the normal battalion square (abolished 1743, but revived in 1752), and a solid square which was formed when the flanking platoons of the battalion fell back in closed column behind the two centre platoons (*Colonne nach der Mitte*).

Despite its impressive appearance, the square remained a formation 'which was beloved by the king but scorned by the generals'.[20] Unless a battalion happened to be

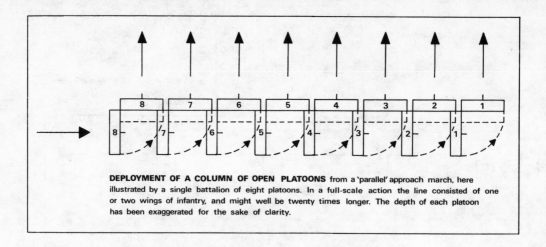

DEPLOYMENT OF A COLUMN OF OPEN PLATOONS from a 'parallel' approach march, here illustrated by a single battalion of eight platoons. In a full-scale action the line consisted of one or two wings of infantry, and might well be twenty times longer. The depth of each platoon has been exaggerated for the sake of clarity.

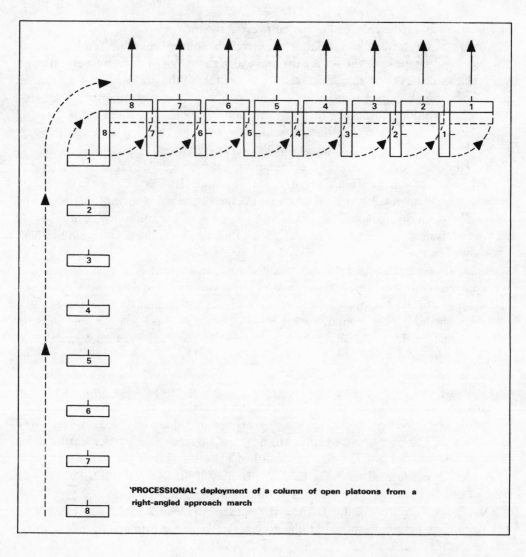

'PROCESSIONAL' deployment of a column of open platoons from a right-angled approach march

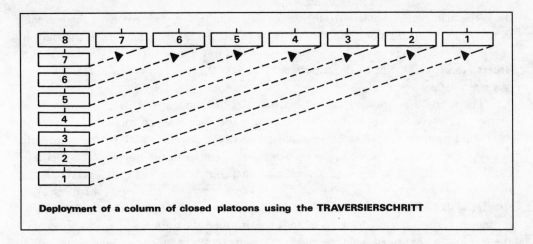

Deployment of a column of closed platoons using the TRAVERSIERSCHRITT

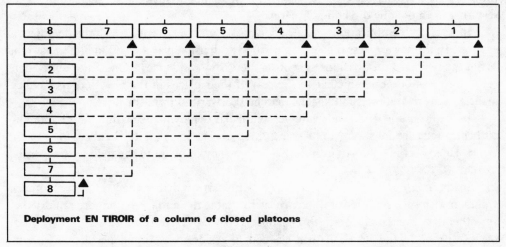

Deployment EN TIROIR of a column of closed platoons

caught on its own in the open, it was infinitely simpler to deal with swarming cavalry by causing the rearward rank to turn about and open fire.

In some ways the battalion was a strangely inflexible formation, being made up of eight platoons which were numbered off in descending order of seniority from right to left, and of three ranks of which the first rank was the one with the tallest and best-favoured men. It would have offended against all sense of military propriety to have reversed a battalion's front simply by causing all the men to make an about turn, for then the junior platoon would have ended up on the right, the position of honour, and the first rank would have been composed of ugly dwarfs. To preserve decorum Frederick introduced the elaborate procedure of the countermarch to the army in 1755.

The most vital of the evolutions were those concerned with shaking the army from column of march into line of battle. Frederick's usual solution was to bring the army on to the field of battle in two or more open platoon columns parallel with the army of the enemy. When the heads of columns reached the assigned station, the component platoons simply wheeled into line and were ready to do battle.

If the parallel march proved to be impracticable, then the columns had to be brought on to the field perpendicularly to the intended line of battle. This involved the platoons in marching in open column up the left flank of the field, then wheeling to the right in succession at a chosen spot. The platoons marched in the new direction until they were ordered to wheel into line by the same procedure as in the parallel march. This was termed 'processional deployment'.

The more direct procedure of perpendicular deployment from a *closed* column of platoons or divisions was first devised in 1745, and incorporated in the regulations in 1748. In this process the component subdivisions of the closed column peeled off to right or left (sometimes simultaneously in both directions) and made obliquely for their stations in the line of battle. The mechanics were somewhat complicated. In the first version of the manoeuvre the troops had to carry out the curious *Traversierschritt* (or *Schrägmärsch*), in which the shoulders were kept rigidly in line while the feet executed a dance-like step. If, for instance, the movement was to be to the right, then the right foot went forward first, the left foot was crossed over the right, the right foot went forward again, and so on, resulting in an oblique direction of march.

In 1752 the complications of the *Traversierschritt* were replaced by the deployment *en tiroir*. In the new process the leading platoon or division marched off in files to its right, as did the rearward subdivisions as soon as their fronts were clear. Once the subdivisions reached a position perpendicular to the rear of their places in the new line, the soldiers made a left turn and the subdivisions marched forward to form the line.

In the event the Prussians made perpendicular deployments on only four reasonably authenticated occasions – at Mollwitz in 1741, Lobositz in 1756, Reichenberg in 1757 and Gross-Jägersdorf in 1757. In every other action they came on to the field by the parallel march.

In the *Political Testament* of 1752 Frederick wrote that he had trained his officers and men with such a degree of diligence 'as to enable them to form up more rapidly than any other troops on earth'.[21] The foreign observers were certainly impressed. To Mirabeau the excellence of the Prussian drill seemed to reside in attaining perfection in some essentially simple movements,[22] while to David Dundas 'although the general movements of the Prussian infantry appear slow and solemn, yet they are so accurate that no time being lost in dressing or correcting distances, they arrive sooner at their object than any others, and at the instant of forming they are in perfect order to make the attack'.[23]

The Prussians themselves knew that the reality, though magnificent, did not always live up to the illusion:

Certainly it sometimes happens that the thing turns out well and the battalion of 200 or 250 files makes a fine impression as it advances on a broad front towards the dilettanti who are standing directly in front. The soldiers' legs, with their elegant gaiters and close-fitting breeches, work back and forth like the warp on a weaver's frame, while the sun is reflected blindingly back from the polished muskets and the whitened leatherwork. In a few minutes the moving wall is upon you. Yet these splendid evolutions are just a luxury of the exercise field, and even there they do not always come off. A ploughed field or a churned up meadow are enough to reduce the harmony to dissonance. Some of the soldiers lose step, and in trying to regain it they make a couple of hops and fall behind. When they fall back into step the others promptly lose it. The advance hesitates and the whole line falters.[24]

No other army surpassed the Prussian in the speed with which it delivered its fire. According to Scharnhorst,[25] the old Prussian musket required eleven seconds to load, and the new model with the 'conical' touch hole and the 'cylindrical' ramrod only eight or nine. Three seconds more had to be allowed for the three commands – 'Ready!' (*Machet Euch fertig!*), 'Present!' (*Schlaget an!*) and 'Fire!' (*Feuer!*), which made for a rate of fire of about four rounds per minute with the old musket and five or six with the new one. Frederick laid increasing stress on musketry after the Seven Years War, and, taking the speed of fire as the measure of its effect, he used to check the performance of his regiments at reviews with his watch. On the drill square a crack battalion could blast off perhaps as many as seven blank rounds a minute, but in battle conditions the rate of fire with ball was unlikely to exceed three. Gaudi complained that 'with this damned "minute fire" the men become exhausted and incapable of doing anything more after loosing off a few of these over-hasty salvoes. You could push them over with your little finger'.[26]

Frederick went to war in 1740 with an army that was trained in the complicated tactics of platoon fire, a technique which had been devised by Marlborough and Leopold of Anhalt-Dessau in the War of the Spanish Succession so as to keep up a continual rattling of volleys and be sure of having a reserve of loaded muskets always at hand. Platoon fire was delivered by the platoons of the battalion in the order 1, 8, 2, 7, 3, 6, 4, 5, and the similar divisional fire in the order 1, 4, 2, 3 (again numbering from the right), in other words progressing from either flank of the battalion towards the middle. The battalion could fire both at the halt and during the advance. In the latter case the battalion waddled forward while loading at about forty-five paces to the minute, with successive platoons taking three long strides forward, giving fire, and waiting for the rest to come up into line.

However, experience showed that the niceties of platoon fire were impracticable in battle conditions.

> You began by firing by platoons, and perhaps two or three would get off orderly volleys. But then would follow a general blazing away – the usual rolling fire when everybody blasted off as soon as he had loaded, when the ranks and files became intermingled, when the first rank was incapable of kneeling, even if it wanted to. The commanders, from subalterns to generals, would be incapable of getting the mass to perform anything else: they just had to wait until it finally set itself in motion forwards or backwards.[27]

Even before the Seven Years War Frederick had to permit almost the whole of the first line of battle to deliver massed battalion salvoes in actual combat, and he confined the platoon firings to the two or three battalions on either flank. This did not prevent platoon and division fire remaining an integral part of parade-ground tactics until the end of the reign, much to the chagrin of the generals. Toulongeon found that the army was solidly in favour of battalion fire, and veteran commanders assured him that 'during long and hot actions, when many troops had been killed, they could not prevent their soldiers from firing at will'.[28]

On occasions a battalion might be plagued by Croats or hussars who did not merit a full volley. In this event the major resorted to *Heckenfeuer*, which was a kind of controlled skirmishing. Two files marched five steps forward from alternate platoons or half-platoons, formed themselves into two ranks, then fired and retired to make way for the next two files in the succession. It all sounds very complicated, but there is the authenticated instance of the fusilier regiment of Bredow resorting to *Heckenfeuer* in the battle of Kunersdorf, when it drove away the Austrian and Russian cavalry.

In normal combat it was difficult for the men in the third, or rearmost rank to have a clear shot at the enemy. That was why the first rank was supposed to flop down on the right knee after loading was completed, while the rearward ranks 'locked on' by stepping to the right – the second rank by eight inches, and the third by fourteen.

The fire was inaccurate even in the best of conditions. In October 1755 Winterfeldt made two platoons of grenadiers fire at a target ten paces broad and ten feet high. At 300 paces the grenadiers scored only between 10 and 13 per cent hits on this not inconsiderable target. At 200 paces the rate increased to only 16.6 per cent, and at 150 paces to 46 per cent.

THE ADVANCE WITH COLD STEEL

For the best part of the first two decades of his reign Frederick was deluded into thinking that the awe-inspiring sight of advancing troops was a more effective weapon than the bullet. This miscalculation must be regarded as his greatest error in his capacity as military technician.

At the start, Frederick was probably influenced by the widespread contemporary revival of interest in classical military history, which inspired a general reappraisal of tactics towards the middle of the eighteenth century. Thus Frederick's preoccupation with cold steel was shared by pundits like the Frenchmen Saxe and Folard and the Austrian generals Thüngen and Khevenhüller. The first sign of the change in Prussian tactics came in April 1741, when Frederick ordered his infantry to have their bayonets permanently fixed when they were on duty. The 'Selowitz' infantry disposition of 25 March 1742 provided further evidence of the way his thoughts were tending, and in the *Reglement* of 1743 he went on to give the army a bold guarantee that no enemy would dare to stand before its bayonets.

The new tactics seemed to receive a bloody confirmation in the campaign of 1745. There was the decisive moment at Hohenfriedberg when the Hereditary Prince Leopold of Anhalt-Dessau ordered the regiment of Anhalt to attack the Saxon position without opening fire or checking its march. The regiment made an impressive breakthrough – and nobody stopped to reflect that the success was due to the supporting fire which came from the battalions to the left and right.

At Soor and Kesselsdorf in the same year the Prussians ran into bad trouble when they attacked batteries head-on, but in both cases the enemy obliged by coming out in pursuit, with the result that the Prussians were able to beat them in the open ground and over-run the batteries in the confusion. Thus in the *General Principia* Frederick suggested that when it was a question of turning the enemy out of batteries the army might go through a deliberate sequence of launching a preliminary attack, then falling back in apparent disorder, and finally dealing the serious blow with the bayonet; he proceeded to commit himself to a full-blooded advocacy of will-power over fire-power, 'because it is a bold front that defeats the enemy, not fire . . . you decide the battle more quickly by marching straight at the enemy than by popping off with your muskets, and the more quickly the action is decided the less men you lose'.

In the attempt to make the cold-steel weapons more effective Frederick introduced a longer and stouter bayonet for the first rank, and in February 1755 he issued a monstrous thirteen-foot *Kurzgewehr* to the NCOs and some of the men of the third rank (see p. 40). This was virtually a bid to re-introduce the pike to warfare and turn back tactics by sixty years.

At the beginning of the Seven Years War the confused and scrappy fighting at Lobositz (1 October 1756) provided Frederick with little opportunity of trying out his new methods. However, the advance without fire was carried out on a large scale at Prague in the following year (6 May 1757), and led to the massacre of several of Frederick's regiments by the Austrian artillery. In his memoirs General v. Warnery puts the responsibility for the bloodbath squarely upon the novel methods.[29]

Frederick was compelled to revise his ideas, and the army returned to the tactics of fire-power. The battle of Rossbach (5 November 1757) was largely decided by the Prussian cavalry before the infantry could get at the enemy, but one month later, at Leuthen, the Prussian musketry was very much in evidence. So it remained for the rest of the war.

In earlier times, wrote Frederick in 1768, it was an advantage to have big soldiers who could make good use of the bayonet, but nowadays 'the cannon does everything and the infantry cannot get to grips with cold steel . . . Battles are decided by the superiority of fire. Except in the attack on defended positions, a force of infantry which loads speedily will always get the better of a force which loads more slowly'.[30]

Thus in the final decades of the reign the infantry were expected to fight almost exclusively by fire. When General d'Hullin toured the army in 1786 he was told by Möllendorff and several other veteran commanders 'that they had never got nearer the enemy than one hundred paces'.[31]

THE CROATIAN THREAT

Frederick took it for granted that the Prussian infantry would emerge victorious whenever they met the Austrian regulars on equal terms in the open field – but the case was very different when the Prussians found themselves in broken country and pitted against the Croatian light infantry in the Austrian employ. These folk were drawn from the populations of Christian refugees which had been settled by the Austrian authorities along the borders with Turkey: agile, hardy and utterly loyal, they excelled in open-order 'Indian-style' fighting, and they sought out difficult country where the close-order skills of the Prussians were at a discount. Almost every regiment owned a horror-story of some episode when it had been caught at a disadvantage by the Croats.

In his *General Principia* Frederick warned his generals that the Croats were a menace in terrain that favoured their kind of fighting, though he was always very careful to conceal the extent of the danger from the army as a whole. In April 1758 General Philip Yorke heard from him that 'he was more upon his guard against them than against any other troops, and that he hoped I did not believe he had that contempt for them that he expressed; but that he had found no other way to inspire confidence into his troops than by treating them as *canaille*, or the lowest of soldiers; that it was impossible for them [the Prussians] to oppose anything equal to them in that kind, and that he did not like to be always sacrificing his regular infantry in that kind of war'.[32]

Frederick sometimes used to remind himself that he ought to do something about finding an answer to the Croats, but the trouble was that he had hardly any men who could be trusted to fight in any way other than in mass formations under the immediate eye of their officers. All the experiments with the 'free battalions' turned out more or less disastrously (see pp. 76–8), and only in his last years did Frederick begin to think about creating something as un-Prussian as a genuine native light infantry (see p. 76).

5

The Cavalry

Frederick's creative influence was probably greater in the cavalry than in any other arm of his forces. After an unimpressive début in the early 1740s the Prussian horsemen gradually acquired proficiency and high morale, and in the Seven Years War they went on to deal the decisive blows at such battles at Rossbach, Leuthen and Freiberg. The credit was due partly to Frederick's own keen understanding of mounted warfare, and partly to the work of his two assistants – the 'hussar king' Hans Joachim v. Zieten, and the sleepy-eyed and dissolute Friedrich Wilhelm v. Seydlitz, who was probably the most gifted leader of men in eighteenth-century Prussia.

The material

There is little in the make-up of Frederick's cavalry to remind us of the beaten, serf-like masses of the infantry regiments. The troopers of the cuirassiers (heavy cavalry) and the dragoons (medium cavalry) were drawn principally from the best material of the regimental cantons – sons of well-set-up peasants who would take their cavalry horses back to their native farms when they were released on leave. The foreign elements, too, were generally of better stock than their counterparts in the infantry. Indeed the security of the army and the effectiveness of the precautions against desertion depended to a large degree upon the loyalty of Frederick's cavalry.

Men like these responded best to a 'modern' style of leadership. One of Seydlitz's lifelong friends wrote that 'he was firmly convinced that the officer must have a superior knowledge and understanding of every detail of the things he demanded of the private trooper. It was only a mastery of such matters that would lend his orders true authority . . . Seydlitz believed that it was not enough for an officer simply to order a man to do something: he must be in a position to show him how it ought to be done, and to do it in an exemplary style'.[1]

The case of the hussars was slightly different, for they were assigned no cantons and the native Prussians were at first unfamiliar with the work of light cavalry. To begin with, Frederick had to look to Hungarian renegades and other wild folk for his recruits, but experience eventually showed that it was easy enough to attract people to the hussar life by the prospect of plunder and the excitement of the service.

Frederick liked to pretend that he sought out a markedly lighter and fitter cuirassier and dragoon than the colossi who were employed by his father. In fact a reasonable stature was needed for a man to wear the heavy iron breastplate of the cuirassiers, and to swing into the saddle of the powerful cavalry horses without assistance. Thus even Frederick

Troopers of Cuirassier Regiment no 22. They are evidently on exercise, as in the event of real action the carbine would have been suspended from the loop of the carbine belt, and not tied to the picket pale. Straw or lemon yellow coat (Kollet), carmine red cuffs, collar and waistcoat, black cuirass with border lacquered in carmine red, carmine red holster covers, saddle cloth and sabretache, straw or lemon yellow breeches, white leather gloves and leather equipment. Hat with narrow gold braid

had to insist on a minimum height of 5 ft 5 in for his cuirassiers and dragoons, and in practice the average height turned out to be noticeably greater.

Among the hussars, however, a weighty man was a decided liability, and recruits were not accepted beyond a maximum height of 5 ft 5 in.

The cavalry horses were acquired sometimes as a result of direct purchases by the individual regiment's, and sometimes as components of great herds which were bought in bulk and then distributed among the cavalry. In the middle of the reign, at least, the stature of the remounts was in proportion to the riders. Frederick decreed that the cuirassier horses should stand at least 5 ft 3 in tall and the dragoon horses at 5 ft 2 in, only the hussars being allowed to accept smaller horses. In 1757 Frederick entered Gotha at the head of the Meinicke Dragoons, and according to an eyewitness 'both men and horses appeared truly Prussian, namely big, strong and handsome'.[2]

The mount *par excellence* of the cuirassiers and dragoons was the powerful native horse of north Germany, and in particular the long-winded Holstein animal – a rather lighter creature than the breed of the same name in the nineteenth century. It was the endurance of the Holstein horse which enabled the twenty-six Prussian squadrons at Soor in 1745 to charge across a ravine, then up the steep slopes of the Austrian position on the Graner Koppe and so on to the valleys beyond.

The darkness of the coat was seen as a sign of quality. Thus in 1751 Frederick stipulated that the very blackest horses should go to the cuirassiers, and those of passable black or blackish-brown to the dragoons. No colour was specified for the light-limbed 'Polish' horses of the hussars, which were purchased in southern Poland, Russia, Moldavia and Wallachia. The 'Polish' horses were excellent for their own kind of work, and their speed and staying power were demonstrated in 1760 when General v. Warnery and his 800 hussars harassed the Austrian dragoon regiment of Archduke Joseph into a state of exhaustion and came away with 400 prisoners.

By a variety of expedients Frederick was able to make up for the dreadful wastage of horseflesh in the Seven Years War. He lost 20,000 horses in the single campaign of 1759, but in the following winter General Werner gathered in 2,000 in Mecklenburg, and in the next spring there was another large round-up in Thuringia. The difference was made up by requisitions in Saxony, and by the very large numbers of 'Polish' horses which the well-paid Jewish dealers managed to send to Frederick throughout the war.

From 1763 'Polish' horses began to appear among the rearward ranks of the dragoon regiments, and finally there were entire regiments mounted upon these animals, in spite of the preference of the men and most of the officers for the German horses. The cuirassiers kept their German horses, though even these began to fall below the standards of the 1750s.

Frederick's own preference was for what he called 'the ancient race of English horses'[3] – strong and tall animals with an easy motion, for which he was prepared to pay the dealer Mr Castle £75 apiece. The generals of his suite rode English horses of the same kind, and the regulations pointed out to the army that this sign was a good way of recognising the royal entourage.

THE CUIRASSIERS

The cuirassiers were the direct descendants of the armoured knights of medieval times. They were given powerful horses and iron breastplates, and they had the ancient task of breaking down the main opposition of the enemy cavalry and crushing the flanks of the infantry.

Frederick owned thirteen regiments of cuirassiers (including the Garde du Corps which was raised in 1740), which gave him a total of sixty-three squadrons. The twelve senior regiments were on an establishment of five squadrons each, but the Garde du Corps owned only three. The administrative division of the squadron consisted of two companies, but for tactical purposes it was broken down into four platoons.

Counting in the twelve supernumeraries per squadron, the cuirassier and dragoon regiments went to war with a strength of about 37 officers, 70 NCOs, 5 farriers, 10 medical orderlies, a score of trumpeters and drummers and the personnel of the regimental staff. This gave a total of about 872 souls, though in February 1755 an augmentation of the supernumeraries brought the total to 890. The cuirassier and dragoon squadron of the Seven Years War therefore consisted of some 185 personnel, comprising 6 officers, a dozen NCOs, 150–60 troopers, 2 trumpeters, 3 drummers, 1 or 2 farriers and a small establishment of orderlies and staff. Throughout the period the 'service horses' of the regiment amounted to about 740, to which we must add the eighty or so mounts (including spares) of the officers.

The cuirassier uniform was both comely and practical. The outfit was crowned by a large black three-cornered hat which looked rather odd on the individual, but made a good impression in the mass. The crown was lined with a cap of iron strips, which afforded the owner some protection from sword cuts. In 1762 Frederick gave his cuirassiers white hat plumes, so as to be able to distinguish them more easily from the Austrian cuirassiers, who wore a similar uniform. Unfortunately the cavalry of almost the whole of Europe proceeded to imitate the fashion, which spoilt the object of the original exercise.

Above his shirt the cuirassier wore a waistcoat (*chemisette*), and on top of that a short coat (*Kollet*) of very strong straw-coloured kersey cloth (which had totally replaced the buckskin jerkin by the end of the Second Silesian War). It was difficult to keep the coats a uniform colour, owing to the variability of the dye, hence coats of white became almost universal in the last years of the reign. The breeches were of soft leather, and the stockings reached two fingers higher than the tops of the buckets of the heavy riding boots. The neck stock was of stiff black or red cloth.

The armour protection consisted of a heavy iron breastplate. It was fastened by straps of yellow leather (white after the Seven Years War) which were passed cross-wise over the back. 'The breastplates must be strapped down very tightly otherwise when a man falls from his horse the breastplate can easily be forced upwards, causing nasty injuries.'[4] The Garde du Corps owned the distinction of wearing breastplates of polished bare metal, but in all the other regiments the iron was painted black. The officers' cuirasses were decorated with a broad border of gilt and a fringe of frilly cloth of the regimental colour. The troopers' cuirasses were bordered with a narrow roll of the same colour.

A narrow leather belt was slung over the right shoulder and held the little cartridge pouch suspended behind and just above the left hip. The box contained eighteen cartridges for the carbine and twelve for the pistols. During action the carbine hung down the right-hand side of the man from a large hook or loop on the separate carbine belt, which was a broad leather strap, usually covered in coloured cloth, passing over the left shoulder. When the carbine was unlikely to be needed for immediate action it was tied to the picket pale, and hung down the right-hand side of the saddle cloth with the muzzle resting in a small leather shoe. All ranks of cuirassiers and dragoons owned two pistols each, which they carried in strong leather holsters which were covered in embroidered cloth and fixed to the front of the saddles. Carbines, however, were not carried by the officers or NCOs.

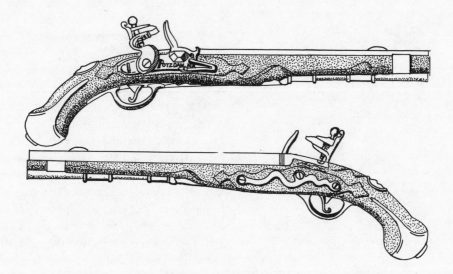

In every category of cavalry the sword hung down the left-hand side from a waist belt. The model of the cuirassier sword dated from the last reign. The blade was between forty and forty-two inches long. It was broad, straight and double-edged, but liable to bend when it was used for pointing instead of cutting. The guard was a massive affair, but the slot for the entry of the hand was so narrow that the men sometimes found difficulty in grasping the hilt when they were in a hurry.

The embroidered royal monogram and the colour of the regimental facings appeared on the saddle cloth, the coverings of the two pistol holsters, and the hanging sabretache pockets of the cuirassiers and hussars.

Among the less glamorous gear of the cuirassiers and dragoons we may mention such items as the forage cap and the smock (*Kittel*) of linen and ticking, which were put on for foraging and stable work, and the riding overcoat of undyed grey wool (which the rank and file exchanged after 1756 for a sleeveless cloak of dark blue).

At the end of every two years the trooper received a new hat, coat, waistcoat, boots and two pairs of stockings. Two shirts, two hair ribbons and two stocks were issued every year. The cloak was expected to last five years.

THE DRAGOONS

Dragoons first came into prominence during the Thirty Years War, when commanders were looking for an arm that would combine the speed of the cavalry with the fire-power of the infantry. However, like most weapons of war, the dragoons became subject to a process of up-rating over the years, and in Prussia old Frederick William converted them into a force that was fit to enter an open cavalry battle in the company of the armoured cuirassiers.

Frederick the Great inherited ten regiments of dragoons. He raised an eleventh in 1744, and a twelfth seven years later. The fifth and sixth regiments in order of seniority were on an extra-large establishment of ten squadrons: all the others stood at five, like the cuirassiers.

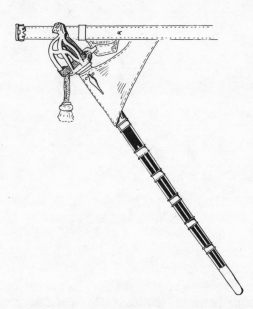

In contradistinction to the cuirassiers, the dragoons lacked the breastplate and wore a long infantry-type coat (originally white; sky-blue from about June 1745). The dragoon carbine was equipped with a bayonet, and in length it stood about half-way between the musket of the infantry and the carbine proper of the cuirassiers and hussars. Both the carbine and the cartridge pouch of black leather hung from a leather bandolier that was looped over the left shoulder. The bandolier was of a yellow colour until the end of the Seven Years War, after which it was whitened. The brass guard of the sword was of a lighter and more open construction than that of the cuirassier sword, and it was surmounted by a pommel in the shape of an eagle's head.

The organisation of the dragoons has been discussed already. Later we shall have the opportunity of seeing these gentlemen in action. It is enough to add for the moment that one of their regiments, the Bayreuth Dragoons (no 5), has a justifiable claim to be considered the most effective single unit in the whole of Frederick's army.

THE HUSSARS

The hussars formed a category of light cavalrymen, originating in Hungary, who were adopted throughout Europe and employed on tasks where speed and mobility were at a premium – patrolling and reconnaissance work, raiding, pursuits, and securing the flank and rear of the heavy cavalry on the battlefield.

The first hussars to appear in the Prussian service were the thirty Preussische Husaren who were raised in 1721 by the dragoon general Wuthenow. Frederick William did not feel inclined to pursue the experiment much further until in 1729 he travelled to see his daughter, the Margravine of Bayreuth, and was much impressed by the local hussars who escorted his coach and lit the way with torches. The first of the new Leib-Corps Husaren were raised in 1731, and six years later they were set up as an independent corps of six squadrons.

For a long time the Prussian hussars could be written off as just another of Frederick William's bad military jokes – more gaudy, perhaps, than the Giant Grenadiers, though not nearly so expensive. The king himself admitted that 'a German lad does not make such a good hussar as an Hungarian or a Pole'.[5] Among the corps of officers were numbered such oddities as the little Hans v. Zieten. He was born in 1699 to a poor landed family in Brandenburg, and he had such a strong military bent that every Sunday morning from the age of nine he went to Ruppin to have his hair dressed and powdered by a grenadier. Following up his first inclination towards the infantry, he entered the regiment of Schwerin. There he stuck, unable to rise above the rank of ensign, on account of his 'small stature and weak voice'.[6] In 1724 he complained to Frederick William of the 'manifold injustices he had suffered', but the king merely wrote back to the regiment, telling the colonel to dismiss him. Entering the dragoon regiment of Wuthenow he promptly fell out with a staff captain, so embarking on a violent quarrel which led to a spell in the fortress casemates of Königsberg and finally, in 1730, to a duel and his cashiering.

The quarrelsome but fundamentally good-hearted Zieten began to find his true vocation only in 1731, when on the recommendation of General v. Buddenbrock he was recalled to the service and appointed commander of a new squadron of the Leib-Corps Husaren. In 1735 he was sent with 120 men to the war on the Rhine 'so as to learn the organisation and methods of the Imperial hussars'.[7] He picked up many useful lessons from the Austrian hussar chief, Lieutenant-Colonel v. Baranyay, and on returning to Prussia he was promoted to major.

Nine squadrons of hussars awaited Frederick's orders upon his accession in 1740 – the Leib-Corps Husaren, now three squadrons strong, and the six squadrons of the Preussische Husaren. These units formed the kernel of four of the five new regiments of hussars which Frederick set up in 1741 (no 1 the Green Hussars, no 2 the Red Hussars, no 3 the Blue Hussars and no 5 the Black Hussars). The other regiment, the White Hussars (no 4) got off to an independent start, being recruited mostly from Polish deserters. Three more regiments of hussars were raised between 1742 and 1745. A ninth regiment (the Bosniaken) was added to their number in 1760, and a tenth in 1773.

The hussar regiments were put on a very powerful establishment of ten squadrons apiece, which gave them a complement ranging from 1,100 to more than 1,500 personnel of all kinds.

The uniforms followed a variation of the absurd fashions that were set by the 'genuine' Hungarian hussars in the Austrian service, namely a dolman shell jacket, a fur-lined pelisse, and tight leather pants and boots which were enclosed in close-fitting trousers of cloth. From 1756 the original busby of wolfskin or bearskin was supplemented, for summer wear, by a felt hat in the form of an inverted flower pot (*Filzmütze*, *Mirliton*, *Flügelmütze* or *Schachelhaube*). A long cloth flap was wrapped round the hat on normal service, but it was allowed to hang loose in battle or on parade.

Most hussars were armed with short, smooth-bore carbines, though before the Second Silesian War the ten best men in each squadron were issued with good horses and rifled carbines and were given special training in target-shooting and reconnaissance work. The hussar sabre had a forty-one-inch curved blade that was light but very good.

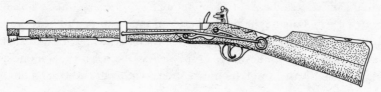

The Prussian hussars made a singularly unimpressive début in the First Silesian War. They saw the Austrian hussars run rings around them in the hill country, and the White Hussars were reduced to impotent fury when the enemy took to the habit of bleating 'Baa! Baa!' at the sight of their furry white pelisses. At Mollwitz the hussars' sole achievement was to ransack their own army's baggage, and after the battle Frederick issued a contemptuous order to the effect that 'women, hussars and baggage drivers, if caught plundering, will be hanged without more ado'.[8]

When the hussars regained their credit, it was largely due to the example of strange little Zieten, who by now had managed to put himself in order. Weighing up his quarrelsome temperament, he took 'a decisive resolve – never to touch alcoholic drink again . . . and for the remainder of his campaigns this man, the first hussar of his century, touched nothing but water'.[9]

A leader of the type of Seydlitz (who, by the way, also did service as an hussar), Zieten was an enemy of corporal punishment, though 'a critical word from him made more impression than fifty blows with a stick'.[10] Frederick learnt to trust him as 'my valiant Zieten. Energetic and bold, he does not allow himself to be elated by success or depressed by misfortune. He is just happy to get to grips with the enemy.'[11]

The raid on Rothschloss on 22 July 1741 was probably the action which more than any other saved the morale of the hussars. Charging with six squadrons, Major v. Zieten routed the Austrians out of the village in short order and compelled his old mentor Baranyay to lay a plank across a stream and scamper over to safety. Baranyay sent back word congratulating his former pupil on his coup.

The first hussar *Reglement* proper dated from 1 December 1743. As one of their first priorities the officers were told to put their men through riding exercises daily, for 'His Majesty demands that mounted hussars should be nimble enough to sweep up an object from the ground at full gallop, or ride at full speed and snatch the hats from each other's heads'.[12] The hussars were then to go on to learn how to fight in dispersed formation, and how to make the best use of their sabres and carbines. One of their most important duties was to go out in swarms of anything from two to four thousand at a time and play the part of 'a spider in his web, which cannot be disturbed without him feeling it'.[13] From the massive size of these patrols we may infer that the Prussian hussars were not yet up to meeting their Austrian counterparts on equal terms.

It was unfortunate for the hussars that Zieten lost some of his influence in the period between the peace of 1745 and the outbreak of the Seven Years War. He made some silly mistakes in the peacetime manoeuvres, which shook Frederick's confidence, and he disappointed the king still further when he refused to be drawn into discussion of any hypothetical military situation. 'My head cannot operate in a void – I must see the actual object. I need facts to inspire me and make an impression on me. Then I know what to do, and I go ahead and do it.'[14]

The temporary eclipse of Zieten left the field open for General v. Winterfeldt, whose ambition it was to make the hussars into an effective arm on the open battlefield. In his instruction to the hussar regiments of 27 September 1747 he suggested a number of techniques by which the hussars might get the better of the infantry and heavy cavalry of the enemy. Frederick was certainly pleased with the progress the hussars were making under Winterfeldt's tutelage, and in the course of the reviews between the wars he noticed one regiment which was at least as well mounted and disciplined as the dragoons.

(above left) *Prince Leopold of Anhalt–Dessau, 'The Old Dessauer'. The sprig of oak leaves in the hat was sported by some of the older generals who had campaigned alongside the Austrians in the time of Prince Eugene;* (above right) *Lieutenant-General Duke Friedrich Eugen v. Württemberg. Active and intelligent, he was one of the best princes of the Empire in the Prussian service;* (below left) *Hans Joachim v. Zieten, 'The Hussar King', wearing the officer's uniform of Hussar Regiment no 2. Fur hat with red flap and eagle's wing, red dolman with tiger skin;* (below right) *Friedrich Wilhelm v. Seydlitz with the uniform of the Cuirassier Regiment no 8 and the orange sash of the Black Eagle*

The vindication of the Prussian hussars as a battle weapon came at Prague, on 6 May 1757, when they intervened at a critical moment and overset the cavalry of the Austrian right. Later on at Torgau (1760) the NCOs and men of the Zieten regiment were seen to rally some of the broken cuirassiers and dragoons and lead them back to the fight.

At the same time it is legitimate to speculate whether Winterfeldt's teaching did not turn the Prussian hussars in a false direction, converting them into a substitute for the heavy cavalry instead of training them up to beat the Austrian hussars at their own game. Frederick's complacency remained unshaken throughout the 1760s and the early 1770s, which left him unprepared for the failure of his hussars in genuine light cavalry work in the War of the Bavarian Succession.

THE BOSNIAKEN

If we had not been concerned with the loss of human lives, it would have been possible to tell the history of Frederick's Bosniaken in terms of pure comedy. The founding father of this strange corps was an Albanian jeweller called Serkis who in 1744, at the age of seventy-five, set off for the Ukraine to round up 4,000 recruits in virtue of a sub-contract with the Saxon government. He returned with a small but varied collection of individuals, who included such luminaries as a Lieutenant Osman and a Cornet Ali. On presenting his band, however, he found that the main contractor had run out of money and left him with the circus on his hands. He addressed himself to Frederick (for whom charlatanism exercised an irresistible appeal) and the result was that the wandering flock was taken into the Prussian service in 1745 and attached to hussar regiment no 5.

The Bosniaken were armed with the lance, 'a weapon which, in the hands of a master, makes him almost unbeatable'.[15] However, their tactics merely consisted of 'setting up a fearful cry, throwing themselves at the enemy and letting go of the reins – for they had to clutch the lance in both hands to deal a really effective thrust – hoping that the fluttering of the pennants on their lances would alarm the enemy horses and cause them to rear up or turn about'.[16]

The Bosniaken duly turned up for the Seven Years War, arrayed in turbans and flourishing their lances. The enemy were at first impressed by the strangeness of their appearance, but they soon discovered that these gentlemen were mostly peasants and deserters and that there were few genuine Easterners among them. Despite a less than distinguished record they attained a total of ten squadrons in 1763, before sinking back again to one squadron after the peace.

In the post-war years the new *Chef* of the Bosniaken, the hussar general Daniel v. Lossow, did what he could to beat the brigands into shape. There was a revealing incident at a Silesian cavalry review when one of the Bosniaken tried to break up a manoeuvre which was being directed by Lossow's old enemy, the rough-spoken General v. Dalwig. Dalwig promptly hit the offending Bosniak and cut down his horse. All of this took place under the eyes of the king, who deprived Dalwig of his cavalry inspection. The other hussars were so angry at the injustice that they threatened to kill the Bosniaken if they so much as dared to appear at a review again.

Quite unabashed, the Bosniaken took the field in the War of 1778 as a full regiment of ten squadrons. The Austrian hussars quickly found that they could evade the thundering Bosniak charge simply by throwing their horses to one side just before the collision. Using

Bosniak in winter garb. Long black coat (Schubban) *trimmed with fur*

these tactics at Trautenau, the hussar regiments of Esterhazy and Wurmser let four squadrons of Bosniaken come on in a great wedge, then gave way to either side and fell on them from the rear. The Bosniaken were wiped out, and their regiment was virtually finished as an effective force.

THE FELDJÄGER-CORPS ZU PFERDE

We move from the disreputable Bosniaken to the much more select company of the mounted *Feldjäger*. Frederick set up the unit on 24 November 1740 when he appointed his *Oberjäger* Joachim Schenck as his *Capitain des Guides*, whose function was to 'obtain good guides and hold them ready, so that when the army advances or a detachment is sent out, the troops may be accompanied by reliable guides who know all the roads and passages'.[17] The first 6 officers and 50 men were recruited before the end of the year. In 1744 the establishment was raised to 6 officers and 112 men, and by the end of the reign the corps stood at a total of 162 picked riders, all the sons of *Ober Förster*. They wore riding boots, but otherwise they were uniformed in much the same way as their comrades in the foot *Jäger*.

On campaign the mounted *Feldjäger* acted as couriers and guides under the immediate direction of the king's first adjutant-general. In time of peace they were stationed at Potsdam, where half their number kept their horses saddled up in instant readiness to carry the royal dispatches.

Peacetime cavalry service

Unlike the infantry, who were herded together in the fortress towns, the cavalry were scattered by squadrons in villages where they could find stabling and fodder on the lavish scale they required. One-third of the cavalry regiments were quartered in Silesia and one-quarter in East Prussia, but the other provinces escaped fairly lightly. The squadrons came together for the spring review, and the autumn manoeuvres, but many of the troopers were released with their horses soon after the first of these assemblies was over. The winter time was not very much more strenuous, being devoted to the care of the horses and the training of the recruits.

At the height of the prosperity of the Prussian cavalry the cuirassier and dragoon horses were fed on a daily ration of 8 lb of oats, 11 lb of hay and 14–15 lb of chopped straw, which by twentieth-century standards is light on oats but heavy on hay and straw. The ration of dry fodder was reduced on grounds of economy after the Seven Years War, and again after the War of the Bavarian Succession, and from 1 June to 1 September the horses were sent home with their riders or put out to graze at the expense of the local peasants. By 1780 a crack regiment like the Bayreuth Dragoons dared to ride its enfeebled horses only once every other day during the stipulated exercise seasons. On the other days the troopers had to go through the evolutions on foot.

The Prussian cavalry possessed no written riding instructions, though it seems to have been a general rule that two years' work were required for the training of a recruit. Seydlitz used to exercise the recruits of his regiment first on foot, then on wooden horses, and when they came to mount the genuine live animals he laid down that 'they must ride without stirrups until they have a faultless posture'.[18] The area of his regimental depot at Trebnitz near Breslau was a scene of endless activity. He used to practice his men in sword exercises against straw dummies (in accordance with the *Reglement* of 1743), in loading their pistols on horseback, and above all in keeping their seats while the squadrons charged over fields, ditches and hedges. Every morning, when Seydlitz left his house at Ohlau, he used to spur his horse over the water trough in front of the door and then leap over the closed gates of his estate. He required all the couriers to do the same.

It was assumed that the officers were already reasonably proficient masters of their horses, though Seydlitz took the precaution of putting candidates for his regiment on unbroken horses and leaving them to their fate: if they survived in the saddle they had passed the first test of admission.

A British observer noted that 'the officers ride well, uniformly, and boldly, and their horses are well trained – in this service they are purposely mounted on lighter and lower horses than the men, as more activity is required of them'.[19] The nobility gained its riding experience in a variety of ways – perhaps in one of the riding academies that were attached to the German courts and universities, but more commonly in the normal course of country life. Seydlitz himself had spent five instructive years from 1734 as page to the 'Mad Margrave' Friedrich of Brandenburg-Schwedt, when he learnt such arts as raising a hat from the ground at sword-point at a gallop, drilling a hat in the air with a pistol shot from the saddle, and riding through the revolving sails of a windmill.

In the regiments the officers were assisted by the *Stallmeister* to acquire the finer points of *haut école*, an art which the textbooks of the period considered to be of direct relevance to combat (see Zehentner's *Kurzer und deutlicher Unterricht zur Anweisung eines jungen Kavaliers im Reiten*, Frankfurt-am-Oder, 1753). Seydlitz himself was a master of *haut école*, and as a squadron commander he once created a sensation by putting his horse through three prodigious caprioles in honour of the king.

The hunting of deer and boar was a favourite amusement of the time, and the necessity of riding through thickets and woods encouraged the Prussian officers to cling to the old continental-style gear of long stirrups, thick boots, and the heavy bolstered-up *Pauschensattel* which pushed the rider forward almost on to the horse's withers (in less horsy language, the bump just to the rear of the base of the neck). The regulations of 1742 and 1743 stated that it was enough for a single hand's breadth of space (two hands' breadth in the case of the hussars) to appear between the seat and the saddle when the rider stood in the stirrups.

Frederick was considered eccentric because he favoured the short stirrups and the flatter saddle that had been evolved by the English for racing and foxhunting. He actually bought an English racehorse in 1764, though he does not seem to have done anything with it. Seydlitz knew that he was going against his master's inclinations when in 1766 he ordered his regiment to ride so 'long' that the leg and the foot would form an almost straight line. The practice caught Frederick's eye in the course of a review in 1770, and he remarked to Seydlitz 'it seems to me that your regiment is riding a good deal longer than the rest of my cavalry'. Seydlitz replied 'Your Majesty, the regiment is riding in the same style as it did at Rossbach'.[20]

The fundamental tactical unit of the cuirassiers and dragoons was the squadron. The squadron owned a field strength of between 140 and 190 officers and men, and it was subdivided into four platoons (*Züge*) of about 40 effectives each. The squadron commander and four of his officers usually took up station in front of the squadron. The standard bearer was sited in the centre of the second rank, with an NCO to his front; one further NCO was positioned on each flank of the squadron, near the trumpeter, and the rest of the officers and NCOs ranged themselves in the rear of the squadron.

The cavalry usually marched by open column of platoons or squadrons, though for passing along narrow roads a column of five or even two files was adopted. The old three-rank line of battle survived until late in 1757, when the men were rearranged in two ranks, in order to compensate for a shortage of cavalry. The thin line worked so well that by 1760 it had become almost universal throughout the Prussian cavalry (the hussars had been in two ranks all the time). As usual the regulations failed to reflect the actual practices of the army, and so the parade-ground line of three ranks continued to be described as the norm in the cavalry *Reglements* of 1764, 1774 and 1779.

The cavalry adopted the same basic techniques as the infantry for shaking themselves out of column of march into line of battle. By May 1756 Frederick had settled on a new way of bringing a column of eleven squadrons into line of battle at right-angles to the direction of march: the sixth squadron alone kept on its course, while the five leading squadrons wheeled in succession to the right and trotted on in that direction until they had gained enough ground to enable them to wheel left into a continuous line of battle; the rearward five columns simultaneously performed the same evolution to the left of the original column. This kind of deployment was certainly carried out at the battle of Gross-Jägersdorf, and possibly also at Lobositz and Reichenberg.

As with the infantry, however, Frederick much preferred the simpler expedient of marching on to the field in open column and parallel with the enemy, and then wheeling all the units into line of battle. The 'parallel' deployment possessed the additional advantage of leaving the squadrons in proper order of seniority, whereas the angular deployment produced a degree of inversion and put the cavalry to the trouble of having to go through countermarches afterwards.

Frederick never entirely recovered from the shock of having seen the slow-moving Prussian cavalry beaten so badly at Mollwitz (11 April 1741). He claimed that

> my father left me a bad cavalry, in which there was hardly an officer who knew his profession. The troopers feared their horses and scarcely ever rode, knowing only how to go through their exercises on foot, like the infantry. The cavalry was too heavy, with its big men and big horses, and the effects in our first war were so bad that I saw that I had to re-make the entire corps.[21]

In all of this Frederick does less than justice to his father's work for the cavalry. Frederick William had raised the horse from 54 squadrons to 114, he had up-rated the dragoons, and he had created the first Prussian hussars. Frederick William's cavalry was slow-moving, certainly, but the old king appreciated very well that the cavalry did much more damage when they charged home with the sword instead of standing still and popping away with their carbines and pistols. In 1734 he had gone so far as to forbid his dragoons on pain of death to use any weapon except the sword.

Even if the contrast between the two reigns has been slightly overdrawn, there can be no doubt that Frederick succeeded magnificently in his aim of teaching the Prussian cavalry to charge as fast and as far as was physically possible. He explained his reasoning to the Comte de Gisors:

> I make the squadrons charge at a fast gallop because then fear carries the cowards along with the rest – they know that if they so much as hesitate in the middle of the onrush they will be crushed by the remainder of the squadron. My intention is to force the enemy to break by the speed of our charges before it ever comes to hand-to-hand fighting: officers become no more valuable than simple troopers in a mêlée, and order and cohesion are lost.[22]

We may trace the following stages in the evolution of the Frederician cavalry charge.

1. On 3 June 1741, in the period soon after the battle of Mollwitz, a report from Leopold of Anhalt-Dessau contained the first reference to the Prussian cavalry moving at the gallop. Frederick went on to teach the cavalry to put in the last thirty paces of their attack at the gallop, and he reminded the troopers that they must rely on the sword.

2. On 17 March 1742 the 'Selowitz' cavalry instruction stipulated that the gallop was to be launched from 100 paces.

3. In 1743 the new cavalry *Reglement* laid down that 'when you attack the enemy . . . you begin at a fast trot and end up at a full gallop, while keeping in compact order . . . As soon as the first enemy line . . . is overthrown, the commanders must re-form their squadrons as soon as possible and lose no time in attacking the second line'. This article was inspired by the experience of the battle of Chotusitz (17 May 1742), which showed that it was inadvisable to spend too long in re-forming the ranks after the first line of the enemy cavalry had been overthrown.

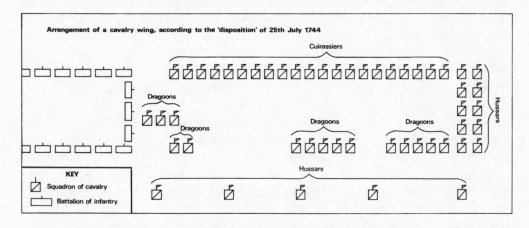

Arrangement of a cavalry wing, according to the 'disposition' of 25th July 1744

Cuirassiers

Dragoons

Dragoons

Dragoons

Dragoons

Hussars

Hussars

KEY
Squadron of cavalry
Battalion of infantry

4. On 25 July 1744 the arrangement of the cavalry on the field was defined in the *Disposition, wie sich die Officiere von der Cavallerie . . . in einem Treffen gegen den Feind zu verhalten haben.* The first line of each wing of cavalry was to be composed of the regiments of cuirassiers, lined up knee-to-knee *en muraille* with a maximum interval of ten paces

between the squadrons. Three hundred paces behind came the main line of dragoons, who were disposed at broader intervals so as to preserve their capacity to manoeuvre. Further squadrons of dragoons were positioned half-way towards the cuirassiers, lending them close support, while the hussars hovered around the flanks and rear of the mass of the heavy cavalry – the cuirassier and dragoon troopers were to be reminded of this faction before every battle, 'so that they will not turn about if they hear an outburst of firing behind them'.[23]

The gallop was to start at 200 paces from the enemy, and towards the end of their course the horses were to be given their head. A special rider held the threat of *infamer Cassation* over the head of any cavalry commander who let himself be attacked by the enemy. The Prussians must always be the ones to attack first.

5. On 4 June 1745 the charge of the Bayreuth Dragoons at Hohenfriedberg demonstrated the efficacy of the shock tactics in a most spectacular manner.

6. In 1747, on the suggestion of Captain Seydlitz, the king stipulated that in future any disordered body of cavalry was to re-group in the direction of the enemy – the *Sammeln nach vorn*. This was a lesson derived from the action at Landeshut on 22 May 1745, when a force of Prussian hussars lost an initial advantage after the signal *Appel* was blown from behind.

7. On 14 August 1748 the *Instruction für die Generalmajors von der Cavallerie* ordained that 'if . . . it happens that somewhere or other the first line runs into difficulties, then the second line must lend immediate support without awaiting further orders'.[24] The instruction was carried out to the letter in the battle of Lobositz (1 October 1756).

8. On 16 March 1759 a new *Instruction für die Generalmajors von der Cavallerie* advised the commanders to let the infantry effect the first breach in the enemy positions, after which 'the general must lead his brigade with all speed to the place where he intends to break in, and then carry out his attack in column of squadrons so as to exploit the confusion of the enemy, like the regiments Garde du Corps, Gensd'armes and Seydlitz at Rossbach, like General v. Seydlitz's wing of cavalry at Zorndorf, and like the regiment Gensd'armes at Hochkirch'.[25] In the *Political Testament* of 1768 Frederick describes the cavalry column as a valuable state secret, and two years later he discussed it again in his *Eléments de Castramétie*.

After the Seven Years War the cavalry continued to devote most of its efforts in manoeuvres to carrying out massive charges *en muraille* under the eyes of the king. However, Seydlitz and other commanders believed that the lengthy and close-packed charges were asking too much of man and beast, and in the last decades of the reign the ill-fed and overloaded horses certainly became less and less equal to the demand.

The Prussian habit during the charge was to stand in the stirrups and hold the sword on high, ready to bring it down on the head of the enemy in a sweeping arc. The purist might have pointed out that in theory the cavalry would have done better to lean forward and point the sword instead, but the experience of the real world showed that it did not really matter how the sword was held. Mirabeau writes that 'veteran and intelligent cavalry officers have told us that when two bodies of cavalry charge one another, it almost always happens that one party flees before the other can meet it. Sword blows are dealt only during the pursuit'.[26]

As a relic of their origins as mounted infantry, the dragoons were expected to learn foot drill with muskets and fixed bayonets to almost the same standard as the infantry proper. Carbines proved useful in various kinds of hussar work, but the cuirassiers were taught to fight on foot only with the purpose of enabling them to win the time to mount up if they came under unexpected attack in their posts or quarters.

6

The Artillery

The status of the technicians

We now take up the unhappy story of Frederick's relations with the technical arms. The king certainly showed a genius for innovation in his capacity as a gunner, and nobody would deny that as a strategist he made a brilliant use of his fortresses. Yet he never showed himself more arbitrary, obtuse and ill-informed than when he was dealing with his gunners and engineers. Why were these relationships so unfortunate?

For a start there was the fact that artillery and engineering were generally regarded as grubby, bourgeois arts, demanding hard and unglamorous toil, constant patience and the precise calculation of physical forces – all of which was alien to the temper of the old European military nobility.

Frederick actively encouraged his own aristocracy in their prejudices. Thus in 1784 he consigned three non-noble cadets to the artillery with the comment, 'they can get on well enough there'.[1] He mentioned the artillery very seldom, if at all, in his battle reports, and it was almost unknown for him to single out an artillery officer for honour or rewards. For most of the reign, in fact, the artillery was left without a recognisable chief. The nearest thing to a head was probably represented by General Christian v. Linger, who had set the armaments industry on its feet in the reign of Frederick William, and who survived in a senile state until he died in his eighty-sixth year in 1755. Lieutenant-Colonel v. Dieskau was designated Inspector-General of the Artillery, thus taking over some of Linger's functions, and in 1762 he was promoted to major-general. All the time, however, Frederick reserved all the important decisions for himself, and left Dieskau with little more than executive powers. An historian has commented 'how odd it was [in the Seven Years War] to have a lieutenant-colonel as Inspector of the entire artillery of an army which was locked in war with five-sevenths of Europe!'[2]

The rest of the army was quick to follow Frederick's lead.

> Live with the Prussian officers [wrote Mirabeau], and you will see the officers of the infantry, cavalry and hussars assume a great superiority over the artillery officers. The latter seem to recognise their lowly status, in a manner of speaking. The other officers intermingle and seek each other out regardless of regiment or arm, but it is altogether exceptional for any friendship to be formed between the gunner officers and the officers of the rest of the army.[3]

So it was that when they returned from campaign against the French in the 1790s the gunners of the horse artillery had to remove the plumes from their hats before they could enter the gates of Berlin, lest it should be thought that they were laying claim to any of the *cachet* of the cuirassiers. For an artilleryman to carry a musket was also considered to be presumptuous, except when it was a question of doing sentry duty in the emergency of the Seven Years War. On 4 October 1766 some artillerymen were certainly issued with muskets to provide a guard of honour for the marriage of the Prince of Orange to a Prussian princess, but immediately after the ceremony the weapons were whisked away again.

In the material sense the artillery captains were at least as well off as the company commanders in the other services, but it is hardly surprising that the morale of the gunners as a whole remained dismally low. Not only did Frederick exclude them from polite society, but he was most unwilling to grant them leave to retire or travel abroad, for fear that they might betray their secrets to a potential enemy. Thrown together on their own company, the gunners lost both the opportunity and curiosity to find out about the latest developments in ballistics and design. The single Prussian theorist to acquire an international reputation was Major v. Tempelhoff, author of *Le Bombardier Prussien*, who was promoted from captain at Frederick's special intervention, and who assumed command of the third artillery regiment in 1783.

The growing complexity of the science of artillery was another agent which exacerbated the relations between the king and his gunners. Accustomed to intervening with real authority in the rest of the army's affairs, Frederick was infuriated to discover that the gunners did not respond to his directions in the same gratifyingly prompt way as the officers of infantry or cavalry. He complained about 'the whimsicality you find among all the gunners in Europe, which leads them to raise pointless difficulties',[4] when he was really touching on the inevitable and growing gap between the military commander and the military technician.

Organisation

During the reign the complement of the Prussian field artillery rose from 789 gunners to more than 8,600. The expansion took place in the following stages.

1740. Frederick inherited one battalion (six companies) of field artillery.

1741. Early in the year he formed a second battalion.

1744. The two battalions were designated the Feld-Artillerie Regiment. The strength of the regiment stood at 72 officers and 2,402 men at the outset of the Seven Years War.

1758. The complement of each company was raised to 300 men. Two new companies were formed, and the regiment was reorganised into three battalions.

1759. The first of the batteries of horse artillery was raised at Landeshut.

1762. A new organisation created two regiments, each of three battalions, each battalion comprising five companies.

1763. After the Seven Years War the two regiments were subdivided into three smaller regiments, each of two battalions. The first and third regiments were stationed at Berlin, and the third at Königsberg. The complement of the company was reduced to 194 gunners, all natives, of whom 94 were usually absent at any given time.

1772. A fourth regiment was formed at Königsberg.

1783/4. Three companies of 'Augmentation' were added to the establishment. By the end of the reign the artillery owned 43 companies of about 200 officers and men each, which was still insufficient to serve the immense mass of the Prussian ordnance.

Each gun or pair of guns stood under the tactical command of a lieutenant or NCO. Of the normal crew of a gun (eight in the case of a battalion piece) only half came from the artillery, the rest consisting of men detached from the infantry as assistants. The common gunners came from the smaller and physically weaker men of the cantons. An intelligent gunner had a reasonable chance of being commissioned an officer, or at least of being made a bombardier, between sixty and ninety of whom were attached to every battalion. The bombardiers had the especial responsibility of managing the howitzers and siege mortars, and they were competent, serious and well-set-up folk, typified by the bombardier Kretschmer who so distinguished himself at Liegnitz. He took a craftsman's pride in his skill, and he was prosperous enough to own a private house in Berlin.

The guns of the fortresses were served by a separate Garrison Artillery, composed of officers and men who were considered physically or morally unfit to take the field. In 1740 Frederick inherited four companies of garrison artillery, owning a total of about 400 personnel. He formed them into a single battalion, and he went on to create a separate battalion, or large company, to take over the fortress artillery of the newly conquered province of Silesia. By the end of the reign the garrison artillery comprised fourteen companies of unequal strength, stationed respectively in the fortresses of Wesel, Magdeburg, Schweidnitz, Neisse, Silberberg, Glatz, Glogau, Brieg, Kosel, Breslau, Stettin, Kolberg, Königsberg and Graudenz.

The artillery wore a blue, infantry-type coat, which was lined with red. The officers were allowed to sport embroidered waistcoats, as befitted a 'learned' and semi-civilian arm. The horse artillerymen were distinguished by the white plumes they wore in their hats, and the riding boots which took the place of the black gaiters of the rest of the artillery.

The ordnance

BATTALION PIECES

In 1731 General v. Linger, the founding-father of the Prussian artillery, reduced the cannon to four calibres – namely the 3-, 6-, 12- and 24-pounders, so called from the weight of the solid roundshot which they fired.

According to the practice of the time, the 3-pounders and 6-pounders were designated 'battalion' or 'regimental' pieces. They were distributed among the battalions of the infantry at the outset of each campaign, and it was their job to lend close fire-support on the battlefield, rather like the machine-gun and light mortar of the two World Wars. In Frederick's first campaigns the 6-pounder proved to be rather too heavy for this purpose, and so on 11 August 1741 the king wrote to Leopold of Anhalt-Dessau, suggesting that it would be a good idea to have all the 6-pounders re-cast into 3-pounders of a new light model which possessed a chambered breech – in other words a sub-calibre powder chamber which required a smaller charge than the fully bored-up breech. Leopold replied that the new 3-pounder was certainly mobile, but he added that he thought that it lacked the power and range of the 6-pounder. Frederick was at first disconcerted, but in the spring of 1742 he introduced the light 3-pounder throughout the army, giving every regiment an average of two of the pieces each. The barrel of the new guns was sixteen calibres (3 ft 8 in) long and it weighed 472 lb. It was served by an eight-man crew and drawn by three horses.

Still convinced of the advantage of chambered pieces, Frederick had eighty-four

The 'Austrian' 12-pounder, showing the Holtzman elevating wedge, here screwed out to maximum extent

light 6-pounders cast in Berlin in 1755 to the designs of Lieutenant-Colonel v. Dieskau. The new barrel was sixteen calibres long and weighed 616 lb, which was light enough to permit the gun to be drawn by a team of four horses – in other words, only one more horse than was required for the 3-pounder, but one less than for the old-model 6-pounder. With its small charge of $1\frac{1}{2}$ lb of powder the chambered 6-pounder carried 1,000 paces point-blank, 1,500 at high trajectory, and up to 400 with canister. The same year saw the introduction of yet another light 3-pounder, this time eighteen calibres long and weighing 455 lb. Frederick's intention was to distribute the new 6-pounder among the first line battalions in the event of a major battle, while relegating the 3-pounders to the second line.

The new guns did not stand up very well to the test of the Seven Years War. Not only did the gunners encounter some difficulty in seating the bagged charges snugly in the constricted chambers, but the pieces were outclassed in range and accuracy by the new and immensely powerful Austrian artillery. From 1758, therefore, Frederick was forced to augment the existing ranges of 3-pounders and 6-pounders with heavy new long-barrelled versions with fully bored-up breeches. Frederick retained the long-barrelled 3-pounder and both versions of the 6-pounder until 1770, when he had them re-cast in new proportions – a twenty calibre long 3-pounder, and a light (eighteen calibre) and a heavy (twenty-two calibre) 6-pounder. Small wonder that Frederick used to complain about the ruinous cost of modern artillery.

BATTERY PIECES

The 12-pounder was classed among the 'battery pieces' – the heavy guns which were grouped in massed batteries on advantageous points of the battlefield – and it was fated to go through the same harrowing history as the lighter guns. As was the case with the battalion pieces, Frederick scrapped the old model in the middle 1750s and embarked on the Seven Years War with a chambered version. This was Dieskau's new gun of 1754, which weighed only 988 lb in the barrel and was drawn by a small team of eight horses.

A high proportion of the Dieskau guns was lost after the battle of Breslau in 1757, which was probably a mercy, and Frederick had to make up his heavy artillery with the help of some splendid and heavy old 12-pounders which Zieten brought up from the fortress of Glogau. The fortress 12-pounder performed with devastating effect at Leuthen, and under its onomatopoeic name of *Brummer* it remained a mainstay of the Prussian artillery throughout Frederick's reign. A third type of 12-pounder was introduced to fill the gap between the weighty *Brummer* and the inadequate chambered piece. Designated the 'Austrian' 12-pounder, it was patterned on the excellent enemy pieces, and cast to the number of eighty in the winter of 1759/60.

The 24-pounder topped the scale of heavy cannon with a barrel weighing around 1,800 lb. It caused considerable execution at Hohenfriedberg and Leuthen, but it was really too heavy to be considered a field piece, and in 1759 Frederick relegated it to siege work, where its hitting-power could be used to knock down fortress walls.

HOWITZERS AND MORTARS

The howitzer was a stubby, heavy-calibre chambered piece, specially designed to throw explosive shells without cracking the brittle cast iron of their casing. In 1740 the Prussian artillery owned just a single model of howitzer, the 18-pounder, and Frederick bent his efforts to increase both the variety and quantity of this versatile weapon. Lieutenant-Colonel v. Holtzmann introduced a 10-pounder howitzer in 1743, and a new type of the 18-pounder followed in 1744. A 7-pounder 'battalion' howitzer appeared in 1758, and it was manufactured in such quantity that by 1762 every battalion of the army was equipped with one of these pieces.

Seventy howitzers of a new kind, the 10-pounder 'battery' howitzer, were produced after the Seven Years War. The 10-pounder could throw its shell the phenomenal range of 4,000 paces, and Frederick designated it as a reserve piece, standing at a general's disposal if he wanted to rout the enemy from a mountain top or some other difficult position.

The mortar was a kind of large howitzer which stood on a solid wooden bed and was used almost exclusively for siege work. Frederick was content for a time to retain the three weights of mortar that had been introduced by Linger in the last reign – the 10-pounder (312 lb), the 24-pounder (758 lb) and the 50-pounder (1,456 lb). In 1755 Dieskau introduced a lighter version of the 24-pounder, which he mounted on a cannon-type carriage, and the 10-pounders were simultaneously dropped from the train.

Equipment and ammunition

The busy Lieutenant-Colonel Ernst v. Holtzmann, *Chef* of the Second Field Artillery Battalion, was responsible for some technical innovations that were imitated all over Europe. Early in the reign he spent his own money to build an experimental 'caisson limber', which incorporated an ammunition box with the limber and thus gave the gun a considerable degree of independence from the ammunition carts. (The limber was the little two-wheeled vehicle which supported the trail of the gun during transport.) The device worked very well, and in 1742 Frederick ordered caisson limbers to be introduced for all his battalion artillery.

In 1747 Holtzmann addressed himself to the problem of elevating and depressing the gun barrel. Up to now this had been accomplished by the expedient of hammering in or withdrawing a wedge which was inserted beneath the breech. This was an awkward and imprecise procedure, especially with the heavy guns, and so Holtzmann devised a new kind of wedge that was forced in and out by the turning of a screw. He went on to produce a screw back-sight for Dieskau's new light 12-pounders, which made for still greater precision in aiming the piece.

The dimensions of the gun carriages remained much as they had been when Linger designed them in 1717. The woodwork was painted in Prussian blue, and the ironwork in black.

The solid iron roundshot was the principal missile of the artillery. In the Prussian service the powder was made up in bags of woollen cloth, which were bound together with a sabot (wooden wad) in the case of the 3-pounder, but loaded separately in all the other cannon. In order to save weight in proportion to calibre, Frederick began to make up some of the cannon ammunition out of hollow, unfilled shot, beginning with the 12-pounder.

For short-range work the artillerymen turned their cannon into monster shotguns by employing canister rounds. These were lightly built cylinders of sheet metal or wood which enclosed scores of shot about the size of walnuts. The cylinder disintegrated as it left the muzzle and the shot sprayed out over a wide arc. The most common canister round was the cylinder of *Büchsenkartätschen*, which came as three-ounce balls of lead which were enclosed in a canister of copper or wood (50 balls in the 3-pounder round, 80 in the 6-pounder, 150 in the 12-pounder and 300 in the 24-pounder). In 1748 the point-blank ranges for canister were reckoned at 550 paces for the 3-pounder, 650 for the 6-pounder, 800 for the 12-pounder and 1,000 for the 24-pounder, though the balls dispersed so widely that the effective ranges were considerably less – as little as 100 paces with the battalion pieces. The ordinary lead balls scattered rather less than those of cast iron, but their range fell off badly because they were liable to jam together and become distorted under the impact of discharge. Hence the old-fashioned cast-iron canister shot came back into prominence towards the end of the reign.

Grapeshot (*Traubenkartätsche*) was a kind of extra-large, long-range canister shot which was manufactured in the size of billiard balls. For the 24-pounder Holtzmann invented the *Klemmkartätsche* round – a wooden cylinder which contained no less than nine 3-pounder shot.

The missile *par excellence* of the howitzer and mortar was the powder-filled shell of cast iron. The bursting was timed by means of a slow-burning fuse which the bombardier adjusted by cutting and plugged into a hole in the shell. The composition took fire automatically from the flame of the discharge.

Howitzers were also capable of firing grapeshot, the light ball (a linen bag which contained an illuminating composition), and the carcass fire-bomb (a pineapple-shaped iron cage stuffed with inflammable material).

Frederick's concern for economy was nowhere more evident than in his scanty arrangements for transporting the artillery. Instead of setting up a separate transport organisation, like the Austrian *Fuhrwesen*, he was content to have the necessary horses, waggons and drivers earmarked by the Commissariat in peacetime. The peasant owners of such 'registered' horses were expected to keep them in good condition while they worked on their farms, and they had to yield them up for forty thalers each upon the mobilisation (the teams for the 12-pounders were simply requisitioned without any payment).

The drivers were raised from the smaller men of the cavalry cantons. They were given no military training whatsoever, and in the earlier wars they were merely supervised by a few retired cavalrymen (called *Artilleriebedienten* or *Schirrmeister*). Thus for the campaign of 1756 Frederick assembled just one *Oberwagenmeister*, 13 *Wagenmeister*, 50 *Schirrmeister* and 49 clerks, smiths and wrights to supervise the efforts of 1,341 frightened and inexperienced drivers. In the horrific battles that ensued, the drivers showed a marked inclination to run away from the scene together with the horses and limbers. Thus in June 1760 Frederick was forced to detach teams of serving cavalrymen (one NCO and four troopers) to every battery of ten or so guns to keep the drivers under some kind of control.

The 'tail' of drivers, horses and vehicles was enormous. The light 3-pounder and its caisson limber (with 108 rounds of solid shot and 22 rounds of canister) were drawn by three horses and required one driver.

The light 6-pounder and its caisson limber (with 70 rounds of solid shot and 20 of canister) required two drivers and four horses. The heavy 6-pounder and its caisson limber demanded at least as much, and in addition it was sometimes accompanied by a separate ammunition cart bearing 120 rounds.

The *Brummer* and the 'Austrian' 12-pounder were drawn respectively by teams of twelve and ten horses. The allowance of ammunition per piece was 70 roundshot and 30 rounds of canister, which were carried on two three-horse ammunition carts. The light chambered 12-pounder and its caisson limber (for 44 rounds) were drawn by eight horses, and 66 further rounds were transported on a separate two-horse cart. Altogether an average battery of ten 12-pounders was reckoned to require 1 captain, 4 lieutenants, 10 NCOs, 120 gunners, 1 *Oberwagenmeister*, 4 *Wagenmeister*, 5 detached cavalrymen, 110 drivers and 226 horses.

The size of the artillery train was swollen still further by its obligation to carry the pontoons, the entrenching tools and (until 1757) the reserve ammunition of the infantry.

The great mass of transport and guns was dispersed as soon as possible at the close of every war. The drivers went thankfully home, and such horses as survived were returned to the plough and the farm cart. The heavy guns were sent back to the fortresses, and the battalion pieces were scattered among their depots (Berlin and Breslau and, from 1753, Magdeburg, Stettin and Königsberg as well). With that, the artillery virtually ceased to exist as a corps until the next mobilisation.

The forlorn gunners huddled together in Berlin, from where they emerged every spring with specially hired teams of horses and went through three or four weeks of firing exercises outside the Oranienburger-Tor. They were given little practice in movement, and none at all in co-operating with the other arms. When the artillery did appear at the big spring reviews and autumn manoeuvres it was only in the shape of a couple of saluting pieces, which were employed to set off the infantry or cavalry on some spectacular movement.

Even on campaign the crews of the heavy guns were the only people who could develop an *esprit de corps*, for the gunners of the battalion pieces were split up among the infantry in penny packets of four men at a time.

Gun drill

The gun drill of the Prussian artillery followed the basic sequence that was laid down for the 3-pounder battalion piece. No 1 stood to the right of the muzzle holding a double-ended mop-cum-rammer. No 2, stationed to the left of the muzzle, withdrew a round (in this case a bagged charge, bound together with the sabot and the shot) from his capacious leather cartridge satchel and inserted it in the muzzle, whereupon No 1 rammed it home. No 4 stood astride the trail immediately behind the breech and kept his thumb pressed over the vent, thus obviating any through-draught while the ramming was going on. Otherwise an ember might have flared up in the barrel and exploded the charge prematurely. As a further precaution the rammer was constructed with a joint near the mop end, like a flail, so that No 1 was able to keep his hands clear of the axis of the bore.

After the charge was firmly rammed home, No 4 pushed a priming tube (a powder-filled reed or sheet-metal cylinder) into the vent and pierced the bag of the charge. To facilitate ignition he sprinkled a little powder from a flask over the top of the priming tube, which now lay flush with the vent. Lastly he adjusted the elevating wedge for range, and signalled changes in traverse with his right hand to the one or more assistants who held the traversing spike. Now that his work was done, No 4 stood out of the way, and No 3 (who was placed by the right wheel) applied the lighted match of a linstock to the vent upon the command of No 1.

Immediately after the discharge No 1 dipped the mop end of his staff in a bucket and swabbed out the smoking bore. Then the sequence began all over again.

No 3 usually held a linstock ready in each hand, and he carried a length of spare match (chemically treated cord) in a long tube of leather or sheet metal which he slung from a strap over his right shoulder.

Nos 5 to 8 were made up of men detached from the infantry. No 5 carried two spare linstocks; No 7 had a spare powder flask, and he was given the special responsibility of opening and shutting the lid of the ammunition caisson for No 8, who had a cartridge satchel and kept No 2 supplied with ammunition. No 6 usually saw to the traversing bar, though two or sometimes three men were required to lift the trail of one of the heavier pieces.

Each gun, or pair of guns, stood under the command of a lieutenant or an NCO. The gun drill was an automatic routine for an experienced crew, and the orders rarely exceeded three: namely 'Attention!' (*Gibt Achtung!*), 'Make ready and load!' (*Macht Euch fertig und ladet!*) and 'Fire!' (*Feuer!*).

The battalion pieces, the 7-pounder howitzer and the light 12-pounder were all unlimbered at about 1,200 paces from the enemy and manhandled the rest of the way by the crew. In the case of the 3-pounder, Nos 1 to 4 hauled on straps (*Avancir-Riemen*) which were attached to hooks on the carriage cheeks and the ends of the axles, and led over their right shoulders, while Nos 5 to 8 inserted a traversing bar transversely through a set of eyes on the trail of the carriage, and pushed from the rear. The piece was capable of being moved at slightly more than the pace of marching infantry, and on each bound the gunners reckoned to push their cannon far enough ahead to enable them to get off two rounds before the infantry caught up.

The heavier pieces were dragged by horse-power all the way to the battery sites.

Tactical development

Artillery took a subordinate place in the battles of the 1740s, and Frederick found himself under no great pressure to increase the quantity of his ordnance or revise the conventional artillery tactics.

After the experience of Mollwitz, where some of the light artillery was lost, the battalion guns were ordered to venture no more than fifty paces in front of the infantry. However, it was not until 1754 that Frederick issued a *Manual* concerning the detailed service of the battalion pieces. They were to open fire with roundshot at 1,200 paces from the enemy, and change to canister once the range closed to 400 paces, all the time keeping up the advance in the way that has just been described.

Frederick was in two minds as to the best way to use his heavy guns. In a *Disposition* of 10 August 1744 he laid down that the 24-pounders and some of the howitzers were to be massed on either flank of the line of battle, thus providing a reasonable concentration of fire, whereas the 12-pounders were to be used in the role of glorified battalion pieces, being scattered among the regiments so as to supplement the fire of the infantry. The same uncertainty was evident in the instructions which Frederick issued at the camp of Alt-Jauernick on 2 June 1745.

The heavy guns performed with varying success in the battles of this last crowded year. At Hohenfriedberg the battery on the Windmühlenberg repulsed the enemy cavalry after it had broken through the first line of the Prussians. At Soor, however, the Prussian infantry took the great enemy battery without any help from their own guns, while at Kesselsdorf the three batteries of Prussian guns failed completely to silence the enemy artillery, which proceeded to crush the Prussian infantry of the right and centre by canister.

In the period between the wars Frederick did not appreciate the great advances that the Austrians were making with their artillery – creating a powerful reserve of fine new pieces, and training up a corps of highly proficient gunners. In 1757, therefore, at the battles of Prague and Kolin, the Prussian infantry was sent forward to be massacred by the enemy batteries, while Frederick's own artillery took hardly any part in the proceedings at all.

Confidence began to return after the eighteen Prussian heavy guns at Rossbach performed so well against the mobs of French and Germans, who represented an admittedly easier foe than the Austrians. The battle of Leuthen was a much more convincing test, for here the Prussians faced a strong and victorious Austrian army. A battery of 12-pounders accompanied the advance guard into action, knocking out two Austrian guns at the outset of the fight, and then pushing on to a site on the Glanzberg. Meanwhile the heavy guns of the centre and left were massed on the Judenberg in support of the main

Horse artillery. The gunners are wearing their distinctive plumes and boots. Blue coat lined with red, light straw waistcoat and breeches. No 1 is standing to the right of the gun (the rammer ought to be shown with a joint near the mop end) and no 2 to the left. No 4 is squinting along the barrel. The piece is a light 6-pounder, with blue woodwork and black ironwork

army. As the battle progressed both groups of guns advanced on to the broad Kirchberg, and then, as the struggle for Leuthen village reached its climax, they trundled on to the south-east slopes of the Butterberg and worked to devastating effect on the closely packed Austrians. Altogether the employment of the heavy artillery at Leuthen remained almost without equal in the eighteenth century for its success in harmonising the two elements of mobility and massed fire-power.

A delighted Frederick now stipulated that the heavy guns should always be brought forward 'continuously, as at Leuthen'.[5] From now onwards the guns were to begin by silencing the enemy artillery, and they were then to fire obliquely (*en écharpe*) on the enemy infantry and cavalry at the point of the intended breakthrough. The battle of Zorndorf turned out to be something of a disappointment in this respect, for the gunners had underestimated the range and so the opening bombardment took little effect. At Kunersdorf, however, the heavy artillery was grouped in a great semicircle and it managed to bring an impressive weight of fire to bear on the salient of the Russian defensive position.

Unfortunately, just when Frederick came near to employing his artillery on a truly Napoleonic scale, the infantry became so badly depleted that he had to break up his concentrations of heavy guns. Hitherto the 12-pounders had travelled as a combined train in the central column of the army, but on the march from Dresden to Liegnitz in 1760 Frederick broke them up and distributed them among the infantry on the basis of one battery of ten guns to every brigade of foot (ie between four and seven battalions).

In their new and unglamorous role the heavy guns performed well enough, as was showed at Liegnitz on 15 August when they shot up Loudon's grenadiers with canister.

Whereas Frederick's brigade batteries were assigned permanently to the infantry, which caused considerable inconvenience on the march, Prince Henry preferred to group his heavy guns in smaller batteries of four or eight pieces at a time, and he distributed them among the brigades only when they were needed. Even then he contrived to keep a reserve of heavy pieces intact, a practice which put sixteen guns at his disposal at the crucial battle of Freiberg in 1762.

The crisis of the Seven Years War was responsible for two further developments in the Prussian artillery – the lavish use of the howitzer, and the invention of the first genuine horse artillery.

The Dutch had devised the howitzer as long ago as the 1690s, but Frederick was the first commander to make full use of the versatility of this weapon in the field. For turning the enemy out of a position, the shell was usually fired at high trajectory: for combat in the open field the shell was fired at low trajectory, when it wrought as much execution by its ricochet effect as by the actual burst. More surprisingly, the howitzer was eminently suitable for the discharge of grapeshot, for the width of the bore (which permitted the use of large shot) more than made up for the shortness of the barrel. Howitzers were employed as battalion pieces, as battery pieces, and (in the 1770s) as horse artillery.

It was a howitzer which furnished one of the rare instances of successful counter-battery fire that we find in the eighteenth century. The scene was the battle of Liegnitz, where an Austrian battery caused considerable annoyance until Major-General v. Saldern ordered Bombardier Kretschmer to silence the offending object with his howitzer.

He threw a first round, which exploded just in front of the cannon and induced the Austrians to fall back from their pieces, thereby gaining us another shot. At the second discharge Kretschmer scored a hit on the Austrian ammunition cart. A man had been standing on top, handing ammunition to the other gunners, and when the shell reached the cart this individual and another man who was standing near him were blown into the air. In addition two further gunners were blown up and eight others were mutilated or killed. Now the enemy finally abandoned their battery.[6]

'Galloping guns' had been employed in foreign armies for more than a century. They were light pieces which went into action with the cavalry. In the middle of the Seven Years War, however, Frederick introduced something different, a fast-moving artillery designed not so much as an auxiliary to the cavalry as to travel 'like the wind' to wherever the commander decided it could be used to the best effect on the battlefield.

Frederick chose the light 6-pounder as the best weapon for his new horse artillery. It was drawn by a team of picked horses, which could be lashed into a gallop if necessary, and the seven-man crew rode into action alongside on horses of their own. Frederick believed strongly in his new kind of artillery, and he was prepared to build it up again and again after repeated misfortunes. The first brigade of *artillerie volante* was set up by Lieutenant Schwebs in the camp of Landeshut in May 1759, and it was lost three months later at Kunersdorf. A replacement battery of ten pieces was created in the camp of Fürstenwalde in August, only to be captured at Maxen. The third of the batteries was created in the spring of 1760, and it survived until the end of the war. Meanwhile Prince Henry had raised a brigade of his own at Landsberg on 1 June 1759.

The trouble was that the horse artillery was extremely vulnerable, being fast enough to race ahead of the infantry, while just too slow to keep up with the cavalry. Berenhorst claims that even the notable successes of the horse artillery (by which he probably meant Pretsch on 29 October 1759 and Reichenbach on 16 August 1762) could have been brought off by conventional artillery with good teams.[7]

Although the surviving two brigades of horse artillery were disbanded after the peace of 1763, Frederick gradually built the arm up again over the following years. A force of twenty 6-pounders and four howitzers was in existence by 1768, and in March 1773 Frederick set up an exercise battery at Potsdam, for the purpose of training relays of gunners who were detached from the foot artillery. Thus in the War of the Bavarian Succession the mounted artillery was able to take the field in the strength of six brigades of nine pieces each.

As he looked back at the development of the military art in the third quarter of the century, Frederick was alarmed to see that he was being drawn into an artillery race – a contest in which the running was being made by his Austrian and Russian rivals. No development could have been less welcome to Frederick, considering his scanty resources and his liking for mobile warfare. He complained in 1768 that artillery was becoming 'an abyss of expense':[8] since the last war he had devoted 1,450,000 thalers to the artillery, including 300,000 he had spent in June of that very year in re-casting the burnt-out pieces, creating a reserve of 100 guns, arming the new fortress of Silberberg and replenishing the stocks of shot and shell.

In 1756 Frederick had allotted just 222 pieces to the force of 70,000 men which invaded Saxony, which gave a ratio of three guns to every thousand men. In the following campaigns he was forced to up-gun his army, in an attempt to keep pace with the Austrians, and on occasion (as at Torgau in 1760) he took the field with more than six guns to every thousand of his troops.

The feeble artillery transport system threatened to collapse altogether under the vast mass of the new ordnance. Whereas only 1,700 horses were needed to mobilise the artillery park at Magdeburg in 1756, Frederick had to gather in 4,000 horses and lose several weeks before he could accomplish the same objective in 1778.

By the early 1770s Frederick had settled on the way in which he intended to employ all this expensive artillery on the battlefield (*Instruction für die Artillerie*, 3 May 1768; *Political Testament*, 1768; and *Eléments de Castramétie*, 1770). The battalion pieces, the 7-pounder howitzers and the ten-gun batteries of 12-pounders were to be dispersed in immediate support of the infantry, as had been the practice in the later stages of the Seven Years War. At the same time it was important to be able to achieve a decisive superiority of fire at the point where the commander intended to break through the enemy line, and with this in mind Frederick recommended the holding-back of a reserve of 12-pounder *Brummer*, the horse artillery and forty of the new 10-pounder howitzers.

In 1771 Frederick circulated a manuscript *Reglement* among the artillery. Further instructions followed in 1778 and 1779, and finally on 10 May 1782 Frederick issued a last, detailed *Instruction*. He warned the gunners against opening fire too early, and, contrary to his doctrine in the Seven Years War, he condemned counter-battery fire. Altogether the advice was notably cautious – the tone of a commander who was crushed rather than inspired by the weight of his own artillery.

7

Engineers and Technical Formations

Engineer officers

In 1740 Frederick took over a small but well-regulated corps of forty-five military engineers. The leading light was a Dutch-born Catholic, Colonel Gerhardt Cornelius v. Walrave (1692–1773), who had put the Prussian engineers on an institutional basis in 1729 and virtually founded the 'Prussian' style of fortress design. At first the king was eminently satisfied with what he found. In May 1741 he promoted Walrave to major-general 'as some recognition of his real services',[1] and in the following year he appointed him head of the new pioneer regiment which was set up at Neisse.

Unfortunately Walrave presumed a little too much on the royal favour. Frederick was willing to put up with Walrave's shameless plundering in Bohemia, and even with the blunders he made in the re-fortification of Prague in 1744, but after 1745 Walrave went on to correspond with the Austrians about the fortifications of Vienna, and he was unwise enough to open negotiations with the Russian and Saxon envoys with the object of buying paintings to add to his collection at Schloss Liliput. Frederick therefore had him arrested.

The court of inquiry could find no proof of actual treachery, but the evidence of fraud was so damning that in February 1748 Walrave was consigned to perpetual imprisonment in the Sternschanze at Neisse, a fort that he had built himself. When the wife of Prince Henry visited the casements in 1759 she was told to look through a little window, and there she saw Walrave, who had been a prisoner of state for all these years. 'He was standing at the door of his cell, surrounded by a whole menagerie of the creatures that he used to feed for his amusement.'[2] Walrave remained there till he died in 1773.

Walrave's disgrace signified much more than the end of an individual career. His pioneer regiment was converted into an ordinary infantry regiment in the course of the Seven Years War, and the Prussian engineering corps, which he had done so much to set up, was as good as broken with him. Thereafter Frederick flattered, exploited and finally cast away a series of engineers in the same manner in which the less industrious monarchs of the time used to work through a string of mistresses.

There was Major-General v. Seers, who lost the fortress of Schweidnitz – and his own reputation – in 1757; there was Frederick's personal friend Giovanni Balbi, who was wrongly accused of mismanaging the siege of Olmütz in 1758; there was the renegade Simon Lefebvre, who underwent a nervous breakdown during the attack on Schweidnitz in 1762; and after the war there were two further foreign technicians, the Piedmontese Pinto and the Frenchman d'Heintze, who ran foul of the king on account of their respective proposals for the rebuilding of Glatz and the construction of the new fortress of Graudenz.

The consequences of all this for Prussian military engineering were deplorable. Frederick ceased to regard his engineers as members of a corporate body, and preferred to discuss projects of fortification directly with fortress commandants or juniors under their command. He allowed little real authority even to the long-enduring Colonel v. Regler,

Engineers. An engineer officer in the centre and a Conducteur to his right. Blue coats, red cuffs, lapels and collars, red waistcoats and breeches. The officer has silver brandenbourgs, and his hat has a broad silver braid

who became the acting head of the corps in the last years of the reign. The rest of the demoralised personnel consisted of five chief engineers, twenty-one captains, twenty lieutenants, and thirteen *Conducteuren*, who were scattered in little groups among the fortresses.

We have a description of the way Frederick used to go about his work:

> When he inspected some newly laid out works in his fortresses, he often used to demand the appropriate plans just as he entered his coach, and proceeded to append 'improvements' and additions that in most cases were detrimental to the security of the place. If an engineer submitted a construction project which cost more than five thousand thalers and would take two years to carry out, he would simply add: 'Good! I allow 2,500 thalers. Get it finished in six months.'[3]

Just as surely the engineers learnt to ask for double their real needs, and thus they became caught up in a self-regenerating cycle of fraud and deception.

Pioneers

Frederick sometimes used to complain about the lack of a body of sappers – specially trained troops who could have helped the engineers to carry on sieges. He failed to appreciate that he had a potentially valuable resource in Walrave's Pionier-Regiment, which was based on Neisse and employed on the making and repair of military roads. He ignored the broad hint that was given him by the failure of his siege of Olmütz, and a little later, on 26 November 1758, he converted the ten musketeer companies of the pioneers into an ordinary regiment of fusiliers (no 49).

Miners

The conversion of the Pionier-Regiment left its two companies of miners in existence as a separate organisation. A third company was raised in 1761, but the experience of the siege of Schweidnitz in the following year showed that the Prussian miners were still lacking in proficiency. After the war Frederick hired some Piedmontese officers to do something to improve the standard, and he raised the establishment by a fourth company in 1783.

The personnel were drawn from the manpower of the mining districts of the monarchy, and in peacetime most of the men returned to their civilian work. The uniform remained the same as that of the parent regiment of pioneers, namely a blue coat lined with red, and a low fusilier-type cap with a frontal plate of tin.

The Pontonier-Corps

The smallest corps of the Prussian army, the bridging train was attached to the artillery and marched and camped with the heavy batteries. The peacetime establishment remained at twenty-seven or twenty-eight officers and men throughout the reign, though the

*Officer and miners of the Mineur-corps. Blue coats, dark orange waistcoats and breeches,
fusilier-type cap with tin plate and dark orange top. The gentlemen are about to enter a counter-
mine in a fortress ditch*

personnel were increased to fifty-three during the Seven Years War. The pontoons were stored at Berlin, Magdeburg and Neisse.

The practice of military engineering

Frederick wrote in the *General Principia* that 'the art of conducting sieges has become a trade like that of carpenter or clock maker. Certain infallible rules have been established, and we carry on an unvarying routine in which we apply the same theory to the same cases.'[4]

However, the execution fell short of the theory to a remarkable degree. Frederick's most ambitious attacks on fortresses turned out to be the destructive but useless bombardments of Prague (1757) and Dresden (1760), and the broken-backed formal sieges of Olmütz (1758) and Schweidnitz (1762). The truth was that the king lacked the troops, the pioneers, the engineers and above all the time which might have made the practice conform more closely with his prescriptions.

In fortress design Frederick borrowed heavily from Walrave, and added some important ingredients of his own.

The close-range defence of the Frederician fortifications depended upon such *motifs* as a star-shaped ground plan *en tenaille*, multiple ramparts, deep and narrow ditches, flanking casemates and a lavish provision of defensive mines.

The long-range defence was characterised by an epoch-making employment of detached forts. For a long time engineers of all nations had been accustomed to planting detached forts outside the perimeter of the main fortress in order to meet some *local* need – to guard the sluice of an inundation, for instance, or to occupy an isolated hill. But Frederick advocated something different – the building of 'large detached works, whether *flèches* (arrow-shaped works), redoubts or little forts . . . so that the enemy is forced to capture them before he can open his trenches against the main fortress'.[5] In other words Frederick used forts to extend the depth of his defences. He showed what he meant when he built a ring of five forts and five *flèches* round Schweidnitz before the Seven Years War. This was a style of engineering that was going to become commonplace in the nineteenth century.

Field fortification was the branch of active military engineering which the Prussians practised with the most conspicuous success, probably because of its close relation with ordinary tactics. The camp of Neustadt, for example, used to protect Upper Silesia and part of Lower Silesia from Austrian incursions over the border mountains, while the position of Bunzelwitz preserved the king and his army during an exceptionally dangerous passage of the campaign of 1761. A quarter of a century later the Bunzelwitz camp was still reckoned to be the 'finest known monument of field fortification'.[6]

The Prussian fortress system

Frederick conceived the fortress as a versatile instrument of war, not a mere slave of the defensive.

In time of war endless convoys of barges used to bring supplies up the Oder to the main magazine at Breslau in the heart of Silesia, from where they were transported to the fortresses of Schweidnitz and Neisse (and Silberberg as well in the War of the Bavarian Succession), and so on to the chains of depots which Frederick established as he advanced into Bohemia or Moravia. Magdeburg acted as the 'Breslau' for operations further west along the Elbe against Saxony.

When Frederick was fighting against odds, and carrying out his prodigous marches across the north German plain, the same fortresses offered him secure river crossings and saved him the labour of having to carry heavy artillery about with him wherever he went.

Frederick would probably have gone under in the Seven Years War if he had not been able to cling on to the two most important of his fortresses. One of these vital strongholds was Stettin on the lower Oder, which served as a barrier against the Russians: the other was the great central fortress of Magdeburg, which commanded the middle Elbe and acted as the foundation of the war in Saxony.

At the same time Frederick appreciated that the survival of his state depended above all on the prowess of his field army, and he was ready to abandon remote and untenable places like Wesel (in Westphalia) and Königsberg (in East Prussia) without a second thought in the early campaigns of the Seven Years War.

Frederick the Great's navy

Almost a century and a half before the era of Tirpitz a Prussian navy took to the water in one of the oddest episodes that maritime history has to show.

The inspiration for this remarkable enterprise sprang from the genial, fat and noisy Duke of Brunswick-Bevern. He had been beaten rather badly by the Austrians at Breslau in 1757, which ruled him out for any future field command, and when he returned from captivity he was appointed governor of Stettin. Bevern chafed in his enforced idleness, and since the Russians did not dare to come near the place, he resolved to go out and strike at the only other available enemy, the Swedes, whose flotillas dominated the region of shallows, sandspits, islands and lagoons where the Oder slid into the Baltic.

With the help of Daniel Schultze, a Stettin merchant, Bevern spent the winter of 1758/9 in converting fishing boats (the local *Zösekahne*) and the vessels of the timber trade (*Kopenhagenfahrer*) into naval craft. The officers seem to have hailed principally from the Land Battalions, and they were smartly uniformed in blue coats and breeches, and black hats with broad gold braid. The crews amounted to 616 men, and were drawn from prime seamen and the troops of the Land Battalions. Prittwitz records that:

> We officers were most impressed with the flotilla, because we had never seen anything like it before. When they sailed up we betook ourselves on board, so as to observe the fleet more closely.
>
> The general effect was by no means unfavourable, for everything was new, and both the sailors and the soldiers were well dressed. When the sailors appeared on parade they wore a white outfit with a red sash around their middles. They sported felt hats, very much like the hussars, and both sashes and hats were adorned with the black eagle.[7]

The Lagoon Flotilla first took to the waters of the Oder on 5 April 1759, to the cheers of the sailors and an exchange of salutes between the vessels and the ramparts of Stettin. By September the little navy had been built up into a force of four galleys and four galliots, armed principally with 12-pounders and 6-pounders, as well as four smaller craft.

The acting admiral was an officer of the Land Battalions, Captain Ernst v. Köller, and using an analogy with land warfare he anchored this mighty armada in two lines off Neuwarp, seeking to block the central narrows of the Stettiner Haff.

The Swedes went over to the attack on 10 September and destroyed the Prussian force in a matter of hours. First they used their superiority in numbers, speed and manoeuvrability to turn the flanks of the Prussian position, and then they chased and overcame the fugitives. The Prussians lost two of the galleys and all four of the galliots, and about thirty of their men were killed or wounded.

The little disaster of Neuwarp confirmed Frederick in his reluctance to take to the sea. He preferred to have 'the first army in Europe rather than the worst fleet among the maritime powers'.[8]

8

Finance, Supply and the Auxiliary Services

Finance

'Three things are necessary for making war – money, money and yet more money.' The words had been spoken by Marshal Trivulzio 250 years before, but the sentiment behind them was purely Frederician. Frederick's most remarkable achievement as a wager of war was not so much in surviving the struggle against most of Europe, with its immensely superior resources, as in emerging from the ordeal with a financial profit.

If Frederick appears at first sight to have arranged his military finances in an unnecessarily complicated way, it is only because he had a squirrel-like habit of salting away little packets of funds in odd corners for future reference. We encounter small treasuries like the *Königliche-Dispositionskasse* (for unforeseeable military expenses, and filled from the surplus revenue of the *General-Domanenkasse*) or the *Kleine Schaatz* which met the cost of mobilisations. However, the basic machinery was simple, being designed to channel a variety of revenues through a main military treasury, the *General-Kriegskasse*.

The principal springs that fed the *General-Kriegskasse* were the taxes on landowners and peasants, the excise dues, an annual 'iron resource' (*eisener Bestand*) of 300,000 thalers from the *General-Domänenkasse* (which administered the royal estates and monopolies), and the contributions that were collected in occupied territory.

The monies were disbursed by the *General-Kriegskasse* principally by way of, first, the huge stores and remounts department called the *Massow-Kasse* or *Wartenberg-Kasse*, which was formed in 1751 by the union of the clothing and remount funds, and second, the *Feld-Kriegs-Kommissariats* which were set up in time of war together with their satellite organs – the *Feld-Kriegskasse* (pay), the *Feld-Proviantamt* (magazines and transport), the *Feld-Bakerei* (bread) and the *Lazarethkasse* (hospitals).

The main state treasury (*Staatsschatz*) was a feeble affair by comparison. It owned 10 million thalers at the time of Frederick's accession, and it survived the wars of the 1740s in a depleted condition though still in credit. By the time of the mobilisation of 1756 it had 13 million thalers in hand, to which we must add the 2,500,000 that were stored away in the little war treasuries (above), giving a total of 15,500,000 thalers. These sums proved to be quite unequal to sustaining the heavy expenditure of the new war. By the end of the campaign of 1756 (not a particularly exacting one by the standards of the Seven Years War) the *Staatsschatz* was already depleted by half, and on 19 March 1758 it ran dry altogether.

The monstrous expenses of the war continued to grow. The single campaign of 1758 cost Frederick 20,046,779 thalers, and by the end of hostilities in 1763 it was reckoned that Prussia had dispensed no less than 139,000,000 thalers in its struggle for survival.

The astonishing thing was that Frederick had covered every thaler of this cost, and was still left with a very healthy balance of 30,250,000 thalers. Where had the 169,250,000 thalers come from? Only 17,300,000 had been contributed by loans and from the original funds of the defunct *Staatsschatz*, and 43,000,000 more were raised by way of taxation, excise duties and the profits of the state monopolies, leaving 108,950,000 thalers which Frederick seems to have conjured from the thin air. In fact the king had been able to tap three important sources of extraordinary income.

First, from the middle of the war until 1762 when the supply was 'treacherously' cut off, Britain supplied Frederick with an outright subsidy. This generosity came in the welcome form of bullion, which Frederick could debase at will, producing a total of 27,000,000 thalers.

Second, in the course of the war Frederick authorised three successive debasements which reduced the worth of the Prussian coinage by a total of $62\frac{1}{2}$ per cent. The profit to the state came from the fact that it discharged its debts in the debased *Ephraimiten* (including the pay of soldiers and public servants), while demanding taxes and contributions at the genuine worth. The mechanics of the fraud were managed by the Jewish merchant concerns of Daniel Itzig and Ephraim & Sons, which provoked a witty soul in Holland to strike a mock coinage showing Frederick and Ephraim *tête-à-tête* and bearing the inscription: 'This is my beloved son, in whom I am well pleased.' Altogether the debasements rendered Frederick a profit of 29,000,000 thalers.

Third, true to the old maxim of 'war must feed on war', Frederick systematically plundered enemy lands of money, cattle, horses, fodder and recruits. In Saxony the king was at first content to leave the administration of these 'contributions' to the local *Stände*, but the revenues fell off so markedly that in 1760 he laid the land under military administration, employing 'generals and officers who were harsher than the Inquisitors of Goa'.[1] These gentlemen cut down the Torgauer Wald, 'the most beautiful of Germany',[2] and sold off the timber, and amongst other barbarities they clapped the leading citizens and merchants of Leipzig in prison as hostages for the payment of a particularly monstrous contribution. Every morning a Prussian official came to see the filthy, bearded and starving inmates, and greeted them with the cry: 'Now, you dogs! Are you going to pay up?'[3]

If anything, the raising of contributions in Mecklenburg was attended with still more cruelty, for the Prussians were not in permanent possession of the country but swept in periodically on raiding expeditions.

In the course of the war the contributions in Mecklenburg and Swedish Pomerania raised 4,950,000 thalers, while the product of the exactions in Saxony amounted to the enormous sum of 48,000,000. In all of this we do not take account of the plundering of these lands for private profit. A courtier saw the engineer Balbi return to Berlin in the winter of 1759 with a cart full of Meissen ware, and commented that 'our officers have laid Meissen under a kind of escheatage. Everybody who passes through fixes himself up with porcelain for life'.[4]

By the middle 1770s the annual revenue had reached the sum of about 21,700,000 thalers, counting in new sources like the state tobacco monopoly, which was set up in 1765, and the taxes from the newly acquired province of West Prussia. Of this at least 13,000,000 was spent every year on the army, and about 3,000,000 more on state administration. The surplus accumulated gratifyingly year by year, allowing Frederick in this post-war period to devote 8,000,000 thalers to fortress construction, and no less than 1,500,000 to jewelled presentation snuff-boxes (an investment in goodwill). Thus the cost of the War of the Bavarian Succession (29,000,000) was borne with little strain.

War industry

The characteristic Prussian bond between the military machine and semi-monopolistic private industry was forged by Frederick William I, or more specifically by Colonel Christian v. Linger, who in 1722 took over the direction of the new small-arms factory at Spandau. It was on his advice that the king entrusted the enterprise to the merchant concern of Splitgerber und Daum. In 1723, the first year of production, the Spandau factory turned out 10,000 muskets and thereby promised to make Prussia independent of imports from Liège. Every one of the weapons, like the muskets of Frederick's reign, bore the initials SD carved on the bevelled lower edge of the lock.

Linger also supervised the work of the powder mill that was established on the Jungfernheide near Berlin in 1717. He turned it into a model of its kind, producing gunpowder that was as fine and powerful as sporting powder in other countries. In both the Spandau and the Jungfernheide establishments the machines were powered by water.

The musket balls were cast in Berlin from the comparatively cheap lead that was available from the Harz Mountains. The royal cannon foundry was likewise established in Berlin. It drew its copper from Rothenburg-an-der-Saale and its tin from Cornwall. Otherwise Prussian industry was in its infancy, the only domestic sources of shot and bombs being the ironworks at Zehdenick and the factory at Schadow on the upper Spree. The high-quality iron for the muskets and pistols was imported from Sweden.

Prussia was self-sufficient in the production of raw wool, and Frederick William encouraged the local textile industries by assigning each regiment to an individual manufacturer, who undertook to furnish blue cloth at a specified quality and price. On visiting Magdeburg an English traveller was told by Prussian officers that 'the dark blue cloth made here, and in other parts of the king of Prussia's dominions, though coarser, wears better and has a more decent appearance when long worn, than the finest cloth manufactured in England or France'.[5]

Officers' uniforms, non-blue cloth, and hats, buttons and certain other items were supplied through the royal warehouses in Berlin, but the regiments were given money to obtain shirts, breeches, shoes, hair ribbons and the like under their own arrangements. In any case, the regiments liked to dye all the smaller items of clothing at one time, so as to be sure of attaining a uniform shade of white or yellow.

Every year on 1 May the NCOs and men of the infantry received one coat, one waistcoat, one pair of breeches, one pair of underpants, two shirts, one dickey, two stocks, two hair ribbons, one pair of stockings, two pairs of shoes, one pair of service gaiters, and one hat. The soldier retained the old coat for one further year, for normal duties off parade, after which he was allowed to cut off the regimentals and sell the garment. The Garde were issued with a special 'bad uniform' to spare their magnificent full dress for really important occasions.

The native industries proved to be well up to sustaining the burden of the two Silesian Wars and supplying the needs of the post-war army. Splitgerber und Daum hired gunsmiths from Liège and set up an additional arms factory at Potsdam, which gave them a total production capacity of 15,000 muskets per year, while in 1743 Colonel v. Holtzmann took over and expanded the municipal cannon foundry at Breslau. Altogether the Prussians produced 444 pieces between 1741 and 1745.

Ten new powder mills came into operation at the same time, and with the parent mill they managed to produce 448,000 lb of explosive in 1746, raising the output to 560,000 lb in 1756. For some time the capacity of the iron industry lagged behind, which compelled Frederick to buy a quantity of shot and bombs from Sweden in 1752, but between that year and 1755 new ironworks came into production in Silesia at Malapane, Kreuzburg, Gottow, Torgelow and Vietz.

The crisis of the Seven Years War was all-embracing. It concerned not just the Prussian army's survival on the battlefield but the ability of the state to keep that army on foot at all. The huge consumption of gunpowder (a total of 81,873,600 lb) far outstripped the capacity of the Prussian mills even before the Jungfernheide establishment was blown up by the Russians in 1760, and Frederick became heavily dependent on purchases from Holland and Britain. In addition, Splitgerber und Daum had to arrange for the import of great quantities of arms of every description – iron cannon from Sweden, bronze cannon and small arms from Holland, muskets from Liège and pistols from Solingen and Suhl.

The regiments were kept adequately supplied with arms and equipment throughout the war, thanks to the efficiency of Lieutenant-General Hans v. Massow's stores department in Berlin. Every year, as the season for winter quarters approached, Massow distributed forms among the regiments of infantry and cavalry and asked them to write down their requirements for the next campaign. His officials took the completed lists around the stores in Berlin and drew out whatever was needed, 'so that,' as Frederick wrote, 'the army never ran short of what it needed, even though we had some campaigns which cost us 40,000 muskets and 20,000 horses'.[6] Having satisfied the immediate demands, Massow laid out new contracts to provide for the campaign two years hence.

Massow died on 24 July 1761, and his post was taken over by his experienced deputy, Colonel Johann v. Stechow. In 1763 the office passed to Colonel Friedrich v. Wartenberg, the later major-general. Wartenberg affected 'a simple air',[7] which did not prevent him from amassing a fortune in the course of his distinguished career.

So it came about that in the Seven Years War the city of Berlin,

this new Palmyra, where splendid and numerous works of architecture sprang out of a sea of sand and lined endless streets, now became the greatest manufacturing town in Germany, the assembly point of all the requisites of war, and indeed the nursing mother of the Prussian army. Here were heaped up great stores of baggage, uniforms, weapons and military equipment of all kinds, and many thousands of men toiled ceaselessly in the workshops to cover any deficiencies or increase the stock still further. Commerce in Berlin never flourished so prosperously as in that period.[8]

The merchant Gotzkowsky, 'a gallant German, stupid and cordial',[9] undertook to furnish the army with 7,500,000 thalers'-worth of supplies upon a single contract, while Splitgerber und Daum was said to have received 4,000,000 thalers in one day in payment for the arms and equipment it had delivered.

At the same time the war brought untold misery to the peasant masses. Even in the capital the nobility and the court circles were hit very hard by the inflation. According to Lehndorff,

we see widows from the best society begging for alms, while children of people of standing grow up without any education . . . But things are different with the bourgeoisie. They are well off and live in great style, especially the Jews, who are building palaces and laying out splendid gardens. Itzig and Ephraim are millionaires, and they are sucking the best blood of the state.[10]

Supply

The army was sustained at remarkably little expense in time of peace. The provincial authorities were obliged to supply the cavalry with dry fodder at fixed prices, and as the reign wore on the peasants found that their fields were being grazed by the cavalry horses for an increasingly long period every summer. The 'registered' artillery and baggage horses simply remained on the land for the duration of the peace. The wretched soldiers were entitled to no free rations at all, though they were able to obtain 2 lb of bread every day at a fixed price or in return for a monthly stoppage of twelve groschen.

Thus Frederick was free to lavish his time and money on making ready for the next war. Flour and grain were heaped up at Berlin, Breslau, Magdeburg and Stettin – all chosen for the excellence of their communications. Altogether in 1752 the magazines held 53,000 bushels. By 1776 the Berlin and Breslau magazines alone contained 72,000 bushels, which was enough to feed an army of 60,000 men for two years (at 1,800 lb to the bushel or *Wispel*). Two-thirds of the contents were always kept in the form of flour (in 450 lb casks) – partly to save the trouble of milling in time of war, and partly because flour kept better than the unmilled grain, which had to be renewed every three years, being subject to damage from rats, insects and the heat. In the Seven Years War bread was actually baked in Stettin from flour that was forty years old.

Frederick obtained as much grain as possible from the nobles and peasants in return for the commutation of their taxes. The rest was purchased in the cheapest market. Since Prussia was not self-sufficient in cereals, considerable quantities were bought in Poland, the granary of Europe, where 1 million thalers would buy about 60,000 bushels. It was largely to facilitate the transport of this grain that Frederick restored the long-disused Finow Canal (between the Oder and the Havel) and dug the Plauen Canal (between the Havel and the Elbe), which gave him direct inland water communication between the Baltic and the Elbe.

Dry fodder could not be stored in the same way, because it was so bulky. However, in 1752 the circles of Silesia were placed under orders to have enough oats, straw and hay always set aside to maintain the horses of a 60,000-man army for one month in the field.

These arrangements were in the hands of the Intendant of the army and his four assistants. 'All of these officers work at nothing else in peacetime,' wrote Frederick, 'hence they have a thorough knowledge of their trade and know how to apply it in wartime.'[11] In the period of Frederick's great wars the vital office of Intendant was held successively by Major-General G. v. d. Goltz, Colonel W. R. v. Retzow (1747–58) and Colonel E. L. v. Amstedt.

The army's hardware was also disposed in readiness – the spare muskets, saddles and other items of equipment in the Arsenal at Berlin, the musket and artillery ammunition in the provincial capitals, the battalion artillery at Berlin, Breslau, Magdeburg, Stettin and Königsberg, the heavy guns in the fortresses, the pontoons at Berlin, Magdeburg and Neisse, and finally the carts and building-materials for the baking ovens at Berlin, Magdeburg, Stettin, Breslau, Glogau and Königsberg.

In the two Silesian wars Frederick confiscated merchant boats to help in transporting the army's grain and fodder, which was found to cause considerable disruption to civilian trade. Before the Seven Years War, therefore, he built thirty barges of a simple design, and stored timber for a good many more at Küstrin, on the Oder, calculating that they could be knocked together in three weeks in the event of war.

The coming of hostilities conjured up an infinitely more complex machine, which demanded constant and careful management. Frederick once complained 'I am not the one who commands the army. Flour and fodder are the masters now.'[12]

The first priority was to mobilise the commissariat train – in other words to requisition all the thousands of extra waggons, horses and drivers that were needed to transport the victuals from the main theatre magazines (usually Breslau or Magdeburg) to the forward 'offensive' magazines like Schweidnitz, and so on to the depots that were established along the line of operations.

The soldier (who received his bread free in wartime) carried between three and six days' ration of bread (at 2 lb per day) ready-baked in his bread bag. Frederick would have preferred biscuit, which was more compact, 'but instead of eating the biscuits like bread the soldiers mix them with water and drink them as a soup, which means that they do not have enough food to sustain them'.[13] A load equivalent to another six days' ration for every man was borne on the company bread waggon. For its further sustenance the army looked to the four-horse commissariat waggons, each of which carried enough flour to keep a company in bread for nine or ten days. The commissariat waggons travelled in 'columns' of fifty-one vehicles at a time, six columns providing flour for 30,000 troops as well as transporting oats for the horses.

Every corps was accompanied by a field bakery column, consisting of the super-intendent (who was usually a colonel), his staff of bakers and material for the construction of the ovens. The son of Intendant v. Retzow wrote that 'the Prussian field ovens consist of hoops of wrought iron which are screwed into a broad oval border, also of wrought iron, thus forming the framework of the standard baking oven. The hearth and the spaces between the hoops are built up with bricks, which means that an oven of this design can be constructed with great speed, always assuming that bricks are available where you happen to be.'[14] Dohna's corps was caught out rather badly in Poland in 1759, for the houses were built of wood and clay and even a brick chimney-breast was a rarity. As for the quality of the ration bread, we have the testimony of one of the royal princesses, who tasted a loaf one day in 1759 and pronounced it 'excellent'.[15]

A single oven was capable of baking a maximum of five batches of 6 lb loaves every twenty-four hours. Taking the size of each batch at between 150 and 200, this gave a maximum of 1,000 loaves, or 3,000 daily rations. Frederick wrote in 1752 that he had assembled the material for forty-eight ovens, for 'we did not have enough in the campaign of 1744, which put me in considerable embarrassment'.[16] However, only thirty-seven ovens were available for the campaign of 1756, and still less appeared in the later years of the great war.

As a general rule the ovens of an army could bake no more than three days' rations in every period of forty-eight hours. This gave rise to some complicated calculations on the part of the commander and his commissariat. In theory, at least, the army had to proceed by bounds of five marches at a time between one magazine and the next, taking into account the circulation of the laden and empty commissariat waggons, the time spent loading and unloading, and the desirability of establishing an intermediate bakery. This was the 'five-march system'.

Fully aware of the importance of their position, the bakers were not above going on strike in the middle of a campaign, or lining their pockets by more underhand means. Retzow's successor as Intendant, Colonel v. Arnstedt, complained that 'it is something of a phenomenon to come across an honest master in a field bakery. You must be very vigilant to be wise to all the frauds that go on in these establishments'.[17]

Some commanders seem to have submitted to the tyranny of the system in its entirety. Bevern, for instance, took three weeks (10 September–1 October 1757) to crawl the sixty-odd miles from Bernstadt to Breslau, counting in the five days he spent baking at Bunzlau and the four he spent for the same purpose at Liegnitz. Frederick, however, rarely allowed himself to be held up by such considerations, and helped himself out with whatever provisions and transport could be picked up along the way. When necessary he could drive his army a dozen miles a day, which was remarkable going by the standards of the time.

In wartime the reliability and quantity of the grain supplies were of more account than economy, and so Frederick was in the habit of laying out large and profitable contracts that would tempt the merchants to scour a large part of Europe for supplies. In the Seven Years War the most important contractors, Schimmelmann and Hagen, bought up grain in Hamburg, Holland and as far afield as Scotland and Norway, and delivered it (at their own risk) to whatever depots were designated by Intendant v. Retzow.

The officers of the commissariat at the same time gathered in whatever supplies of grain were to be had in the actual theatre of war – if possible by agreement with the local administration (even in enemy lands), but if necessary without it.

The tiny peacetime establishment of the Intendant's department was far too small to manage these operations alone, and Retzow and his successor were forced to recruit large numbers of temporary commissariat officials without enquiring too closely into their backgrounds. A favourite trick of these gentlemen was to persuade local authorities that they had failed to supply grain in the specified quantity and quality, and then demand blackmail money as the price of keeping silent. In the Seven Years War Frederick was taken aback to hear of a commissariat official called Rose who was so untypically honest that he refused to accept his allowance of four horses' rations on the grounds that he could not ride. The strange incident stuck in Frederick's mind, and he appointed the upright Rose as the first President of the new Staatsbank in 1764.

The gathering in of fodder for the horses was a vital operation of war. While powerful escorts of hussars stood guard, large parties of troopers (in smocks) and infantry mowed the hay, bound it in trusses and loaded it on to horses or carts. At the same time other detachments would comb the villages for stores of dry fodder. A commander could never be at his ease while this kind of operation was going on – the enemy might challenge him to battle while a high proportion of his cavalry was scattered over the hayfields, or they might cut up his foraging parties and thereby threaten his army with starvation. The Austrians had elevated this kind of disruptive warfare into a fine art.

The exacting of contributions of cash was an interesting activity that was sometimes associated with foraging. It is best described as a process of authorised blackmail, by which towns and villages were threatened with the destruction of hostages and property if they failed to yield up the demanded sums. The hussars were usually made responsible for raising such 'contributions', which was one reason why their service was so popular.

The supplies of meat were obliging enough to march with the regiments on their own feet. In wartime the soldier was entitled to a free weekly ration of up to 2 lb of meat, the company commander being made responsible for buying, herding, and slaughtering the necessary animals from a special allowance (*Fleischgeld*). The company was permitted to herd no more than ten days' supplies of cattle at a time, all the surplus being turned over to the commissariat.

Brandy, beer, tobacco, food in great variety (and sometimes other, more personal services) were sold by the sutlers, and in particular the formidable female variety, the *Marketenderinen*. Though the reality was usually much less glamorous than the 'Daughter of the Regiment' we encounter in Donizetti's opera, the *Marketenderin* wore an undeniably saucy outfit that was composed of a skirt, a military-style tunic and a busby or three-cornered hat. Both female and male sutlers were under orders to wear a distinguishing light blue cockade in the hat. Their stock-in-trade was carried in kegs and containers that were tied to the saddle, or stored in a cart along with a tent and stall.

The sutlers enjoyed a semi-official status. Frederick used to put all the available breweries and distilleries to work in wartime to help to replenish their flasks, and he provided them with escorts to help them to plunder the enemy villages. Conversely they had to put up with having the soldiers turned out of their tents and stalls at Tattoo (*Zapfenstreich*), which was beaten at eight o'clock every evening, and they had to abide by whatever restrictions were imposed by the commander or his staff. The female sutlers proved to be a good deal less amenable to direction than their male counterparts. One day during some manoeuvres near Potsdam the king and his staff espied a little hill from which they would have a good view of what was going on. When he reached the top Frederick found it occupied by the stalls of two *Marketenderinen*, who informed him that this pitch was ideal for their trade, whereas he could watch his puppet soldiers from wherever he liked. Frederick had to beat a retreat.

Other commodities – firewood, straw for bedding, pigs and poultry – the troops simply requisitioned for themselves as they marched through the countryside.

The mass of animals and vehicles that sustained the army was imposing in the extreme. There was the train of heavy artillery, with its guns, ammunition carts and pontoons. There were the flour waggons and baking ovens of the commissariat. At the unit level there were the company bread waggon and the company baggage waggon and pack-horses (bearing tents and tent-poles, twenty-two field flasks and, from 1748, the twenty field kettles as well), not to mention the officers' coaches, carts and pack-animals. Every battalion drew with it two light guns, the coach with the strong-box (*Commandeur-Chaise*) and (from late 1757) three or four four-horse ammunition carts, each containing 15,000 musket cartridges. On top of that we have the herds of cattle and the horses and carts of the sutlers.

All of this leaves out of account the special trains that were formed to transport vast additional quantities of victuals or ammunition. Convoys of 1,000 vehicles at a time were commonplace, while three or four times that number of carts were sometimes assembled in the Seven Years War – the train that Schwerin took to Bohemia in 1757, for instance, or the ill-fated convoy that set out in the following year to replenish Frederick's siege artillery at Olmütz.

To provide an adequate escort for a medium-sized convoy demanded eight or ten battalions, two regiments of cavalry and several hundred hussars: heavy concentrations of infantry and artillery marched at the head, centre and tail of the convoy, while further infantry were disposed by platoons evenly along the sides; all the while the hussars and dragoons kept watch on the head and tail and fanned out into the country on either side of the road. As many waggons travelled abreast as the road would permit, so as to shorten the length of the convoy. Every night the waggons were leaguered up into a defensive *Wagenburg*, which was sometimes reinforced by light earthworks. On the field of battle the army's baggage was drawn together in the rear into a *Wagenburg* of the same kind, and it was usually designated as the dressing station for the wounded.

The conscripted peasant drivers were the only people whose needs passed unnoticed. Saueracker wrote that 'on campaign no one has to undergo such fatigue as a pack-horse leader or a driver, especially in the artillery, not to mention the fact that in a battle their lives stand in as much danger as any of the soldiers. If bad drivers run away, and good drivers become bad, it is only because they are poorly paid, poorly clad and poorly provided for'.[18]

It is evident that the apparent predominance of 'teeth' over 'tail' in eighteenth-century armies is very deceptive, once we take into account the size of the non-military 'logistical support' (sutlers and the requisitioned drivers, animals and carts), and the amount of effort which the 'fighting soldier' had to devote to maintaining himself and the army.

On the whole Frederick succeeded remarkably well in mobilising these very mixed resources. C. F. v. Barsewisch testifies that in the regiment of Wedell in the Seven Years War 'we were never short of bread, and it frequently happened that we had a surplus of meat. It is true that coffee, sugar and beer were often not to be had even at high prices, while in Moravia we sometimes ran out of wine. But in Bohemia we had local wine in plenty, especially in the camp at Melnik in 1757. You know how things are in wartime: if you want to be really comfortable, you ought to stay at home'.[19]

Medical services

Frederick cared for the welfare of his soldiers only in so far as they were likely to repay that attention by taking their place in the line of battle. There was little room in the king's scheme of things for the crippled, the aged, or the seriously sick or wounded.

Frederick was content to run the medical services on the same modest footing as in the last reign, making little attempt to adapt them to meet the exigencies of the new wars. Two functionaries stood at the head of the hierarchy – the *General-Chirurgus*, and the *General-Stabs-Medicus*, the most prominent holder of the latter post being Frederick's personal physician, the able Dr Christian Cothenius, who became deputy to Dr Johann Eller in 1750, and then took over as chief from 1760 to 1788.

At the regimental level medical affairs were in the hands of the regimental surgeon-major (*Regiments-Feldscheer*), a doctor who had qualified at one of the two medical schools in Berlin. He was paid 200 thalers at the outset of each campaign, from which he was expected to fit out his medicine chest, and he received a monthly sum which was supposed to enable him to provide beds and accommodation for the sick and wounded, and to hire the collection of semi-skilled company *Feldscheer*.

A field surgery (*Feldapotheke*) looked after the needs of the army as a whole when it went on campaign – the establishment for a corps of 30,000 men being reckoned at 160 surgeons and hospital *Feldscheer*, 9 six-horse *Apothekenwagen* and 12 four-horse supply waggons. First aid after an action was rendered at the *Wagenburg* dressing station or the field hospital (*Feldlazarethe*), and the surviving wounded and the sick were sent on to standing hospitals that were established in towns and villages.

If the enumeration of the facilities and personnel seems impressive enough, the reality was nothing short of appalling. Bad staffing was at the root of the problem. There were certainly dedicated men among the regimental surgeons, like the chief surgeon of the regiment of Meyerinck who bound up the wounds of three or four hundred men a day after the battle of Leuthen, but in time of war Frederick was ready to take on barbers' assistants – 'raw young lads who could scarcely shave a beard tolerably well, and were not even up to applying a plaster'.[20] In 1744 Frederick bestirred himself to recruit twelve surgeons in Paris, hoping that they would set an example to their Prussian counterparts, but not long after they arrived at their destination these gentlemen had to be dismissed because they were 'far too prone to disorderly conduct'.[21]

As for transport, the wounded were carted back to the rearward hospitals in whatever waggons could be spared by the Commissariat. The preacher Carl Daniel Küster has a harrowing description of how the men who were wounded at Hochkirch were transported to Glogau in the second half of October 1758: the walking wounded ransacked the villages along the way, since no provisions whatever were issued for this *via dolorosa*, and they waited for the casualties on the carts to die off so that they could plunder their clothes and claim their places.[22]

The worst misdeeds of all were perpetrated in the standing rearward hospitals, where orderlies and the specially hired *Kommissarien* and *Inspektoren* plundered and neglected the sick and wounded at will. The *Kommandant*, the nominal chief of the hospital, was a serving officer who was usually devoid of all medical experience. Young Christian v. Prittwitz made the acquaintance of this, one of the most hideous aspects of King Frederick's service, when he was struck down by fever at the outset of the campaign of 1757 and found himself consigned to the *Kadettenhaus* at Dresden, which had been requisitioned as a hospital. At first Prittwitz was glad to arrive at the place, 'but I was horrified when I entered this house of misery and saw a great quantity of corpses heaped on top of each other along the walls, with their rigid feet poking through the straw which had been scattered over them . . . Whole rooms were filled with sick of every category, who were stacked up in layers and afforded the most inadequate treatment'.[23]

Dr Cothenius claimed that 220,000 sick and wounded were discharged as cured and healed from the hospitals in the course of the Seven Years War. We can only trust that the ratio of those who died in those establishments was lower than in the War of the Bavarian Succession, when out of every five sick who entered the hospital at Neisse, only one emerged alive.

Something more sinister than mere neglect lay behind the dreadful mortality. Warnery writes that after Torgau,

the cold killed off most of the wounded, as usually happens in the Prussian service, where the hospitals are so badly served and so malodorous that the soldier considers himself dead once he enters the portals. It is not altogether surprising that so few disabled men were to be seen in the states of the king of Prussia after such a cruel war: I have it on good authority that the hospital directors and surgeons were under orders to let men die if they were wounded in such a way that they would be incapable of serving after they were healed.'[24]

The name for this licensed murder was 'conservative surgery'.

Field preachers

Frederick (if he believed in precious little else) was a firm believer in the fundamental absurdity of all religion. At the same time he valued the cohesive force of religious practices among simpler folk, and he expected his generals to give their full support to at least the outward trappings of religious observance. Even Seydlitz, the notorious rake, used to forbid his young officers to joke about religion and the clergy, and he lent what assistance he could to the labours of Balke, the excellent *Feldprediger* of his regiment.

In wartime, of course, the words of the preachers took on new authority. On the question of the immortality of the soul Carl Küster noted that 'after the battle of Prague I could still find many wounded officers who maintained that the soul died with the body and that there existed no state of divine retribution. Few officers held to this opinion after the battle of Leuthen, and none at all after we were attacked by surprise at Hochkirch'.[25]

In the field it was the duty of the preachers to hold fifteen minutes of prayers every morning and evening, to preach a sermon every Sunday, and to celebrate a communion service on alternate Sundays. On 7 June 1758 the courtier Lehndorff saw a regiment at its prayers in the field, and he testifies that 'you could imagine nothing more elevating than to see this band of heroes, who make provinces and kingdoms tremble, bow down before the Almighty. The generals, the officers and all the rank and file stand in a circle around the preacher, who makes his altar out of two drums, and they all pray to the Lord with bowed heads'.[26] Victory celebrations were ushered in by a *feu de joie* from the muskets and artillery and the singing of the chorale *Ein feste Burg ist unser Gott*. One of the field preachers would then deliver an appropriate sermon, and the service was completed by a rendering of the *Te Deum* on the trumpets and drums of the cuirassiers.

The clerical hierarchy was headed by a kind of field bishop (*Feldprobst*) who simultaneously held the office of preacher to the First Battalion of the Garde. One of his most important functions was to ordain candidates for the cloth, a large proportion of whom were graduates of the university of Halle. These gentlemen, Frederick stipulated, should be 'of good repute, learned, and if possible still wearing their own hair'.[27]

The field preachers as a whole were young and active men, far removed from the image of the crabbed old pastors who appear in Menzel's nineteenth-century engravings of the Frederician army. In fact Ortmann had to warn a young field preacher of his acquaintance that 'to begin with, a number of the officers, especially the younger ones, seize on the kind of preacher who is unwise enough to accompany them in their pleasures, and they tell him that he is a man who knows how to live . . . Some of them go on to try him out and place all sorts of temptations in his path. But if, through good-heartedness and immaturity, he allows himself to waver, it is not long before all these false compliments are turned into scorn and contempt'.[28]

The Protestant field preachers wore civilian clothes until December 1742, when

Frederick prescribed a uniform garb. Samuel Benedikt Carstedt, preacher of the regiment of Kalckstein, describes it as:

> A three-cornered hat. Hair worn naturally or a short and well-kept wig. A blue collar with a narrow white edge, and a black velvet cravat. A black silk robe which reached down only to the calf. Small cuffs. Black silk stockings and round shoes. This was our clothing. It had a great deal, if not everything, in common with the dress of a French abbé.[29]

Lutheran, Calvinist, Catholic and even Greek Orthodox chaplains lived together amicably in the tolerant atmosphere of Frederick's Prussia. An English pamphleteer sourly commented that even the most bitter enemy of the Reformation could not have done the Protestant cause such disservice as Frederick, who had founded the new Catholic church in Berlin, and begun the Seven Years War with the invasion of Saxony – the first Protestant state of Germany.

Field music

The infantry had a generous allowance of drummers and fifers (about fifteen per battalion) who thumped out commands in the field and sounded Tattoo every evening to clear the inns and the sutlers' tents. The cuirassiers, too, were capable of creating an impressive noise, for they had an establishment of trumpeters and kettle-drummers. For most of the time, however, the army marched and paraded in perfect silence, for the Prussians were proud of being able to keep in step without a beat to assist them.

The 'music' proper of the infantry and dragoons consisted of 'chapels' of up to six woodwind at a time, who created a gentle, unaccented and to twentieth-century ears quite unmilitary sound. A trumpeter sometimes marched in front of the woodwind, to add a little variety and brightness to the music, and horns (an importation from Poland) and clarinets came into prominence from about 1770. Otherwise only the Prussian artillery felt the influence of the 'Janissary music' of drums, tom-toms, triangles, cymbals and tambourines, which became all the rage elsewhere in Europe. Even characteristically 'Prussian' features of military music like the glockenspiel and the jingling-johnny (*Schellenbaum*) were imported after Frederick's death.

The Prussian 'music' had some historic tunes to play, even if the instrumentation was decidedly unadventurous. The name of Prince Leopold of Anhalt-Dessau was indissolubly linked with the 'Dessauer-Marsch', which came from a simple melody which Leopold heard on campaign in Italy in 1705. Frederick himself composed the 'Mollwitzer-Marsch' in camp a few days after his first action, and according to tradition he made up the famous 'Hohenfriedberger' after the great battle of 1745 and awarded it to the Bayreuth Dragoons.

In action the woodwind were supposed to keep together behind the company colours, which were grouped between the fourth and fifth platoons of the battalion. Once the artillery and musketry opened up in competition, however, the musicians' sense of duty gave way to their famous and highly-developed instinct for self-preservation. Prittwitz noted how his battalion's *Hautboisten* vanished at the outset of the battle of Zorndorf, upon which he compared them to 'the coming and going of swallows . . . who disappear in autumn before the onset of cold weather, and reappear in springtime in fine condition without anybody being able to divine where on earth they stay and hide during the winter'.[30]

On the retreat from Kunersdorf one of the *Hautboisten* was rash enough to be caught in the open by a cossack, who hunted him across a meadow. Frederick drew the attention of his staff to this rare event, and remarked 'Now I just wonder whether Apollo and the Muse of Music are going to do anything to save their disciple.'[31] At the last moment the musician turned about in desperation and presented the monstrous muzzle of his bassoon at the cossack, who promptly fled in terror.

9

Staff Work and the Control of the Army

Staff

In staff work, as in the control of finances, Frederick initiated or controlled everything that was done in his name. Thus the titles of the functionaries remained of much less account than the relationship in which they, as individuals, stood to the king.

At the heart of the management of the army resided the king and his First Cabinet Secretary, the faithful Eichel, who wrote out the royal orders and memoranda. At one remove stood a small body of aides-de-camp and draftsmen, and the eight or so clerks of the *Geheime Kriegskanzlei* (Secret War Chancellery) who copied out the more extensive correspondence.

The responsibility for what we would now call the work of the general staff was mostly divided between two offices, those of the *Generalquartiermeister* and of the *Generaladjutant*.

The origins of the *Generalquartiermeister's* post date back to 1657 when the Great Elector set up a staff on the Swedish model to help him with planning the movements of the army. The first effective holder of the office in Frederick's reign was Karl Christoph v. Schmettau, who came from the Austrian service in 1741, and was promoted major-general and given the official title of *Generalquartiermeister* on 28 May 1743. On Schmettau's urging the king appointed Captain Wilhelm v. d. Oelsnitz as his assistant or *Quartiermeisterlieutenant* (he was elevated to *Generalquartiermeisterlieutenant* in 1752). Four more *Quartiermeisterlieutenants* were created on 22 December 1756.

Oelsnitz was killed at the siege of Prague in 1757, and Schmettau was sent to the doghouse after he yielded up Dresden two years later. However, the department survived the loss of its founding fathers, and the number of *Quartiersmeisterlieutenants* was built up steadily after the war, reaching a peak of twenty-nine in 1783.

The *Generalquartiersmeister* and his staff were responsible for finding out about the theatre of war, devising the orders of battle, policing the army, directing the field intelligence, arranging winter quarters, planning march routes and determining the sites of camps. To make absolutely sure that the army took up the designated camp site without confusion, the *Generalquartiermeister* used to ride ahead with the 'major-generals of the day' of the infantry and cavalry under an hussar escort, and show the generals the position of the camp and the lie of the surrounding country. He then staked out the camp, and sent back officers with clear marching instructions to guide the army to the site.

To help him in his work the *Generalquartiermeister* had the commandant of the staff dragoon regiment (which policed the camp and the marching columns), and the staff provosts who policed the headquarters, kept up the lists of prisoners of war and of troops under arrest, negotiated the contracts for the exchange of prisoners, fixed weights and measures and kept the sutlers under some kind of control.

On 22 October 1772 Frederick drew up an instruction at the request of the hard-worked *Quartiermeisterlieutenants*. He warned them that 'a nobleman who devotes himself to this trade must have considerable natural activity, if he is not to find the labour too hard for him'.[1] He added that in compensation a good man was well set on the path of promotion, for in the course of his business he got to know all the duties of a commander.

The second division of our 'general staff' comprised the *Generaladjutanten* and their assistants, whose prime function was to manage the army as an institution. Frederick appointed seven *Generaladjutanten* at his accession, of whom the senior saw to *das Detail von der Armee* – keeping the records of the army's strength up to date, administering pensions, preparing reviews and manoeuvres, and directing the Feldjägercorps. Frederick abolished the juniors in 1758, thus strengthening the authority of the senior *General-adjutant*. A further concentration of staff work was achieved in 1765, when the acting *Generalquartiermeister*, the notorious 'Wilhelmi' Anhalt took over the *Generaladjutant*'s department. This hated figure combined both functions from then until 1781.

In compensation for the cutting down of the *Generaladjutanten*, Frederick raised the number of assistants, or *Flügeladjutanten*, to about twenty. The younger adjutants acted as galloping aides-de-camp, while some of their seniors were given field commands or put in charge of grenadier battalions.

Before we leave the central staff it is worth mentioning that affairs were managed so 'unofficially' that Hans v. Winterfeldt, the all-powerful figure of the middle 1750s, held no higher appointment in the staff than one of the *Generadjutanten*.

Brigademajors were selected captains who assisted individual commanders in transmitting orders, and in making sure that these orders were carried out. This did not satisfy Frederick, who was anxious to create a category of staff officers who would enable the king to exercise a more direct control of the army at brigade or divisional level. After the Second Silesian War he appointed twelve special aides-de-camp for this purpose (*Adjutanten bei den Generalen*), and in 1759 he went on to create his first set of royal adjutants (*Officiers in der Koniglichen Suite*) – best described as royal commissars or narks who ran the affairs of aged or ineffective commanders.

The mass of officers hanging about the king was swollen still further by the dozen or so subalterns whom Frederick was training up as staff officers (see p. 37), by the young orderly (*Ordonnanz*) officers who represented the individual regiments at the royal headquarters, and by the reserve of major-generals, colonels and majors whom the king held in readiness for the command of detachments.

Taking into account the existence of the Intendant and his assistants, the commissariat, the Massow-Wartenberg department, all the apparatus of the staff, as well as a separate civil and military administration in Silesia, it is strange that Frederick felt the need to complicate matters still further by setting up yet another body in 1746. This was a sixth, or military department, which was attached to the *General-Directorium* (the organ of state administration). In 1761 the head of the department was glorified by the title of 'War Minister', but in fact his work was unglamorous in the extreme. The functionary in question, Lieutenant-General v. Wedell, merely directed the recruiting, paid the *Servisgeld* for the billeting of the troops, arranged for the regiments to be fed when they were marching to and from the peacetime reviews and manoeuvres, and administered the Potsdam Military Orphanage. 'This minister never actually appointed anyone to any rank or exercised authority over any personnel. Hence you can live with the military for a long time on close terms and never hear him come up in conversation.'[2]

The Prussian intelligence system was at its most impressive, or at least at its busiest, when it was gathering information for the long term. Immediately after the end of the First Silesian War Colonel v. Bornstedt and twenty-six other officers took off as *Volontairs* to accompany the Austrians in their campaign in Bavaria. Commissariat officials simultaneously seized the opportunity to examine the Austrian supply system, while Prussian bakers tried to find out how it was that ten Austrian ovens were capable of baking 50,000 loaves in a single day.

Again after the Second Silesian War Winterfeldt employed the ex-Austrian colonels Gellhorn and Rebentisch to send him reports on military developments in the Habsburg territories, and he briefed all the Prussian officers travelling to take the 'cure' at Karlsbad to reconnoitre the roads, passes, rivers and bridges in the Bohemian border country.

In 1754 Winterfeldt took the road to Karlsbad in person. He sketched the mountain passes in his own hand, and from what he saw he concluded that the Aussig route offered the best path for an invasion of Bohemia. On the way back he dropped in on his old friend General v. Pirsch, the commandant of the Saxon fortress of Königstein. 'He had a very clear view of the whole neighbourhood from this rock, which reached almost to the clouds',[3] and he noted with interest that the Saxons were building formidable new works round the edge of the plateau. Frederick himself used to pump travellers for news of the tactics and weapons of his potential enemies, and indeed for any information that might enable him to build up character-pictures of their rulers and generals.

One particularly enterprising spy network was set up in Poland by the Jew Sabatky. It was by this channel that Frederick hoped to receive information from Colonel Tottleben and some other Russian officers who had been corrupted in the spring of 1760 by Colonel de Pechlin, a Prussian agent who was planted in St Petersburg.

Where Frederick encountered more obvious difficulty was in obtaining reliable information on campaign. For a start, the people of Bohemia, Moravia and his own Upper Silesia fled to the hills on the approach of the Prussian army. Then there was the obstacle presented by the Austrian hussars and Croats, who swarmed over the countryside and intercepted the Prussian spies and informants. Most important of all, as Mitchell noted, there was the fact that 'in this army the spies are paid too sparingly, and consequently the intelligence is none of the best'.[4] Winterfeldt often complained of the same thing, and so did another spymaster, the *Capitaine des Guides* Gaudi, who remarked that it was not easy to get hold of informants who would 'expose themselves to the danger of being hanged for a prize of ten thalers at the most'.[5]

Rather than pay for good spies Frederick preferred to wring information out of such well-informed civilians as coachmen, carters, drovers, foresters and local officials. 'Only with harsh and violent treatment,' he wrote, 'can we get the Bohemians and Moravians to perform this service for us.'[6] He thought it amusing when in 1760 he had some Wendish peasants in Lusatia beaten until they were willing to sing 'like canaries'.[7]

Failing this, Frederick was sometimes driven to following in the tracks of the enemy, and keeping on the lookout for some sign that might tell him what they were up to. This was a very clumsy and dangerous way of collecting intelligence, and in 1758 all Frederick's powers of observation did not save him from being attacked and over-run at Hochkirch.

One suspects that Old Fritz got a good deal of satisfaction by drawing on the vast repertoire of tricks and ruses which served to conceal his own intentions. He was capable of having roads repaired as if in preparation for a retreat (before Hohenfriedberg), or of assigning fictional names to regiments (before Rossbach), or of arranging to have a courier captured with a false message (which gained him a day's march on the retreat from Olmütz in 1758).

The Prussian officer corps became a singularly uncommunicative one, and Frederick was at pains to keep prying foreigners at a distance from all but the most routine of military activities. When two foreign officers came to see the important Spandau manoeuvres of 1753 he instructed prince Henry to make sure that 'these people will see a plain near Spandau and nothing else'. He went to the trouble of publishing a totally misleading description of the same manoeuvres, in the hope that it would keep any other curious folk amused.

MAPS

The shortage of adequate maps compounded the difficulties which Frederick encountered in orientating himself on campaign. He had to embark on the war in 1740 with only the sketchiest knowledge of the theatre, and in the next year he made it his business to commission a general map of Silesia on the scale of 1:200,000. The new map still failed to meet his purposes, and so he instructed Major v. Wrede, an engineer, to compile a more detailed map of the Silesian borders with Bohemia and Moravia. Wrede began work in 1747, and by 1753 his labours were complete, except for filling in a gap in the centre around Strehlen and Neumarkt. Other projects were set in train in due course, and the work of the Prussian military cartographers eventually reached a very high standard, the peak probably being attained by Dietrich de Haas, who drew three maps of the theatre of operations of the Russo-Turkish campaign of 1770. Field-Marshal Samuel v. Schmettau had already been inspired by the work of Cassini in France to begin a trigonometrical survey of Prussia in 1750, but Frederick discouraged the experiment because he feared the consequences if such accurate maps should fall into the hands of the enemy.

The labours of the Prussian map-makers were supplemented by judicious acquisitions abroad, such as of the *magnifique Landkarten* which Winterfeldt saw on sale in Dresden, or the maps which the French envoy was obliging enough to collect for Frederick in Prague. Selected maps were left in the Silesian fortresses, so as to remain at the disposal of corps commanders, and in the Seven Years War the royal headquarters was accompanied by a travelling *Plankammer* which was managed by the engineer major Griese.

For all the diligence of Frederick and his draftsmen, it was very seldom indeed that the Prussians went into action with a really accurate knowledge of the terrain over which they were fighting – which was a severe disadvantage for an army that was accustomed to attacking the enemy at short notice. The battle of Leuthen offers the one notable exception, for the terrain had been a favourite stamping-ground for the peacetime manoeuvres, and Zieten knew every yard of the scene of the cavalry action on the right.

Kolin was more typical. On the morning of that fatal day, when Frederick was giving out the orders in the inn of Slati Slunce, he announced 'Gentlemen, many of you must still remember this neighbourhood from the time when we stood here in 1742. I am certain I have the plan somewhere, but Major v. Griese cannot find it.'[8] As it turned out, peoples' memories of the ground were very hazy, and the Austrian position turned out to be more extensive than had been expected. Two years later at Kunersdorf Frederick was led by his ignorance of the terrain to make another bad misappreciation, even though the field lay just outside the university- and garrison-town of Frankfurt.

The blame cannot be laid at Frederick's door. The cartography of the time showed villages and roads well enough, but it had no adequate means of representing broken ground and hills before the invention of contours, and all but the very best maps were poor at indicating the nature of woods or swamps. All of this was at a period when a gap of two hundred yards was reckoned to be a 'narrow defile', because it interfered with the advance of a line of infantry.

Inspectors

The provincial inspectors were a body of royal commissioners who were established on 9 February 1763, when Frederick was tightening up the discipline of the army at the close of the Seven Years War. The inspectors stood outside the staff proper, but they represented one of Frederick's most important instruments of military control in the last decades of his reign. Originally numbering five for the cavalry and six for the infantry, they reached the respective totals of seven and ten by the time of Frederick's death, which meant that individual inspectors were responsible for watching over anything between twenty and seventy-five squadrons of cavalry, or between five and twenty-one battalions of infantry.

The job of the inspector was to tour his province, or 'inspection', making sure that the regiments were up to the stipulated strengths, seeing that they performed the exercises in a proficient and uniform way, and noting the names of officers who conducted themselves particularly well or particularly badly. The setting-up of the inspectors represented a praiseworthy and almost unique attempt on the part of Frederick to delegate a measure of his authority, and he tried to choose the very best men for these posts, regardless of their seniority.

It was a pity that it all turned out so badly. To set against the outstanding figure of Seydlitz, who performed wonders with the Silesian cavalry, there were the despotic Stutterheim and Ramin, who delighted in relegating officers to the garrison regiments at every spring review, and the pedantic Saldern, tyrant of the Magdeburg Infantry Inspection, who set the tone for the whole army in the final period of Frederick's reign. The king was certainly saved the labour of corresponding directly with the regimental commanders, but as a consequence the administration of the army became more roundabout and slow.

Reviews and manoeuvres

Twice a year in peacetime the regiments of every province were put through their paces under the eyes of the king or (later in the reign) one of his inspectors.

The first of these gatherings was the spring or summer review – four days of concentrated activity which represented the culmination of the two-month 'exercise season'. In each province in turn the native cantonists were recalled to the colours and the full regiments marched off to the chosen field – the Berlin and Potsdam regiments in mid-May, the Magdeburg, Pomeranian, East Prussian (and later also the West Prussian) regiments in May and June, and the Silesian regiments in July or August.

The phenomenon made a deep impression on foreign visitors. Dr Moore arrived in Berlin at the height of the preparations for one of the reviews.

> Nothing was to be seen in the streets but soldiers parading, and officers hurrying backwards and forwards. The town looked more like the cantonment of a great army, than the capital of a kingdom in the time of profound peace. The court itself resembled the levee of a general in the field . . . every man there (for there were no women) was dressed in a military uniform.[9]

The Marquis de Toulongeon, as a professional officer, was struck by the fact that the 40,000-strong garrison of Berlin could march off to the reviews in perfect order in silence; he was accustomed to the state of affairs which prevailed in the French army, when there was a near-riot when even the smallest garrison had to turn out.[10]

Early on the morning of the first day of the review it was the custom for the entire body of regiments to march past the king. The troops then returned to the camp, where the colonels lined up the new ensigns, the new NCOs, the recruits, and the men who were to be dismissed on account of their age, wounds or ill-health. Knesebeck remembered the scene outside Magdeburg in 1783, when he was present as a *Junker* in the regiment of Kalckstein.

> The regiments were deployed in the following order: the commandant stood with his spontoon in front of the first battalion (for only the generals were on horseback). Behind the commandant were arrayed such regimental *Junker* as had not yet been presented to the king, and behind them again the recruits of the present year, drawn up in three ranks according to size. It was a splendid day, and the wide heath was covered with spectators in coaches and on horseback. A fragrance arose from the thyme that was trodden under the horses' hooves. Then we saw a dense cloud of dust in the distance. It was coming in our direction, and people became quieter and quieter the closer it approached. It was Frederick's coach. He alighted at Korbelitz and mounted horse. It was an enormous English grey that he was riding this year . . . As soon as he was in the saddle he set off at a gallop, so that his whole suite had to follow in a headlong rush behind his huge, long-striding beast.
>
> Such was the arrival of the seventy-year-old veteran. Some thirty paces from the line he pulled up to a halt, took up his telescope and examined the whole extent to make sure that the alignment was correct. He stopped immediately in front of us *Junker* – a little old man with huge great eyes and a penetrating gaze.[11]

On the second day of the ordeal the cavalry went through some basic evolutions, then presented its remounts, harness and saddles for the king's inspection. After that the infantry came on in two or three columns, and deployed into line to carry out advances by platoons or battalions. At the end of the day the regimental and battalion commanders assembled at the royal headquarters to hear Frederick's comments on their performance.

The reviews ended in two days of large-scale exercises. Kaltenborn describes the tension among the officers when they put eighteen or twenty thousand troops at a time through their movements in a holy silence, knowing that their career hung upon the will of one man. During those frightful days 'wives, mothers, children and friends addressed their most fervent petitions to Heaven, lest, as happened only too often, their husbands, fathers, sons or companions met with some disaster'.[12]

In military terms the usefulness of the reviews was very limited. Where their true importance resided was in the ceremonial aspect, in the execution of the tribal ritual which bound the Prussian army to its king.

In contrast the other great gatherings, the autumn manoeuvres, could be turned only too readily to an immediate military end.

Frederick staged the first assembly of the kind at Potsdam in 1743. He spent the next two seasons on campaign, but after the peace he resumed the manoeuvres on a still more ambitious scale. An English observer reported to his government in August 1748 that 'these inferences, worthy of the attention of Europe, are to be drawn, from the very frequent practises of reviewing large bodies of troops at Potsdam, that the king of Prussia is determined to hold his army in a constant readiness for action: and that, from often repeating the same kind of orders, for reviews, which would be necessary for taking the field, nobody will be able to discover, when His Prussian Majesty is really earnest'.[13]

No less than 44,000 troops were brought together for the Spandau manoeuvres of 1753, causing alarm throughout Central Europe. Foreign observers were generally kept away, which served only to heighten suspicions, and Burgoyne noted that if Frederick intended to 'manoeuvre ten thousand men in private, he shuts up the country as effectively as his palace'.[14] The other powers of Europe began to follow suit, and so for the next two centuries the season of the autumn manoeuvres became notorious as a period of heightened international tension.

The autumn manoeuvres represented a considerably more realistic performance than the springtime pageant. Not only did the native cantonists usually remain at home, leaving the field to the highly proficient foreign mercenaries, but the space for movement was so much greater.

> The environs of Berlin and Potsdam seem particularly well calculated for this end only, but great care is taken that no essential injury shall be done. The whole is a corn country, and a light dry soil, and the operations only take place before the crop is sown, and after it is off the ground. The movements of these troops are performed in the ploughed or stubble fields, in the woods and under such circumstances as actually present themselves in service.[15]

Now the chief objectives were to try out new tactics, and to train the commanders in planning and directing the movements of large bodies of troops. Contested manoeuvres between 'rival' armies (as opposed to attacks against flagged positions) were first introduced before the Seven Years War.

10

Operations of War

We have recruited our army, dressed it, trained it up and furnished it with a commissariat of sorts. Before we see it in action, however, we ought to stop for a while and consider how it was arranged and managed in some of the more common eventualities of war.

Camps and field routine

We begin with the army at rest in a simple camp. The tents of the infantry were arrayed in two parallel ranks, immediately behind the position designated for the army in the event of combat. The cavalry had their tents further to the rear, arranged in depth and forming streets perpendicular to the lines of infantry.

The company was usually allotted two tents for the NCOs and twenty-two for the men, and the piled muskets were sheltered under two bell-shaped *Gewehr-Mantels* which were emblazoned with the regimental coat of arms.

The troops slept by six- or seven-man *Kameradschaften* in simple ridge tents which rose to a height of six feet. The material was of canvas, and the seams were covered on the outside by strips of blue linen. The tents of the NCOs were somewhat roomier and possessed straight sides. Then we progress by way of the common tent of the junior subalterns, the individual tents of the lieutenants and the multi-chambered dwellings of the senior officers until we finally arrive at the grand marquee of the king. With the possible exception of the lieutenants' tents, all the tents of the officers seem to have been oval in plan.

The whole was arranged with obsessional neatness. On entering the Prussian service in 1741 the ex-Austrian general Schmettau was surprised to find that

> the camps were invariably drawn up in uninterrupted straight lines. The men laboriously dug up turfs and laid them in front of each battalion and squadron so as to indicate the positions that would be taken up by the troops, the NCOs and the officers when the army stood under arms. As if to increase the work the soldiers had to construct a royal monogram out of green turfs by the colours and standards of every battalion and cavalry regiment, as well as turning over the surrounding soil as meticulously as in a garden.[1]

The security perimeter was designed as much to intercept deserters as to hold off the enemy. At the immediate disposal of the major-generals of the day (see p. 33) there was available the powerful central *Generalwache*, which stood guard over the treasury and the provisions. The inner circle of the perimeter proper was held by a contribution of one lieutenant, two NCOs, one drummer and forty-eight men from every regiment of the army: these troops were divided into little pickets, each of which was stationed on the right flank of the tents of the parent battalion. In the event of an alarm four regiments'-worth of pickets at a time could be concentrated under the command of a captain.

Feldwache of infantry or cavalry were stationed a little further afield in groups of twenty or thirty men apiece. The *Feldwache* were always drawn up ready for action, but Schmettau noted that with a distinct lack of imagination the Prussians used to place them a uniform 300 paces into the country and align them directly in front of the colours or standards of the parent regiment.

More distant security was provided by powerful pickets of cavalry which took up station on the flanks of the army, by outlying chains of hussars, and by little garrisons of grenadier battalions in the villages about.

Reveille was beaten as soon as daylight permitted a man to be seen at fifty paces, the regimental drummers taking their cue from the first ruffle that came from the First Battalion of the Garde. The men duly emerged from their tents to answer the roll call and receive their assignments to fatigues or other duties. The completed rolls were then forwarded by the NCOs to the subalterns, who collated them and gave them to the senior lieutenant, who had the responsibility of delivering a written report to the captain's tent. If the army was due to march, the companies now turned out completely armed and equipped. Otherwise the new guards marched off to relieve the old, after which the regiments gathered in circles, each around its *Feldprediger*, for fifteen minutes of prayers.

At about nine in the morning the king or the commander-in-chief received reports on the military situation from the two major-generals of the day and from any officers who had been sent out on reconnaissance. Two hours later the king issued the *Parole* and all necessary instructions to the new major-generals of the day. These two gentlemen took the orders down in writing, then stepped outside the royal tent and conveyed the king's intentions first to the royal aides-de-camp, and then to the majors of the day, the brigade-majors and the aides-de-camp of the individual generals, all of which officers were drawn up in a circle. As a final check the senior royal aide-de-camp repeated the *Parole* to the king and read out the orders as they had been transmitted to him by the major-generals. After this the officers dispersed to circulate the orders among the army.

The troops passed the rest of the day on drill or fatigues, or indulging in whatever off-duty pleasures the camp had to offer. At six in the evening, after a further prayer session, the regimental pickets were turned out. Two hours later the drummers beat Tattoo and the men were cleared from the sutlers' tents. Another two hours on, and it was time for the major-generals of the day to undertake the first of their 'grand rounds' (tours of the first line of the camp). Smaller 'rounds' were performed by the colonels, lieutenant-colonels and majors of the day.

Marches

Three watchful hussars, riding in single file, represented the most distant outriders of the Prussian army as it crawled, scores of thousands of troops strong, across the landscape of Central Europe. Eleven comrades followed in close support of our three heroes, after which further groups of hussars came in successively larger bodies – first a platoon, then a

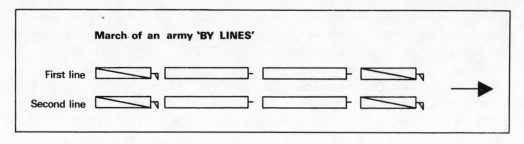

March of an army 'BY LINES'

First line

Second line

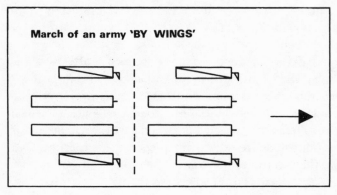

March of an army 'BY WINGS'

miniature advance guard of two or three hundred men, and finally the main force of hussars. The infantry of the advance guard marched about 1,000 paces behind.

The purpose of the advance guards, as originally constituted, was to occupy features of the ground, help the *Generalquartiermeister* to stake out the camps, and provide the first warning of the proximity of the enemy. In the course of the Seven Years War, however, Frederick considerably expanded both the size and purpose of his advance guards, which were now supposed to spearhead his 'oblique attack' as well as keep in constant contact with the enemy.

As long as the enemy remained at least three marches distant, the army moved in loose formation of up to eight columns at a time, with the cavalry columns on the wings, and the artillery and baggage towards the centre. The infantry marched (as nearly always) in column of platoons, taking full advantage of the width of the ill-defined roads of the period. Footsore soldiers were piled on to baggage waggons, and the NCOs were under instructions to accompany all soldiers who had to step out of the ranks to relieve themselves. A small rearguard followed the army, sweeping up deserters and stragglers.

Whenever the enemy were known to be within three or four marches, the advance guard fell back to within one mile or less of the columns of the main army, which now marched 'by lines' (*Treffenweise*) or 'by wings' (*Flügelweise*), with the baggage and the pack-horses tucked away on side roads on the flank furthest away from the enemy. Of the two conformations the one 'by lines' was preferable, for the component platoons needed merely to wheel to right or left to form the lines of battle. It is true that Frederick came on to the field of Leuthen 'by wings', but by some clever re-shuffling he managed to shake himself out into lines before he came into contact with the enemy.

On occasion Frederick's army was capable of moving a dozen miles a day for a week or two at a stretch. In normal circumstances half of that distance was a more reasonable average, given the exigencies of supply and the necessity of resting for one day in three or four. The rate sank still lower in the spring and autumn on account of the shortness of the days and the heavy rainfall.

Battle

According to the *Normal-Schlachtordnung* of the period, the army on the battlefield was disposed in two lines, each consisting of a central block of infantry, with a wing of cavalry placed on either flank where there was more room to manoeuvre. Leopold of Anhalt-Dessau was so obsessed by the prevailing ideas that at Kesselsdorf in 1745, when he found himself by chance on the western flank of the Saxon line, which put him in a wonderful position for rolling up the enemy from the left, he chose to lead his army all the way round to the front of the enemy line, from where he could attack head-on in the conventional way. This by no means accorded with the notions of Frederick, who disliked the frontal battle and was striving to find some way of bringing a crushing superiority of force to bear against one sector of an enemy army.

Frederick discovered a source of information in the slantwise 'oblique attack' which had first been propounded by the ancient Greek author Epaminondas. The idea of the oblique attack had been taken up by such writers as the first Duke of Prussia in the sixteenth century, by Montecucculi in the seventeenth century, and more recently by the experts Folard, Puységur and Khevenhüller. The famous 'oblique' attack of Frederick was there-

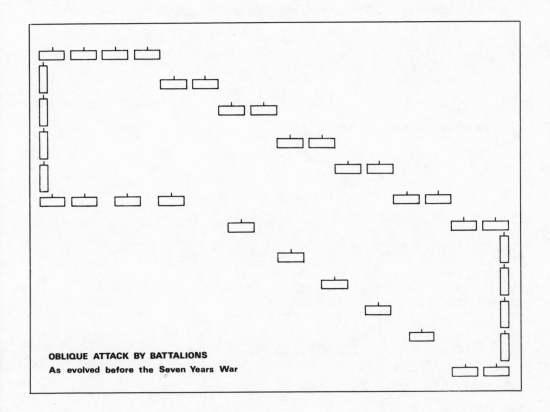

OBLIQUE ATTACK BY BATTALIONS
As evolved before the Seven Years War

fore no innovation, but what Old Fritz succeeded in doing was to translate the hoary old idea into an instrument of war.

Frederick's 'oblique attack' went through a continuous process of evolution, starting with a first tentative peacetime experiment in 1747. To begin with, Frederick's idea was to hold back an entire wing, or gradually turn the whole army in a partial wheel as it approached the enemy. Both of these devices proved to be feeble and clumsy, but four years later Frederick arrived at a much more promising solution – that of arranging the army in a staggered formation (*in Staffeln, en échelon*) from the outset of the attack. The new technique was first put into practice by the Potsdam garrison on 19 August 1751, and it was developed at the Berlin review of the next year and in the Spandau manoeuvres of 1754 and 1755.

By 1756, therefore, a large proportion of the army was versed in the basic principles of the 'oblique attack'. The main striking force was concentrated in the form of an advance guard on whichever of the two wings was to be hurled at the enemy. The rest of the army was 'refused' in a staggered line of regiments, each successive regiment marching to the flank of, and between twenty and fifty paces to the rear of, the regiment before. Thus Frederick hoped to be able to preserve the freedom to break off the action if things went unexpectedly badly. Of course the 'oblique attack' would gain immensely in effect if Frederick ever managed to march the whole army round to the flank of the enemy position before he delivered his assault.

Frederick's belief in the efficacy of the 'oblique attack' was unshaken by some of the difficulties he met in carrying it out in the course of the Seven Years War. At the battle of Prague the beautiful order of the Prussian advance was wrecked by the difficulties of the ground, while at Kolin the army was defeated because the 'refused' wing waded into the combat contrary to orders.

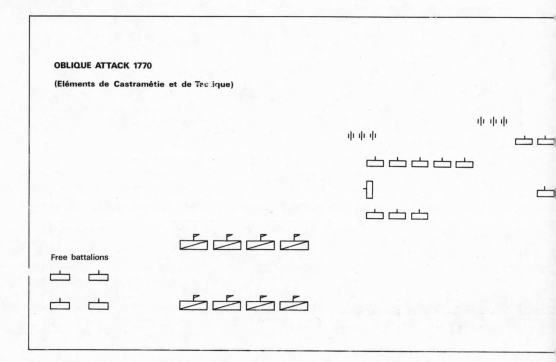

OBLIQUE ATTACK 1770

(Eléments de Castramétie et de Tac.ique)

Free battalions

The credit of the army and of its 'oblique attack' were at last restored at Rossbach, where the infantry not only outmarched the Franco-German host but managed in the process to deliver a beautiful advance *in Staffeln*. At Leuthen, one month later, the 'oblique attack' was carried out to textbook perfection. An army drawn up in this formation used to take up comparatively little space, and 'from a distance the intermingled uniforms, colours and standards looked like a disorderly mass of men. But it required only a nod from the commander for this restless throng to array itself in the finest order, moving with a speed that seemed like a racing torrent'.[2]

In 1758 Frederick marched to do battle with the Russians at Zorndorf. With the mistakes at Kolin still in mind he emphasised that 'we shall attack with one wing only, while refusing the other wing altogether'.[3] General Dohna took the king at his word, with the result that the left wing was massacred without support from the right. After these varied experiences Frederick was at some trouble to maintain a proper balance between the extremes of a 'Kolin' and a 'Zorndorf'.

After the Seven Years War Frederick amended the shape of the 'oblique attack' so as to take account of the powerful enemy artillery that he was likely to encounter in a future war. In 1770 he described a new conformation in which the echelons were represented by entire brigades, staggered by intervals of 100 paces. The cavalry of the attacking wing was held back in reserve, out of reach of the enemy shot and shell, and four battalions were told off to form a square and lend the cavalry their support against any possible counter-attack.

Just when the oblique attack was reaching its furthest development we encounter faint signs that the Prussians were already searching for a more flexible scheme of battle tactics. Assaults by semi-independent columns were carried out at Burkersdorf and Freiberg at the close of the Seven Years War. More significantly still, Frederick outlined a truly Napoleonic sequence of combat in the *Political Testament* of 1768: to begin with he

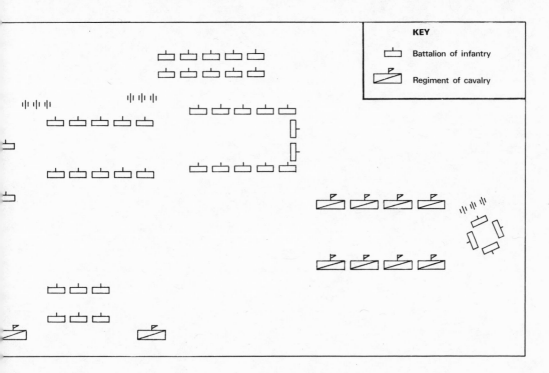

KEY

⊏⊐   Battalion of infantry

▱   Regiment of cavalry

would order the new long-range howitzers to lay down a heavy bombardment, then he would send forward the free battalions in open order (*en débandade*), and last of all he would throw in the cavalry in columns and achieve a decisive breakthrough in the enemy line.

It was ironic that Frederick commanded an army which, from his own strenuous efforts, was totally incapable of ever putting such an operation into effect – an army where the infantry had been beaten into bovine submission, and where the generals had lost the capacity for independent command.

11

Frederick's Army in Peace and War

The First Silesian War 1740–1742

On 22 June 1740 the salvoes of the 'Long Lads' echoed through the vaults of the Garrison Church at Potsdam as the old king was laid to rest. Crown Prince Frederick, or King Frederick II as we should now call him, inherited a kingdom of barren and scattered provinces, and a population of 2,500,000 souls. The army was made up of 83,000 troops, who were probably the best disciplined in Europe, though still largely untried in battle.

Frederick took over the army at a time when the leadership was subject to two strong and conflicting influences.

On the one hand the stern and inward-looking Prussia of the late king was represented by the Dessau princely clan. Its leader was the moustachioed and dark-visaged Prince Leopold of Anhalt-Dessau (1676–1747). The Old Dessauer's intellect was a limited but creative one, and he was famed as the virtual founder of the Prussian infantry. He had shown himself to be eminently fair to Frederick, during the bleak years the Crown Prince had spent in the early 1730s, but Leopold was never able to arouse the same friendship and trust in the new king that he had once inspired in the heart of his bosom companion Frederick William.

Three of Leopold's sons in particular were responsible for perpetuating the Anhalt-Dessau family influence into a new generation. The eldest, the Hereditary Prince Leopold Maximilian, was known as an intelligent and resolute officer who had made his name by commanding the Prussian infantry on the Rhine campaign with Prince Eugene. He died in 1751. The third son, Prince Dietrich, was by far the most sympathetic of the tribe. Frederick valued his friendship and soldierly qualities and made him a field-marshal in 1747. Dietrich, however, was weary of the military life, and in 1750 he was finally allowed to retire to his beloved Dessau, where he could spend his days hunting the deer through the oak forest beside the Elbe. Boswell came across him there in 1764, and describes him as 'just one of the old Germans, rough and cordial'.[1]

Prince Moritz, the fifth son, was a violent but good-natured buffoon and the favourite of his father. Old Leopold used to take him as a child to the hunts and reviews, but he conceived the disastrous experiment of bringing him up without any formal education. As an adult, therefore, *le prince sauvage* was just about capable of drawing his own signature, but he was unable to put down anything else on paper at all. According to a contemporary he possessed a 'great inclination to the military service; he loves his soldiers as a commander, and he loves his horses and his dogs. He treats them all in more or less the same way'.[2] His natural military talents gained him the Black Eagle on the field of Kesselsdorf and the promotion to field-marshal at Leuthen, but he remained unfit for independent command without the help of a good staff.

It was fortunate for the Prussian army that the power of the Dessau tribe was nullified to some degree by the humane and civilising influence of Kurt Christoph v. Schwerin

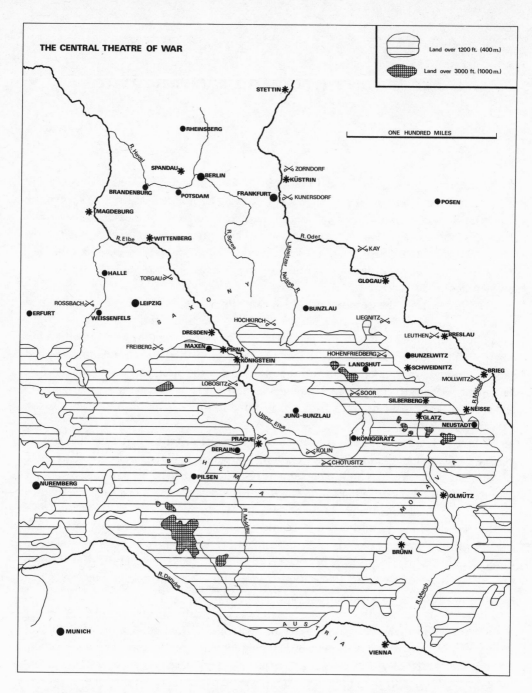

(1685–1757). A true man of the wider eighteenth-century world, Schwerin was born in what was then Swedish Pomerania, and he studied in his youth at the university of Leyden. He established excellent relations with Crown Prince Frederick, and he was promoted to field-marshal upon the new king's accession in 1740.

Everything conspired to set Schwerin and the Old Dessauer at odds. 'The gentle, philanthropic character of Schwerin, his humanity, his attractive appearance, his choice of educated company – all came into conflict with the raw, soldierly, rather harsh ways of the Prince.'[3] Oddly enough, it was Schwerin who excelled in the heat of battle, and Leopold who in Frederick's words ran about 'like a wet hen'.

Leopold and Schwerin collected fellow-spirits about themselves, which served to institutionalise their quarrel in the Prussian army for years to come. Prince Adolf v. Bernburg and the generals Fouqué and Goltz inclined to the Dessau party, while Ferdinand of Brunswick, Bevern, Duke Friedrich Eugen of Württemberg, General Forcade and the royal brothers Augustus William, Henry and Ferdinand were drawn by their temperament to Schwerin's side.

Carrying its factions with it, the Prussian army was launched into a war of conquest on 16 December 1740.

Frederick came to the throne with the determination to *corriger la figure de Prusse* after all the years during which his father had stood at the beck and call of the Habsburgs. He was presented almost at once with the opportunity of doing something profitable and dramatic, for in October the Habsburg dominions were inherited by a totally inexperienced ruler, the twenty-three-year-old girl Maria Theresa. Very soon powers like France, Bavaria, Saxony and Piedmont began to show an interest in snatching a prize from what seemed to be the imminent collapse of that enormous state, where the army was demoralised and the central administration was feeble and run-down.

The most suitable object for Frederick's own ambitions was undoubtedly the most northerly of the Habsburg possessions, the province of Silesia, 'a fine land, inhabited by an industrious population'.[4]

Strategically speaking, Silesia (now part of Poland) formed a part of the great north European plain which swept without interruption from the Urals to Ypres. The central tract of this plain was intersected by two considerable rivers, the Oder and the Elbe, which flowed transversely from south-east to north-west and passed through Prussian territory before they reached the sea. All this was very convenient from Frederick's viewpoint, for he could send armies with equal facility up the Oder into Silesia or further west up the Elbe into the heart of Saxony and Bohemia.

The Oder–Elbe plain was bordered along its southern edge by the long range of hills which separated the northern theatre from the Austrian provinces of Bohemia and Moravia (now part of Czechoslovakia).

Bohemia, the western province, was easy enough to conquer. It possessed no modern fortresses and the Prussians could bring their supplies up the Elbe to within three marches of the capital, Prague. By the same token, however, the Prussians had nowhere secure to establish their magazines in this part of the world – and well-stocked magazines were a necessity if Frederick wanted to follow the circuitous and difficult route south-east to Vienna.

After some unfortunate experiences in Bohemia Frederick concluded in later years that there was no way of finishing off the Austrians except by a direct drive on Vienna. This brought him to the necessity of pushing south through Moravia, the eastern province, and thus of dealing with the two fortresses of Olmütz and Brünn. Since Olmütz in particular was strong, and the Prussians were rather bad at sieges, the prospect of campaigning in Moravia was singularly unpleasant.

Making a crude generalisation, one might say that it was both easy and profitable for Frederick to snatch Silesia and invade Saxony. It was simple enough for him to carry the war on into Bohemia, though the exercise was somewhat pointless. Moravia, in contrast, was difficult to over-run, but offered Frederick a direct route to the seat of Habsburg power.

In December 1740, 27,000 Prussian troops assembled for the invasion of Silesia. Frederick was with old Leopold as he saw them gather, row upon row, and he remarked that it seemed strange that this multitude of men, resentful, and better armed and physically stronger than the king and his generals, should nevertheless shiver in their presence. The Old Dessauer simply replied: 'That's the marvellous effect of order, discipline and narrow supervision.'[5]

The Austrian garrison of Silesia was tiny, and by the end of January 1741 the bluecoats had swept all the way down to the border mountains with Moravia. Schwerin spearheaded the final push, and he regretted only that he had run out of his beloved Rhine wine in the process and was left with 'miserable beer'.[6]

Frederick meanwhile had made his entry to the Silesian capital of Breslau on 3 January. A citizen writes that the whole town was

> thronged with Brandenburg-Prussian officers and men – splendid and well set-up specimens who sported dashing uniforms. They attracted admiring gazes from everyone, and our Silesian women were excited with such passion that many of them must have been left with a little Brandenburger. Thus the Brandenburg–Prussian blood was imported into Silesia at the same time as the Low German dialect. While marching along the Ring a soldier saw the tower of the Elizabeth Church and called out to his comrades: 'Broder dat is eene schmuck Stadt, wann wy man dorfften hier blieven!' ('Now that's what I call a splendid town! It would be nice to stay here!')
>
> The Schweidnischer Keller was crammed with the Brandenburgers and sparkling with grenadier caps. The landlord did not know the Brandenburg six-pfennig piece and was unwilling to accept it until he received orders to take it with good grace. Our foreign guests smoked tobacco in the Keller, which had never been allowed before, and there was one witty grenadier who lit all the candles at two in the afternoon: they burned well into the night.[7]

Early in the spring the Austrian field-marshal Neipperg put an end to the celebrations by leading a force down from the hills, and the Austrians went on to pitch a camp in the snowy fields round the village of Mollwitz.

Frederick responded by throwing his army into the attack early on the morning of 10 April. Unfortunately there was some delay and confusion in arranging the army in order of battle, and before the Prussian infantry could get to grips the Austrian horse overthrew the slow-moving cavalry of Frederick's right. General v. d. Schulenburg, the cavalry commander, carried out a brave but hopeless counter-attack, and he was killed in horrible circumstances.

> First of all his horse was shot from beneath him, and then he took a cut across his face which left an eye hanging half-way down the cheek. He applied a handkerchief in an attempt to stanch the blood, but when he was mounting a fresh horse a flying shot smashed through his head and stretched him on the ground.[8]

Things were going so badly that Schwerin advised the young king to leave the field. Frederick took off at some speed, and the army did not see him again until the following night, by when he had ridden a circuit of thirty miles.

It was the engrained discipline of the Prussian infantry which saved the day. They opened a platoon fire and moved doggedly forward until the raw Austrian troops began to mass in terrified flocks around their colours. Field-Marshal v. Neipperg was glad when darkness fell and he could withdraw his army from the field.

Frederick set up camp at Mollwitz after the battle and embarked on the long process of putting right the shortcomings that had been revealed by the combat. He taught the cavalry to charge, he tried to make the artillery more mobile, and most important of all he set out to inculcate a sense of urgency and professionalism among the officers. Frederick set an example of diligence by embarking on his tours of the camp at four o'clock every morning, and he imposed a régime so spartan that over four hundred officers are said to have asked to resign. The French commander, Marshal de Belle-Isle, was impressed to see him drilling a battalion of the Garde in person.

> The weather was frightful and the snow was falling in large flakes, which did not prevent the battalion from exercising as if it had been a fine day. I had some inkling before I came of the army's discipline, obedience and exactitude, but I must say that they were driven to such a degree that I was ill-prepared for the reality.[9]

Frederick was not particularly anxious to try conclusions with the Austrians again for the moment. Hence the war in Silesia was prolonged in a stalemate until he came to terms with the Austrians on 9 October, walking off with the considerable prize of Lower (northern) Silesia. He thereby flouted an offensive alliance he had made with the French and Bavarians in June, a circumstance which did not bother him in the slightest.

By the end of 1741 Frederick had built up his army by five new regiments of foot, five of dragoons and five of hussars to a very respectable total of 117,600 combatants.

Assuming that the Austrians would be tied down by their war against the French and Bavarians, Frederick resumed operations in February 1742 and struck directly at Vienna by way of the almost unguarded province of Moravia. Zieten's hussars actually ranged to within sight of the towers of Vienna, but by then the main army's communications were dangerously threatened by a mass rising of the Moravian peasantry and the sorties that were being launched by the very active garrison of Brünn. Frederick accordingly drew back his army to Bohemia in the hope of finding a little rest.

In May there came unwelcome but unmistakable signs that the main Austrian army was on the move against him. Frederick ordered his scattered forces to assemble, and on the 14th he betook himself with two battalions of the Garde to the top of a hill near Chrudim.

> The weather was splendid [wrote a Prussian officer] and from our hill we had a wonderful view over the plains and mountains . . . our columns were converging on the plain from every side, as we could clearly make out from headquarters, but since they had to march through several gorges and valleys on the way, they seemed to be issuing from the heart of the mountains and the very bowels of the earth. *Parturiunt montes*, etc, as Horace wrote. But now, instead of the poet's 'mouse' the labouring mountains gave birth to strong and fine soldiers. The king himself seemed to be affected by the sight. As for me, I was in transports, though I could not help reflecting with a little bitterness about the mutability of human affairs, and how in fifty years there would be nothing left of these brave men but dust and ashes.[10]

Three days later the Austrians almost succeeded in bringing off a 'Mollwitz' in reverse when they descended unexpectedly on the Prussian camp at Chotusitz. The Prussian cavalry made a spirited but not particularly effective response: the regiments on the left broke clean through the Austrian lines and disappeared from view: on the right the cavalry stopped short after routing the first enemy line, and were themselves driven from the field.

By half past nine in the morning the cavalry battles were over and attention began to focus on the village of Chotusitz. The Prussian troops fell back under the first assault, but Hereditary Prince Leopold of Anhalt-Dessau managed to claw back the lost ground, and Frederick (unaccountably late) began to advance with the hitherto unengaged right wing of the Prussian infantry. The Austrian commanders appreciated that they had now lost whatever advantage they had gained from the first surprise, and so they withdrew their whitecoats from the field.

The instructive little victory of Chotusitz showed Frederick that his cavalry, though much improved, was still the least proficient element of his army. He saw that he must continue to build up his hussars, to prevent himself from being taken by surprise again, and he told his cuirassiers and dragoons that they must press on with the attack after the initial breakthrough without bothering overmuch to re-form their lines.

In order to avert any further unpleasantness Frederick put out feelers for a proper settlement. The Peace of Breslau (11 June 1742) rounded off Frederick's first military adventure, and established him as the rightful owner of the whole of Silesia and the adjacent county of Glatz. 1,300,000 new subjects were now to know the delights of Prussian rule.

The Second Silesian War 1744–1745

While the Austrians turned west to pursue their quarrel with the French and Bavarians, Frederick put his army through a series of strenuous reviews and raised nine field battalions and seven garrison battalions, two companies of foot *Jäger*, one squadron of mounted *Jäger* and twenty squadrons of hussars. By the late summer of 1744 he had at his disposal a combatant force of 94,500 infantry and 29,200 cavalry.

The Austrians meanwhile had been making spectacular progress against the allies, and in August 1744 Frederick saw it was time to embark on a new adventure beyond the mountains. He browbeat the Saxons into allowing him to march through their territory, and by taking this roundabout route he was able to break into Bohemia from the north-west. He encountered virtually no opposition, and on 16 September he reduced Prague after a short siege. His casualties to date numbered 50 dead and 110 wounded.

After this encouraging start Frederick lost his way. He struck south from Prague but was quite unable to find out where the main force of the Austrian army was hidden, let alone bring it to battle. Meanwhile the Austrian hussars and Croats swarmed on all sides, cutting the Prussian communications, intercepting couriers, and wiping out the vital foraging parties. When, at last, the Austrian army and a corps of Saxon auxiliaries did make a stand near Beneschau, Frederick discovered that the position was so well covered by ponds, streams and swamps that it would have been suicide to attack.

The second half of November found the Prussians in full retreat in Silesia. The hussar colonel v. Lojewsky recalled

> in this dreadful weather the snow, rain, storm and cold alternated every day. The ploughed-up roads were scarcely practicable, even for the riding horses, and with every mile we travelled the wheels of the many carts and guns made the mud still deeper. Remember also that we were in an exhausted land where each bundle of straw or hay cost a skirmish, and where the soldiers lacked for every necessity. It is not surprising that the number of sick mounted daily. The starving horses fell down in the shafts of the waggons, obstructing the narrow mountain paths and augmenting the difficulties the army encountered on the march.[11]

The losses were multiplied by a galloping desertion, which was particularly noticeable in the command of General v. Einsiedel as it withdrew from Prague, and there were scenes of anarchy when the shattered army finally reached Silesia. Estimates of the total cost of Frederick's Bohemian adventure range from 10,000 men to 30,000.

The near-catastrophic campaign of 1744 showed up once again the inability of the Prussians to cope with the enemy light troops. That at least was something which might be remedied to some degree by time and effort. What was much more alarming was the realisation that the Prussian army was an extremely brittle machine, liable to break up with frightening speed once the bonds of discipline were snapped. The spectre of 1744 remained at Frederick's shoulder for the rest of his life.

In the eventful year of 1745 the Austrians and their new-found friends the Saxons three times took the offensive in the border country, but on each occasion the Prussian army was able to steal back the initiative.

The fresh and starry night of 4/5 June found the Prussians marching across Lower Silesia to catch the enemy at Hohenfriedberg. The bluecoats passed across the front of the Austrian camp without mishap, and early in the morning the right wing bore down on the Saxons, who were ensconced behind an area of ponds, dykes and bushes. Here the decisive blow was dealt by the regiment of Alt-Anhalt, which advanced with shouldered muskets and turned the Saxons out of their position. By seven o'clock the Saxons were beaten and their allies were left without support.

On the left wing General v. Kyau, supported by General v. Zieten, threw forty-five squadrons of horse against the sixty-six squadrons of the Austrians and drove them back. Both the Prussian cavalry and the adjoining left wing of the infantry pushed some way on, veering further and further from the right wing of the army. Thus the Prussians split themselves asunder, and left a number of veteran regiments of Austrian infantry holding firm between the villages of Gunthersdorf and Thomaswaldau.

Fortunately the super-large regiment of Bayreuth Dragoons had been cunningly planted by General v. Gessler and their colonel Otto v. Schwerin in the gap in the Prussian line. Now that the attack on the left had run out of impetus the Bayreuth Dragoons put in one mighty charge, and as the smoke lifted the rest of the army saw that they were hacking their way through a mass of fleeing whitecoats. Twenty Austrian battalions were ridden down in the process, and the Bayreuth Dragoons returned with 2,500 prisoners and 66 captured colours. The defeat of the allied army was now complete.

Hohenfriedberg must be reckoned the first great victory of Frederick and his army. The discipline of the infantry had never been shown to greater advantage (even if some

The seal of the Bayreuth Dragoons. Granted in recognition of their charge at Hohenfriedberg

baleful tactical precedents were set, see p. 90). More gratifying still, the cavalry had at last repaid all the attention that had been lavished on them over the last few years. Not only had the Bayreuth Dragoons charged to stupendous effect, but the cavalry as a whole had got the better of the Austrian horse in an unequal combat. Zieten had performed well in his first battlefield command, and his regiment of hussars had not hesitated to join in the quarrels of their big brothers of the heavy cavalry.

The Austrians and Saxons came on again in September, and showing unusual enterprise the allied host tried to catch Frederick at a disadvantage in his strung-out camp at Soor on the 30th. They reckoned without the Prussian army's extraordinary speed of reaction: the twenty-six squadrons of the Prussian right evicted forty-five Austrian squadrons from a hilltop, while the Prussian infantry pushed manfully up the steep and open slopes to the left under a withering fire. By one in the afternoon the enemy had been pushed back into the woods from which they had only just emerged.

Just before the close of the year the enemy made one final effort, this time in the region of Dresden. Frederick and the main army were too distant to intervene, but Leopold of Anhalt-Dessau hastily gathered in the regiments that were quartered in Saxony and on 15 December he was able to bring the Saxons to battle at Kesselsdorf. With a grunt of 'In Jesu Nahmen Marsch!' the Old Dessauer set the bluecoats crunching over the frozen snow in a frontal attack, and two hours later the Saxons were in rout.

After Kesselsdorf the Dessau tribe reigned supreme, and the belief took root that no power could withstand a body of Prussian infantry advancing with shouldered muskets.

This time there was no question of an allied recovery. Dresden, the Saxon capital, surrendered two days later, and the Austrian army and the remnants of the Saxons fell back to the Bohemian border. On Christmas Day the combatants signed a treaty of peace at Dresden. The Saxons agreed to make over 1 million thalers as reparations, while the Austrians agreed to acknowledge Frederick as legitimate owner of Silesia. Frederick's Prussia could now take its place as one of the foremost military powers of Europe.

The inter-war period 1745–1756

Frederick needed to enlist scarcely 7,000 native Prussians to supply the losses of the last war. He made up the rest simply by holding on to the best of the Austrian and Saxon prisoners of war.

A dozen years later Frederick went to war again in the company of just 141,496 infantry and cavalry and some 1,700 gunners (84,770 infantry, 29,466 cavalry, with 4,080 infantry and 3,180 cavalry as additional supernumeraries; also 122 heavy guns and 250 battery pieces; 20,000 garrison troops). These 143,000-odd troops were very little more than he had had at the end of 1745, and they seemed very little to set against Austria's horde of 177,500 troops, not to mention the forces of Maria Theresa's potential allies.

In compensation Frederick's men had been schooled to a peak of proficiency in the inter-war reviews and manoeuvres, and their morale and solidity were never to be higher. Frederick later looked back with regret on that golden time when 'all the battalions, all the cavalry regiments were led by veteran commanders and tested officers – people of bravery and worth'.[12]

As for the higher leadership, Frederick was deprived of the services of Prince Leopold of Anhalt-Dessau, who went to his grave in 1747. Zieten's performance in the peacetime manoeuvres proved to be something of a disappointment (see p. 100), but Field-Marshal v. Schwerin won his way back to favour after the disasters of 1744 (for which he was unfairly blamed), and Frederick strengthened the ranks of the field-marshalate still further by attracting over to his side James Keith, who was one of the most outstanding of the Russian generals and 'a sensible, amiable man'.[13]

Keith spoke German badly and he was never able to win the complete trust of the Prussian officers, 'for they were accustomed to obeying only such leaders who were native Prussians and had risen through every rank of the military hierarchy'.[14] This in no way detracted from the esteem in which Keith was held by the king, who prized him for his professionalism, his conversation, his knowledge of the world and his unassuming ways.

> Keith was no lover of grandeur and state, and he gave almost his entire income to his mistress, a Finnish woman called Eva. She had good looks, intelligence and winning manners, and she lived in great style. She took his horses and his cooks, but Keith was content to drive around in a tiny cart and fetch his food from a small eating house.[15]

However, the field-marshals Keith and Schwerin, the younger generation of the Dessau clan and in fact the whole corps of generals were compelled to take second place to that mysterious figure, Generaladjutant Hans Carl v. Winterfeldt. 'Out of all the commanders whom Frederick chose to admit to his special confidence, he was undoubtedly the one who owned it in the fullest sense of the word.'[16]

Winterfeldt was born near Demmin in 1707, and he was brought up in a characteristic 'Pomeranian' fashion, lacking all education save the few scraps of knowledge that were imparted to him by a poor theological student and an old sergeant of grenadiers. In the early 1730s he was sent to Russia to help to train the army on Prussian lines, and he took the opportunity to make a useful marriage with Fräulein v. Maltzahn, the step-daughter of the Russian field-marshal Münnich. On his return to Germany, Winterfeldt accompanied Crown Prince Frederick on his Rhine campaign of 1734, which cemented a still more promising connection.

In the new reign Winterfeldt fought with distinction as a major at Mollwitz, and by the time of the Second Silesian War he had won a secure place in the royal trust. After the war Winterfeldt became a military factotum. He put the hussars in order, tested innovations in weapons, tactics and regulations, enticed foreign officers into the service, collected intelligence, and set in train the mobilisation of 1756.

'Few men,' wrote Warnery, 'have ever been endowed with such happy gifts, with such a pleasant countenance or a more warlike air; his orders were short and to the point.'[17] He was hard-working and intelligent, as well as brave, sociable and generous to his friends. But what many officers could not forgive in him was 'an overweening ambition which, when he was provoked, made him vengeful or even implacable'.[18] Winterfeldt was accused of sowing an antagonism between Frederick and his younger brothers, and, more seriously still, he was blamed for launching Prussia into the Seven Years War. This drastic step was variously attributed to his mortal hatred for everything French or to a personal feud with the Empress Elizabeth of Russia.[19]

It was through his listening posts in foreign parts that Winterfeldt detected what seemed to be ominous stirrings in international politics. Under the influence of Chancellor Kaunitz, Maria Theresa had been striving to wean the French away from their age-old hostility towards the house of Habsburg. The French remained unresponsive until early in 1756, when they got wind that Frederick had concluded a convention of neutrality with Britain. Fearing that they had been betrayed by Old Fritz, the French signed a defensive alliance with Austria at Versailles on 17 May.

Kaunitz harboured hopes of drawing Saxony and Russia into the new alignment of forces, though it is hardly likely that he would have been able to embroil these powers in a new war if Frederick had not precipitated matters by putting his army on an operational footing. The Austrians belatedly began to respond in kind, but the Saxons chose to cling to their neutrality despite all the sinister activity in the Prussian territory.

The Prussian concentration was complete by the last week of August 1756, and on the 29th the first elements of 63,000 troops crossed the Saxon border. War on a European scale was now inevitable.

Perhaps Frederick and Winterfeldt would not have dashed into their adventure quite so readily if they had taken better stock of their opposition. The Saxons, it is true, were feeble and riddled with treachery, while the Swedes (another potential enemy) were only a shadow of their former selves, but Frederick refused to see that the main antagonist, the Austrian army, had been transformed over the last ten years by the hard-working Empress Maria Theresa and her generals. As for the Russians, Frederick assumed that they must still be the same mob of *muzhiks* that Winterfeldt had seen in the 1730s.

The Seven Years War 1756–1763

Frederick envisaged his first campaign as a short, sharp, preventive action that would put him in possession of Saxony, eliminate a potential threat to Brandenburg (the Saxon border ran to within thirty miles of Berlin) and win him a valuable base for any further operations. 'Saxony,' he wrote, 'is like a sack of flour. You can beat it as often as you like and something will always come out.'

Frederick entered the city of Dresden without opposition, and he pushed the main body of the army forward to encircle the Saxon troops in their refuge at the camp of Pirna and Königstein, overlooking the sandstone gorge of the Elbe to the south of Dresden.

Meanwhile Prince Ferdinand of Brunswick led the right wing of the army into the Austrian territory of Bohemia, hoping to stake out quarters there for the winter. One of the eighteen-year-old lieutenants, Jakob v. Lemcke, took the opportunity to visit the little town of Aussig in order to taste 'the Bohemian wine, for which this neighbourhood is famous. But I had hardly entered one of the cellars than I was overcome by the concentration of vapours and had to be dragged out . . . I staggered back to the camp, not least because it was dangerous to stay in Aussig. The high hills on the far side of the Elbe were swarming with Croats, who shot down many individuals in the town'.[20] Finally the build-up of Austrian forces in north Bohemia became so threatening that Frederick had to leave Pirna under a reduced blockade and join Ferdinand with the main army.

Early on the morning of 1 October 1756 the Prussians emerged at the edge of the north Bohemian plain near Lobositz. There was little to be seen of the enemy, apart from some Croats who had ensconced themselves on a hill to the left, but the plain in front was shrouded in mist and Frederick sent forward a body of cavalry to sound out the way.

The horsemen returned in some disarray, having been mauled by a powerful body of Austrian cavalry. After this provocation the whole of the Prussian cavalry, more than 10,000 troopers altogether, surged forward out of control. A quarter of an hour later they were back, 'pursued by the Austrians until they were almost under our guns; then we witnessed the spectacle of horses dragging their riders along by one stirrup, or trailing their own intestines on the ground'.[21] Only now was it evident that the main Austrian army was present, drawn up cunningly behind a line of ponds, swamps and villages.

The only place where the Prussians could get at the enemy was on the hill on the left, where the Austrians had their Croats, and both armies began to feed more and more troops into what ultimately became the decisive struggle. Bevern's secretary Kistenmacher described the turning point.

> From the ditches came one salvo after another, but our troops could see nothing of the enemy through the thick growth of vines and bushes, for they were firing and reloading all the time on their knees . . . our boys had shot off all their ammunition, and they soon emptied the cartridge boxes of their dead and wounded comrades as well . . . In this sad state of affairs the Duke of Bevern came galloping . . . up to his regiment, and saw how the difficult terrain was forcing the men to fight in little groups instead of in close order . . . 'Lads!' he called to them, 'shoot, for God's sake! Shoot and get at them!' The men replied that they were out of ammunition. 'What!' shouted the duke, 'haven't you got bayonets? Go out and skewer the swine!' In an

167

The capitulation of the Saxons at Pirna

instant the soldiers stormed blindly at the enemy and bayoneted them in the ribs or reversed their muskets and smashed their heads with the butts.[22]

Prussians, Croats and Austrians, all intermingled, poured down the slopes into the plain in front of the village of Lobositz. Here the combat was taken up by the advance guard of the main Austrian army. Once more Bevern settled the issue. He poured howitzer fire into the houses, and then the troops broke into the village by individual battalions and drove the Austrians out.

The next morning revealed that all the enemy had stolen away from the field.

Such was the outcome of the first, and in some ways the most curious action of the war. This was an accidental 'encounter' which was none of Frederick's seeking, and indeed at one juncture the king had 'done a Mollwitz' and disappeared from the scene altogether. This did not prevent the Prussian army from acquitting itself well. The infantry got the better of the fight on the Lobosch hill, under very adverse circumstances, while the cavalry had shown that it was imbued with the right instincts, even if it had run out of control.

As for the enemy, they had shown their usual skill in choosing good defensive positions. What was new and somewhat ominous was the unexpected tenacity, confidence and precision of movement that they had shown in the fight. After the battle the saying went round in Frederick's army that 'they're not the same old Austrians!'[23]

In fact the Austrian commander, Field-Marshal v. Browne, had deliberately broken off the action. His purpose in fighting at Lobositz had been to fix the attention of the Prussians on the western side of the Elbe, thereby enabling him to slip a picked force up the east bank and help the Saxon army to escape into Bohemia. Browne duly marched a little corps to within sight of the Saxon camp, but all the Saxon generals managed to do was to pile up their soldiers in a sodden and starving mass under the cloud-wreathed height of Lilienstein. Finally on 17 October the whole Saxon army of 16 or 17,000 men laid down its arms.

The whole of civilised Europe was shocked by the scenes which followed. Colonel v. Katzler of the Gensd'armes began the sport by snatching 100 men from the Saxon Horseguards to make up for the losses his regiments had suffered at Lobositz, but then Frederick arrived at the scene and announced that he intended to incorporate the Saxon regiments as intact units into the Prussian army. The protesting soldiers were beaten into submission with sticks.

The Saxon troopers were scattered among the Prussian horse, but altogether ten regiments of Saxon infantry were taken over entire and shared among the generals, 'which gave rise to a tremendous promotion. Young men who would have considered themselves lucky to make lieutenant at thirty, were now advanced at sixteen'.[24]

Frederick certainly counted on a measure of desertion from the ex-Saxon units, but over the course of the following months the Saxon troops defected by entire battalions at a time. By the end of 1757 Frederick was left with just three regiments of infantry and one grenadier battalion, and even these were mostly composed of recruits raised individually in Saxony.

Frederick would have done much better to have split the Saxons up and incorporated them among his reliable old regiments, as Winterfeldt had suggested. It is difficult to understand why Frederick chose the other course. Perhaps he believed, like Prince Moritz, that the Saxons would be eager to fight for a Protestant king. Perhaps he was led astray by his own crass indifference to the feelings which move the hearts of ordinary men, or perhaps he was blinded by his inveterate hatred of things Saxon. Certainly there were times when Frederick seemed to be pursuing a private feud against the Saxons rather than a regular war.

THE INVASION OF BOHEMIA—PRAGUE AND KOLIN 1757

During the winter and spring of 1756/7 the Austrian diplomats were hard at work, and in the atmosphere created by Frederick's invasion of Saxony they encountered no great difficulty in persuading the greater part of Europe to enter the war on their side. It was not long before France, Russia, Sweden and the states of southern and western Germany were ranged with the Austrians and the refugee Saxons in a league that had as its object the dismemberment of Frederick's Prussia.

Calculating that the nascent coalition would be slow on its feet, Frederick resolved to get in a damaging blow at the Austrians before the other powers could intervene. Between 18 and 22 April 1757, 113,000 Prussian troops struck across the Bohemian border at four widely separated points. Frederick joined Moritz of Anhalt-Dessau inside Bohemia, and their combined forces passed by way of the field of Lobositz, where 'it was scarcely possible to stay on account of the evil stench which arose from the dead who had lost their lives in the recent action. The many graves were sufficient proof of the cost of this dearly-won victory of the Prussian army'.[25]

The Austrians fell back in confusion to a camp immediately to the east of Prague, and they made no attempt to disturb the proceedings when *notre vieux papa* Schwerin came up from eastern Bohemia with 54,000 troops and united with Frederick's army on the early morning of 6 May.

Frederick at once sent the combined force on a circuitous march south-east then south, intending to roll up the Austrian position from its right, and the movement of the thousands of horses and troops threw up great clouds of dust which made the day seem 'like the end of the world'.[26]

The cavalry of the Prussian left wing was leading the way, and soon it was hotly engaged with the Austrian horse in what the hussar colonel Warnery called

> a real mêlée, such as you see in battle paintings. Since I had lost my own trumpeter I used a trumpeter I had captured from the Austrians instead, and I had one of my hussars hold the bridle of his horse. When I had succeeded in rallying a squadron I discovered I was almost upon a large part of the enemy army, for the dust had prevented me from seeing more than four paces. Finally we began to retire – or more accurately to flee in confusion to put a distance between us and the enemy artillery.[27]

At this critical juncture General v. Zieten led twenty-five squadrons of fresh hussars round from the reserve and took the Austrian cavalry in the right flank. The resistance of the Austrian horse collapsed. Only 3,600 kept together in any kind of order, and all the rest scattered over the landscape of Bohemia.

Meanwhile the Austrian commanders were fast lining the remainder of the eastern edge of the plateau with infantry and batteries. Winterfeldt appreciated the urgency of the situation, and threw in an improvised attack of fourteen battalions. The result was a massacre. The troops were under orders to advance with shouldered muskets, and as they floundered in the boggy meadows they had no means of hitting back at the Austrians, who were showering them with bullets and canister. Winterfeldt was hit in the neck by a musket ball and fell unconscious from the saddle, whereupon the regiments behind him began to give way.

From a little distance old Field-Marshal v. Schwerin saw his own regiment fall back and he knew it was high time to intervene. Riding forward he seized a green regimental colour from the hand of a *Junker* of his second battalion and called to his men 'Heran mein Kinder!' He had scarcely covered twelve paces when he was deluged in a charge of canister shot. One ball took him behind the ear, one in the heart and three in the stomach. His dying hand let the colour fall to the right of the horse, and he himself toppled over to the left. His horrified regiment took to its heels.

Meanwhile a wide gap was opening at the crucial angle between the main Austrian army, which was still facing north, and those regiments which had been moved to the south-east and had fought to such effect against Winterfeldt and Schwerin. Now that the enemy had pulled themselves off balance Frederick threw eighteen battalions into the breach and cut the Austrian host in two – a move that was going to inspire Napoleon at Austerlitz in 1805.

After this masterpiece of opportunism the Prussians took the main Austrian army in the right flank and began to push it towards Prague. The Austrians resisted desperately all the way, and in the bitter fighting Lieutenant v. Lemcke (our friend from Aussig) received a bullet in the behind. 'I crawled away on all fours behind a hill, where I was astounded to encounter a great number of officers and NCOs. Some were wounded, but most were just looking for cover. I espied the sergeant-major of my regiment's *Leibcompagnie*, though I dare not mention his name because he afterwards became a *Kriegsrat*.'[28]

Prince Henry, the king's brother, proved to be one of the genuine heroes. He rode from one battalion to another in his sodden uniform (he had been submerged in a stream) and he urged the exhausted men forward with his sword until the Austrian army was reduced to a milling mass outside the gates of Prague.

Thus Frederick had taken on an Austrian force of approximately equal size and had driven it from its prepared position in the face of almost every conceivable obstacle and accident. In every way the battle of Prague represented Frederick's most notable victory to date. At the same time the Prussians had plenty of food for thought. They had lost over 14,000 men (actually more than the Austrians) and among that number were included Field-Marshal v. Schwerin and what Frederick called 'the pillars of the Prussian infantry'.

After his stupendous if costly victory Frederick hoped that the Austrians would ask for peace. However, the 49,000 refugee troops in Prague managed to put themselves in some kind of order, and Frederick's army raged powerlessly outside the ramparts, surrounded by all the hideous aftermath of the battle.

Thus the initiative gradually passed back to the Austrians. Under a new commander, the imperturbable Field-Marshal v. Daun, they built up a new army of 54,000 men from recruits, some of the fugitives from the field of Prague and such regiments as had been unable to arrive in time for the battle. Daun hovered annoyingly about the upper Elbe, only thirty or forty miles to the east of Prague, and Frederick became so concerned at this growing threat that he left Field-Marshal Keith to watch Prague while he took the main army off in search of Daun.

Early on 18 June Frederick found the Austrians in possession of a low range of hills which ran to the south of the *Kaiserstrasse* near Kolin. In essentials the king aimed to follow the scheme he had adopted at Prague. That gruff *Naturkind* Major-General v. Hülsen was to lead the way with an advance guard of seven battalions and pass round the right, or eastern flank of the Austrian army. Frederick told off Tresckow to march in close support with nine battalions of the left wing of the main army, and he instructed Prince Moritz to follow in Tresckow's tracks with the remainder of the wing. The rest of the army was to be 'refused'.

After a tedious wait Hülsen and the left wing got under way at noon, and to the Austrians it seemed that the sudden flash of the sun on the shouldered weapons ran through the enemy regiments like a lightning strike. Hülsen's battalions stormed through the flaming streets of the village of Krzeczhorz, and with the support of Tresckow's command they went on to capture two batteries of heavy guns in the rear.

Under circumstances that are still unclear (though it seems that Frederick had a hand in them) Moritz hung back with the rest of the left wing instead of following in the wake of the advance guard. So it was that the troops had to wait a little longer in the appalling heat, while the Austrian guns continued to bombard them with shot. When the advance was finally resumed the regiments made straight for the front of the range of hills, the whole extent of which was now covered with Austrian troops.

Major-General v. Manstein, with the division next in line, had meanwhile halted under a galling fire from the Croats who were infiltrating through the fields of tall corn. Misunderstanding a comment from a *Flügeladjutant*, Manstein detached one of his battalions to clear out the Croats. Once the forward movement had begun, however, four more battalions followed suit and headed directly for the Austrian position.

Thus the advance guard remained without support, and the intended flanking movement was converted into a frontal battle in which the Austrian superiority in numbers, guns and position was bound to tell.

Lieutenant v. Prittwitz records that at first the Prussian troops were glad to be on the move again, but scarcely had they advanced a few steps when

> we began to feel the effect of the enemy artillery . . . A storm of shot and howitzer shells passed clear over our heads, but more than enough fell in the ranks to smash a large number of our men . . . I glanced aside just once and I saw an NCO torn apart by a shell nearby: the sight was frightful enough to take away my curiosity . . . we had to wind our way through the long corn, which reached as far as our necks, and as we came nearer we were greeted with a hail of canister that stretched whole clumps of our troops on the ground. We still had our muskets on our shoulders, and I could hear how the canister balls clattered against our bayonets.[29]

While the commands of Moritz and Manstein battled their way up to the ridge, the issue of the day was already being decided on the left wing. The Prussian cavalry in that part of the world was commanded by the octogenarian General v. Pennavaire (called 'The Anvil' because he was beaten so often), and it showed such passivity that the Austrian and Saxon horse swept it from the field. The only units which acted with any spirit were the well-tried Normann Dragoons and Colonel v. Seydlitz's regiment of Rochow Cuirassiers. The enemy cavalry now swept down on the Prussian battalions and took them in front, flank and rear.

Prittwitz believed that the day was won right up to the moment when hoof-beats pounded up from behind. 'The cavalry were upon me before I could really make them out. The animal that hit me was executing a flying jump, and I felt the knee in my back as I was flung to the earth. I received a cut on my head, whereupon a mass of horses came up from behind and stormed over me without causing me the least injury.'[30] This was the work of the Austrian cavalry. To his right the Saxons were riding over the regiment of Prince Henry, where 'some of the poor *Junker* were still children. The colours were snatched from their hands, and they themselves were cut down or wounded'.[31]

By now the catastrophe was general. Nineteen battalions of the left wing and advance guard were being chopped up by the cavalry, and Manstein's command was decimated by the artillery. The cavalry of the left wing and reserve were in disorder, and Zieten, who had not been on his best form in this battle, was laid unconscious by a canister shot which struck him in the head.

At this interesting turn the First Battalion of the Garde arrived on the scene in their immaculate regimentals. Their presence was doubly welcome, for they and the Gemmingen grenadiers were virtually the only troops in a fit state to hold off the enemy. As they protected the retreat of the shattered army the guardsmen were three times surrounded by the hostile cavalry, but on every occasion the third rank turned about and delivered volleys to the rear. In the course of this dignified withdrawal the battalion left behind a trail of 24 officers and 475 men.

Altogether some 10,000 Prussian dead and severely wounded remained on the field of Kolin. The prisoners, about 5,000 of them, were marched away under an escort of cavalry.

> From every point of view we formed a pitiable parade. Everybody had to march to the destination on foot – staff officers, captains, subalterns and men all mixed together.

A number of people had lost their coats and paraded in their white waistcoats and breeches, some of which were stained with blood. One of the prisoners was limping, another had his arm in a sling that was improvised from a handkerchief, while a third appeared with a handkerchief wound about his head.[32]

The full implications of the defeat at Kolin made themselves felt over the course of six or seven agonising weeks. The Prussians had to give up the blockade of Prague, but Prince Moritz did his oafish best to restore the army to some kind of order and Frederick harboured hopes of being able to keep his forces in northern Bohemia. Unfortunately the second royal brother, Prince Augustus William, was forced to abandon an important position at Jung-Bunzlau, and late in July all the Prussian forces recoiled across the border into Saxony.

Frederick was furious, and on 29 July he arrived at Bautzen to settle accounts with the Crown Prince and his generals. In a ferocious tone Frederick ordered Augustus William and General v. Schmettau to leave his presence on the instant and never dare to appear before him again. The prince was weeping as he rode off. 'The army regretted him, but in one or two days it had forgotten all about him, just as it forgot about Field-Marshal v. Schwerin after he had been killed.'[33] The wretched prince died of a brain tumour on 12 June 1758.

With the Austrians full of fight, and the Prussian army back in Saxony, Frederick now had to face up to the realities of war with the enormous hostile coalition. By the middle of September the Swedes were in Prussian Pomerania, the Russians had invaded East Prussia, and the French had brought about the surrender of the only friendly force on the Continent – the Duke of Cumberland and his British-subsidised army of Protestant German contingents.

The disaster at Kolin, which precipitated Frederick into this crisis, had been the consequence of a chapter of misunderstandings and accidents, as well as the result of the passivity of the cavalry and infantry tactics of the same murderous kind that had cost Frederick so many men at Prague. Out of his generals Krosigk and Manstein were now dead, Zieten and Ingersleben wounded, and Tresckow and Pannwitz in the hands of the enemy.

The one consolation which Frederick could draw from the affair was that he had lighted upon the 'first commander he had yet seen who could exploit the capabilities of cavalry to the fullest degree'.[34] This paragon among commanders was Colonel Friedrich Wilhelm v. Seydlitz.

Seydlitz was born in 1721 at Calcar in Cleves, the son of an officer of dragoons. He spent his formative years as page to the Margrave of Brandenburg-Schwedt, with wonderful consequences for his horsemanship but disastrous results for his morals. He passed into the army and came to know all three branches of the cavalry service – as an hussar (*Rittmeister* in the Natzmer Regiment 1743), as a dragoon (commandant of the Württemberg Regiment 1752) and lastly as a cuirassier (commandant of the Rochow Regiment 1753).

As the sole cavalryman who had shown any dash in the last battle Seydlitz was awarded the Black Eagle and promoted to major-general. The advancement to lieutenant-general followed a few months later, which was very rapid promotion indeed, though 'nobody resented his good fortune, such was the warm esteem in which he was held in the circle of Frederick's army'.[35] J. A. v. Retzow, who was then a very young officer, wrote:

> He was distinguished among the other commanders for his personal bravery, sure *coup d'oeil*, and capacity for judicious and swift movements. No less remarkable were his cheerfulness and his striving, not simply to avoid injustice to others, but to put forward their services in their real light and contribute to their reward. It is not surprising that he won the hearts of his subordinates.[36]

At once chivalrous and realistic, Seydlitz admired the tenacity of the Russians, and he even found a good word to say about the French at Rossbach, whom he described as good troops who were poorly led. On top of this we have the elusive element of style. 'His hat, his coat, his boots, his breeches, all were imitated. A graceful rider, as well as a winning speaker, he attracted approval, admiration and friendship.'[37]

The worst enemy that Seydlitz had was himself. He could rarely refrain from speaking his mind to the king (who was not one to relish honest talk), and by his drinking and whoring he sometimes contrived to put himself out of action for weeks at a time.

THE 'BERLIN WATCH PARADE' AT BAY – ROSSBACH AND LEUTHEN 1757

In his desperate situation Frederick appreciated that it would have been fatal for him to try to hold on to every last yard of territory. Making the best of his central position, he evolved instead a strategy of interior lines, by which he aimed to strike with a concentrated army against each enemy force in turn, destroying it on the spot or at least preventing it from joining up with the other hostile armies.

Thus in the later summer of 1757 Frederick left the Duke of Bevern in Silesia to look out for the Austrians in the east, while he himself held the main army in Saxony and tried to settle accounts with a large allied army that was approaching from the opposite direction. This latter force constituted the most bizarre set of enemies that Frederick ever had to deal with. One element consisted of an army of 24,000 French – a military people who had declined suddenly and sadly since the 1740s. The German townspeople were scandalised by the sybaritic style of life of the officers, and the way in which the soldiers were allowed to march along with loaves of bread stuck on their bayonets. The rest of the force was made up of a wild assortment of German contingents, known officially as the *Reichs-Truppen* but with more accuracy as the *Reissaus-Truppen* ('bug-out troops').

The French and Germans united in August in a strength of 50,000 men, but they were extremely unwilling to come to grips with Old Fritz. They not only evacuated Erfurt in the face of Frederick's main army, but on 19 September they pulled a large force out of Gotha in some panic when Seydlitz materialised outside with just 1,500 cavalry.

> Only a few soldiers were captured, but in compensation the Prussians took all the more valets, lackeys, cooks, *friseurs*, courtesans, field chaplains and actors – all the folk inseparable from a French army. The baggage of many commanders also fell to the Prussians – whole chests full of perfumes and scented powders, and great quantities of dressing gowns, hair nets, sun shades, nightgowns and parrots.[38]

Frederick could not afford to waste any more time in that part of the world, and so he fell back eastwards to a more central position at Butstädt and allowed his troops a little rest. There was, however, a brief outburst of excitement towards the middle of October when the Austrians, who had meanwhile entered Silesia in considerable force, sent General Haddik with 3,500 light troops on a raid against Berlin. Haddik raced across the sandy plain and reached the defenceless city on 16 October, causing considerable consternation in the royal palaces.

Haddik was content to demand a 'contribution' of 215,000 thalers, and 'after everything was agreed, he asked the Magistracy for a dozen pairs of ladies' gloves stamped with the municipal coat of arms, for he wanted to give a present to his Empress'.[39] Prince Moritz and 8,000 Prussian troops were now pounding up the road to Berlin, and so the Austrians stole away with their cash and their gloves on the 17th. The episode is interesting on account of its very irrelevance, for it showed how little the survival of Prussia depended upon the capital and how very much upon the king and his army.

Emboldened by the absence of Frederick, the *Kombinierte Kaiserliche Reichs-Exekutions-Französische Armee* marched east and showed its nose beyond the Saale. This time the king was not going to let the allies escape. He executed a rapid about turn, chased the enemy over the Saale, forced a crossing at Weissenfels, and by 4 November was facing them across a swampy valley near the village of Rossbach.

The allies' confidence began to return (after all, they had odds in their favour of nearly two to one), and the commanders hatched a great scheme for marching round the southern flank of the Prussian army and unseating Frederick from his position. The German chief Hildburghausen intended to bring on a fight in the process, but the French marshal Soubise merely hoped that Frederick would pick up his bags and go away. At half past eleven on the morning of 5 November 1757 the allied army duly lurched off to the beating of drums and the shrilling of bugles and fifes.

Frederick was at first slow to respond to the threat, but at half past two in the afternoon the tents of the Prussian camp collapsed 'just as if they had been pulled by a string in some theatrical scene', and three-quarters of an hour later a battery of sixteen heavy cannon and two howitzers rang out from the Janus Hill: the anxious country-people testified that at that moment the ground miles away 'trembled under our feet, and the noise exceeded the worst roll of thunder'.[40]

While the crawling allied army was still strung out in column of march, Seydlitz swept over a ridge with thirty-eight squadrons and scattered the advance guard of cavalry. The Prussian infantry, racing along behind, wheeled into the path of the allied army like a pivoting gate, and reduced the French and German infantry to disorder in less than fifteen minutes.

Seydlitz now launched his cavalry in a final and devastating charge, and the Prussian troopers hewed away at the defenceless mobs without mercy. Far more of the allies were cut down in the pursuit than in the actual combat, and 'the roads were strewn with French cuirasses and hats, and great riding boots which their owners had thrown aside in order to escape more easily in their shoes and socks. The sunken track at Markwerben was full of hacked-down Frenchmen'.[41]

The Prussians had suffered a total of 548 casualties in *la bataille amusante*, but the allies lost 5,000 dead or wounded in the battle, and a further 5,000 who were captured afterwards or delivered up by the peasants. In Frederick's army we are evidently dealing with a very formidable military machine indeed.

For the immediate future Frederick knew that his success had done little more than win him the freedom to settle accounts with the Austrians in the east, where the war had been going badly. On 7 September a force of 28,000 Austrians had swooped down on Moys (near Görlitz) where Winterfeldt had 13,300 men guarding the communications between Saxony and Silesia. Winterfeldt had never completely recovered from the wound he had sustained at Prague, and quite probably this circumstance accounts for the ease with which the Austrians were able to surprise him in broad daylight and push three of his grenadier battalions from the vital Jäckelsberg height. Winterfeldt led the regiments of Manteuffel and Tresckow in a desperate counter-attack, but he was shot from his horse and the move promptly collapsed. After the action the enemy found the body on the hillside. He had been shot in the back, which may not be unconnected with the fact that the regiment of Tresckow was made up largely of Catholics from Upper Silesia.

The detachment which had overwhelmed Winterfeldt now went on to capture the brand new fortress of Schweidnitz on 13 November, which gave the main Austrian army of 54,000 men a secure communication with its base in Bohemia. Finally the Austrian host closed in on Breslau, where the unfortunate Bevern stood at bay with just 28,000 troops, whom he disposed in a wide arc to the west of the city. The Austrians launched their attack on 22 November. The Prussian flanks held firm for a time, but at two in the afternoon the centre of their over-extended position collapsed and the army flowed back on Breslau.

Bevern decided to withdraw out of harm's way to Glogau in north-eastern Silesia, but before the retreat began he was captured while making a reconnaissance on 24 November. The orphaned army marched away 'any old how, without order or formation, pillaging the villages on the way. There were no punishments – we excused ourselves by claiming that we were denying provisions to the enemy, but the truth was that we never expected to come that way again'.[42] The city of Breslau was abandoned to its fate, and the garrison capitulated on 25 November.

Frederick had set out with his army from Leipzig on 13 November, and he was marching due east into Silesia at a rate of a dozen miles a day. He was too late to avert the catastrophe which overtook Bevern, but General v. Zieten gathered up what was left of the defeated force and rejoined Frederick, giving him a total of 35,000 men. On 3 December 1757 the army reached Neumarkt, which lay within striking distance of the camp which the Austrians had taken up near Breslau.

Frederick informed his assembled generals that he intended to attack the three-fold stronger Austrian host wherever he found it, and he asked the commanders to spread the news among the regiments. He ended by threatening that 'if any regiment of cavalry shall fail to crash straight into the enemy, when ordered, I shall have it dismounted immediately after the battle and turned into a garrison regiment. If any infantry battalion so much as begins to waver, it will lose its colours and its swords, and I shall have the braid cut from its uniform'.

This heartening utterance represented the nearest that the austere Frederick ever came to appealing to the spirit of his men. It tells us a lot about the Prussian army that his words engendered scenes of emotional enthusiasm in the camp. 'The old warriors, who had already won so many battles under Frederick, shook each other by the hand and promised to stand by one another loyally. They made the young troops swear not to shrink before the enemy, but to go straight at them regardless of the opposition'.[43] Many years after the war the cynical Kaltenborn joined that army and he solemnly testifies that he saw hardened old veterans reduced to tears whenever they repeated the magical speech.[44]

A mist hung over the snow-dusted ground as the Prussian army made for the Austrian camp near Leuthen at first light on 5 December 1757. The cavalry of the advance guard got the proceedings off to a good start by repulsing a body of enemy horse near the village of Borne. The Austrian army at once responded by advancing a thousand yards from its camp to its battle position – a line which stretched across four miles of open country from the hamlet of Nippern in the north to that of Sagschütz in the south. The large village of Leuthen (which gave its name to the coming battle) stood on the left centre. 'The Austrians, for once, were giving battle in the open field. They stood in endless great lines, and they could hardly credit their senses when they saw the little body of Prussians advancing to attack them.'[45] They gave Frederick's army the name of the 'Berlin watch-parade'.

Frederick rode forward some distance from Borne in the company of Prince Moritz. From what he saw he decided to send his army on a long march south and then roll up the Austrian army from its left. A low line of hills extended in that direction, and he counted on the ridge giving him cover for part of the way. It was, however, very important to keep the enemy in a state of anxiety for their *right* wing, which lay behind and to the right of Borne, and to this end he made parts of the first and second columns of his army go through a show of deploying into battle order. The Austrian high command took the bait, and obligingly moved the generals Lucchese and Serbelloni with the disposable reserve of cavalry and infantry to bolster up the 'threatened' right wing.

Meanwhile the Prussian army executed a right turn round and through Borne, and by some complicated manoeuvres the king managed to juggle the original formation of four columns 'by wings' into an order of two columns 'by lines'. As the move to the south gradually became evident to the Austrians they merely assumed that Frederick must have renounced all thought of battle for that day, but soon after noon, when the sun dispersed the last of the mist, Frederick's army executed another turn, this time half-left, which brought it into a deadly attacking position at right angles to the Austrian left flank.

Poised to strike the first blow were the six battalions of the advance guard under Prince Karl of Bevern, with Zieten and the right wing of the cavalry guarding his open flank. Then came Major-General v. Wedell with three further battalions, and lastly the main army, which was echeloned away to the left in battalion *Staffeln* at fifty-pace intervals. Now that he was so close to bringing off what he had failed to achieve at Prague and Kolin, Frederick was determined not to spoil the effect by too much haste. He rode slowly from right to left, pointing out the objectives to the officers, and finally at one in the afternoon the somewhat anxious Prince Moritz rode with his watch in his hand to announce that there remained only four hours of daylight.

A free corporal in the advance guard regiment of Meyerinck describes the moments that followed. 'In front we had the whole Imperial army, whose size we could scarcely take in, and behind us there was the entire Prussian army . . . drawn up in battle order. Our army advanced with sounding music, as if on parade. Its order was as magnificent as at any review at Berlin, for it was marching under the eyes of its great monarch.'[46]

As luck would have it, the Prussian attack fell upon the least reliable troops in the Imperial army – fourteen battalions of Württembergers, with some Bavarians in support. Marching half-left Wedell's command threw three battalions of the Württembergers from the Kiefenberg at bayonet-point, while on the right Karl v. Bevern helped Zieten's fifty-three squadrons to repulse a determined counter-attack by the Austrian general Nádasti. The whole operation was supported by the heavy artillery, which was advancing rapidly from one battery site to the next.

The Austrians march out of Breslau, 21 December 1757. They are piling their muskets to the left of the centre. Note the fifer (a negro) and drummers on the flank of the Prussian battalion in the foreground

The Austrians retreated on Leuthen village, 'whither a whole mob of fugitives retired, filling every house, garden and corner in the place'.[47] Now at last the Austrian commanders appreciated how badly they had been tricked by Frederick, and they sent successive bodies of troops to shore up the collapsing left flank: first of all some individual battalions of the second line, then the reserve corps and finally the entire army. In the haste and disorder the troops were in some places piled 100 deep, but the officers eventually contrived to build up the semblance of a new line, extending on either side of Leuthen along a frontage of 1,800 paces.

After a brief pause the Prussian army moved forward again at half past three. There was a particularly hot fight for the walled churchyard at Leuthen, where the Franconian regiment of Roth Würzburg was holding fast, but the Germans were finally overcome after the Third Battalion of the Garde under Captain v. Möllendorff (the future field-marshal) broke down the gate at the western side. After Leuthen had been cleared the Prussian advance came to a halt in a standing fire-fight along a line to the north of the village.

The decision came towards five o'clock, when the snow was gleaming red with the setting sun. The Austrian cavalry general Lucchese gathered seventy squadrons and manoeuvred to carry out an attack on the left flank of the struggling Prussian infantry. This dangerous development was detected by Lieutenant-General v. Driesen (the commander of the left wing of the Prussian cavalry) and before the Austrians could launch their charge they were themselves taken in the right flank by thirty-five squadrons of cuirassiers and the ubiquitous Bayreuth Dragoons. Thirty further squadrons hastened up from the Prussian reserve to join in the fight, and the mass of struggling cavalry bore down on the Austrian infantry, which finally broke and fled.

The night was closing fast, but Frederick determined on one last push north to the bridge at Lissa, to prevent the Austrians from planting themselves behind the line of the Weistritz. He collected three battalions of grenadiers and the Seydlitz Cuirassiers and hastened through the falling snow to Lissa, where at seven in the evening the grenadiers turned the Austrians out of the houses which covered the bridge. The whole army followed in Frederick's track.

The troops marched on in a silence that could only have been produced by their reflections on having survived that great bloody day. But suddenly the quiet was broken by a grenadier who wounded the familiar hymn *Nun danket alle Gott*. Every man was awakened as if from a deep sleep, and, transported with gratitude to Providence, for their survival, more than twenty-five thousand troops sang the chorale with one voice through to the end. The darkness of the night, the voices of the troops, and the horror of the battlefield, where you stumbled upon a corpse at almost every step, combined to give the episode a solemnity which was easier to feel than describe.[48]

In his headquarters at Lissa the king assembled Moritz of Dessau, Driesen, Zieten, Retzow, Wedell and his own young brother Ferdinand, and gave them the *Parole* and the orders for the following morning. He added that 'This day will transmit the glory of your name and our Nation to all posterity.'[49]

Frederick's circles believed that Leuthen was the finest of the king's victories. Historians are inclined to agree. His 'oblique attack', evolved over the years, was here used to the fullest effect, and the army that he beat at Leuthen was not a mob like the one he had defeated at Rossbach a month before, but a highly professional force which had three times got the better of the Prussians in recent combats.

Within his own army each of the elements had given of its best. The cavalry earned the credit of deciding the final issue in the Prussian favour, but what was more significant was the new emphasis that was given to fire-power, a tactical component which had been sadly neglected by the Prussians since 1745. The infantry battalions had taken their ammunition waggons into action for the first time, and they were able to sustain what was possibly the hottest fire-fight of Frederick's reign (some men fired over 180 rounds). As for the gunners, they moved their *Brummer* and other heavy pieces from one position to another with remarkable facility, and managed to lend effective support to the rest of the army throughout the action.

Lastly the Prussian army had gone into action in a highly emotional state, which probably came from the fact that the 'Berlin watch-parade' was the thinned-down, purged and refined native remnant of the less selective hordes that had been beaten at Kolin, Moys and Breslau.

The defeated Austrians recoiled towards the border mountains, and in his mental confusion their commander Prince Charles of Lorraine left 17,000 troops stranded at Breslau. These surrendered as prisoners of war on 20 December.

Thus ended the extraordinarily eventful year of 1757. After the triumph of Prague and the disaster of Kolin Frederick had contrived to eliminate both the Franco-German and the Austrian armies from the vital theatre of war in the northern plain. He could now think of carrying the war once again into Austrian territory and of settling matters with the Russians, who still loomed in the east.

After the distressing experiences of 1744 and the early summer of 1757, Frederick made up his mind that it was pointless to make war in the empty expanse of Bohemia. He resolved instead to strike by way of Moravia directly at the heart of the Austrian monarchy.

Schweidnitz, the last Austrian foothold in Silesia, fell on 18 April after a tiresome siege. Now that their rear was clear, the Prussians swept over the Moravian border hills at the end of the month. Frederick had stolen a clear week on the enemy commander Daun, and on 3 May the blue columns united in the plain of the upper March in the strength of 55,000 troops. Frederick's objective was to reduce Olmütz, which was the best-found of all the Austrian fortresses, and the one important obstacle on the route to Vienna.

Frederick placed Olmütz under blockade on 20 May, and entrusted the direction of the siege to Colonel v. Balbi, the one technician who had emerged with an enhanced reputation from the recent siege of Schweidnitz. Unfortunately the king was unable to restrain his natural instinct to meddle in what was better left alone. He ordered the artillery to fire with reduced charges (which meant that the guns could not carry to the fortress), and he misaligned a new trench (which brought the wretched troops under enfilade fire from the Austrian cannon). All the time Field-Marshal v. Daun lurked dangerously in the neighbourhood with the Austrian army of relief.

With the siege of Olmütz dragging out at inordinate length, Frederick had to summon up a fresh ammunition convoy from Silesia. The resourceful Lieutenant-Colonel v. d. Mosel was made responsible for the operation, and he contrived to collect 4,000 waggons and send them south under the escort of 9,000 troops, who were mostly recruits and reconvalescents hailing from a variety of regiments. The Austrians got wind of the move from their sympathisers in Silesia, and early on 30 June two of their most enterprising commanders closed in on the convoy near Domstadtl – Loudon from the east and Siskovics from the west. 'They directed their cannon against the *Wagenburg*, shot the horses dead, blew up the powder carts and created the most appalling confusion.'[50] The escorting force was cut clean in two, with losses of 2,386 troops, and all save 100 waggons were destroyed or lost.

Frederick at once raised the siege of Olmütz and abandoned his great design of the offensive against Austria. Indeed the enemy managed to get across the most convenient route to Silesia and wreck the magazine at Königgrätz, and Frederick was only too thankful to be able to slip back to Silesia unscathed early in August.

AGAINST THE RUSSIANS – GROSS-JÄGERSDORF 1757 AND ZORNDORF 1758

The abortive campaign of Olmütz represented the last of Frederick's adventures south of the border mountains. Yet again he had been reminded that the Austrians were virtually unbeatable in their own sphere of strategic dominance, and now he could no longer put off the task of dealing with yet another antagonist – the much-improved army of the Russian empire.

At the end of June in the previous year the Russian field-marshal Apraksin had moved into the isolated province of East Prussia with a green-coated horde of 55,000 troops. He took the little coastal fortress of Memel on 5 July and advanced by way of Insterburg on the provincial capital, Königsberg. Near Gross-Jägersdorf the way was barred by Field-Marshal v. Lehwaldt and a corps of 26,000 Prussians.

As we have seen, Frederick's 'strategy of interior lines' involved the monarch in taking personal command of a powerful and mobile striking-force. It was an unfortunate consequence of the system that small Prussian corps were scattered in penny packets over the other theatres of war, where their commanders waited to be crushed by overwhelming hosts (as at Moys and Breslau), or plunged into semi-suicidal attacks for which they were temperamentally unfitted. Thus on 30 August 1757 the old and worthy Lehwaldt committed his rather bad little army to an assault on the milling mass of the Russians.

The enemy enjoyed a two-fold superiority in men and an almost five-fold superiority in guns, and in the attempt to get to grips with the great extent of the Russian line Lehwaldt's command became split in two. Such was the confusion in the wood of Norkitteln that the Prussian battalions ended up firing into each other, and some of the officers were convinced that they had run into a position which was beset with entrenchments and fortified batteries (in fact the Russians did not employ field fortifications until the encounter at Kay in 1759).

Lehwaldt drew his battered army from the field, but for a variety of reasons Field-Marshal Apraksin did not follow up his advantage: his army, too, had been badly knocked about, and its supply arrangements were in disarray; moreover, he was waiting to see how political affairs turned out in Russia, where Empress Elizabeth was said to be dangerously ill.

Thus in October 1757 East Prussia was evacuated by both the combatants. Apraksin pulled back to Poland, while Lehwaldt turned into Pomerania to confront the Swedes, who were putting on one of their rare shows of bellicosity.

In January 1758 a new and more aggressive Russian commander, General Fermor, invaded East Prussia with 34,000 men. On the 22nd he received in the name of his empress the by no means unwilling home of the East Prussian *Stände* at Königsberg. The cossacks and kalmuks certainly earned a bad reputation by their atrocities, but most of the Russian regulars conducted themselves like perfect gentlemen.

> Open-handed and easy-going, the Russians promoted commerce and social life. At Königsberg the drinking of punch became fashionable, and the Russian government gave balls which the local ladies were all too delighted to attend at the invitation of 'gallant, nimble and good-looking adjutants'.[51]

Frederick was furious at the conduct of the East Prussians, and made up his mind never to visit the province again. He ought to have been deeply concerned as well, for the easy acquiescence of the people in Russian rule betrayed the trait that was going to bring about the submission of the Prussian nation as a whole to the French conquerors in 1806.

Not surprisingly, the Russians were slow to get off the mark again. Fermor gathered 66,000 men in February 1758 for the march across West Prussia against Pomerania and Brandenburg, but it was not until the late summer that he seriously threatened the line of the Oder, which Dohna (Lehwaldt's successor) defended by means of his camp at Frankfurt and the garrison he had downstream at Küstrin.

Since the Austrians remained supine, Frederick decided that he could advantageously take a hand in affairs in the north-eastern theatre. He left Landeshut in Silesia on 11 August, and in ten days he drove his 14,000 troops all the way to the Oder, which he crossed below Küstrin.

Frederick spent a couple of days feeling out the Russian position, which faced eastwards in a region of swampy valleys and low, rounded hills. Following what by now was his almost invariable scheme of battle, he aimed to take his army on a circuitous march round one flank of the opposing army, in this case the Russian right. After spending a short night under arms, the Prussian army set off at three on the morning of 25 August 1758.

Frederick marched his troops westwards 'by lines', ignoring the tempting target that was offered on the way by the Russian baggage in its *Wagenburg* at Klein-Kammin – he was interested only in knocking out the Russian army. Fermor, however, responded to the Prussian move with commendable speed, and redisposed his army in a cramped but orderly battle array facing south. As a finishing touch he set fire to the village of Zorndorf, which lay in front of his new position.

Frederick rode on to the high ground north of Zorndorf and saw that he would have to make a frontal attack after all. He therefore decided to lay down a prolonged bombardment and throw a concentrated force against the Russian right wing. The attack was to be led by Lieutenant-General v. Manteuffel with an advance guard of eight picked battalions. Lieutenant-General v. Kanitz came up behind with the main body of the left wing, with twenty squadrons in reserve, while Lieutenant-General v. Seydlitz was disposed with thirty-six further squadrons on the left flank. The right wing of the army was to be 'refused'.

After two hours of cannonade the attack of the Prussian infantry got under way. There was a Protestant pastor in the Russian ranks who described their advance.

> The Prussian hose came near – magnificent and splendid, and marching in calm and silent order. Then we heard the frightful noise of the Prussian drums, though at first we could not make out their woodwind – they were playing *Ich bin ja Herr in deiner Macht!* Anybody of feeling can appreciate that through the rest of my long life I have never been able to hear that melody without the deepest emotion.[52]

The advance guard forged ahead in aggressive style, while the main body of the left wing did its best to follow in its tracks. But then the Prussian army began to drift apart in a peculiar fashion. First of all the advance guard lost contact with Kanitz's command in all the smoke and dust, and walked into the Russian army without any support. About one-third of the troops were casualties before the battalions finally crumbled in the face of a charge of the Russian cavalry. Lieutenant v. Prittwitz, who was with the main body of the left wing, describes how the fugitives from the advance guard 'crashed into our ranks like madmen, and threw our men into such confusion that we began to open fire as well, causing more casualties to our own troops than to the Russians who were following on behind'.[53]

The left wing itself began to veer off half-right and encountered the centre of the Russian army. This was plainly counter to the royal plan, even though Kanitz had some initial success and smashed through three lines of the enemy. A lieutenant in the regiment of Below remembered how in the process he had his spontoon shot from his hand and his face spattered with the brains of a decapitated soldier, while a bullet drilled his hat, another pierced his coat and a third bounded off his gorget.

> Now I came upon a battery of twelve cannon. All the Russians had fled except for the men at the guns, who crouched under the pieces and let themselves be massacred. There was just one splendid lad who stood immovable, clutching a colour embroidered

with the Russian eagle. I shouted out, offering him quarter, but he shook his head. I was raising my sword to deal him a mighty blow when he threw the flag under a cannon and was cut down along with the rest. I took up the colour and called out: 'We're winning lads, we're winning! Just a bit more, for God's sake, and we'll finish them off!'[54]

The fourth line of Russians was beginning to waver when a fresh enemy force appeared in the flank and rear and came at the Prussians with the bayonet. The bluecoats promptly fled. Now the entire infantry of Frederick's left wing was in a state of collapse.

General v. Dohna and the 'refused' right wing had not only failed to take any part in the action, but had inclined to the right and further and further away from the scene of the fighting on the left. Frederick accordingly rode over to Dohna's command at half past one in the afternoon, and did what he could to get the battle re-started. Seydlitz enterprisingly brought his cavalry over, and launched an attack at about half past three. Without the support of Dohna's infantry, however, he was unable to make any impression on the stolid Russian foot.

At last at four o'clock Dohna and the right wing began to move. While Seydlitz held off the counter-attacks of the Russian horse, the Prussian infantry pushed forward by short and desperately resisted bounds. After four hours of fighting the Prussians were almost out of cartridges, but they had driven the Russian infantry from the greater part of their position. Only the Russian gunners disputed the ground until they were shot or bayoneted, or blown up when their ammunition carts exploded.

The two armies drew apart under cover of darkness. Both the Prussians and the Russians had suffered appallingly in the battle, and they waited almost motionless in their positions for the whole of the next day. Lieutenant v. Hülsen was sent to the royal headquarters at Neudamm during these anxious hours. There he discovered Frederick 'standing in front of his tent, outside which the captured colours had been planted. You could not imagine a more splendid sight. The king was with General v. Seydlitz. The dust and sweat of the day before still lay on Seydlitz's face. He was in a cheerful mood and he looked magnificent'.[55]

Finally on 27 August the failure of the supply arrangements, the bane of the Russians, compelled Fermor to march away and leave the hideous field to the Prussians. Prittwitz travelled over the ground and discovered the Prussian wounded assembling in their thousands.

> They came from all directions. Some were crawling on hands and feet, others were limping on muskets with the butts tucked under the armpit to serve as crutches . . . Further on there were the remains of blown-up ammunition waggons and powder carts, and nearby a multitude of half-roasted gunners who were giving off an unpleasant smell of burning, as well as a number of wounded *in extremis*, who in their fear and agony had dug their hands and feet deep into the earth. Elsewhere I saw a whole train of two-wheeled Russian carts, with the horses shot in the traces, and around the whole battlefield ran wounded horses, with their intestines dragging along the ground or hopping about on three legs.[56]

As for the Russian wounded, many of them were buried alive by the enraged Prussian soldiers and peasants, while the rest hobbled away or died over the course of the next two weeks, strewn across fields and tracks, or propped up against the trees. All the able-bodied men of the neighbourhood were called up to bury the thousands of corpses as they lay 'all naked, blackened and hideous – mutilated trunks, severed arms and legs, hacked-off heads, torn-out entrails – horses and men lying across one another'.[57] In the hot weather the corruption had already progressed so far that many of the arms and legs came away as the squashy bodies were being dragged to the pits.

Such was the outcome of the first real trial of strength between the Prussians and the Russians. 'Never had troops sold their lives so dearly as the Russians on that day. In a transport of joy Frederick asked Seydlitz on the following day: "When you come down to it, don't you think the Russians are scum?" "Sire," replied the general, "I am not sure whether you can apply this name to infantry like the Russians, who fought so well and managed to repulse our own troops."'[58]

Frederick had lost over 12,000 men, or more than one-third of his army, and the morale of his exiled East Prussian regiments was finally broken.

Frederick detached General v. Dohna with 17,000 troops to follow in Fermor's tracks, and in November the Russians retreated to winter quarters behind the Vistula. In the northern part of the Baltic theatre the Swedes made their annual excursion from Swedish Pomerania, but by January in the next year they were back again under the walls of their base at Stralsund.

THE STING IN THE TAIL OF THE YEAR – HOCHKIRCH 1758

Frederick marched back to the southern theatre with a small nucleus of the 'Zorndorf' army and rejoined Margrave Karl of Brandenburg-Schwedt, who had been covering Silesia against the Austrians with 33,000 men. After the king's appearance the rival armies remained virtually inactive for five weeks – Frederick hoping to manoeuvre Daun out of south-east Saxony, and the Austrians apparently content to be holding Frederick fast.

In the second week of October the king decided to settle himself into a position in the hills and woods near the village of Hochkirch. The new camp was perilously exposed, and on the night of 13 October the field preacher Karl Küster was wandering about Hochkirch hill, on the right of the position, looking for somewhere to rest his head, when he was astonished to see the Austrian left flank scarcely five or six hundred paces away. 'Meanwhile darkness fell, and the army lit its watch fires, which gave the scene a gloomy and solemn aspect: in this damp weather the area of both camps looked like a clouded sky, through which the fires, like stars, could be dimly discerned.'[59]

Frederick was unperturbed. He had become accustomed to sticking close to the enemy, so that he should know exactly where they were (see p. 145). Also he was aware that Daun was a phlegmatic kind of person, who was probably incapable of making a night attack. Last of all he had confidence in his 30,000 troops, who were mostly Brandenburgers and Pomeranians and had been spared the harrowing experience of Zorndorf.

Suddenly, at five in the morning of 14 October, dense Austrian columns fell on the Prussian regiments around Hochkirch village. 'The Austrians seemed to spring out of the earth among the stands of the Prussian colours, in the sanctuary of their camp. Several hundred Prussians had their throats cut in their tents, before they could so much as open their eyes, while others sprang to arms half-dressed.'[60]

The brunt of the first attack fell upon the regiment of Markgraf Karl, which came under murderous artillery fire in the village. Worst of all were the howitzer shells, which arched into the crowded main street and 'shattered heads and shoulders, or, bursting on the ground, smashed the troops' feet. Many of the dead could fall to the earth only after the press had thinned out'.[61]

At the first alarm Frederick had merely cried out to the infantry: 'Lads, go back to your tents, they're only Croats!'[62] He hastily revised his ideas when some of the Austrian missiles carried over Hochkirch and landed in the Prussian centre. Meanwhile the field-marshals Keith and Moritz of Dessau had taken charge of the battle for Hochkirch hill. Keith first threw in the regiment of Itzenplitz, but before long the troops were driven from the village by artillery fire and fell back to safety with the Pomeranian regiment of Kannacher, which was standing in support outside.

Next came the regiment of Prinz v. Preussen, which swept the Austrian grenadiers from the streets and relieved the troops holding out in the churchyard. Beyond the village, however, the Prussians were met by deployed lines of Austrian infantry, and by the muzzles of their own captured guns, which had been turned against them and were firing canister. Prince Moritz fell wounded, and the Prussians recoiled into the village.

Field-Marshal Keith, too, was close at hand, watching the progress of the battle, when he suddenly plunged dead from his horse. *Feldprediger* Küster did his best to reach him, but the regiment of Prinz v. Preussen crashed out of the street under a hail of bullets and Küster was carried away in the throng. Only the second battalion of the regiment of Markgraf Karl remained in Hochkirch, holding out behind the churchyard wall under the command of Major Simon v. Langen. This heroic band was finally wiped out by the last of three Austrian attacks.

The resistance of the Prussian right ended in a murderous fire-fight to the right and rear of Hochkirch village. Frederick's own horse was hit in the shoulder, and near him Major v. Haugwitz was drilled through the left arm. Most horrific of all, Major-General Prince Friedrich Franz of Brunswick, the twenty-six-year-old brother of the queen, was beheaded by a cannon shot in front of the second battalion of the regiment of Wedell. 'The duke's horse, a pure white grey, was decked with his parade saddle-cloth. After its master fell it galloped for a good half hour between the Austrian lines and ours, without finding a place of refuge – a most sorry sight.'[63]

Meanwhile at seven o'clock the four-and-a-half grenadier battalions on the Prussian left had come under attack from further Austrian columns, which compelled them to abandon a battery of thirty heavy cannon that was standing in front of their camp.

With both the flanks in a state of collapse the Prussians began to fall back to the north-west. This was the first time that some of the veteran regiments had turned their backs on the enemy, and many old officers had to be dragged away from the scene by force. In these sad minutes it was the brazen-lunged Lieutenant-Colonel Christoph v. Saldern who prevented the retreat from degenerating into total rout. 'This was a commander of rare gifts, whose boldness and skill in moving infantry was as unique in its way as Seydlitz's mastery of cavalry.'[64]

This one day cost Frederick 9,000 troops, or one-third of his army, as well as two of his field-marshals. The Prince de Ligne found Keith lying among the Austrian and Prussian dead, still oddly impressive with his scarred and majestic face. The other field-marshal, the newly promoted Moritz of Dessau, was captured in a cart by a detachment of Austrian hussars, who accepted his parole and allowed him to travel to Bautzen to have his wounds dressed. Moritz never returned to service. He recovered from his wounds well enough, but a lesion on his lip developed into a cancer, from which he died on 11 April 1760. With this the direct line of the Dessau tribe abdicated the power it had exercised over the Prussian army for three-quarters of a century.

Frederick retrieved his fortunes with astonishing speed and address. He summoned Prince Henry and his corps from the west to make up the losses, then slipped past Daun and raced eastwards into Silesia, where he compelled an Austrian detachment to raise the siege of Neisse on 5 November. Daun lumbered off in the other direction to threaten Dresden, but General v. Schmettau refused to be browbeaten into surrendering the place and he held on until Frederick returned to this theatre in the second half of November. Daun thereupon took his army back to Bohemia, and Frederick remained master of all the ground to the north of the border hills.

1759, THE TERRIBLE YEAR – KAY, KUNERSDORF AND MAXEN

Not even the most ruthless recruiting could fully make up the gaps which had been left in the Prussian army by the bloodletting and hardships of the last campaigns. In 1759, therefore, Frederick had only 127,000 troops on foot, the first appreciable diminution that we notice in the army in the present war. Moreover, Frederick, the great lover of concentration of force, was compelled by the hostile coalition to keep a number of separate armies or corps in being. First of all the 'main' royal army of some 50,000 men had to shuttle between the Elbe and the Oder, according to whether the Austrians showed their noses in Saxony or Silesia. Then there was what we might call the 'eastern' army of about 30,000 men, which kept watch on the Russians and Swedes in the area of the lower Oder. On the other flank Frederick constituted a separate command (again of about 30,000 troops) which counteracted the *Reichsarmee* in Saxony. This 'western' army was left in the capable hands of Prince Henry, the third of the royal brothers, whom Frederick once toasted as 'the faultless commander'. Realistic and cautious, the long-faced Henry practised an almost 'Austrian' style of generalship and excelled in the choice of strong positions. In part his circumspect ways were dictated by the relatively poor quality of his army, which Frederick loaded with a large number of the 'free battalions'.

In addition there was usually in existence a small 'drifting' corps, of the kind commanded by Winterfeldt in 1757 or Finck in 1759. It was supposed to guard the communications between the different armies, but it was dangerously liable to be crushed by whatever powerful enemy force happened to be passing through the locality.

Lastly Frederick maintained a contingent of between 2,500 and 3,500 troops with the British and Protestant German army under Prince Ferdinand of Brunswick, a Prussian general, which confronted the French in western Germany. The composition varied considerably from one year to another, though the most enduring element was probably represented by the squadrons of the formidable Black Hussars.

For 1759 the immediate problem was to clear up the ugly situation that was developing on the eastern theatre. Frederick had always encountered some difficulty in finding a proper man to take charge in that part of the world – and in the summer of 1759 his need was all the more acute because Daun had moved into Silesia and was holding the 'main' royal army down. Frederick had suspected for some time that General v. Dohna was lacking in enterprise, and after the battle of Zorndorf in 1758 he had left him with Major-

General Moritz v. Wobersnow as his adviser. Wobersnow did not enjoy a particularly high reputation in the army. According to Warnery, 'this gentleman was old enough to have a son who was a captain. This did not prevent him from gambling, drinking, arguing and whoring. My brother, who was then a major of hussars, delivered a report to him on the eve of the battle of Kay. He found him reclining on a bale of straw with a prostitute, whom he did not even have the decency to send away'.[65]

In 1759 the Dohna–Wobersnow combination proved to be incapable of staying the Russian advance through Poland. In July, therefore, Frederick placed them under the command of the tall, athletic and stupid Lieutenant-General Johann v. Wedell, who had spearheaded the advance at Leuthen.

Wedell had never commanded an independent detachment, let alone an army, and now he considered no other course of action except to carry out Frederick's commission to attack the Russians wherever he found them. The Russian general Saltykov obliged on 23 July by making a circuit round to Wedell's rear and taking up position on a range of hills which faced eastwards over the broad and swampy valley of the Eichmühlen-Fliess near Kay. Wedell at once made his own army execute an about turn and advance to the attack. The astonished troops were forced to throw away their steaming soup and stuff the half-cooked meat into their knapsacks, and they marched west into a hot wind which threw dust into their faces.

None of Wedell's flanking detachments could make any headway in this difficult terrain, and so the army was fed bit by bit up the same narrow ridge that led to the position of the Russian right wing. The Russians were arrayed in two lines, with six hastily en-trenched batteries in front, and they were able to massacre the bluecoats as they bunched together between the ponds and bushes. First came the main body under Manteuffel and Hülsen. Lieutenant v. Lemcke was serving in the regiment of Dessau during this episode, and he tried to drive on his shrinking men, 'who refused to move from behind the trees, and kept up a fire on the enemy from there. I was carrying my sword instead of a spontoon, and I had already bent it double on my disobedient troops . . . when a cannon ball came bouncing along and smashed the sole of my left foot, throwing me to the ground. My little body of men at once took to flight'.[66] The Prussian second line was thrown into the hopeless battle in the late afternoon, and last of all Wobersnow followed in the same bloody track with the rearguard. The suicidal proceedings came to an end after Wobersnow was mortally wounded by a canister shot in the side.

Saltykov had now knocked Wedell's command out of the reckoning as an effective force, and two weeks later the Russians linked up with 20,000 Austrian troops under General Loudon, who was the liveliest of all the imperial commanders. Frederick was now taken between two powerful armies – Daun's main force of Austrians, and the joint Russo-Austrian force of Saltykov and Loudon.

At this grave juncture Frederick summoned up Prince Henry with the 'western' army to hold off Daun in Silesia, while he himself marched with the 'central' army to join the remnants of Wedell's force in the east. Transpose Dohna for Wedell, and Frederick was placed in almost the same situation that had faced him in the Zorndorf campaign of 1758; and, just as occurred in that year, he found that the Russians were ensconced in a position on the far side of the Oder – in this case a camp which extended in a long salient almost due east of Frankfurt.

Frederick brought his army across the river below Frankfurt, and on the afternoon of 11 August 1759 he looked south across a swampy heath towards what seemed to him to be the front of the Russo-Austrian camp, stretching along a row of sandy hills. A region of wooded heights extended to the left, as he saw it, but there appeared to be no reason why he should not be able to take the army on a march round that flank of the Russian line and come at the enemy from the rear. Following what was by now his well-established routine, he planned to send a diversionary force (under Lieutenant-General v. Finck) directly across the heath, while creeping with the main army round to the start line of his intended attack in the neighbourhood of the village of Kunersdorf.

The army set off 'by lines' at two in the morning of 12 August 1759. After a long and tiring march through the wooded terrain Frederick at last arrived opposite what should have been a stretch of open ground that led up to the enemy 'rear'. Instead he found that the enemy had another complete line of defences, stretching clean across his intended line of advance. Moreover the outfield was obstructed in a very annoying fashion by some ponds south of Kunersdorf – reconnaissance had never been one of Frederick's stronger points.

The Prussian advance guard over-ran the eastern salient of the position with no great difficulty, but the enemy consolidated behind the hollow of the Kuh-Grund, and held their truncated position against everything that Frederick could throw against them. After repeated attacks the Prussian infantry gained a little ground on the far side of the hollow in the middle of this very hot afternoon, but before the cavalry could be fed into the action Seydlitz was wounded by a canister shot which shattered his sword hilt and mangled his right hand. Bleeding profusely, the great cavalryman had to leave the field in a state of considerable pain and shock.

The left wing of the main army now carried out a number of sporadic and unco-ordinated attacks against the front of the ridge behind the Kuh-Grund, while on the far side Finck twice threw in the 'diversionary' corps to no effect. Now that the infantry were almost played out, Lieutenant-General v. Platen brought the cavalry in one great mass round the south of Kunersdorf and tried to get at the enemy defences behind the village. The Prussian cavalry was decimated by the guns of the Grosser Spitzberg, a hill which the enemy had turned into one of the strongest points of their position, and the survivors were counter-attacked by the Russian and Austrian horse. After half an hour of wild fighting in the smoke and dust the Prussian cavalry broke and fled, and the rout of Frederick's army became general.

Immediately after the battle Frederick was able to rally just 5,000 troops and 50 guns. Nineteen thousand men (nearly two-thirds of his army) were lost for good, as well as nearly all the heavy pieces and the fine new battery of horse artillery. He put the blame for the catastrophe on his soldiers, a 'mob of cowards' who lacked all 'feelings of honour', and he was inclined to believe that his own career and the Prussian state were about to go down in the general wreck.

There now supervened what Frederick was to call the 'miracle of the House of Brandenburg'. Saltykov certainly brought his army across the Oder four days after his victory, but he believed that the Russians had already contributed more than enough to the allied war effort, after the two bloody battles of Kay and Kunersdorf, and he was unwilling to push on any further unless Daun came north to offer him support. Daun made no move of the kind, and so at the end of the month Saltykov pulled his army back over the river. Thus the badly shaken Prussian army was saved from destruction, and

Frederick was able to survive the two further shocks which the year had in store for him.

With Frederick committed on the lower Oder against the Russians, the main body of the Austrians and the *Reichsarmee* had deemed it safe to move against the great city of Dresden. While he was still shaken by the impact of his defeat at Kunersdorf, Frederick had written to the governor, General v. Schmettau, advising him to capitulate on good terms and save the garrison, the magazine and the Saxon field treasury. Frederick changed his mind once he saw that the Russians were not going to fight, but his countermanding order came too late to prevent Schmettau surrendering this vital point on 4 September.

Frederick returned from the Oder to Saxony and spent the rest of the campaigning season of 1759 in vain manoeuvres to evict the Austrians from their positions in the tangled border mountains south of Dresden. One particularly unhappy episode broke the career of a deserving commander, Lieutenant-General Friedrich August v. Finck. He had come from the Russian service in the 1740s with impeccable credentials as part of the Münnich–Manstein–Winterfeldt connection (he was actually a cousin of Winterfeldt's), and he had recently done Frederick the valuable service of putting the army in some kind of order after the rout at Kunersdorf. Finck was 'beyond any shadow of doubt an able commander – brave, active and extremely competent; his one misfortune was that he was dealing with a master who would never admit himself to be in the wrong'.[67]

Much against Finck's own judgement, and that of Prince Henry, he was detached with a corps to hold the dangerously isolated plateau of Maxen. In the afternoon of 20 November four columns of Austrian infantry attacked from the south-west in overwhelming force. The Prussian cavalry under Major-General v. Gersdorff did nothing to help their comrades of the infantry, and the centre of Finck's corps caved in under the pressure. Since there was no escape down the narrow tracks that led down from the plateau, Finck was compelled to order his entire command to lay down its weapons. Thirteen thousand troops were removed from the strategic map just as surely as if they had been destroyed in battle, and Frederick found plenty of reasons for blaming everybody but himself for a disaster which in statistical terms exceeded the one at Kolin. He deleted the hussar regiment of Gersdorff from the army list, and he held the remainder of the 'Maxen regiments' in everlasting contempt. Finck himself was cashiered and sentenced to one year's fortress arrest in Spandau.

The depleted Prussian army clung on in its positions in the hills round Dresden until February 1760. The snow lay knee-deep for weeks, and there was not nearly enough room in the little villages for the shivering troops. A veteran of the regiment of Forcade remembered how, 'in an attempt to get their frozen blood to flow some of the soldiers ran about the camp like madmen. Others huddled together in their tents, not even venturing out for food, in the hope of warming at least some of their members from the bodies of their comrades . . . They were carried to the grave in heaps, and this one winter campaign cost as many men as two major battles'.[68] Counting in the men who died from cold and hunger at the turn of the year the total cost of the campaign of 1759 was more than 60,000 troops.

THE PRUSSIAN ARMY IN THE LATER SEVEN YEARS WAR

It seemed scarcely possible for the Prussian army to continue to bear the burden of this war, a struggle that was devouring men and resources at a rate which would have seemed out of the question when Frederick first embarked on his adventure in 1756.

Frederick had 5,500 officers at his disposal in October 1756. Of these about half were lost in the first three years of the war, another 1,328 at the triple disasters of Kay, Kunersdorf and Maxen in 1759, and 771 more in the actions at Landeshut, Liegnitz and Torgau in 1760. A proportion of the officers recovered from their wounds or returned from captivity, but all told 4,000 officers were permanently lost to Frederick in the course of the war, of whom 1,500 had been killed. The shortage of officers was all the more keenly felt because the tight Prussian discipline demanded heavily officered regiments, and because Frederick insisted on keeping every unit (save the grenadier battalions) as a separate entity.

The appalling deficiencies were supplied by a variety of expedients: commissions were bestowed upon bourgeois and suitable NCOs, a number of footloose officers were hired from abroad, and in the winter of 1758/9 Frederick began to commission boys and the younger intakes of the Cadet Corps. The future historian Archenholtz was thirteen when he was sent with thirty-nine other cadets to Frederick's headquarters at Breslau in December 1758; the king in person assigned them to their regiments, where they were told off to train the recruits, command small detachments or serve as adjutants.

The toll among the higher commanders was correspondingly heavy. Schwerin, Winterfeldt and Keith were dead, Moritz of Dessau was dying, the careers of Bevern, Schmettau and Finck were blighted, and the irreplaceable Seydlitz was accident-prone and liable to recurrences of his syphilis, which left Zieten as the only senior cavalry commander of any real stature. Of the second-rank generals Saldern was winning golden opinions, while Wunsch and 'Green' Kleist were making their names under the leadership of Prince Henry: none of them, however, were capable of taking the places of the dead heroes of 1756.

A detached eye might look upon the institution of the regiment as a machine that is designed to ingest healthy young men and disgorge corpses and cripples. Thus in the course of the Seven Years War nearly all the Prussian regiments had worked through 3,000 recruits, and some had absorbed a good many more. And yet, after the assorted catastrophes of 1758 and 1759, the quality of the men tended to improve rather than regress, and the size of the active army was stabilised at more than 100,000 troops.

The foreign mercenary element had borne much of the brunt of the first couple of campaigns (as Frederick intended), and only after these folk had run away or been killed off did the king draw at all heavily on the resources of native manpower. Officers agreed that the young cantonists who were being summoned to the colours were devoted and brave, and responded well to the hurried training to which they were subjected. 'The drilling on foot and horseback went on without let in the market places, in the fields, in the stables and barns, so that the recruits arrived at their regiments fully trained and looking something like soldiers.'[69]

Frederick, of course, set no great store by enthusiasm or idealism among the troops, and he still resorted to all kinds of shifts and devices to fill up the ranks. He continued to impress large quantities of enemy prisoners of war, and in 1760 he made a particularly useful contract with Colonel Collignon and a group of free-enterprise recruiting agents who undertook to scour the Empire for likely specimens. For every recruit who arrived at Magdeburg the resourceful Collignon received fifteen thalers, of which he disbursed ten to his sub-contractors. Altogether Collignon and his gang are said to have trapped 60,000 recruits.

Where honour and ambition were inclined to fail, Frederick knew that more disreputable motives still held their power to bind men to the colours. Little attempt was made to prevent the soldiers from pillaging at will, and in Silesia the coming of the Prussians came to be feared as much as that of the Russians. It is significant that these years also saw the 'free battalions' spring up in rank profusion, though the king was careful to consign most of these gangs of brigands to the army of his brother, Prince Henry. He was not inspired by fraternal love.

The strength of the cavalry was maintained at a fairly constant 30,000. Horses were obtained in adequate quantity through round-ups in enemy territory, or by way of purchase in eastern Europe, and Frederick experienced no great difficulty in enlisting recruits for this attractive service. The Prussian cuirassiers were now a very formidable force on the battlefield, while the dragoons and more especially the hussars reached a high state of general proficiency, thanks to their frequent brushes with the enemy. It is true that the hussars were liable to lose half their effectives or even more in a single campaign, but the numbers were just as regularly made up again from infantry or peasants who believed that they could make their fortune by plunder.

The strain of the war probably told most heavily on the artillery. It was given fewer and fewer horses to drag around its increasingly heavily ordnance, and as always it was assigned the very worst of the recruits.

1760 – FAILURE AT LANDESHUT AND DRESDEN, REPRIEVE AT LIEGNITZ AND TORGAU

For the opening of the campaign of 1760 Frederick devoted his main army once more to the bid to recapture Dresden in the teeth of the Austrians and the *Reichsarmee*. Prince Henry with what we called the 'western' army was switched to Silesia to keep an eye on the Russians, while the unenviable command of the 'drifting' corps was entrusted to General de la Motte Fouqué, the tyrannical governor of Glatz.

Fouqué was another of those intelligent, tough and rather nasty officers who appealed to Frederick more than they did to the rest of the army. He had an alert eye and a quick tongue, and he affected an old-fashioned uniform which harked back to the days of the Old Dessauer, his mentor in the military trade. Retzow's judgement is harsh but accurate: 'Fouqué had almost no friend save the king, his master, who had the highest opinion of his military talents. Even his children behaved towards him like cringing serfs.'[70]

Fouqué's job was to keep up the communications between the Prussian armies in Saxony and Silesia. To this end Frederick directed him to occupy Landeshut in southeastern Silesia, near the Bohemian border, where there was an important crossroads. Fouqué was not the man to argue with his master's orders, and he arrayed his 12,000 or so troops along a front of four miles on a ridge to the east and south-east of the little town.

In this vulnerable position Fouqué was assailed by General Loudon and 30,000 Austrian troops on the early morning of 23 June. The Prussians were driven from the heights and towards the river Bober, and such survivors as reached the far side were run down by the Austrian cavalry. Fouqué was isolated with the free battalion of Below and a company of the regiment of Braun, which formed square and tried to withstand the Austrian charges. Finally the Prussians ran out of powder and were over-run by the enemy horse, Fouqué himself being wounded and taken prisoner.

The attack of the Regiment of Bernburg at Liegnitz

Once again Frederick had allowed an isolated corps to be overwhelmed by the enemy, though the damage could not be compared with that sustained at Maxen the previous year: fewer troops were involved, for a start, and Fouqué had certainly put up a magnificent fight.

After having eliminated Fouqué, the irrepressible Loudon turned south into the rocky box of the county of Glatz and laid siege to the fortress of the same name, which was manned by a 'Prussian' garrison of 3,200 troops, mostly deserters and impressed prisoners of war. These folk mutinied on 26 July, and the Austrians walked into the place virtually without opposition. Thanks to the appalling quality of the garrison troops, the Austrians had been allowed to gain one of the most important posts of the border region.

Loudon hastened north to Breslau, hoping to capture the city as easily as he had brought down Glatz. Luckily for Frederick, the place was in the hands of Major-General Bogislaw v. Tauentzien, who was one of the very few officers he could unreservedly trust in a detached command.

Tauentzien was well aware of his duty to deny the great Breslau magazines to Loudon, who arrived outside at the end of July. When the Austrians swore to pluck the very babes from their mothers' wombs, unless Breslau capitulated at once, Teuentzien replied 'I am not pregnant. Nor are my soldiers.'[71] Loudon did not really have the means to put his horrible threats into effect, and the Austrians had to abandon their blockade on 4 August, when Prince Henry came marching from the north.

While Loudon was roaming so destructively about Silesia, Frederick addressed himself to the task of routing out the 14,000 Austrians and troops of the *Reichsarmee* who were still in Dresden. He put any idea of a formal siege out of his head, and calculated that two or three days' bombardment would suffice to put him in possession of the city. The Prussian field artillery opened fire on 14 July, and on the 19th the heavy guns from Torgau joined in the chorus. The cannonade worked to terrible effect in this beautiful city, which was the fullest flowering of the German baroque. 'Many of the foremost streets were burning from end to end, and wherever you looked you could see houses crashing to the ground . . . the Prussians noticed that Austrian officers were observing their movements from the Kreuzkirche. They accordingly opened fire on the tower. It caught alight, and as it collapsed it caused a wide conflagration.'[72]

Frederick had little talent for siege warfare, and towards the end of the third week of July he decided that he could no longer hang on uselessly before Dresden while the main Austrian army was hovering in the hills and Loudon and the Russians were wreaking all sorts of depredations in Silesia. On the night of 21/22 July the Prussians removed the guns from their batteries, whereupon the Austrians sallied forth from Dresden and broke and scattered the regiment of Anhalt-Bernburg. Frederick was furious, and the punishment was 'without precedent in Prussian military history. The common soldiers had to give up their swords, while the officers and NCOs were deprived of the braid of their hats.'[73]

Frederick lingered in the neighbourhood of Dresden until 29 July, when the accumulation of bad news from Silesia made it imperative for him to do something to save the situation in that part of the world. Armies now converged on Silesia from every direction, and the Prussians began to pass through one of the most dangerous passages in the Seven Years War.

As Frederick hastened eastwards to join Prince Henry, the king had Daun at his heels and Loudon and a Russian force under Chernyshev somewhere to his front. Daun and Loudon managed to link up before Frederick could reach his brother, and the Austrians decided to use their vast superiority of force (90,000 against 30,000) to envelop Frederick on the north bank of the Katzbach stream near Liegnitz: Loudon was to cross the water and fall on the Prussian camp from the east, while Daun and the main force would move up from the south-west and complete the destruction.

Suspecting that something was afoot, Frederick left his camp on the night of 14/15 August and moved a short distance to the plateau of Liegnitz. Towards three in the morning he received a report to the effect that Loudon had reached the 'Prussian' side of the Katzbach and was advancing against Frederick's left and rear. Frederick was now faced with the necessity of warding off an enemy attack, the first since the day of Soor in 1745. Leaving the second line of the army in the charge of Zieten, he marched his first line to the left and rapidly formed a new front to meet Loudon's advance.

In the early morning mist Loudon three times threw his grenadiers at the Prussians, and each attack was repulsed by salvoes of musketry and storms of canister from the deadly 12-pounders that were distributed among the Prussian brigades (see p. 120).

Frederick saw that the time was ripe for a counter-attack. On the left flank the more enthusiastic members of the humiliated regiment of Bernburg were burning for revenge, and Ensign v. Göchausen wrote later:

I can still see brave old General v. Bülow spring forward and mark out the brigadier, Prince Bernburg, and call out to him from some distance: 'My dear sir, what is your regiment up to? For God's sake, hold your brigade together!' But shouts and orders were now powerless to influence events. The three battalions of the regiment of Bernburg leapt forward and deafened themselves, the generals and the enemy with the dreadful cry of 'Honour or death!'[74]

The Bernburgers broke through the Austrian lines, assisted by the Prinz Ferdinand

Regiment and two regiments of cuirassiers, and they forced Loudon to withdraw his battered command over the Katzbach. Thus the battle on the plateau was fought and decided within two hours, before Daun could so much as begin to move the main Austrian army across the Katzbach.

The Austrians were never again in a position to achieve such an overwhelming tactical concentration of force as on the early morning of Liegnitz, and yet they had fumbled their opportunity. As for Chernyshev and his Russians, they had heard the sound of the battle but made no attempt to intervene.

Frederick had every right to be generous. He conveyed his congratulations to the army in unusually warm terms, and he restored the regiment of Bernburg to favour, undertaking to buy the braid for the hats at his own cost.

Frederick remained in Silesia for several weeks more, which gave the Russians and Austrians the opportunity to send a number of detachments hastening towards his capital of Berlin. The Russian general Tottleben arrived before Berlin on 3 October. The Austrian commander Lacy came on the scene a little later with 15,000 Austrians and Saxons, which, together with further Russian detachments under Chernyshev and Panin, brought the combined allied force to about 35,000 men. Thirteen thousand Prussian troops retired to safety in the citadel of Spandau on 8 October, leaving 3,000 more in Berlin to surrender as prisoners of war when the placed was yielded up on the 9th.

The Russians wrecked the royal cannon foundry, the military workshops, the powder mills and most of the royal factories, and confiscated 100,000 thalers from the treasury in addition to the city's 'contribution' of 1,700,000 thalers.

All the same, the damage ought to have been much greater. The rich Berlin merchant Gotzkowsky enjoyed some credit with the Russians, from his kindness to their officer prisoners after Zorndorf, and as well as negotiating the reasonable 'contribution' he was able to persuade the Russians to spare such establishments as the *Lagerhaus* and the *Gold-und-Silber-Manufaktur*. Even the fine Arsenal escaped destruction. The Russians decided to bring some powder from the outlying mills to blow it up, but before they could reach their destination all the powder was lost in an accidental explosion. They had to be content with carrying away some of the equipment and weapons, and breaking or burning the rest or throwing them into the Spree.

The Austrians proved to be much more vindictive than their Russian allies. As for the Saxons, they had many old scores to settle and wreaked their vengeance on the royal palace of Charlottenburg.

The allies pulled out of Berlin on 12 October, taking with them their loot and 5,000 prisoners. The captives included the younger boys of the Cadet Corps, who underwent starvation and many other hardships on their march east with the Russians.

With his enemies grouped so closely round him, Frederick could scarcely move in any direction without being uncomfortably aware that the allies must be up to some mischief behind his back. While the Prussians were marching and counter-marching in Silesia, Daun took the opportunity to move the main Austrian army back to Saxony and march down the Elbe to Torgau, where he was joined by Lacy's corps from Berlin on 24 October. Daun was under strict instructions to stand and fight, and he accordingly made himself comfortable in one of Prince Henry's old positions, which extended along a row of heights on the left (west) bank of the Elbe fifty miles below Dresden. The Austrians looked south-west over the steep, vineyard-covered slopes, with Lacy's corps on the left (east), nearest the Elbe, and Daun's main army on the heights of Süptitz and Grosswig to the right. The front was garnished with 275 guns.

Frederick at once marched to the attack, for he could not possibly allow the Austrians to remain sitting on the resources of Saxony. Already outnumbered (44,000 against 53,000) he accepted the further risk of splitting his forces in two: while Zieten moved into position to strike at the Austrians from the south, Frederick took the rest of the army on a long march round the west flank of the enemy with the intention of coming at Daun from the rear.

Towards noon on the cold, wet and windy day of 3 November 1760, while Frederick's command was still crashing through the woods, the crafty Daun detected what was afoot and drew out the regiments of his first line into a new front which faced towards the north-east. It was like Liegnitz, with the roles reversed.

Not only had Frederick seen his original plan of attack thwarted, but the strong south wind brought an alarming noise of cannon fire from Zieten's direction. Frederick exclaimed to his generals: 'My God, Zieten's attacking already and we're still a league and a half short! What's going to happen? My infantry's still not there!'[75] He did not know that Zieten too was well short of his objective, and that the sounds of 'battle' merely proceeded from a brush between Zieten's advance guard and the Croats.

Acting from the mistaken sense of urgency, Frederick brought his advance guard of ten grenadier battalions out of the woods early in the afternoon and threw them at the centre of Daun's position. There were no other troops within supporting distance, and so the isolated grenadiers were driven back with appalling losses. Over 5,000 men fell within half an hour.

Only after the massacre was complete did Lieutenant-General v. Bülow come on the scene with the main body of infantry. A subaltern in the regiment of Forcade described the scene as Bülow's command followed in the tracks of the grenadiers through the pouring rain:

> Even before the Prussians caught sight of the enemy the tree tops were severed by the enemy shot and fell on their heads, and the thunder of the cannon reverberated fearfully through the forest. They were deafened by the discharges of the artillery, which seemed to them like harbingers of death. And then when they emerged from the trees they saw not a victorious scene . . . but a slaughter ground, full of corpses and mutilated bodies, panting and swimming in their blood.[76]

This attack too was pressed back, after Daun brought up his reserves. It was at about this critical time that a canister ball hit Frederick in the chest. The fur-lined coat softened the impact to some extent, but the king was bruised and knocked breathless, and he was escorted from the field in tears.

The Duke of Holstein brought up the cavalry and tried to revive the attack, and he managed to break through the right flank of Daun's line before he was bundled back as well. Finally the last available battalions of the main army put in a suicidal assault over the heaps of dead and wounded. Daun was looking on, and he exclaimed to a group of captured Prussian officers: 'My God, why is the king throwing so many men away? Doesn't he know it will do him no good?' Daun himself was in considerable pain, from a wound in his foot, and as the light began to fail he had himself carried to Torgau town, where he composed the announcement of his victory. His royal enemy Frederick spent the same night sitting on the bottom step of the altar in the village church of Elsnig, unaware of the outcome of the battle but fearing the worst.

What had been happening to Zieten all this time? For several hours the veteran hussar kept his command almost motionless in front of Lacy's corps, engaging in an artillery duel and waiting for Frederick to make some obvious impression on the masses of Daun's infantry, which extended over to his left. As he rode slowly along the front of his immobile cavalry a cannon shot beheaded a cuirassier, whereupon he called out: 'Don't worry, lads! He had an easy death!'[77]

Finally towards dusk Zieten pushed his corps half-left across broken country against Daun's left. Many of the Prussian officers knew this ground fairly well, from the time they had spent there with Prince Henry's army in 1759, and an orderly officer hastened to report to Lieutenant-Colonel v. Möllendorff, the commandant of the Garde, that the Austrians had not bothered to guard a vital causeway which lay between two ponds. He in turn transmitted the news to Major-General v. Saldern, who pushed over the dam with his brigade of five battalions. Saldern's troops were checked for a time in a heavy fire-fight which broke out on the far side of the causeway, but Zieten exploited this first breach by sending in the rest of his infantry, part of which followed over the causeway, while the rest fought their way through Süptitz.

The noise and flashes from Zieten's action carried over to the battered remnants of Frederick's command, where the *Flügeladjutant* v. Gaudi persuaded the hearty old Lieutenant-General v. Hülsen to gather his forces for yet another assault. All of Hülsen's horses had been shot from under him, and 'since his age and his wounds prevented him from going on foot, he set himself on a cannon and had himself dragged into the enemy fire'.[78] The troops crowded up the sandy slopes, hauling the artillery by main force, and the battle ended in total darkness and confusion, but with the Austrians driven off their position.

The losses of the victorious Prussians (16,670) actually exceeded those of the enemy, and amounted to a higher proportion of Frederick's army than in any other of his battles. Such was the cost of storming a defensible position that was beset with artillery. Even after all this bloodletting the battle of Torgau decided little in strategic terms, for Daun still held Dresden and southern Saxony, while the troublesome Loudon was free to take up winter quarters in Upper Silesia.

Frederick exorcised the frustrations of the campaign by resuming his china-smashing contest with the Saxons. He was seeking revenge for the sack of Charlottenburg, and since he had already reduced the interior of the castle of Krogwitz to smithereens his eye lighted upon the exquisite fittings of the royal Saxon hunting lodge of Hubertusburg. General v. Saldern refused to carry out the unholy commission, which forced Frederick to summon up his crony Charles Guichard, a wandering soldier and enthusiast for classical military history, whom Frederick had re-christened 'Quintus Icilius' after the centurion of the 10th Legion at Pharsalus (48 BC). 'Quintus Icilius' carried out his task with thoroughness, if no great enthusiasm, and within a few hours nothing was left of the interior save the bare walls.

1761 – THE YEAR OF ATTRITION

For the campaign of 1761 Frederick contrived to build up his field army to a size of 104,000 troops. This was a truly remarkable figure, considering all the wastage of the last year, and Frederick attained it by making further heavy drafts on the cantons and by increasing the number of free battalions from eleven (in 1760) to twenty-five.

Even so Frederick found himself hemmed in on all sides by superior allied forces. Not only was Daun still in control of much of Saxony, but in the high summer Loudon and Buturlin assembled a powerful army of Austrians and Russians in the centre of Silesia and posed a dangerous threat to Breslau and Schweidnitz.

Frederick was in no position to withstand the Austro-Russian host in the open field. Instead he decided to throw up an entrenched camp at Bunzelwitz, from which he could bid defiance to the enemy while living off the rich magazines nearby at Schweidnitz. Each half of the army took turns in working round the clock on the fortifications, and after three days the troops occupied the completed camp (20 August).

Frederick had his little tent pitched near one of the main batteries, as if to underline the urgency of the situation, and the army spent the whole of each night under arms. In the daytime the troops slumped down to snatch what rest was allowed them by the crushing heat and their own hunger and thirst. The allies were worse off still, for they were standing in the open and shimmering plain, far from their own bases. Finally on 9 September Buturlin made off for Poland with a large number of the Russian troops, leaving Loudon with what seemed to be an inadequate force for any kind of aggressive action. Now that the immediate danger was past, Frederick struck camp on 26 September and marched for his other Silesian magazine at Neisse.

Loudon's sense of adventure was awakened by the report that Frederick had left a paltry garrison of four weak battalions in Schweidnitz, and on 1 October he took the place by storm.

The capture of this key fortress left Frederick with no alternative but to yield the greater part of southern Silesia, and he retreated first to Strehlen and finally on Breslau. More bad news came in the winter. A new government came to power in Britain, and declined to renew the subsidy to Prussia. Meanwhile to the north-east the Russians were laying siege to Kolberg, a fortified town on the coast of eastern Pomerania. The Russians had failed at Kolberg twice before, but on 16 December 1761 the place finally capitulated, giving them a useful port of call on an otherwise inhospitable stretch of the Baltic coast.

Frederick had ensured the immediate physical survival of the 'main' royal army, but the ability of his state to sustain the war was now in serious question. For the first time his officers were allowed no *Wintervergütigungen* – the fitting-out allowance for the next campaign – and in some regiments the hardships were so great that the captains had to sell off their muskets to the free battalions. Frederick himself spent the early winter in sullen retirement at Breslau. He seldom ventured out of doors, and he kept his favourite flute neglected in its box. 'His soldiers, and even the Gensd'armes – who were survivors of the old army because they had suffered little in the war – pronounced that they would lay down their arms if they came under attack.'[79]

1762 – THE YEAR OF SALVATION

One day in January 1762 a remarkable change was evident in Frederick's conduct. He arrayed the Garde for inspection, retrieved his flute and summoned up his French cooks from Berlin. The transformation had been accomplished by the news of a change of régime in Russia, where his bitter enemy the Empress Elizabeth had died on 5 January and was succeeded by the snub-nosed and crazy Peter III, who was besotted with things Prussian.

The new tsar made peace with Frederick on 5 May. Sweden followed suit on the 22nd, and in June Peter went so far as to conclude an offensive alliance and put an auxiliary corps of 20,000 troops at Frederick's disposal. Frederick meanwhile had restored his army to a strength of more than 100,000 combatant troops.

The war in Silesia at last took on the appearance of an equal contest, with the main armies of Frederick and Daun sportingly matched at 80,000 troops each. Big battles were out of fashion, after the bloodbath at Torgau, but Frederick was determined to win back southern Silesia, and he began the process by manoeuvring Daun out of his successive camps at Zobten and Munzendorf.

Daun finally drew back to a chain of rocky hills at Dittmannsdorf, a position which covered the whole of the plain of Schweidnitz. He stuffed the fortress of Schweidnitz itself with 10,000 picked troops. Just when Frederick needed the Russians most, to winkle the Austrians out of their position, he received the appalling news that Peter III had been murdered. The Russian contingent, however, was persuaded to stay on in reserve for a few days longer, and on 21 July Frederick attacked the Austrian camp. The Prussians accomplished a breakthrough at Burkersdorf, on the right of Daun's position, and thereby drove the Austrians from the last tenable ground in the south of Silesia.

Frederick followed on Daun's heels, as he began a hasty retreat towards the county of Glatz, and he left Lieutenant-General v. Tauentzien with 12,000 troops to see to Schweidnitz. The king assumed that Schweidnitz would surrender ten or twelve days after the attack had got under way. All the same, Schweidnitz was worthy of more serious attention, for its siege represented the ultimate effort of both parties in the contest for the possession of Silesia, and upon that issue hung the outcome of the struggle for the upper hand in Central Europe.

The siege of Schweidnitz got off to an ominously bad start. The Prussians began to dig their 'first parallel' on the night of 7/8 August, only to see the working parties over-run at once by a massive sortie of 5,000 Austrians. The Prussians' morale was depressed still further when they failed in two assaults against the Jauernicker Flèche, which was one of the smaller and weaker fortifications. In addition the chief engineer, Simon Lefebvre, ran into considerable difficulties when he set the inexperienced Prussian miners at work to tunnel beneath the fortifications.

All of this placed heavy demands on regiments that were some of the worst of an already battered army. The ranks were largely made up of frightened boys, who were liable to burst into tears whenever the Austrians launched a sortie, and the hunger was so extreme that some of the troops were driven to collect grains of barley from amid the horse dung.

The place surrendered only on 9 October, after the main Jauernicker Fort had been wrecked by a lucky mortar bomb, which blew up its magazine, and a mine blast which levelled the outer wall of the ditch.

The epic contest for Schweidnitz closed the war in Silesia. However, the fighting in Saxony went ahead with all the more urgency, for both sides knew that peace was in the offing. Prince Henry was spurred on by his royal brother to take the offensive, and on 29 October he attacked and beat the *Reichsarmee* at Freiberg.

The peace negotiations went ahead in the devastated hunting lodge of Hubertusburg – an odd choice of venue – and on 15 February 1763 the Prussians, Austrians and Saxons concluded a peace which restored their borders to the lines they had followed in 1756.

THE COST OF THE WAR

According to modern estimates,[80] the titanic struggle of the Seven Years War cost the warring parties half a million troops in dead, of whom 180,000 were Prussian. As for the prisoners, the Austrians reckoned that by themselves they had captured 62,889 of Frederick's officers and men.[81]

One regiment alone, the Jung-Braunschweig Fusiliers, had run through 4,474 men in the course of the war, which indicates that it must have been wiped out three times over. The noble family of Belling had lost twenty males out of twenty-three, while many years later Frederick encountered a widow at Silberberg who told him that six of her sons had died in the same terrible war. The population of Prussia as a whole sank by at least half a million.

In terms of material waste the Prussians had lost 60,000 horses and 13,000 dwellings, and Frederick had dispensed no less than 139,000,000 thalers (all of which, and more, he recovered from other sources). To the Austrians alone the army had yielded 204 colours, 52 standards, 430 cannon, 34 howitzers and 23 mortars, not to mention a huge number of transport waggons – 4,000 of them on the single day of 30 June 1758.

The Prussian army after the Seven Years War

THE CONDITION OF THE ARMY IN THE POST-WAR PERIOD

Looking back from the end of the century, one of Frederick's officers concluded that 'beyond doubt the true golden era of the army extended from the accession of the king up to the Peace of Hubertusburg'.[82] In later years the army showed unmistakable signs of decay.

This is not to deny that the numerical losses of the Seven Years War were made good with almost indecent haste. Much of the manpower of the disbanded free battalions was impressed for the permanent army, and in addition 300 officers and 40,000 men chose to come back from Austrian captivity, which helped to fill the worst of the remaining gaps. So as to repopulate the military stock in general, Frederick decreed that as many soldiers as possible should find themselves wives in Saxony before they left for home.

After the demobilisation and reorganisations of 1763 the field army stood at $105\frac{1}{2}$ field battalions, 215 squadrons and 30 artillery companies, which gave a strength of 130,000 troops, of whom 82,000 were absent on leave at any given time outside the exercise season. The garrison troops amounted to 32 battalions, 9 companies of garrison artillery and a number of Land Regiments, a total of 25,000 men.

More difficult than the counting of heads was to restore the old standards of enthusiasm and efficiency. Frederick summed up his task: 'We must begin to recruit and discipline our army anew, and educate the young officers to honour.'[83]

Unfortunately Frederick's preoccupation produced a force in which everything was subordinated to a perfection in outward appearances, a mechanical proficiency in drill and the application of a code of unthinking discipline – in short, an army which reflected the obsessions of its overworked master rather than any tactical necessity. The wandering Scot James Boswell caught the mood of the king when he visited Potsdam in 1764.

> I . . . went to the parade. I saw the king. It was a glorious sight. He was dressed in a suit of plain blue, with a star and a plain hat with a white feather. He had in his hand a cane. The sun shone bright. He stood before his palace, with an air of iron confidence that could not be opposed. As a loadstone moves needles, or a storm bows the lofty oaks, did Frederick the Great make the Prussian officers submissive bend as he walked majestic in the midst of them.[84]

Among the rank and file the sense of cohesion and honour was dying fast. Frederick only hastened its death when he sent uniforms of increasingly poor quality to the regiments, when he extended the already wide exemptions from the cantonal draft, and when on 14 October 1780 he made military service a punishment for civilian criminals.

There was no compensating inflow of good foreign recruits. In 1763 Frederick promulgated a badly conceived Recruiting Ordinance (*Werbe-Etat*) which replaced the earlier system of direct recruiting by the officers on behalf of their own companies by a general recruiting for the state. General v. Gaudi claimed that the damage was immense. In earlier times, he said, the captains had an interest in recruiting good men for their own companies, but 'now the officers and NCOs who are sent on recruiting know very well that they are not gathering recruits for their own regiment, but simply throwing them together in one mass . . . they do not bother about the moral qualities of the men, but take on the most disreputable folk'.[85]

The quality of the foreign recruits was probably at its very worst in the late 1770s and early 1780s, for then the best German material was being drawn into the British service for the war against the American rebels.

There seemed to be no escape from the atmosphere of constraint. Frederick instituted an ever harsher régime, so as to compensate for the declining worth of the manpower, but the brutal punishments themselves drove men to desert. Finally the king had to station bodies of cavalry in every large garrison, so as to deter the infantry from running off.

The cavalry itself underwent a sad decline. The horse establishment was drastically cut immediately after the war, and the rations of dry fodder were progressively reduced. For a time the old spirit was kept alive by Seydlitz, who commanded the important Silesian cavalry inspection, and whose salutary influence extended over the whole cavalry arm. In 1772 he was afflicted by a stroke, and in the summer of the following year he was laid low again, as the consequence of a debauch. Frederick visited him in August. Seydlitz turned his face to the pillow so as to avert his nose, which was ravaged by syphilis, but Frederick spoke urgently to him for an hour and several times exclaimed: 'I cannot spare you! I cannot spare you!'[86] Seydlitz died on 7 November at the age of fifty-three, and his departure was a disaster for the Prussian cavalry.

Seydlitz had been eager to hand over the Silesian inspection to Colonel v. Wackenitz, whom he reckoned was the one man who was really suited to carry on his work. Unfortunately that gentleman had fallen into disfavour with the king for showing mercy to a Russian officer at Zorndorf, and Frederick instead split the inspection in two and turned the Lower Silesian cavalry over to Seydlitz's bitter enemy, the unpleasant little General v. Röder, who did his best to undo everything his rival had achieved. It was not easy to preserve the spirit of Rossbach when in some years a regiment might ride twenty-five times or even less, or when the animals were turned out to graze in the summer months like donkeys.

Frederick was disturbed to see that the war had accomplished something like a social revolution in the officer corps. In the 1760s, therefore, he dismissed nearly all the commissioned NCOs and the disreputable foreign officers of the free battalions, and he instituted a thoroughgoing purge of such bourgeois as had become officers in the infantry or cavalry. The deficiencies were made up to some degree by importing noble officers from the states of the empire. Thus in 1777 the regiment of Alt-Stutterheim could count sixteen foreign officers out of its establishment of fifty-one.

Frederick's concern for the officer corps did not extend in other directions. The *Werbe-Etat* of 1763 was bitterly resented, for in all except some favoured regiments the captain was permitted to retain the pay of only a proportion of the men who were absent on leave – between twenty-five and thirty per company, according to the regiment's war record – whereas under the old system he had been allowed to pocket the lot, on the understanding that he would devote some at least of the proceeds to recruiting for his company in foreign parts. The company commander was now driven to a variety of underhand expedients, since he could hardly live on his basic captain's pay of thirty-three thalers per month, and even the inspectors were ready to connive in the enlistment of 'falsified foreigners' (*Gemächte Ausländer*) – Prussian natives who were recruited contrary to the royal prohibitions. Carl Daniel Küster testifies that he often encountered captains who were deeply disturbed by the trickery which had entered their lives.

Officers tended to hang on in the regiments as long as their physical powers lasted, and sometimes a good deal longer, so as to postpone the day when they were thrown into civilian life with little or no pension. Almost every regiment owned a proportion of officers who were in advanced bodily decay, or were mentally crushed by years of drudgery. In the absence of a couple of strenuous campaigns (the War of the Bavarian Succession hardly counts) there was no means by which the incompetents could be weeded out, or the good young officers pushed up the ladder of promotion. Ironically enough, a system for the purchase of commissions, such as existed in England and (unofficially) in Austria, would have done something to help the youngsters. John Burgoyne shrewdly observed:

Most of the generals who eminently possessed the great parts of their profession perished in the war or are worn out by the fatigue of it, or have sought occasions to retire. The greater part of the present set have recommended themselves by their assiduity upon the parade, and are men of very confused education. The severity, with which command is carried; a long attention to trivial duties; the smallness of pay in the lower ranks: the oeconomy of table imposed upon the high [but see p. 44]; the want of the French language, and many other causes which prevent the intercourse officers of other countries enjoy with superiors and strangers, concur to keep the mind contracted.[87]

The officers found it increasingly difficult to see in Frederick the man who had led the 'Berlin watch-parade' as his private army in the worst days of the Seven Years War. They were liable to be withered by a blast of the royal scorn, whenever they crossed his path, and more and more they discovered that they had to have dealings with such objectionable intermediaries as the district inspectors and that curious creature 'Wilhelmi' v. Anhalt.

Heinrich Wilhelm v. Anhalt was a by-blow of the Dessau clan, having been born of a liaison between Prince August of Anhalt-Dessau (the eldest son of the Old Dessauer) and the beautiful but indiscreet daughter of a clergyman. He spent his youth in the suite of Prince Moritz, where he cultivated an interest in military engineering and topography. It was his skill in these arts that brought him to the notice of the king, after his first patron had died in 1760, and before the end of the war he was promoted to lieutenant-colonel and ennobled with his brother under the title of 'von Anhalt'. Wilhelmi reorganised the nascent horse artillery in the last stages of the war, and from 1765 to 1781 he combined the offices of *Generalquartiermeister* and *Generaladjutant*, thus becoming the nearest thing to a chief of staff that the Prussian eighteenth century had to offer.

Mirabeau met Wilhelmi in later years and describes him as 'an able tactician, endowed with a superior *coup d'oeil*. Unfortunately he is hard to the degree of ferocity, and perhaps his talent and even his common sense have been impaired by a fall from his horse, for which he was trepanned'.[88] Wilhelmi used his powers in the crudest possible fashion, and he was responsible for the departure from the service of a large number of officers, ranging from Steuben (the future drillmaster of Washington's army) to no less a personage than Prince Ferdinand of Brunswick, who had prevented Wilhelmi from striking a *Stallmeister* at a review at Magdeburg. Prince Ferdinand declared that there was no room in the same army for both himself and Wilhelmi, to which Frederick replied: 'You have already made your choice, I can't do without Anhalt.'[89]

Another man of the same stamp was the savage General v. Ramin, whom Frederick chose as governor of Berlin after the war. 'The king conceived that every now and again it was important to appoint to the capital a chief who was capable of inspiring fear, so as to maintain discipline in all the severity necessary for his service.'[90] To endow this barbarian with a little dignity, Frederick staged an informal ceremony at a review at Potsdam and hung his own order of the Black Eagle around Ramin's neck. Frederick was only too aware of the ridiculous aspect of his gesture, and he turned his face aside so that Ramin would not see his smirk.

Monsters like these commanded little respect in the army. Seydlitz disliked Wilhelmi intensely, which was a fairly damning indictment in itself, and Prince Henry believed that this newly created 'Herr v. Anhalt' had taken Winterfeldt's place as the king's evil genius.

Prince Henry's own humanity and common sense presented a pleasing contrast to the searing sarcasm of the king and the uncouth ravings of Wilhelmi. Unfortunately this circumstance helped to encourage the spirit of division in the army, and led officers to attribute Prussia's survival in the war to Prince Henry's cautious stratagems rather than to the boldness of his royal brother.

Prominent among the new generation of generals was the urbane and popular Möllendorff, former commandant of the Garde, who had paved the way to victory at Torgau, and who was one of the few commanders to emerge with credit from the War of the Bavarian Succession. In later years he resided in considerable state at Berlin, as one of Ramin's successors as governor.

Möllendorff's influence in social life was paralleled in tactics and discipline by that of his bosom friend, Major-General Friedrich Christoph v. Saldern. Saldern excelled at moving troops about with speed and precision, as he had proved at Hochkirch, Liegnitz and Torgau, and as head of the important Magdeburg Infantry Inspection from 1763 until 1785 he managed to persuade the rest of the generals that regularity in tactical evolutions was the essence of all military training. Foreign officers came to Prussia with the express purpose of seeing Saldern put his infantry through their paces, and they read avidly in his memoranda (*Taktik der Infanterie*, Dresden 1784, and *Taktische Grundsätze und Anweisung*, Dresden 1786. Both these works appear to have been published without Saldern's authorisation).

Saldern was a priggish, nose-to-the-grindstone kind of person who seems oddly out of place in the eighteenth century. As a good Christian he had refused to carry out Frederick's order to devastate the Saxon hunting lodge at Hubertusburg (see p. 196). He kept his books in as good order as his conscience, 'for he was well aware that in a great machine, if so much as a single cog of a wheel is bent or broken, the whole mechanism will suffer'.[91] He reviewed the list of his wine cellar every day, lest anybody should be taking a surreptitious swig at the contents, and he kept the account book locked away from everyone except a single trusted steward. We can see why people were willing to credit him (wrongly, so it seems) with the authorship of the following statement: 'It is certainly laid down that we should march at seventy-six paces to the minute, but upon mature consideration and much reflection I have come to the conclusion that seventy-five steps would be even better.'[92]

All the same, Saldern was able to win a wide admiration in the later Frederician army. He looked like 'a picture of the God of War, tall, very well formed, full of majesty and dignity'.[93] He entranced Frederick by devising new manoeuvres for almost every review, and on the great Neumarkt at Magdeburg he was capable of commanding three battalions at a time, his voice echoing across the square from the tall cathedral tower.

As for active command in the field, the army began to look once more to the House of Brunswick. The great Prince Ferdinand had fallen foul of Wilhelmi Anhalt and left the service after the Seven Years War, as we have seen. The presence of the line was, however, maintained by the Hereditary Prince Karl Wilhelm Friedrich, who won golden opinions by the way he commanded a corps in the War of the Polish Succession. He charmed the soldiers by his open manners and his concern for their welfare, while military pundits were lost in admiration for his perception, for the clarity of his dispositions and the precision of his orders. After Frederick's death the new king therefore made it one of his first concerns to promote this paragon of the military virtues to field-marshal.

It was a measure of the change in the character of warfare that Brunswick, the same man, should have commanded the Prussian army in the inglorious Valmy campaign of 1792, and that in the company of Möllendorff he presided over its destruction in the catastrophe of Jena–Auerstedt in 1806.

THE FIRST PARTITION OF POLAND 1772

The chaotic constitution of the Polish state had long offered an affront and temptation to the tidy-minded and greedy monarchs of Central Europe. In August 1772, after a period of high tension, Prussia, Austria and Russia banded together to share out large regions of this defenceless kingdom. West Prussia fell to Frederick, which gave him an augmentation of 600,000 subjects and a direct overland communication between Pomerania and East Prussia.

This windfall enabled Frederick to establish a fourth regiment of field artillery, and raise a hussar regiment (no 10) and four regiments of fusiliers (nos 51, 53, 54, 55).

The old generals assumed that the Polish troops must be 'some kind of orang-utans', and they were surprised to find that they looked exactly the same as the veteran regiments. However, the young officers were 'almost all Polish nobles . . . who were unable to read or write in German'.[94]

THE WAR OF THE BAVARIAN SUCCESSION 1778-1779

In the summer of 1778 Frederick suspected that the young Austrian Emperor Joseph II (co-regent with his mother Maria Theresa) was trying to arrange an exchange of the remote and strategically useless Austrian Netherlands with the electorate of Bavaria. The deal, if it had gone through, would have more than made up for the loss of Silesia and tilted the balance of power in Central Europe once more in favour of the Austrians.

Frederick had the support of most of the German states in objecting to the scheme, and since the Austrians would not give way he committed Prussia to a new war.

If statistics and the lessons of history counted for anything, then the contest should have been decided in favour of Prussia in a matter of weeks. Austria, which had been the heart of a coalition in the Seven Years War, now stood without a friend. Frederick, who was accustomed to emerging victorious in the face of the heaviest odds, now enjoyed the support of 22,000 Saxon troops and planned to put 154,000 of his own into the field. This great mass of men was divided into two groups, with the object of carrying out a pincer movement: Frederick assembled 87,000 in southern Silesia and made ready to strike by way of Moravia directly for the Danube; Prince Henry, meanwhile, was to gather 85,000 troops to the west and advance up the Elbe into Bohemia.

A good four months had been spent in making ready for the campaign, and yet some alarming deficiencies were evident even before the forces reached their assembly areas. Along some of the march routes the transport arrangements virtually collapsed, and the artillery in particular was in a bad way, for the quantity and weight of the ordnance had increased over the last years, and, as always, the teams of horses had to be raised anew in the event of war. Many roads which had been perfectly practicable during the Seven Years War were now found to be too steep for the guns.

The Austrians cunningly placed their main force in northern Bohemia between the two widely separated Prussian armies. The right rested on the rebuilt fortress of Königgrätz, and the front was protected by the line of the upper Elbe, where every crossing point was guarded by a triple redoubt. The trees along the hills were hewn down to form abattis, and the tangled countryside was swarming with Croats.

Early in July 1778, Prince Henry and his Second Army irrupted into Bohemia by way of the Lusatian passes, gaining an initial advantage over the Austrians, but after this promising start he ran out of supplies before he could turn the line of the upper Elbe.

Over to the east, on 5 July, Frederick led the advance guard of the First Army over the little stream near Nachod which marked the border. He at once rode ahead with a regiment of dragoons and a squadron of the Black Hussars. Most of the young hussars had never seen Frederick before, and they were disappointed to discover that he was much older-looking and more sullen than they had been led to expect. When they emerged into the plain the veterans promised them some action. But there were no Austrians to be seen – they had all retired behind the upper Elbe. The little party turned back at noon, and the hussars gave loud vent to their disappointment in the war and in Frederick himself, who rode on in silence.

The army penetrated a few miles into enemy territory, then spent the rest of the campaigning season in idleness in front of the enemy positions. A heavy desertion set in as soon as the troops found how well the Austrians were living in their camp nearby at Jaromiersch, and on 1 September Frederick ordered his officers to say aloud in the hearing of their soldiers that the Austrians were beating a dozen men to death daily (which was a complete fabrication).

The *Feldjäger* in particular were demoralised, for Frederick had deprived them of their beloved short rifles and issued them with the ordinary bayoneted smooth-bore muskets instead. They deserted in such numbers that the king had to employ two battalions of the garrison regiment of Bremer as 'free battalions'. The experiment proved to be a disaster, for one officer and two hundred men made off on the first night of duty alone. Thus the Croats waded the upper Elbe and roamed about on the 'Prussian' side almost unmolested.

Among the other *Fehler und négligences* which Frederick noted among the infantry were the three occasions on which whole detachments allowed themselves to be surprised and beaten by the Austrians (at Dittersbach 8 November 1778, Habelschwerdt 18 January 1779 and Cämmerswalde 7 February 1779).

The cavalry performed still worse. The hussars sat smoking in their billets, rather than going out to torment the enemy, while the regiments of heavy cavalry devoted most of their energies to battling among themselves for the foraging rights. The price of fodder, indeed, rose so high that the officers of the Bayreuth Dragoons left their horses to starve and sold off the bundles of hay to the sutlers. Everywhere the animals 'looked like skeletons, and stood up to the knees in the mud which they were churning up in the search for fodder. Whenever the artillery horses and other draught horses were harnessed up and set to work, they threw themselves into the traces then sank exhausted to the ground in their hundreds'.[95]

Prince Henry had ordered affairs more sensibly, over in the western theatre, for he carefully parcelled the foraging areas among the individual regiments.

In November 1778 the Empress Catherine II of Russia offered to mediate between the warring parties. Both Frederick and Joseph were quick to take her up on this proposal, and in the spring of the next year Old Fritz drew back his dejected forces from Bohemia. A full treaty of peace was signed at Teschen on 13 May 1779: the Austrians gave up their grand design on Bavaria, though they were allowed to save their honour by walking off with the little district of Burghausen. All told, Frederick emerged with more profit than might have been expected from the way the war had gone.

Frederick had lost 40,000 troops from sickness, desertion and enemy action during this, his last campaign. Historians dignify the contest by the name of the 'War of the Bavarian Succession', though the soldiers remembered it as the *Kartoffelkrieg*, the 'Potato War', from the newly introduced vegetable which they uprooted to allay their hunger.

THE FINAL YEARS OF THE REIGN

In numerical terms the Prussian army had never been more powerful than at the time of Frederick's death in 1786, no less than 190,600 troops standing at the disposal of his successor (140,000 infantry, 40,000 cavalry and 10,600 gunners; 110,000 were foreigners

The last encounter of Frederick and Zieten. Frederick William, Prince of Prussia (later Frederick William II) is the large figure standing behind the king. Möllendorff is looking from the right of the picture with his hands folded on top of his stick

and 80,000 natives, and of the total force 90,000 were on leave at any given time outside the exercise season).

One suspects that in these last years the old king's mind was crowded with ghosts rather than the endless blue ranks he saw before him. In 1785 he held a special review of the Pomeranian troops at Stargard. He was unable to mount horse, and so he had the regiments march past him in succession. He raised his hat every time a set of colours went by, and as the final battalions came up he remarked to the inspector, General v. Brünning: 'It's true, they're splendid troops, my dear Pomeranians!' The officers were taken aback by his weak, melancholy voice, but he added almost pleadingly, 'Just let them march past once more!' Now he kept his head uncovered all the time the regiments passed by.[96]

Sometimes when he was passing through Silesia Frederick would turn aside to the estate of Minkowitz near Namslau and meditate for a few minutes before Seydlitz's tomb – a black marble slab which was lettered with gold. He seems to have felt the loss of Winterfeldt more keenly still, after all those years, for that man had been the most understanding of all his confidants.

Zieten clung on longer than any other of the great men of the 1750s, and Frederick often numbered the old 'hussar king' among his guests at table. There was one evening when Zieten nodded off, and the conversation turning on the battle of Torgau Frederick remarked: 'The Old Man nearly played me a stupid prank there!'[97] At the evocative word 'Torgau', Zieten started up and looked so intently at the king that Frederick had to dismiss the table in his embarrassment.

Frederick and Zieten spoke for the last time at Christmas 1785. Frederick immediately singled him out as he stood in the company of several princes and ushered him to a chair. They talked together for several minutes, and Frederick, deeply affected, had to leave the room without saying a word to the other dignitaries. Zieten died one month later. Frederick commented to some of his generals:

> Our old Zieten has showed himself very much the general even when he died. In wartime he always commanded the advance guard, and now he has taken the lead in death. I always used to lead the main army, and now I shall follow after him, just as on campaign.[98]

The Marquis de Toulongeon was received in audience in April 1786, and noted unmistakable signs of suffering in the king – the white, lined face, the reverberating cough, and the bandages that were bound about one leg. Frederick was carried away after five minutes and to Toulongeon it seemed he had witnessed 'the ghost of some hero who had appeared to me from the other world'.[99]

Those terrifying blue eyes closed for the last time in the early morning of 17 August 1786.

12

Influence and Legacy

Foreign observers admired what Frederick was doing with his army, but the more perceptive among them asked themselves whether the achievement would long survive his death.

> Was it possible [wrote Mirabeau] that all the successors of Frederick will be as tireless as he? Will they go every year to preside over military reviews in every corner of the state? Will they read, examine and weigh up every report that the Inspectors send in on every regiment?[1]

Frederick himself had written in a surprisingly pessimistic tone in 1782, when he expressed his fears that his soft and uncaring nephew would allow the House of Brandenburg to be trampled down by Austria.[2]

This same nephew acceded in 1786 as King Frederick William II. He was the son of the unlucky Prince Augustus William who had died in disgrace in 1758, and as Crown Prince he had himself suffered repeated humiliations at the hands of his royal uncle. Small wonder that he was bald and toothless before he reached middle age, and came to the throne bearing what seemed to be the physical signs of a defeated man. These circumstances did not prevent Frederick William from addressing himself to the work of correcting some of the worst abuses of the old reign. He converted many fusilier regiments into units of genuine light infantry, he endowed each regiment with a depot battalion, he regularised and increased the pay of the officers, he gave the engineering corps a proper chief, he reformed the staff, and he reorganised the medical services.

Unfortunately Frederick William lacked the determination and the sheer nastiness that were needed to carry through a complete transformation of an army that was still spellbound by the memory of the old king. Too many of the old preconceptions remained undisturbed: not only did the Saldern-type tactics still hold sway, but Prussian society lived on in sublime indifference to the changes that were being wrought in western Europe by the French Revolution.

In 1806 Napoleon took the offensive in central Germany and routed the slow-moving Prussian army at the dual battle of Jena–Auerstedt. The ensuing collapse proved to be more than just a military one, for the entire Prussian nation showed itself willing to submit to the victorious French. An historian has commented:

> If a people is accustomed blindly to accept authority, it will experience no great difficulty in transferring its allegiance from one authority to another. The institutional framework of the absolute military state did not permit the members of the middle and lower classes to identify themselves in any real sense with the state machine. When that machine collapsed it was only natural that they should accept this fact and adjust their narrow lives to the new circumstances forced upon them.[3]

Queen Luisa put it more poetically. 'We went to sleep on the laurels of Frederick the Great. We awoke, and we found ourselves in a new world.'

And yet, in space and time, the influence of Frederick's army was extremely potent.

Whereas the two Silesian wars of the 1740s were soon lost to mind amid the other dynastic contests of the century, the Seven Years War presented itself to foreigners as something fearsome and extraordinary. Even in Venice society divided into the factions of the *Prussiani* and *Teresiani*, who pursued their arguments in the squares, in the coffee houses but most violently of all in the monastery of SS Giovanni e Paolo, where the monks 'struck out manfully in their dining hall for the honour of Maria Theresa or Frederick, using plates, basins and mugs as their weapons'.[4]

In Europe generally military men sought to express their admiration for things Prussian by imitating every conceivable external of Frederick's army, rather as a savage might adorn himself with the feathers of an eagle in an attempt to endow himself with the creature's qualities. Now the tailors 'liked to diminish the amount of fabric in the coat skirts, while shortening the waistcoats and narrowing the sleeves and lapels. Now the little hat of the Prussian musketeers perched on the heads of *gens comme il faut*'.[5] Inspired by Prussia, the public subjected itself to a process of militarisation. 'Everyone had himself made uniforms of martial cut and military combinations of colour – officials of the forests, posts and mines, the provincial nobility, and members of knightly orders and corps down to canons of the cathedral; no Englishman would go abroad but in the uniform of his county militia.'[6]

In more genuinely military matters a foreigner could cap almost any discussion by exclaiming: 'Mais je l'ai vu en Prusse!'

The whole exercise was patently absurd. The Prussian uniforms could not 'possibly contribute to gain one battle',[7] and, as Burgoyne pointed out, Frederick had run his army so tightly only because his mercenary rank and file were unreliable: it was harmful for foreigners to try to manage their armies on this principle 'when the disposition of their country offers the best groundwork of national character or public spirit'.[8]

Not even the French public could suppress its glee at the discomfiture of their generals at the hands of the Prussians in the Seven Years War. As for the military men, they began to search about for whatever features of the Prussian system could be adapted to the French army. The *Règlement* of 1764 borrowed a good many articles on drill and discipline from the Prussian practice, while in the 1770s the Comte de Guibert and the Prussian renegade Pirch introduced the army to the Frederician deployment from the closed column, a device that was incorporated in the Ordinance of 1791, the drill-book of the French Revolution.

In one respect at least the army of the *ancien régime* clearly won an advance on its Prussian masters. In 1760, recognising that the French could never rival the Prussians in the exactitude of their movements, Marshal de Broglie had the inspiration of breaking down the field army into half a dozen sub-units, or 'divisions', which could reach their assigned stations more conveniently than the conventional army, with its two lines of battle. Thus the French began to move away from the concept of the army as an indivisible *bloc*, and the foundation was laid for the evolution of the corps system of the 1800s, which gave Napoleon the means of attaining in strategic terms what it had cost Frederick so many pains to effect on the battlefields of the Seven Years War – namely the envelopment of the enemy armed force.

In other places in Europe spirits became Prussianised to a more extreme degree. The enthusiasm in Britain reached its peak after the news arrived of Frederick's great victories of 1757: 'women and children are singing his praises: the most frantick marks of joy appear in the publick streets'.[9]

Taken together with the Jacobite rebellion of 1745 and the fears of French invasion in the 1750s, the admiration for Frederick's achievements helped to dissipate some of the old English aversion to the institution of the standing army.[10]

English translations of the Prussian infantry regulations were published in 1754 and 1757, and a rendering of the cavalry regulations appeared in the latter year. On 24 April 1756 the sergeants of the First Foot Guards put their troops through the Prussian drill for the first time, an example followed by the companies of 'Prussian Volunteers' which sprang up in the Seven Years War.

One would have thought that the experience of the war against the American rebels (1775–83) would have taught the British to revise their ideas. Certainly Cornwallis, having returned from America, was singularly unimpressed by what he saw of the Prussians when they went through their paces at Berlin, Potsdam and Magdeburg in 1785. 'Their manoeuvres were such as the worst general in England would be hooted at for practising; two lines coming up within six yards of one another and firing till they had no ammunition left; nothing could be more ridiculous.'[11] It was a pity that the sceptical marquis was accompanied to the field by Colonel David Dundas, who was entranced by the proceedings. A hungry and ambitious Scot, Dundas was fired with the ambition to work out a Prussianised drillbook of his own, and in 1792 he persuaded his masters to enforce his 'Eighteen Manoeuvres' throughout the infantry.

In Russia the admiration for things Prussian was twice driven beyond all sane limits. The besotted Tsar Peter III was disposed of in 1762 before he could do too much damage, but between 1796 and his assassination in 1801 Tsar Paul I not only introduced the old Prussian drillbook and the Saldern waddle of seventy-five paces to the minute, but he contrived to have his entire army dressed up in honour of the dead Frederick in all the pomaded grandeur of the middle of the eighteenth century.

Oddly enough, it was a 'genuine' Frederician officer who accomplished what was by far the most successful transformation of a foreign army. This was Baron Friedrich v. Steuben. He had functioned as one of the *Quartiermeisterlieutenants* towards the end of the Seven Years War, but also – and more significantly – he had spent some time as a lieutenant in the Mayr Free Battalion (no 2). Steuben ran foul of the infamous Wilhelmi Anhalt at the end of the war and left the service with the rank of captain. After he had spent a number of years wandering about Europe he came to the notice of the inventive Benjamin Franklin, who recommended him to Washington as a Prussian lieutenant-general, no less. He arrived in America at a time when the rebel cause was at a low ebb, and in February 1778 he was faced with the task of re-fashioning Washington's demoralised force at Valley Forge into the semblance of an army.

Conveying his orders through interpreters, or shouting in his own fractured English, Steuben put the rebel troops through a skilfully modified version of the Prussian drill. He explained his thinking to another Prussian officer in the following terms. 'The genius of this nation is not in the least to be compared to that of the Prussians, Austrians or French. You say to *your* soldier: "Do this!" and he does it. But I am obliged to say: "This is the reason why you ought to do that", and then he does it.'[12]

The troops appreciated what Steuben was doing for them despite (or perhaps because of) the original quality of his invective: 'Sacre! Goddam de gaucheries of dese badauts! Je ne puis plus, I can curse dem no more!'[13] He selected a company of officers for special training, and sent them off to spread his doctrines through the army, and in 1779 he drew up his *Regulations for the Order and Discipline of the United States* – the famous *Blue Book* that determined the tactics and routine of the American service for more than three decades.

The reputation of Frederick in Prussia itself suffered an eclipse in the period from 1808, when a generation of enlightened military reformers was rebuilding the army after the catastrophe of Jena–Auerstedt. To Scharnhorst, Gneisenau, Blücher, Clausewitz and people of that kind it seemed that it had been the mentality of the Frederician era, with its mindless discipline and its divorce of the people from the government, that was account- able in large measure for Prussia's humiliation by the French.

The cult of Frederick was revived, strange to say, by the National–Liberal movement which caused so much unrest throughout Germany and culminated in the revolution of 1848. Indeed the Prussian bureaucracy of the Holy Alliance period was so alarmed at the trend to present Frederick as the all-German hero that the officials actually set about destroying quantities of documents relating to his reign. The return of Old Fritz to respectability was accomplished, as much as anything else, by the unimpeachably con- servative J. D. E. Preuss, who brought out his massive biography *Friedrich der Grosse* in nine volumes between 1832 and 1834. The results of the awakening of scholarly interest in Frederick were presented in a more popular form in Franz Kugler's *Geschichte Friedrichs des Grossen* in 1840, and two years later the work was republished with illustra- tions by Adolf Menzel, whose detailed and on the whole very accurate portrayal of men and events has fixed the image of the Frederician army for succeeding generations.

The Prussian government now began to reclaim Frederick for itself, an interest that was first expressed in the publication of the *Oeuvres de Frédéric le Grand* in thirty volumes (1846–56), and found its last expression in the General Staff's *Kriege Friedrichs des Grossen*, an enormous enterprise that was begun in 1890 and went ahead until the publica- tion was brought to an end by World War I.

At the same time it is difficult to believe that the new Prusso-German régime de- liberately followed the example of Frederick's doings in anything save the most superficial aspects, despite the concept of the 'strategy of the central position' that underlay the so- called Schlieffen Plan with which Germany went to war in 1914. Schlieffen himself (Chief of the General Staff 1891–1914) had little genuine historical awareness, and he was quite ignorant of the fact that patriotic German historians were working for years to show that Frederick had sprung to arms in 1756 only in self-defence, and not with the intention of putting into effect any vast scheme of aggrandisement. When, at last, the fruits of all their researches were laid before him, all he could say was: 'What a pity!'[14]

After the collapse of the Hohenzollern monarchy the Nazis enlisted the trappings of Fredericiana in their support. Films like *Anthem of Leuthen* recalled the great days of the 1750s, while posters displayed Frederick's head alongside those of Bismarck and the Führer. Thus an historian could write:

In January 1918, somewhere on the Western Front, an unknown corporal of German- Austrian blood saw for the first time, and at a distance, the commander of Prussian

Germany, Erich Ludendorff. He was struck with admiration. Later, as a statesman, Hitler greeted this tradition once again, when he bowed to Field-Marshal v. Hindenburg in the Garrison Church at Potsdam. Thus the living force of Frederick, the creator and leader of the army, reaches to our present day.[15]

Not only did Hitler believe in this bogus spiritual genealogy, but he began to detect more and more parallels between his own career and that of Old Fritz. He justified his intention of attacking the Low Countries to his generals by recalling the example of Frederick in 1740. In later years, when the war began to turn against him, he looked for inspiration to Graff's portrait of Frederick, which hung in his study. Goebbels, for one, was ready to draw a direct parallel between the death of the Empress Elizabeth of Russia in 1762 and that of President Roosevelt in 1945, and he expected that the enemy alliance would collapse in exactly the same way as Frederick's enemies had broken apart near the end of the Seven Years War. This time the omens played the Nazis false.

After the war the nascent West German Bundeswehr of the 1950s put its trust in the decidedly non-Frederician concepts of 'inner leadership' and the 'citizen in uniform': and yet the East Germans, having pretended to disavow everything that savoured of Prussianism, proceeded to adopt the codes and discipline of the old army almost intact. The Communist authorities at least had the advantage of taking over folk like the Pomeranians and Brandenburgers, while the West Germans had to fill their army with folk like the Baders, Württembergers and Westphalians, about whom Frederick was known to speak on occasion in disparaging terms.

Some West German historians (notably Ludwig Dehio) were inclined to group the Frederician army together with the SS State as basically identical manifestations of a spirit of militarism, but others pointed out that to some degree the Nazi movement was an aberration and represented a 'betrayal of Prussianism'.[16] There was certainly something very odd in the spectacle of the ex-corporal Hitler – Austrian, lapsed Catholic, lower-middle-class and irredeemably vulgar – appropriating for his own purposes the shade of the snobbish Prussian Frederick, a Freemason who was able to maintain his military machine only with the help of Jewish financiers.

The case for the rehabilitation of Frederick and his army was put most cogently by Gerhard Ritter,[17] who saw the aggressive militarism of recent times in Germany as essentially a phenomenon of the post-Bismarck period. In the earlier age, he claimed, the worst excesses of militarism were usually restrained by the higher political wisdom that German historians term *Staatsräson*. He reserved his particular admiration for Frederick, who sought to wage war as far as possible without disturbance to the people or their work, and curbed his power-drive 'by insight and reason, by political wisdom'.[18] The picture is perhaps a little overdrawn. Ritter leaves out of account Frederick's instinct (which grew rather than diminished) to settle the quarrel with Austria by an advance to the Danube, and he presents the War of the Bavarian Succession as a deliberate cabinet war of manoeuvre, which ignores the sheer physical difficulties of waging any other kind of war with the muscle-bound Prussian army of that period.

Perhaps it is more useful to dismiss the preoccupations of the day altogether, and look upon Frederick and his army purely as manifestations of their own time. That is something which the old devil surely has a right to demand of us.

KEY TO THE MAPS

(a)   ⊏⊐   Prussian infantry

      ⊿   Prussian cavalry

      ⟋⟍⟋⟍⟋⟍   Prussian battery of heavy guns

Enemy forces shown as above but in red

(b)   Prussian units are identified by number (see the list of regiments Appendix 2) thus:

     ▯-4   Infantry regiment no 4

     ▯20/22   Battalion of grenadiers from infantry regiments no's 20 and 22

     ▯CR5   Cuirassier regiment no 5

     ▯DR3   Dragoon regiment no 3

     ▯HR7   Hussar regiment no 7

(c)   Prussian units are shaded from their left flanks to give an immediate visual impression of losses sustained in battle

Field strengths of units varied considerably, though in the Second Silesian War the averages stood at about:

1,100 for an infantry regiment
450 for a grenadier battalion
550 for a regiment of cuirassiers or dragoons

At the outset of the Seven Years War the equivalent strengths were:

1,400 for an infantry regiment
625–650 for a grenadier battalion
720–860 for a regiment of cuirassiers or dragoons

Example: An infantry regiment shaded thus ■⊐ in 1745 would have lost just over 500 men in dead, wounded, missing and prisoners

(d)   Heights are given in metres

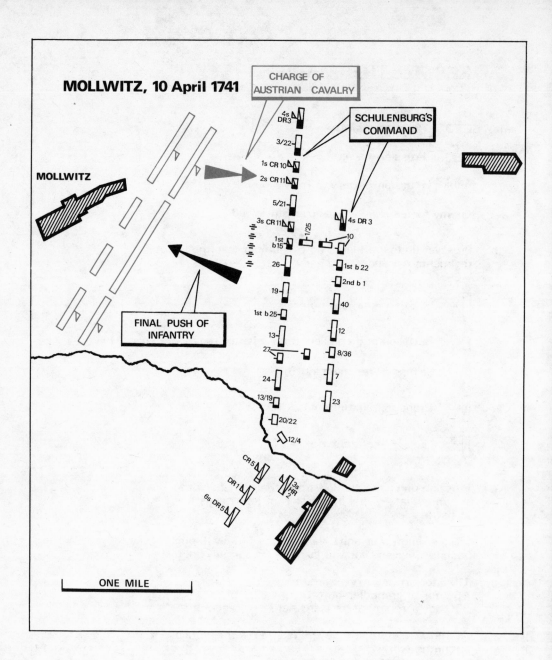

MOLLWITZ, 10 April 1741

CHARGE OF AUSTRIAN CAVALRY

SCHULENBURG'S COMMAND

MOLLWITZ

FINAL PUSH OF INFANTRY

4s DR3
3/22
1s CR 10
2s CR11
5/21
3s CR 11
1st b15
26
19
1st b 25
13
27
24
13/19
20/22
12/4
CR 5
DR 1
6s DR 5

4s DR 3
1/25
10
1st b 22
2nd b 1
40
12
8/36
7
23
3s HR 2

ONE MILE

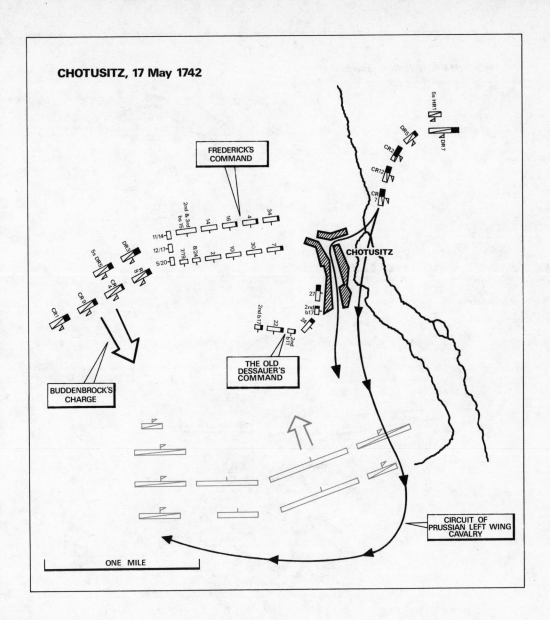

CHOTUSITZ, 17 May 1742

FREDERICK'S COMMAND

5s HR1

DR8
DR7

CR2

CR12

CR
7

CHOTUSITZ

34

4

16

14

2nd & 3rd
bs 15

11/14

12/17

5/20

7/19

8/24

2

10

30

7

27

2nd
b17

2/

5s DR5

DR3/

R

CR

CR 9/

CR1

2nd b17

22/

2nd
b11

BUDDENBROCK'S
CHARGE

THE OLD
DESSAUER'S
COMMAND

CIRCUIT OF
PRUSSIAN LEFT WING
CAVALRY

ONE MILE

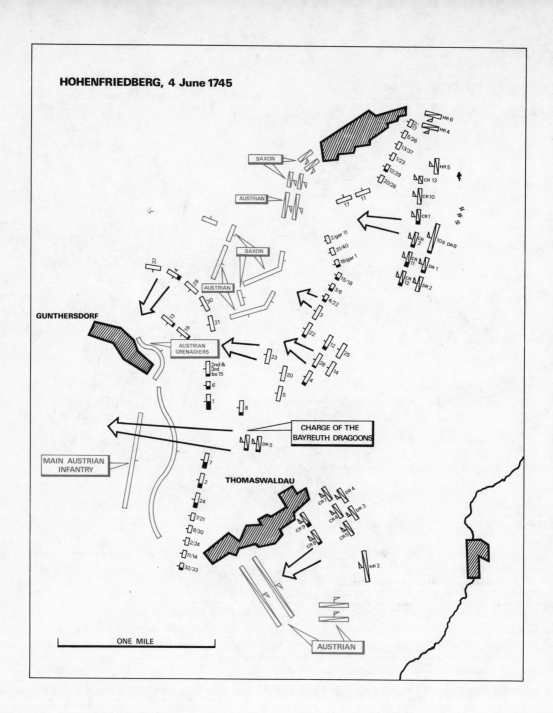

HOHENFRIEDBERG, 4 June 1745

GUNTHERSDORF

SAXON

AUSTRIAN

SAXON

AUSTRIAN

AUSTRIAN GRENADIERS

HR 6
HR 4
HR 5
CR 13
CR 10
CR 1
CR 2
10S DR 6
CR 11
DR 1
CR 12
DR 2

2/17
5/36
13/37
1/23
12/29
20/26
17 11

2/gar 11
31/40
16/gar 1
15/18
3/6
4/22
3
22
12 25
28 14
4

37
4
29
30
3 19
21
23
20
5

2nd & 3rd bs 15
6
1
8

CHARGE OF THE BAYREUTH DRAGOONS

DR 5

MAIN AUSTRIAN INFANTRY

7
2
24
7/21
8/30
2/24
11/14
32/33

THOMASWALDAU

CR 7 DR 4
CR 4 DR 3
CR 9
CR 8 CR 5
HR 2

ONE MILE

AUSTRIAN

216

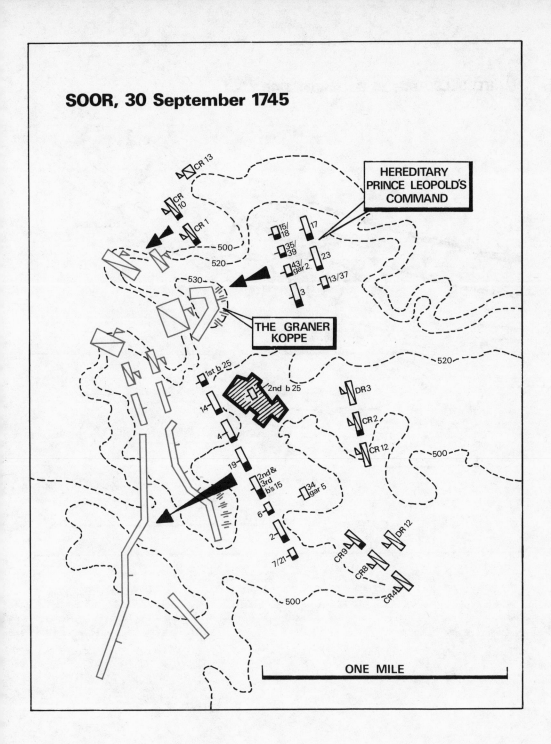

SOOR, 30 September 1745

CR 13

CR 10

CR 1

500

520

15/18   17

35/39

530   43/gar 2   23

13/37

3

HEREDITARY PRINCE LEOPOLD'S COMMAND

THE GRANER KOPPE

520

1st b 25

2nd b 25

14

4

19

2nd & 3rd b's 15

DR3

CR 2

CR 12

500

34 gar 5

6

2

7/21

CR9   DR 12

CR8

CR4

500

ONE MILE

217

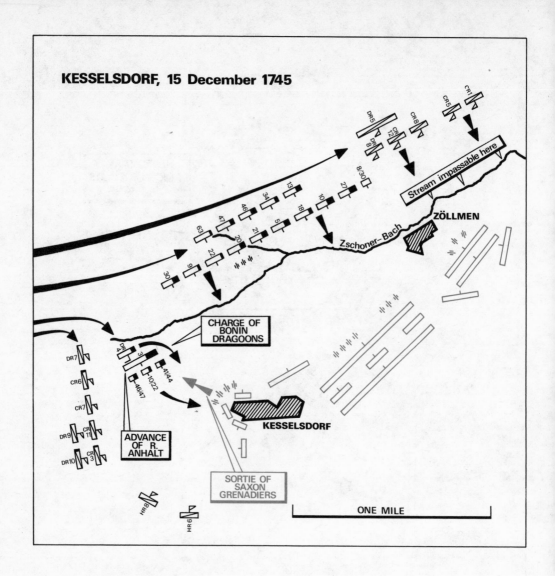

KESSELSDORF, 15 December 1745

DR5 | CR 12/9 | CR8 | CR5 | CR1

Stream impassable here

ZÖLLMEN

8/30 · 27 · 10 · 18 · 13 · 5 · 34 · 46 · 21 · 47 · 63 · 30 · 9 · 22 · 20

Zschoner-Bach

CHARGE OF
BONIN
DRAGOONS

DR7 · CR6 · CR7 · DR9 · CR 11 · DR10 · CR 3

DR4 · 3 · 41/44 · 10/22 · 46/47

ADVANCE
OF R.
ANHALT

KESSELSDORF

SORTIE OF
SAXON
GRENADIERS

ONE MILE

HR8 · HR6

218

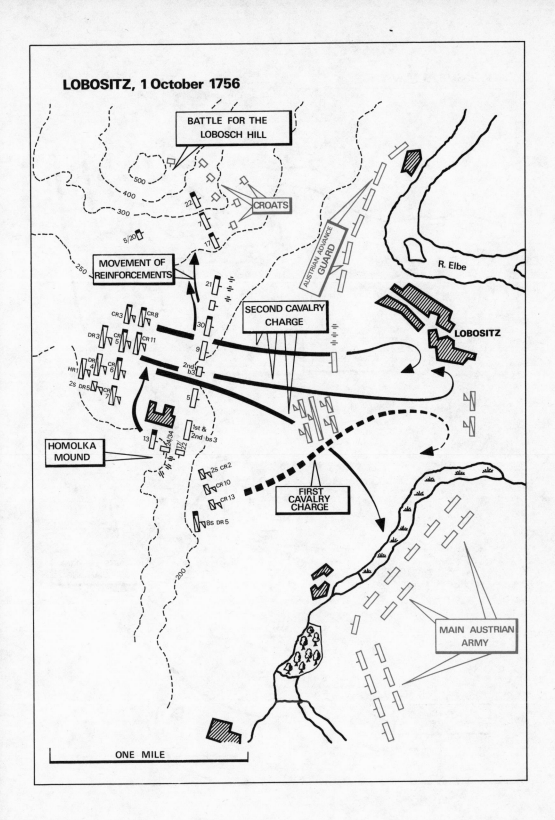

LOBOSITZ, 1 October 1756

BATTLE FOR THE
LOBOSCH HILL

CROATS

AUSTRIAN ADVANCE GUARD

R. Elbe

MOVEMENT OF
REINFORCEMENTS

SECOND CAVALRY
CHARGE

LOBOSITZ

HOMOLKA
MOUND

FIRST
CAVALRY
CHARGE

MAIN AUSTRIAN
ARMY

ONE MILE

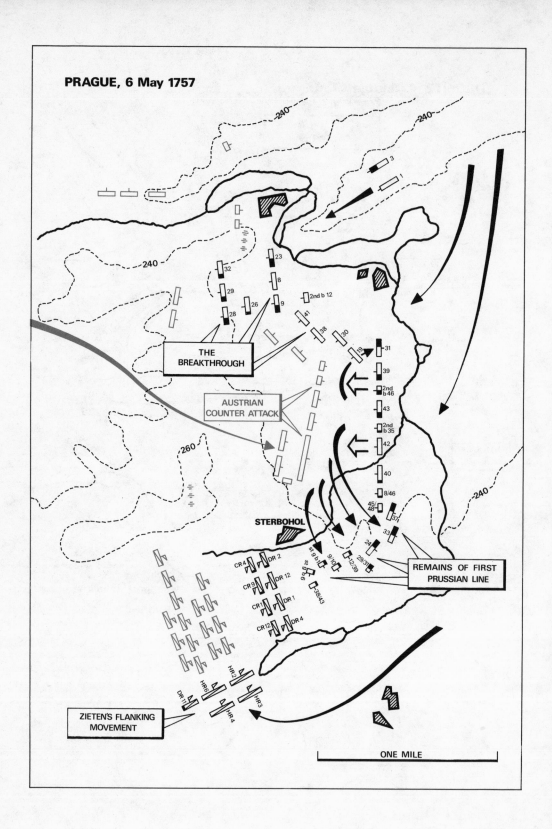

PRAGUE, 6 May 1757

THE BREAKTHROUGH

AUSTRIAN COUNTER ATTACK

STERBOHOL

REMAINS OF FIRST PRUSSIAN LINE

ZIETEN'S FLANKING MOVEMENT

ONE MILE

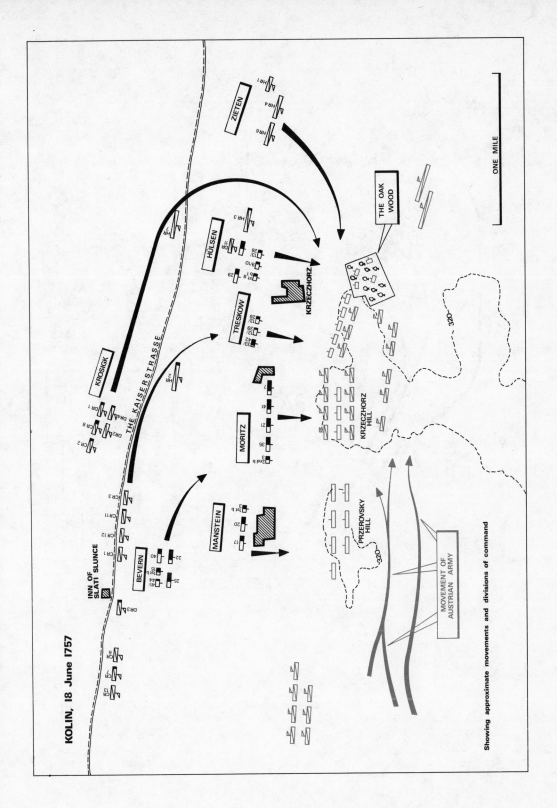

KOLIN, 18 June 1757

Showing approximate movements and divisions of command

ONE MILE

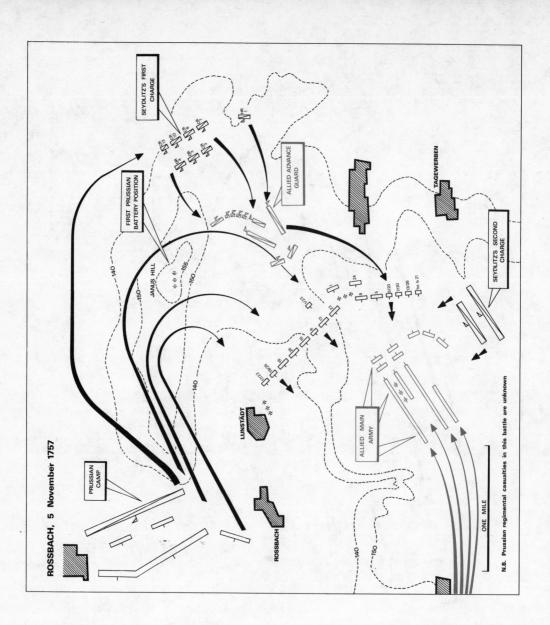

ROSSBACH, 5 November 1757

SEYDLITZ'S FIRST CHARGE

FIRST PRUSSIAN BATTERY POSITION

ALLIED ADVANCE GUARD

TAGEWERBEN

SEYDLITZ'S SECOND CHARGE

JANUS HILL

LUNSTÄDT

PRUSSIAN CAMP

ROSSBACH

ALLIED MAIN ARMY

ONE MILE

N.B. Prussian regimental casualties in this battle are unknown

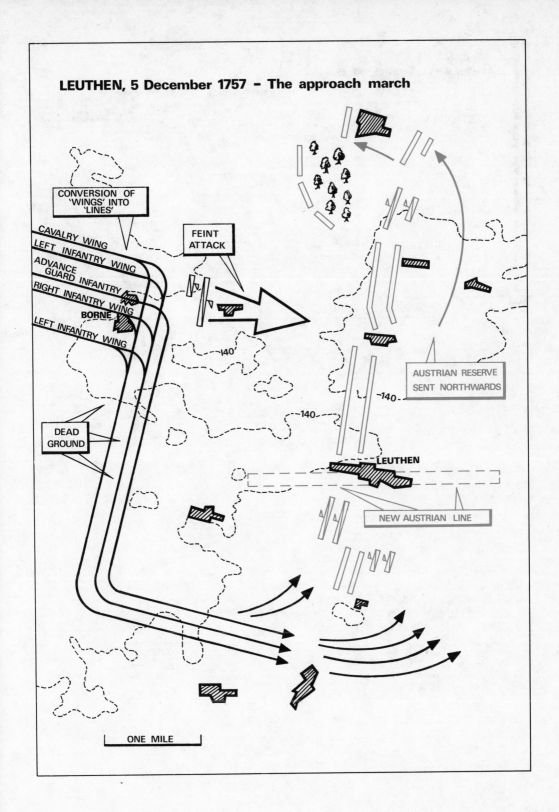

LEUTHEN, 5 December 1757 - The approach march

CONVERSION OF 'WINGS' INTO 'LINES'

FEINT ATTACK

CAVALRY WING

LEFT INFANTRY WING

ADVANCE GUARD INFANTRY

RIGHT INFANTRY WING

BORNE

LEFT INFANTRY WING

DEAD GROUND

AUSTRIAN RESERVE SENT NORTHWARDS

LEUTHEN

NEW AUSTRIAN LINE

140

140

140

ONE MILE

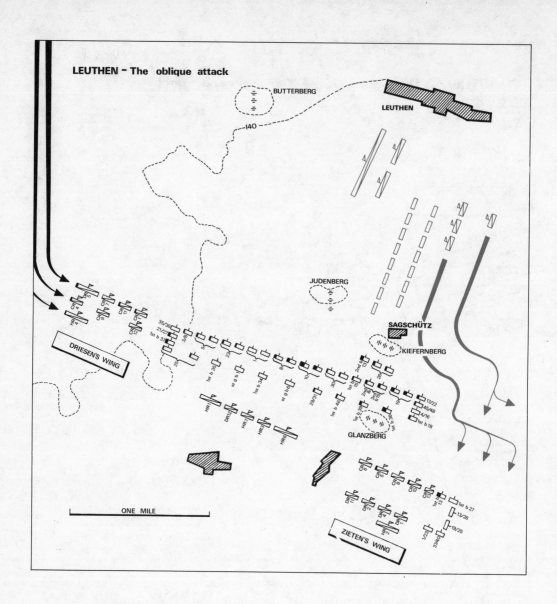

LEUTHEN - The oblique attack

BUTTERBERG

LEUTHEN

140

JUDENBERG

SAGSCHÜTZ

KIEFERNBERG

DRIESEN'S WING

35/36
21/27
1st b 37
3/6

17/22
45/48
4/16
1st b 18

GLANZBERG

ONE MILE

1st b 27
13/26
19/25

ZIETEN'S WING

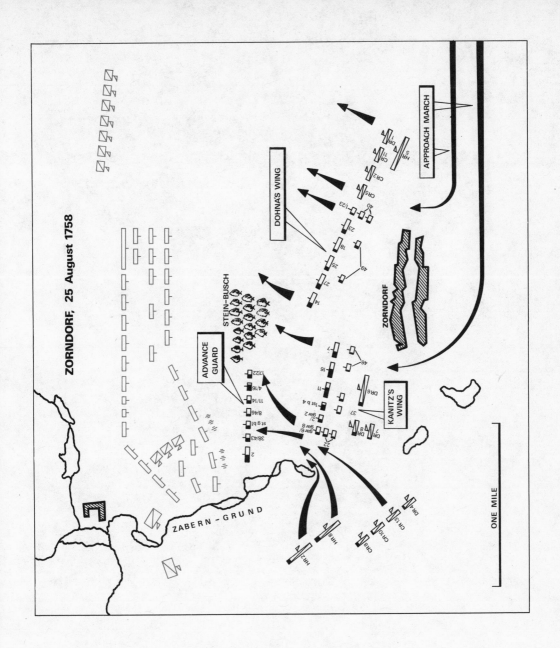

ZORNDORF, 25 August 1758

APPROACH MARCH

DOHNA'S WING

ZORNDORF

STEIN-BUSCH

ADVANCE
GUARD

KANITZ'S
WING

ZABERN – GRUND

ONE MILE

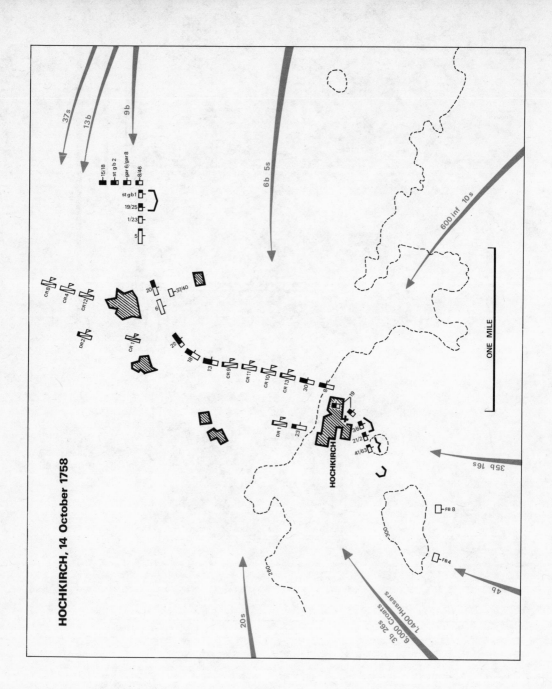

HOCHKIRCH, 14 October 1758

37s

13b

9b

6b 5s

600 inf 10 s

15/18
st g b 2
gar 6/gar 8
8/46

st gb1

19/25

1/23

5

CR 8

CR 4

CR 12

DR 2

CR 1

20

6

37/40

28

18

13

CR 9

CR 11

CR 10

CR 13

30

8

19

DR 1

23

3/6

21/2

41/63

HOCHKIRCH

ONE MILE

35b 16s

300

FB 8

4b

260

FB 4

20 s

3b 26s
6,000 Croats
1,400 Hussars

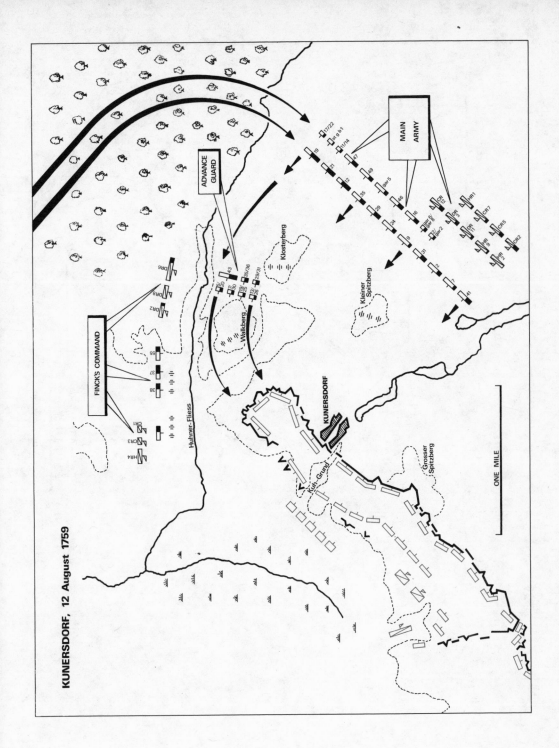

KUNERSDORF, 12 August 1759

ADVANCE GUARD

MAIN ARMY

FINCK'S COMMAND

Klosterberg

Walkberg

Kleiner Spitzberg

KUNERSDORF

Kuh-Grund

Grosser Spitzberg

Huhner-Fliess

ONE MILE

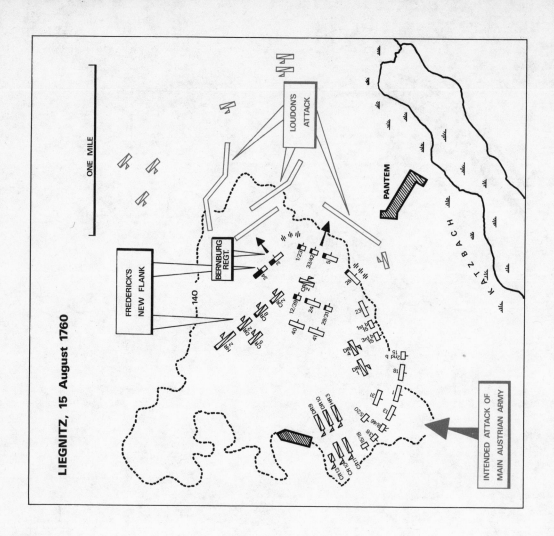

LIEGNITZ, 15 August 1760

ONE MILE

LOUDON'S ATTACK

PANTEM

FREDERICK'S NEW FLANK

BERNBURG REGT.

140

K A T Z B A C H

INTENDED ATTACK OF MAIN AUSTRIAN ARMY

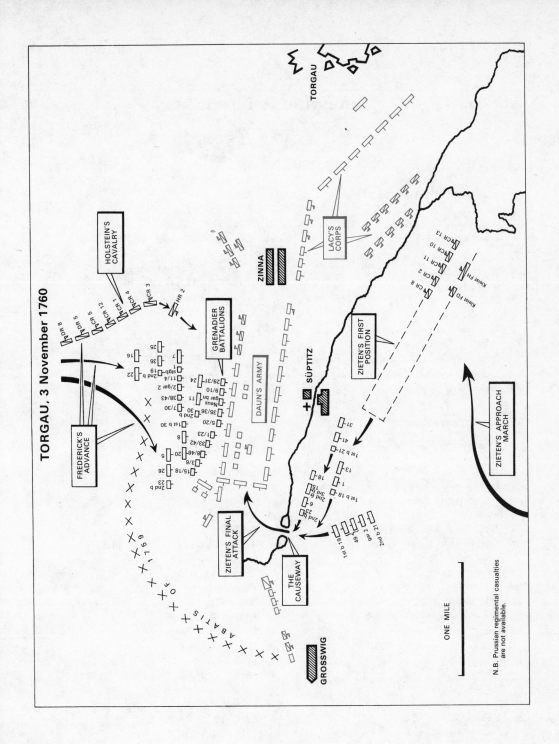

TORGAU, 3 November 1760

TORGAU

LACY'S CORPS

ZINNA

HOLSTEIN'S CAVALRY

DR 8
DR 5
CR 5
CR 12
CR 4
CR 1
CR 3
HR 2

GRENADIER BATTALIONS

FREDERICK'S ADVANCE

DAUN'S ARMY

ZIETEN'S FIRST POSITION

SÜPTITZ

ZIETEN'S APPROACH MARCH

CR 8
CR 2
CR 11
CR 10
CR 13
Kleist FH
Kleist FD

ZIETEN'S FINAL ATTACK

THE CAUSEWAY

ABATIS OF 1759

GROSSWIG

ONE MILE

N.B. Prussian regimental casualties
are not available.

229

Notes and References

1 The Land, the Age, the Man

1 Görlitz, 2
2 Ligne, XXVIII, 59
3 Osten-Sacken, I, 127
4 Knesebeck, quoted in Jany, III, 102
5 Wraxall, I, 110
6 Kaltenborn, I, 80
7 Lossow, 94
8 Yorke, III, 210
9 *Testament Politique* 1768, 149
10 Hildebrandt, IV, 108
11 Anon, *Idée de la . . . cour de Prusse* June 1753, British Museum Stowe MSS 307 f60
12 Ligne, IX, 132–3

2 The Officer Corps

1 Jany, II, 230
2 Lossow, 19
3 Jany, III, 42
4 *Instruction* 11 May 1763, in Frederick's *Militärische Schriften*, 275
5 Ibid, 274
6 *Testament Politique* 1768, 130
7 Frederick, in *Oeuvres*, I, 192
8 Kaltenborn, I, 47
9 Mirabeau, 128
10 Guibert *Observations*, 47
11 Scharfenort, 57
12 Anon, *Drei Jahre im Kadetten-Corps*, 88
13 Ibid, 88–9
14 Ibid, 90
15 Lemcke, 21
16 Prittwitz, 51
17 Küster, *Saldern*, 159
18 Prittwitz, 118–19
19 Mirabeau, 86
20 Toulongeon, 166
21 Lossow, 96
22 *Kriege Friedrichs*, I, 30
23 Jany, II, 228
24 Yorke, III, 226
25 Lehndorff, *Dreissig Jahre*, 93, and *Nachträge*, I, 175

26 Retzow, 164
27 Schmettau, II, 303
28 Kalckreuth, 144
29 *Testament Politique* 1768, 156
30 Hildebrandt, I, 79
31 *Testament Politique* 1768, 156
32 Berenhorst, II, 129–30
33 Scheelen in *Urkundliche Beiträge*, X, 37
34 Ortmann, 633
35 Prittwitz, 175–6
36 Kaltenborn, II, 32
37 *Zweite Schlesische Krieg*, II, 124
38 Jany, III, 47
39 Sack, 25–6
40 Anon, *Erinnerungen*, 23
41 Ibid, 27–8
42 Yorke, III, 222
43 Scheffner, 108
44 Prittwitz, 57
45 Kaltenborn, II, 46
46 Hülsen, 28–9
47 Mirabeau, 181
48 Toulongeon, 146–7
49 Lossow, 62–3
50 Instruction 11 May 1763, in Frederick's *Militärische Schriften*, 316
51 Lossow, 64–5
52 Lemcke, 33
53 Moore, II, 190–1
54 Küster, *Saldern*, 62
55 Varnhagen v. Ense, 70
56 Lehndorff, *Nachträge*, II, 174
57 Schlözer, 105
58 Hildebrandt, I, 79
59 Ortmann, 626
60 Kaltenborn, I, 85
61 Catt, 278
62 Laukhard, I, 239; Scheffner, 103
63 Scheffner, 91–2
64 Lossow, 65
65 Kaltenborn, II, 29–30; Trenck, I, 126
66 Natzmer, 20
67 Laukhard, 256
68 Anon, *Erinnerungen*, 35

69 Ligne, XXVIII, 60
70 Yorke, III, 227
71 Moore, II, 152
72 Burgoyne, 66
73 Schwarze, 174

3 The Men

1   Warnery, 111
2   *Testament Politique* 1768, 140, 179
3   Kaltenborn, I, 109
4   Bräker, 122
5   Witzleben, 54
6   Ortmann, 143
7   Toulongeon, 170
8   Mirabeau, 78
9   Jany, II, 239
10 Scheffner, 89; Laukhard, I, 248–9
11 Bräker, 118–19
12 Moore, II, 144–5
13 Berenhorst, II, 199
14 Moore, II, 121
15 Guibert, *Observations*, 132
16 Prittwitz, 57
17 Bräker, 135–7
18 Laukhard, I, 259
19 Ibid, I, 289
20 Archenholtz, II, 45
21 Bräker, 143
22 *Testament Politique* 1768, 82
23 Laukhard, I, 250
24 Toulongeon, 106
25 Lossow, 92
26 Kaltenborn, I, 42–3
27 *Testament Politique* 1752, 86
28 Berenhorst, I, 128
29 Scheelen in *Urkundliche Beiträge*, X, 40
30 Toulongeon, 294
31 Moore, II, 144
32 *Testament Politique* 1752, 84
33 Mirabeau, 82
34 Laukhard, I, 245–6
35 Schnackenburg, 98
36 Hullin, in Toulongeon, 293
37 Warnery, 534
38 Kaltenborn, I, 31
39 Ibid, 34
40 Hildebrandt, IV, 51
41 Kaltenborn, I, 22
42 Lossow, 3
43 Hildebrandt, VI, 33

4 The Infantry

1   Hullin in Toulongeon, 216
2   Schnackenburg, 100

3   Lossow, 144
4   Ibid, 139
5   Warnery, 256
6   Jany, II, 142
7   'Betrachtungen', in *Militärische Schriften*, 123
8   Mirabeau, 14
9   Kaltenborn, I, 123
10 Guibert, *Journal*, I, 165
11 Toulongeon, 171
12 Lossow, 135
13 Kling, I, 51
14 *Zweite Schlesische Krieg*, I, 46
15 Lossow, 157
16 Guibert, *Observations*, 88
17 Bräker, 138
18 Toulongeon, 194
19 Berenhorst, *Betrachtungen*, II, 199
20 Toulongeon, 203
21 *Testament Politique* 1752, 87
22 Mirabeau, 131
23 Dundas, *Remarks*
24 Berenhorst, *Betrachtungen*, II, 424–5
25 Scharnhorst, III, 268ff
26 Jany, III, 86
27 Berenhorst, *Betrachtungen*, I, 255
28 Toulongeon, 197
29 Warnery, 113
30 *Testament Politique* 1768, 146, 148
31 Toulongeon, 355
32 Yorke, III, 224

5 The Cavalry

1   Hohenstock, in Unger, 69
2   Ibid, 32
3   Mitchell, I, 403
4   Lossow, 147
5   Unger, 47
6   *Erste Schlesische Krieg*, II, 269
7   Unger, 46
8   Hahn, 26
9   Thiébault, III, 295–6
10 Kaltenborn, II, 100
11 Catt, 83
12 Unger, 49
13 *Zweite Schlesische Krieg*, I, 49
14 Thiébault, III, 298
15 Lossow, 158
16 Kaltenborn, II, 82
17 Jany, II, 17
18 Unger, 81
19 Dundas, *Remarks*
20 Buxbaum, 117
21 *Testament Politique* 1768, 152
22 Gisors, 104

23 *Militärische Schriften*, 305
24 Ibid, 307
25 Ibid, 312
26 Mirabeau, 104

6 The Artillery

1 Goltz, 211
2 Decker, 6
3 Mirabeau, 162
4 *Testament Politique* 1752, 88
5 *Oeuvres*, XXVIII, 149
6 Barsewisch, 115
7 Berenhorst *Betrachtungen*, I, 267
8 *Testament Politique* 1768, 142

7 Engineers and Technical Formations

1 Jähns, 2, 702
2 Prinzessin Heinrich, 152
3 Schmettau, *Feldzug*, 161
4 In *Oeuvres*, XXVIII, 65
5 'Aphorism' in ibid, XXX, 228
6 Mirabeau, 181
7 Prittwitz, 264
8 'Exposé du gouvernement Prussien' 1776, in *Politischen Testamente*, 244

8 Finance, Supply and the Auxiliary Services

1 Warnery, 532
2 Archenholtz, II, 33
3 Ibid, II, 123
4 Lehndorff, *Nachträge* I, 226
5 Moore, II, 111
6 *Testamente Politique* 1768, 138
7 Guibert, *Observations*, 98
8 Archenholtz, II, 84–5
9 Boswell, 75
10 Lehndorff, *Nachträge*, I, 252, 354
11 *Testament Politique* 1752, 99
12 To Podewils 25 Sept 1745, *Politische Korrespondenz*, IV, no 1, 995
13 *General Principia* (ed of 1936), 20
14 Retzow, II, 82
15 Prinzessin Heinrich, 153
16 *Testament Politique* 1752, 96
17 Jany, II, 266
18 Ibid, III, 79
19 Barsewisch, 63
20 Dr Fritze in Anon, *Erinnerungen*, 146
21 *Zweite Schlesische Krieg*, I, Appendix, p 22
22 Küster, *Bruchstück*, 133
23 Prittwitz, 71–2
24 Warnery, 430
25 Küster, *Bruchstück*, 84

26 Lehndorff, *Nachträge*, I, 175
27 *Zweite Schlesische Krieg*, I, Appendix, p 19
28 Ortmann, 703
29 Graewe, 'Feldprediger', 208
30 Prittwitz, 218
31 Hildebrandt, V, 34

9 Staff Work and the Control of the Army

1 'Über Kriegsmarsche', *Militärische Schriften*, 199
2 Thiébault, III, 205
3 Retzow, I, 44
4 Mitchell, I, 418
5 *Siebenjährige Krieg*, II, 165
6 'Über Kriegsmarsche', *Militärische Schriften*, 197
7 Ibid, 197
8 *Siebenjährige Krieg*, III, 93
9 Moore, II, 133
10 Toulongeon, 155
11 Jany, III, 100–2
12 Kaltenborn, I, 18
13 Legge to Newcastle, 23 Aug 1748, in Schlenke, 276
14 Burgoyne, 68
15 Dundas, *Remarks*

10 Operations of War

1 Schmettau, *Lebensgeschichte*, II, 280–1
2 Archenholtz, I, 136
3 *Siebenjährige Krieg*, VIII, 141

11 Frederick's Army in Peace and War

1 Boswell, 104
2 Lehndorff, 46–7
3 Schmettau, *Lebensgeschichte*, II, 292
4 Archenholtz, I, 2
5 Hildebrandt, V, 46
6 Schwerin, 104–5
7 Steinberger, 52–3
8 Friedrich v. Geuder, in Meyer, 95–6
9 *Erste Schlesische Krieg*, II, 42
10 Anon, *Les campagnes du Roi*, 69
11 Jany, II, 111
12 *Oeuvres*, IV, 5
13 Yorke, III, 225
14 Retzow, I, 258
15 Lehndorff, 399
16 Retzow, I, 42
17 Warnery, 214
18 Retzow, I, 43
19 Warnery, 214; Retzow, I, 41; Kalckstein, 151; Lehndorff, 336; Prince Henry in a note written on a copy of Frederick's *Histoire de*

Mon Temps

20 Lemcke, 24
21 Bräker, 148
22 'Briefe preussischer Soldaten', in Generalstab, *Urkundliche Beiträge*, II, 9–10
23 Archenholtz, I, 20
24 Lehndorff, 306–7
25 Krogh, 167
26 Letter of a musketeer of the regiment of Anhalt, in 'Briefe preussischer Soldaten', in Generalstab, *Urkundliche Beiträge*, II, 51
27 Warnery, 109
28 Lemcke, 28
29 Prittwitz, 128–31
30 Ibid, 137
31 Ibid, 136
32 Ibid, 154–5
33 Warnery, 202
34 Catt, 83
35 Lehndorff, 371
36 Retzow, I, 196
37 Berenhorst, *Betrachtungen*, I, 280
38 Archenholtz, I, 108
39 Ibid, I, 93
40 Wiltsch, 163
41 Ibid, 183
42 Warnery, 227–8
43 Retzow, I, 243
44 Kaltenborn, I, 53
45 Archenholtz, I, 135
46 Barsewisch, 33
47 Archenholtz, I, 138
48 Retzow, I, 253
49 *Siebenjährige Krieg*, VI, 39
50 Archenholtz, I, 159
51 Scheffner, 67
52 Jany, II, 489
53 Prittwitz, 219
54 Hülsen, 90
55 Ibid, 92–3
56 Prittwitz, 234–6
57 Ortmann, 421
58 Warnery, 275
59 Küster, *Bruchstück*, 32
60 Archenholtz, I, 182
61 Küster, *Bruchstück*, 39–40
62 *Siebenjährige Krieg*, VIII, 283
63 Barsewisch, 75
64 Archenholtz, I, 185
65 Warnery, 30
66 Lemcke, 36–8
67 Warnery, 346–7
68 Archenholtz, II, 9–10
69 Ibid, II, 129

70 Retzow, II, 198
71 Archenholtz, I, 334
72 Ibid, I, 327–8
73 Ibid, II, 52
74 *Siebenjährige Krieg*, XII, 210
75 Hildebrandt, I, 34
76 Archenholtz, II, 107–8
77 Hahn, 80
78 Archenholtz, II, 110
79 Warnery, 492
80 Groehler, 168
81 Schmidt, II, 322
82 Kaltenborn, II, 155
83 Osten-Sacken, I, 263
84 Boswell, 23
85 Jany, 'Gefechtsausbildung', 8–9
86 Varnhagen v. Ense, 225
87 Burgoyne, 66
88 Mirabeau, 27
89 Kaltenborn, II, 11
90 Thiébault, III, 308
91 Küster, *Saldern*, 85
92 Goltz, 336
93 Archenholtz, II, 82
94 Anon, *Erinnerungen*, 26
95 Schmettau, *Feldzug*, 285
96 Hildebrandt, V, 149
97 Ibid, III, 166
98 Ibid, III, 168
99 Toulongeon, 131

12 Influence and Legacy

1 Mirabeau, 238–9
2 'Considérations', *Politischen Testamente*, 250
3 Craig, 21
4 Archenholtz, I, 241
5 Berenhorst, *Betrachtungen*, II, 329
6 Ibid, II, 147
7 Anon, 'Reflections', 170
8 Burgoyne, 65
9 Earl of Holdernesse to Mitchell, 20 May 1757, Mitchell, I, 249
10 Schlenke, 281
11 Cornwallis, I, 205
12 Dupuy and Dupuy, 272
13 Palmer, 148
14 Jany, II, 343
15 Frederick's *Instruktion*, ed Franke, vii–viii
16 Eg E. Kessel, 'Adolf Hitler und der Verrat am Preussentum', in *Das Parlament*, 15 Nov 1961
17 *Staatskunst und Kriegshandwerk*
18 Ibid, Eng trans, I, 24

Appendix 1

Battle Statistics

The following abbreviations are used: b=battalions of infantry, cav=cavalry, g=grenadier, gn=guns, inf=infantry, r=regiments, s=squadrons of cavalry. Totals are approximate, as the sources rarely indicate how many gunners are included in the totals.

Mollwitz, 10 April 1741

(a) Prussians: 31 b (17,000), 30 s (4,000), 500 hussars, c. 50 gn. Total: c.22,000. Losses: 4,850.

(b) Austrians: 16 b (9,000), 11 regular cav r (nearly 8,000), 2 hussar r (over 1,000), 19 gn. Total: c.18,100. Losses: 4,551.

Chotusitz, 17 May 1742

(1) Prussians: 33 b (17,000), 70 s (7,000), 82 gn. Total: c.24,500. Losses: 4,819 (including 2,566 cav).

(b) Austrians: 13 inf r (16,000), 12 cav r (7,000), 3,000 hussars, 2,500 Croats, about 40 gn. Total: c.29,000. Losses: 6,332 (including c.1,200 prisoners).

Hohenfriedberg (Striegau), 4 June 1745

(a) Prussians: 12 g b, 52 b (38,600), 111 s (19,900), 192 gn (including 54 heavy). Total: c.50,000. Losses: 4,737.

(b) Austrians: 47 b, 126 s (37,654 regular inf and cav), 2–3,000 hussars and Croats. Total: c.41,200. Losses: 10,332.

(c) Saxons: 18 b, 24 s (22,500 regular inf and cav), 2,600 uhlans. Losses: 2,844

Allied total forces: c.66,000, 121 gn (including 40 heavy). Losses: 13,176, 63 gn (including 29 Saxon).

Soor, 30 September 1745

(a) Prussians: 31 b (16,710), 41 s (5,852). Total: 22,562. Losses: 3,876.

(b) Austrians and Saxons: 25,300 regular inf, 12,700 regular cav, 4,000 Croats and light cav. Total: c.41,000. Losses: 7,444.

Kesselsdorf, 15 December 1745

(a) Prussians: 35 b (21,000), 93 s (9,000), 33 gn. Total: c.31,000. Losses: c.5,000.

(b) Saxons: 39 b (24,000), 58 s (7,000), 42 gn. Total: c.31,200. Losses: 6,630.

Lobositz, 1 October 1756

(a) Prussians: 25 b (c.18,000), 59 s (10,500), 300 hussars, 97 gn. Total: c.29,000. Losses: 2,906.

(b) Austrians: 15 inf r and 4 b of Croats (c.26,500), 12 cav r (7,500), 94 g. Total: c.34,500. Losses: 2,873.

Prague, 6 May 1756

(a) Prussians: 66 b (47,000), 113 s (17,000), 214 gn (including 82 heavy). Total: c.65,000. Losses: 14,300.

(b) Austrians: 54 regular b, 5 Croat b (48,500), 12 heavy cav r, 5 hussar r (12,600), 177 gn (including 59 heavy). Total: c.62,000. Losses: 13,400 (including over 4,500 prisoners), 60 gn.

Kolin, 18 June 1757

(a) Prussians: 32 b (17–18,000), 116 s (14,000), 88 gn (including 28 heavy). Total: c.32,000. Losses: 13,768, 45 gn.

(b) Austrians: 42 b (28,960), 17 cav r (14,000), 145 gn. Total: c.44,000. Losses: c.9,000.

Gross-Jägersdorf, 30 August 1757

(a) Prussians: 22 b (17,000), 50 s (8,200), 55 gn. Total: c.25,600. Losses: 4,520.

(b) Russians: 90 b, 11 cav r, c.260 gn. Total: 70–75,000. Losses: c.5,250.

Rossbach, 5 November 1757

(a) Prussians: 27 b (16,600), 45 s (5,400), 79 gn (including 23 heavy). Total: c.22,000. Losses: 548.

(b) *Reichsarmee*: 14 b, 42 s, 12 heavy gn. Total: 10,900. Losses: 3,552.

(c) French: 49 b, 40 s, 32 heavy gn. Total: 30,200. Losses: 6,600.

Allied total: c.42,000. Total losses: c.10,150.

Breslau, 22 November 1957

(a) Prussians: 39½ b (19,000), 101 s (8,000), 80 gn. Total: c.28,000. Losses: 6,350, 29 gn.

(b) Austrians: 60,381 inf, 23,225 cav, 220 gn. Total: c.84,000. Losses: 5,851.

Leuthen, 5 December 1757

(a) Prussians: 48 b (c.21,000), 129 s (11,000), 167 gn. Total: c.33,000. Losses: 11,589.

(b) Austrians: 85 b, 125 s, 210 gn. Total: 65,000. Losses: c.22,000 (including c.12,000 prisoners), 131 gn.

Zorndorf, 25 August 1758

(a) Prussians: 38 b (25,000), 83 s (10,500), 193 gn (including 117 heavy). Total: c.36,000. Losses: 12,797, 26 gn.

(b) Russians: 55 b (36,308), 21 s (3,382), c.3,000 irregulars, 136 gn. Total: c.43,300. Losses: c.18,500.

Hochkirch, 14 October 1758

(a) Prussians: 35 b (20,000), 73 s (10,000), 200 gn. Total: c.31,000. Losses: 9,097, 101 gn.

(b) Austrians: 50,000 inf, 28,000 cav, 340 gn. Total: c.80,000. Losses: 7,587.

Kay (Paltzig, Züllichau), 23 July 1759

(a) Prussians: 19,600 inf, 7,800 cav, 56 heavy gn. Total: c.28,000. Losses: c.8,300, 13 gn.

(b) Russians: 54 b, 34 s of heavy cav, 29 s of hussars, 8 r of cossacks, 186 gn (including 46 heavy). Total: 40,000, including 7,000 irregulars. Losses: 4,804.

Kunersdorf, 12 August 1759

(a) Prussians: 53 b (36,900), 95 s (13,000), 140 heavy gn. Total: c.50,900. Losses: c.19,100, 172 gn.

(b) Russians: 68 b, 36 s, 200 gn. Total: c.41,000. Losses: 13,477.

(c) Austrians: 18 b, 35 s, 48 gn. Total: 18,523. Losses: c.2,000.

Allied total: c.59,500. Losses: c.15,500.

Liegnitz, 15 August 1760

(a) Prussians: 36 b, 78 s, 74 heavy gn. Total: c.30,000. Losses: 3,394.

(b) Austrians: main army c.66,000, Loudon's corps c.24,000. Losses: c.8,500, 80 gn.

Torgau, 3 November 1760

(a) Prussians: Main army 41 b, 48 s, Zieten's corps 21 b, 54 s, altogether 35,000 inf, 13,500 cav, 309 gn. Total: c.50,000. Losses: 16,670.

(b) Austrians: 42,000 inf, 10,000 cav, 275 gn. Total: c.53,400. Losses: 15,697 (including more than 7,000 prisoners), 49 gn.

2

List of Regiments

The asterisks refer to Frederick's grading of his regiments in the 1760s according to their performance in the Seven Years War – * signifies good, and ** very good.

For details of uniforms the reader is referred to C. Jany and A. Menzel, *Die Armee Friedrichs des Grossen in ihrer Uniformierung*, Berlin 1908 (British Museum Library press mark 1899.k.4), and the superb (and very expensive) work of F.-G. Melzner and H. Bleckwenn, *Die Uniformen der Infanterie 1753–1786*, in the series *Das altpreussische Heer* (publication still in progress, Biblio Verlag, D45 Osnabrück, Jahnstrasse 15).

Infantry regiments

IR NO 1

Station   Berlin.
Designation   1740 Glasenapp, 1742 Hacke, Winterfeldt, 1758 Lattorff, 1760 Zeuner, 1768 Koschenbahr, 1776 Bandemer, 1778 Kalckreuth, 1778 Bornstedt.
Uniform   Blue coat, red cuffs and lapels, white waistcoat and breeches.
Record   Distinguished at Soor, Prague and Hochkirch. A regiment with an extremely high reputation. 'It's true, I always considered the Winterfeldt regiment was brave, but to-day it has surpassed all my expectations. I shall never forget it' (Frederick at Hochkirch).
Grenadier battalion   1740 Kleist, with no 25; 1742 Kleist, with no 22; 1744 Tauentzien, with no 23. Seven Years War with no 23: 1756 Bandemer, 1757 Wedell, 1758 Rathenow, 1762 Posek, 1778 Schlieben, with no 13. A famous battalion, used for a variety of dangerous enterprises in the Seven Years War.

IR NO 2 *

Station   Rastenburg (East Prussia).
Designation   1740 Roeder, 1743 Schlichting, 1750 Kanitz, 1769 Stutterheim, 1783 Anhalt.
Uniform   Blue coat, red cuffs and lapels, yellow waistcoat and breeches.
Record   Unusually hard-fighting (especially for an East Prussian regiment), with consistently high casualties. One battalion captured at Meissen 4 December 1759.
Grenadier battalion   1740 Pfuhl, with no 4; 1744 Kahlbutz, with no 24; 1744–5 Kleist 'v. Württemberg', with no 17. Seven Years War with Garrison Regt no 2: 1756 Manstein, 1758 Nesse, 1760 Natalis. 1778 Rautter, with no 16.

IR NO 3 * (THREE BATTALIONS STRONG)

Station   Halle.
Designation   1740 Alt-Anhalt, 1758 Kahlden, 1759 Anhalt-Bernburg, 1784 Leipziger.
Uniform   Blue coat, red cuffs, white waistcoat and breeches.
Record   Famous in the 1740s as the Old Dessauer's regiment, and distinguished at Hohenfriedberg and Soor. In the Seven Years War it was filled up with impressed Saxons and performed erratically, disgracing itself at the siege of Dresden in 1760 but redeeming its name at Liegnitz later in the same year.
Grenadier battalion   1740 one coy with Bolstern, no 27, the other with Sydow, then Burghausen, no 14; 1742 Finckenstein, with no 36; 1744 Buddenbrock, with no 6. Seven Years War with no 6: 1756 Kleist, 1757 Hacke, 1758 Plotho, 1759 Hacke. 1778 Blomberg, with no 6.
Almost wiped out at Torgau.

IR NO 4

Station Prussian Holland (East Prussia).

Designation 1740 Groeben, 1744 Polentz, 1745 Dohna, 1745 Kalnein, 1757 Rautter, 1758 Kleist, 1761 Thadden, 1744 Pelkowsky, 1782 Egloffstein.

Uniform Blue coat, red cuffs, yellow waistcoat and breeches.

Record A poorish regiment, badly knocked about at Gross-Jägersdorf and Zorndorf. Of its *Chefs*, Rautter was disgraced for his performance at Zorndorf, while Thadden was known as a drunkard.

Grenadier battalion 1740 Pfuhl, with no 2, later no 6; 1744 Sydow, with no 22. Seven Years War with no 16: 1756 Polentz, 1757 Kleist, 1758 Willemy, 1762 Thielau. 1788 Hausen, with no 53.
Severe losses at Zorndorf, and captured at Maxen.

IR NO 5 *

Station Magdeburg.

Designation 1740 Wedell, 1742 Bonin, 1755 Alt-Braunschweig, 1766 Saldern, 1785 Lengefeld.

Uniform Blue coat, with straw cuffs, lapels and collar, straw waistcoat and breeches.

Record Solid and well-disciplined. Distinguished at Liegnitz.

Grenadier battalion 1740 Winterfeldt, with no 21; 1742 Hagen (also called 'Geist'), with no 20; 1744 Jeetze, with no 36. Seven Years War with no 20: 1756 Jung-Billerbeck.
Winterfeldt founded the tradition of one of the army's best grenadier battalions. Distinguished at Lobositz and Kunersdorf. Heavy losses at Torgau.

IR NO 6 GRENADIER-GARDE-BATAILLON

Station Potsdam.

Designation The name 'Grenadier-Garde-Bataillon' was always linked with that of the contemporary *Chef*, namely: 1740 (year of formation) Einsiedel, 1745 Retzow, 1759 Saldern, 1766 Lestwitz, 1779 Rohdich.

Uniform Blue coat, red cuffs and collar, straw waistcoat and breeches.

Record Distinguished at Hohenfriedberg, heavy losses at Hochkirch.

Grenadier battalion 1740 one coy with no 29, Itzenplitz, the other with no 4, Pfuhl; 1744 with no 3. Seven Years War with no 3. 1778 with no 3.

IR NO 7

Station Stettin.

Designation 1740 Bredow, 1741 Braunschweig-Bevern, December 1756–November 1757 Alt-Bevern, 1757 Bevern, 1781 Winterfeldt, 1784 Goltz.

Uniform Blue coat, rose-red cuffs and lapels, straw waistcoat and breeches.

Record Saw especially heavy fighting at Hohenfriedberg, Kolin and Zorndorf. The first battalion captured at Schweidnitz 1757. Frederick regarded it as a typically reliable Pomeranian regiment, and one that had 'done honour to the House of Brandenburg from time immemorial'. The genial Duke of Bevern was *Chef* for forty years. For conditions in the 1750s see the Prittwitz memoirs.

Grenadier battalion 1740 Düring, with no 30; 1742 Uchländer, with no 19; 1744 Grumbkow, with no 21. Seven Years War with no 30: 1756 Kanitz, 1757 Lubath. 1778 Owstien, with no 8.
Distinguished at Kunersdorf.

IR NO 8

Station Stettin.

Designation 1740 Anhalt-Zerbst, 1747 Tresckow, 1754 Amstell, 1757 Geist, 1759 Queiss, 1769 Hacke, 1785 Keller, 1786 Scholten.

Uniform Blue coat, red cuffs and lapels, white waistcoat and breeches.

Record Distinguished at Hochkirch. In 1784 Frederick said (probably unfairly) that the troops looked like 'a mob of ignorant peasants'.

Grenadier battalion   1740 Saldern, with no 36; 1742 Itzenplitz, with no 24; 1744 Schöning, with no 30.
Seven Years War with no 46, Alt-Billerbeck. 1778, with no 7.
Captured at Gabel 15 July 1757. Raised again but badly battered at Hochkirch.

IR NO 9 **

Station   Hamm and Soest (the Ruhr region of Prussian Westphalia).
Designation   1740 Leps, 1747 Quadt, 1756 Jung-Kleist, 1758 Oldenburg, 1758 Puttkamer, 1759 Schencken-
dorff, 1760 Jung-Schenckendorff, 1763 Wolfersdorff, 1782 Budberg.
Uniform   Blue coat, red cuffs and lapels, white waistcoat and breeches.
Record   A Westphalian regiment, though usually in good odour with the king. Distinguished at Prague.
Captured at Maxen after a creditable fight. Raised again but shattered in Pomerania in 1761.
Grenadier battalion   1745 Henning v. Langen (later Hagen), with no 10; 1745 Sydow (later Kleist), with
no 27. Seven Years War with no 10: 1756 Möllendorff, 1758 Bähr. 1778 Bandemer, with no 10.
Captured at Gabel 15 July 1757, but exchanged 1758. Heavy losses at Torgau.

IR NO 10 **

Station   Bielefeld, Herford.
Designation   1740 Anhalt-Dessau, 1750 Knobloch, 1757 Pannwitz, 1768 Petersdorff, 1781 Stwolinsky.
Uniform   Blue coat, lemon yellow cuffs, lemon yellow waistcoat and breeches.
Record   Distinguished at Kesselsdorf, Leuthen and Burkersdorf. First battalion captured at Landeshut.
Another good Westphalian regiment, and notable for the enthusiasm of its cantonists. At the beginning
of the Seven Years War Frederick questioned whether it would fight well against the French: an officer
put his mind at rest, citing the superiority of 'pumpernickel and Westphalian ham' over the 'cakes and
frogs' legs' of the French.
Grenadier battalion   1745, with no 9; 1745 Hagen (then Plotho), with no 27. Seven Years War with no 9.
1778 with no 9.

IR NO 11

Station   Königsberg.
Designation   1740 Holstein-Beck, 1749 Below, 1758 Rebentisch, 1763 Tettenborn, 1776 Zastrow, 1782
Rothkirch, 1786 Voss.
Uniform   Blue coat, red cuffs, white waistcoat and breeches.
Record   Distinguished at Chotusitz and Prague. Large numbers of Austrian and Russian prisoners were
incorporated in the course of the Seven Years War. The regiment did notably badly at Zorndorf, and
at Maxen, where it broke up before being captured with the rest. (See the Carl v. Hülsen memoirs for
life in the 1750s.)
Grenadier battalion   1740 Lattorff, with no 33; 1742 Kanitz, with no 14; 1744 Trenck, with no 14. Seven
Years War with no 14: 1756 Gohr, 1757 Petersdorff, 1759 Beyer, 1760 Oppen. 1778 Hertzberg, with
no 14.
A generally reliable battalion.

IR NO 12 *

Station   Prenzlau (Pomerania).
Designation   1740 Markgraf Heinrich, 1741 Selchow, 1743 Darmstadt, 1747 Alt-Darmstadt, 1757 Finck,
1763 Wunsch.
Uniform   Blue coat, red cuffs and lapels, straw waistcoat and breeches.
Record   Broken at Prague, shot up at Kunersdorf, ridden down and captured at Maxen. Surprised at
Cammerswalde 7 February 1779. Brave but unfortunate.
Grenadier battalion   1740 Puttkamer, with no 24; 1742 Jeetze, with no 17; 1744 Luck, with no 29. Seven
Years War with no 39: 1756 Woldau, 1758 Pieverlingk, 1760 Stechow, 1760 Görne. 1778 Brösigke,
with no 13.
Distinguished at Liegnitz, but suffered heavy losses.

IR NO 13 **

Station Berlin.

Designation 1740 Truchsess, 1745 Polentz, 1746 Schwarz-Schwerin or Bogislaw-Schwerin, 1750 Itzenplitz, 1760 Syburg, 1762 Kaiser (ie Tsar Peter III of Russia), 1763 Wylich und Lottum, 1774 Braun.

Uniform Blue coat, light straw cuffs and lapels, light straw waistcoat and breeches.

Record Distinguished at Leuthen, and at Hochkirch where it suffered 820 casualties. A tightly run regiment, known as the *Donner und Blitzen* regiment under the régime of General Itzenplitz, who was mortally wounded at Kunersdorf. For life in the other ranks, see the Bräker memoirs.

Grenadier battalion 1740 Reibnitz, with no 19; 1742 Lattorff then Hagen (also called 'Geist'), with no 28; 1744 Hagen, with no 37. Seven Years War with no 26: 1756 Finck, 1757 Bornstädt, 1759 Humboldt, 1759 Schwerin, 1761 Kalckstein. 1778 with no 1.

Captured at Maxen. Raised again, and captured at Brandenburg 14 October 1762.

IR NO 14

Station Friedland and Bartenstein (East Prussia).

Designation 1740 Lehwaldt, 1768 Graf. v. Anhalt, 1777 Steinwehr, 1782 Henckel v. Donnersmarck.

Uniform Blue coat, red cuffs and lapels, white waistcoat and breeches.

Record Lightly engaged in the Silesian wars, but suffered heavily at Gross-Jägersdorf and Kunersdorf. One battalion lost at Maxen.

Grenadier battalion 1740 with no 3; 1742 with no 11; 1744 with no 11. Seven Years War with no 11. 1778 with no 11.

BATAILLON-GARDE, OR LEIB-GARDE-BATAILLON (THE FIRST BATTALION OF IR NO 15, THE FUSS-GARDE REGIMENT)

Station Ruppen, Nauen and Potsdam. Recruited generally.

Designation As above. It had no *Chefs*, only commandants. These were: 1740 Markgraf Wilhelm of Brandenburg, 1744 Prince Ferdinand of Brunswick, 1755 Ingersleben, 1757 Tauentzien, 1763 Prince Frederick William of Prussia, 1764 Billerbeck, 1765 Laxdehnen, 1773 Scheelen (till 1786).

Uniform Blue coat, red cuffs, light yellow waistcoat and breeches.

Record Its *forte* was peacetime parading, though it performed magnificently at Mollwitz and Kolin. It consisted 'principally of foreigners. The private soldiers were badly paid and served unwillingly, but they were held to the colours by principles of honour and discipline' (Archenholtz). The rule of Scheelen was notably sadistic.

IR NO 15 REGIMENT-GARDE

Station Ruppen, Nauen and Potsdam. Recruited generally.

Designation As above. It had no *Chefs*, only commandants. These were: 1740 Bredow, 1743 Schwerin, 1745 Schultze, 1747 Meyering, 1749 Beschwitz and Merseberg, 1754 Merseberg, 1756 Saldern, 1760 Möllendorff, 1771 Buttler, 1776 Rohdich, 1779 Brüning, 1785 Roeder.

Uniform Blue coat, red collar, lapels and cuffs, lemon yellow waistcoat and trousers. The Third battalion wore grenadier caps with white plates and red tops.

Record Distinguished at Soor, and at Leuthen, where the Third battalion captured the churchyard.

Grenadier battalion 1744 Wedell, with no 18. Seven Years War with no 18: 1756 Bülow, 1757 Kleist, 1759 Graf v. Anhalt. 1778 Apenburg, with no 18.

Knocked about at Soor, captured at Hochkirch.

IR NO 16

Station Königsberg.

Designation 1740 Flanss, 1748 Christoph Dohna, 1762 Syburg, 1771 Borck, 1777 Buddenbrock, 1782 Schottenstein, 1785 Romberg.

Uniform   Blue coat, red or light brick-red cuffs and lapels, straw waistcoat and breeches.

Record   Heavy losses at Zorndorf and Kunersdorf. A middling East Prussian regiment.

Grenadier battalion   1740 Hauss (then Ruitz), with no 34; 1742 Kahlbutz, with no 34; 1744 Kleist v. Jung-Schwerin, with Gar R (Garrison Regiment) no 1. Seven Years War with no 4. 1778 with no 2.

IR NO 17

Station   Coslin and Rügenwalde (Pomerania).

Designation   1740 La Motte (ie La Motte Fouqué), 1748 Jung-Jeetze, 1752 Jeetze, 1756 Manteuffel, 1764 Rosen, 1772 Billerbeck, 1786 Könitz.

Uniform   Blue coat, white cuffs, lapels and collar, white waistcoat and breeches.

Record   A good Pomeranian regiment, distinguished at Soor, Prague and at Neustadt 15 March 1760. Frederick wrote to General v. d. Goltz on the latter occasion: 'I wish you to convey a compliment to the officers of Manteuffel in my name. They have acted in our old, honourable way, and not according to the infamous modern example of other folk . . .'

Grenadier battalion   1740 Wedell, with no 18; 1742, with no 12; 1744, with no 2. Seven Years War with no 22: 1756 Puttkamer, 1757 Wrede, 1757 Kremzow, 1759 v. d. Thann, 1760 Wobersnow, 1760 Rothenburg. 1778 Below, with no 22.

Warnery says of these grenadiers at Prague that they were 'the only ones who did not open fire, but pressed home the attack at bayonet point! After all they were Pomeranians . . . who are beyond doubt the best infantry in the world'. Mauled and captured at Landeshut.

IR NO 18 **

Station   Spandau and Nauen. Recruited in the Altmark.

Designation   1740 Derschau, 1742 Prinz v. Preussen, 1764 Prinz Friedrich Wilhelm.

Uniform   Blue coat, rose-red cuffs, lapels and collar, white waistcoat and breeches.

Record   An excellent Brandenburg regiment. After Zorndorf Frederick commented of this regiment and that of Forcade: 'I owe my salvation to these regiments and General Seydlitz. I could do anything with commanders and troops like these.'

Grenadier battalion   1740 with no 17; 1744, Seven Years War and 1778 with no 15.

IR NO 19

Station   Berlin.

Designation   1740 Markgraf Karl (ie Friedrich Karl, Margrave of Brandenburg-Schwedt), 1763 Tettenborn, 1763 Braunschweig-Wolfenbüttel.

Uniform   Blue coat, red cuffs and collar, straw waistcoat and breeches.

Record   Heavily engaged at Mollwitz, Leuthen, siege of Breslau 1757, Kunersdorf, Torgau and above all at Hochkirch, where the Second battalion under Major v. Langen was wiped out in the defence of the churchyard. After the Seven Years War Frederick failed to do justice to this remarkable regiment.

Margrave Karl took over all the Irish troops who were captured with the Saxon army at Pirna. 'To begin with they were most unwilling to serve among the Prussians, but now the decent treatment they receive from the Margrave has won them over so completely that they would be in despair if they were ordered to be sent to any other regiment' (Lehndorff, 1757).

Grenadier battalion   1740 with no 13; 1742 with no 7; 1744 Finck v. Finckenstein, with no 25. Seven Years War with no 25: 1756 Ramin, 1757 Heyden, 1759 Schwerin, 1761 Woldeck. 1778 Löben, with no 25. Distinguished at Kunersdorf. Captured at Maxen but restored.

IR NO 20 *

Station   Magdeburg.

Designation   1740 Graevenitz, 1741 Voigt, 1742 Hertzberg, 1746 Jung-Borcke, 1747 Borcke, 1756 Zastrow, 1757 Bornstedt, 1759 Jung-Stutterheim, 1778 Kalckstein, 1784 Below, 1786 Bornstedt.

Uniform   Blue coat, red cuffs and lapels, white waistcoat and breeches.

Record   Heavy losses at Kolin and Hochkirch.

Grenadier battalion   1740 Buddenbrock, with no 22; 1742 with no 5; 1744 Lepel, with no 26. Seven Years War with no 5. 1778 with no 5.

IR NO 21

Station   Halberstadt and Quedlinburg (Magdeburg).
Designation   1740 Marwitz, 1744 Bredow, 1756 Hülsen, 1767 Schwerin, 1773 Erbprinz v. Braunschweig.
Uniform   Blue coat, red cuffs and collar, straw waistcoat and breeches.
Record   Badly hit at Kolin and Kunersdorf, and became one of the 'Maxen regiments'.
Grenadier battalion   1740 with no 5; 1742 Bolstern, with no 23; 1744 with no 7. Seven Years War with no 27: 1756 Lengefeld, 1757 Diringshofen, 1761 Budberg.
   Distinguished at Moys, and storming of Schweidnitz 1758. Mostly lost at Greiffenberg 26 March 1759. Restored.

IR NO 22

Station   Stargard and Pyritz (Pomerania).
Designation   1740 Alt-Borcke, 1741 Prinz Moritz, 1760 Alt-Schenckendorff, 1768 Plötz, 1777 Schlieben.
Uniform   Blue coat, brick red cuffs and lapels, straw waistcoat and breeches.
Record   Massacred at Kolin and suffered heavily at Zorndorf. On 5 January 1741 the regiment entered Breslau 'in blue and red uniforms with straw-coloured waistcoats . . . a splendid collection of men, with fine shining weapons that were a delight to see' (Steinberger).
Grenadier battalion   1740 with no 20; 1742 with no 1; 1744 with no 17; 1745 with no 10. Seven Years War and 1778 with no 17.

IR NO 23

Station   Berlin.
Designation   1740 Sydow, 1743 Blanckensee, 1745 Christoph Dohna, 1748 Forcade, 1765 Puttkamer, 1766 Rentzel, 1778 Thüna, 1786 Lichnowski.
Uniform   Blue coat, red cuffs, white waistcoat and breeches.
Record   Distinguished at Soor, Prague and Zorndorf (see IR no 18). Forcade was a favourite of the king's, and one day Frederick remarked of his troops: 'When I want to see real soldiers, I watch for this regiment' (Archenholtz). In the army, however, Forcade was known as 'that old granny' (*dat alte Mutterchen*) (Lehndorff). The historian Archenholtz was an officer in the regiment.
Grenadier battalion   1740 Diersfort, with no 26; 1742 with no 21. Seven Years War with no 1. 1778 Eberstein, with no 26.

IR NO 24

Station   Frankfurt, Fürstenwalde and area (Pomerania).
Designation   1740 Alt-Schwerin, 1750 Schwerin, 1757 Goltz, 1763 Diringshofen, 1776 Leopold v. Braunschweig, 1785 Beville.
Uniform   Blue coat, red cuffs and lapels, straw or white waistcoat and breeches.
Record   The regiment of Field-Marshal Schwerin, and famous for its quantity of beer-swilling Mecklenburgers. Badly knocked about at Prague, Kay and Torgau.
Grenadier battalion   1740 with no 12; 1742 with no 8; 1744 Kahlbutz, with no 2, then Gar R no 5, then no 27; 1745 Finck, with no 27. Seven Years War with no 34: 1756 Grumbkow, 1757 Graf v. Anhalt, 1757 Naumeister, 1760 Sobeck, 1761 Drache. 1778 Grolman, with no 39.
   Captured at Landeshut, but restored.

IR NO 25

Station   Berlin.
Designation   1740 Kalckstein, 1760 Ramin, 1782 Möllendorff.

Uniform   Blue coat, red cuffs and lapels, white waistcoat and breeches.

Record   Rebuilt after being almost annihilated at Kolin.

Grenadier battalion   1740 with no 1; 1742 Trenck, with no 27; 1744 with no 21. Seven Years War and 1778 with no 19.

IR NO 26

Station   Berlin. Recruited from Pomerania and the Wendish Slavs.

Designation   1740 Kleist, 1747 Alt-Kleist, 1749 Meyerinck, 1758 Wedell, 1760 Linden, 1764 Steinkeller, 1778 Woldeck.

Uniform   Blue coat, red cuffs and collar, white waistcoat and breeches. The *Brandenbourgs* of the officers' coats were copied in the collar patches of German generals of the two world wars.

Record   Performed bravely at Mollwitz, Prague, Leuthen (fifteen awards of the *Pour le Mérite*), Hochkirch and Torgau. See the Barsewisch memoirs for conditions in the Seven Years War. Moritz of Dessau once remarked to the king: 'Your Majesty may safely entrust your crown and sceptre to the keeping of this regiment. If it ever runs before the enemy, I know it must be time for me to make myself scarce as well' (Barsewisch).

Grenadier battalion   1744 with no 20. Seven Years War with no 13. 1778 with no 23.

IR NO 27 *

Station   Stendal and Gardelegen (Altmark).

Designation   1740 Prinz Leopold, 1747 Jung-Kleist, 1749 Kleist, 1756 Alt-Kleist, 1757 Asseburg, 1759 Lindstädt, 1764 Stojentin, 1776 Knobelsdorff.

Uniform   Blue coat, red cuffs, lapels and collar, white waistcoat and breeches.

Record   Distinguished at Chotusitz, Lobositz and Breslau. Frederick once saw it fall out of step while returning from a review, whereupon he called out to the inspector: 'Saldern, let the regiment be! It was never very good at falling back – it has only ever known how to attack!'

Grenadier battalion   1740 with no 3; 1742 with no 5; 1744 with no 24; 1745 with no 9. Seven Years War and 1778 with no 21.

IR NO 28 *

Station   Wesel, then Brieg (Silesia). Recruited generally.

Designation   1740 Alt-Dohna, 1742 Hautcharmoy, 1758 Jung-Münchow, 1758 Jung-Kreytzen, 1759 Kreytzen, 1759 Ramin, 1760 Thile, 1770 Zaremba.

Uniform   Plain blue coat, straw waistcoat and breeches.

Record   *Distinguished at Prague*

Grenadier battalion   1744 Finck, with no 38; 1745 Ellert, with no 38. Seven Years War with no 32: 1756 Kreytzen, 1758 Arnim, 1762 Schätzel. 1778 Kamecke, with no 32.

Distinguished at storm of Schweidnitz 1758. Captured at Landeshut, but restored.

IR NO 29 *

Station   Anklam and Demmin (Pomerania), then Breslau.

Designation   1740 Jung-Borcke, 1746 Alt-Borcke, 1747 Schultze, 1758 Wedell, 1758 Knobloch, 1764 Stechow, 1778 Flemming, 1782 Wendessen.

Uniform   Blue coat, red cuffs, white waistcoat and breeches.

Record   Badly mauled at Kolin, Hochkirch and Kunersdorf. One battalion lost at Maxen.

Grenadier battalion   1740–1 with no 6, then no 33; 1742 Byla, with no 30; 1744 with no 12. Seven Years War with no 31: 1756 Ostenreich, 1759 Falkenhayn. 1778 Kowalsky, with no 31.

Distinguished at Liegnitz. Suffered heavily at Kunersdorf and Torgau.

IR NO 30

Station   Anklam and Demmin (Pomerania).

Designation   1740 Jeetze, 1748 Alt-Jeetze, 1752 Uchländer, 1755 Blanckensee, 1756 Pritz, 1757 Kannacher, 1759 Stutterheim, 1759 Alt-Stutterheim.

Uniform   Blue coat, red or carmine red cuffs, white waistcoat and breeches.

Record   Highly distinguished at Kesselsdorf. Frederick called it 'a good and brave regiment'.

Grenadier battalion   1740 with no 7; 1742 with no 29; 1744 with no 8. Seven Years War with no 7. 1778 Restorff, with no 47.

IR NO 31 *

Station   Wesel, then Breslau. Recruited generally.

Designation   1740 Dossow, 1743 Varenne, 1744 Schwarz-Schwerin or Bogislaw-Schwerin, 1746 Lestwitz, 1763 Tauentzien.

Uniform   Blue coat, rose-red cuffs, white waistcoat and breeches.

Record   Suffered very heavily from desertion in 1744. Heavy losses at Prague, distinguished at Breslau.

Grenadier battalion   1744 Jäger, then Lindstedt, with no 40. Seven Years War and 1778 with no 29.

IR NO 32

Station   Minden and Geldern, then Neisse (Upper Silesia).

Designation   Formed 1743, Jung-Schwerin, from battalions Beaufort and Kroecher; 1747 Jung-Tresckow, 1755 Tresckow, 1763 (as new regiment) Lestwitz, 1770 Rothkirch, 1786 Hohenlohe-Ingelfingen.

Uniform   Plain blue coat, with blue cuffs, white waistcoat and breeches.

Record   First battalion distinguished at Domstädtl, but the regiment as a whole performed badly at Moys and Kay, due to the large element of Upper Silesian Catholics. Captured at Schweidnitz 1761, and replaced by the regiment of Horn (formerly no 56).

Grenadier battalion   1744 Kleist, then Hertzberg, with no 33. Seven Years War and 1778 with no 28.

IR NO 33 (FUSILIER)

Station   Brandenburg, then Glatz.

Designation   1740 Persode, 1743 Schlichting, 1743 Bredow, 1744 La Motte, 1774 Thadden, 1784 Goetzen.

Uniform   Blue coat, white cuffs and lapels, white waistcoat and breeches, fusilier cap with orange top.

Record   Badly cut-up at Prague, captured at Landeshut.

Grenadier battalion   First Silesian War with nos 29 and 11; 1744 with no 32. Seven Years War with no 42: 1756 Nimschöfsky, 1762 Mosch.
Suffered heavily at Kolin.

IR NO 34 **

Station   Ruppin (Mittelmark).

Designation   Prinz Ferdinand.

Uniform   Blue coat, red cuffs, lapels and collar, lemon yellow waistcoat and breeches.

Record   A good reputation. The recruits fought well at Domstadtl, and the regiment excelled at Liegnitz.

Grenadier battalion   1740 with no 16; 1744 Stangen, with Gar R no 5. Seven Years War with no 24.

IR NO 35 (FUSILIER) **

Station   Magdeburg, then Potsdam. Recruited generally.

Designation   Prinz Heinrich.

Uniform   Blue coat, sulphur yellow cuffs and collar, sulphur yellow waistcoat and breeches, fusilier cap with sulphur yellow top.

Record   In heavy fighting at Kolin and Kunersdorf.

Grenadier battalion   1744 Tresckow, with no 39; 1745 Strantz, with no 39. Seven Years War with no 36:
   1756 Schenckendorff, 1759 Schwartz. 1778 Brünow, with no 46.
   Distinguished at Breslau.

IR NO 36 (FUSILIER)

Station   Potsdam, then Brandenburg-am-Oder.
Designation   1740 Münchow, 1758 Alt-Münchow, 1766 Kleist, 1780 Zitzewitz, 1785 Brünning.
Uniform   Blue coat, white cuffs and collar, white waistcoat and breeches, fusilier cap with white top.   .
Record   Badly hit at Kolin. Captured at Maxen, raised again, but captured at Schweidnitz 1761. An un-
   enviable record.
Grenadier battalion   1740 with no 8; 1742 with no 3; 1744 with no 5; Seven Years War with no 35. 1778
   Scholten, with Gar R no 7.

IR NO 37 (FUSILIER)

Station   Potsdam, then Glogau (Silesia).
Designation   1740 Camas, 1741 Moulin, 1755 Kurssell, 1758 Braun, 1770 Keller, 1785 Wolframsdorf.
Record   Heavy casualties at Prague, Second battalion captured at Schweidnitz 1757, heavy casualties at
   Zorndorf and Kunersdorf, First battalion captured at Landeshut. An unlucky regiment.
Grenadier battalion   1742 La Motte, with no 38; 1744 with no 13. Seven Years War with no 40: Manteuffel.
   1778 Götz, with no 38.
   Distinguished at Breslau. Captured at Maxen, but restored.

IR NO 38 (FUSILIER)

Station   Berlin, then Liegnitz (Silesia) then Frankenstein (Silesia).
Designation   1740 Jung-Dohna, 1749 Brandes, 1758 Zastrow, 1766 Falkenhayn, 1781 Anhalt, 1783 Hager.
Uniform   Blue coat, red cuffs, lapels and collar, white waistcoat and breeches, fusilier cap with light blue top.
Record   Severe casualties at Kunersdorf, one battalion captured at Maxen.
Grenadier battalion   1742 with no 37; 1744 with no 28. Seven Years War with no 43: 1756 Burgsdorff, 1760
   Heilsberg. 1778 with no 37.
   A hard-fighting battalion which suffered heavily at Prague and Zorndorf.

IR NO 39 (FUSILIER) **

Station   Prenzlau and Mohrin (Pomerania), then the Neumark. Recruited generally.
Designation   1740 Braunschweig, 1751 Franz v. Braunschweig, 1755 Jung-Braunschweig, 1771 Möllen-
   dorff, 1783 Könitz.
Uniform   Blue coat, lemon yellow cuffs and collar, lemon yellow waistcoat and breeches, fusilier cap with
   lemon yellow top.
Record   Almost three-quarters of the complement were foreigners. Fought well in action, but suffered from
   heavy desertion. Severe losses in Pomerania 1761.
Grenadier battalion   1744 with no 35. Seven Years War with no 12. 1778 with no 24.

IR NO 40 (FUSILIER)

Station   Breslau, then Schweidnitz.
Designation   1740 Sachsen-Eisenach, 1741 Graevenitz, 1743 Kreytzen, 1758 Alt-Kreytzen, 1759 Gablentz,
   1777 Erlach.
Uniform   Blue coat, rose-red cuffs, rose-red waistcoats and breeches, fusilier cap with rose-red top.
Record   Captured at Schweidnitz 1757, but restored. In 1784 Frederick said the men hardly resembled
   soldiers. The regiment originally came from the service of Sachsen-Eisenach.
Grenadier battalion   Seven Years War with no 37. 1778 Lölhöffel, with no 43.

IR NO 41 (FUSILIER) **

Station   Minden.

Designation   1741 Bevern, 1741 Riedesel, 1746 Wied, 1765 Lossow, 1782 Jung-Woldeck.

Uniform   Blue coat, light carmine red collar, lapels and cuffs, straw waistcoat and breeches, fusilier cap with light carmine top.

Record   Taken from the Württemberg service and entrusted to General v. Riedesel, as an effective disciplinarian. Heavy losses at Kolin, distinguished at Kunersdorf.

Grenadier battalion   1745 Holstein-Beck, then Münchow, with no 44. Seven Years War with no 44: 1756 Gemmingen, 1757 Beneckendorff. 1778 Romberg, with no 44.
Distinguished at Kolin, and storm of Schweidnitz 1758. Captured at Maxen, but restored.

IR NO 42 (FUSILIER)

Station   Frankenstein (Silesia), then Breslau.

Designation   1741 Markgraf Heinrich, 1764 Lettow, 1776 Lichnowsky, 1786 Köthen.

Uniform   Blue coat, orange cuffs, lapels and collar, white waistcoat and breeches, fusilier cap with black or light carmine red top.

Record   A very ordinary regiment. The First battalion was captured at Landeshut, but restored. Markgraf Heinrich (of Brandenburg-Schwedt) was not allowed to exercise actual command. General v. Lettow was an honest and uncommunicative Pomeranian.

Grenadier battalion   1744 with Gar R no 8. Seven Years War and 1778 with no 33.
Almost destroyed at Kolin.

IR NO 43 (FUSILIER)

Station   Schweidnitz, then Liegnitz (Silesia).

Designation   1744 Zimmernow, 1744 Kalsow, 1757 Kalckreuth, 1758 Bredow, 1760 Zieten, 1767 Krockow, 1773 Schwerin.

Uniform   Blue coat, brick red cuffs and collar, white waistcoat and breeches, fusilier hat with white top.

Record   Converted from a garrison regiment. Distinguished at Kunersdorf.

Grenadier battalion   1744 Brandes, then Finck, with Gar R no 7. Seven Years War with no 38. 1778 with no 40.

IR NO 44 (FUSILIER)

Station   Wesel. Recruited generally.

Designation   1744 Alt-Dohna, 1749 Jungkenn, 1759 Hoffmann, 1760 Grant, 1764 Brietzke, 1779 Gaudi.

Uniform   Blue coat, red cuffs, straw waistcoat and breeches, fusilier cap with black top.

Record   Raised from recruits from Württemberg and other German states. Lightly engaged in most of its actions.

Grenadier battalion   1745 with no 41. Seven Years War and 1778 with no 41.

IR NO 45 (FUSILIER)

Station   Wesel. Recruited generally.

Designation   1743 Dossow, 1757 Hessen-Cassel, 1786 Eckartsberg.

Uniform   Blue coat, scarlet cuffs, white waistcoat and breeches, fusilier cap with black top.

Record   Captured at Maxen.

Grenadier battalion   1745 Ingersleben, with Gar R no 9. Seven Years War with no 48 and Gar R no 9: 1756 Ingersleben, 1757 Unruh. 1778 Meusel, with no 48.
Captured at Glatz 1760 and unrestored for the duration of the war.

IR NO 46 (FUSILIER)

Station   Berlin.

Designation   1743 Alt-Württemberg, 1757 Bülow, 1776 Lettow, 1779 Pfuhl.

Uniform   Blue coat, cuffs and lapels of black plush, straw waistcoat and breeches, fusilier cap with top of straw above and black plush below.

Record   Heavily engaged at Kunersdorf, captured at Landeshut. A large proportion of the many Württemberg recruits deserted in 1744, as did six hundred Frenchmen in 1778–9.

Grenadier battalion   1745 Osten, then Kleist 'v. Prinz Leopold', then Aulack, with no 47. Seven Years War with no 8. 1778 with no 35.

IR NO 47 (FUSILIER)

Station   Burg, then Brieg (Silesia). Recruited in Upper Silesia.

Designation   1743 Prinz Georg or Jung-Darmstadt, 1747 Derschau, 1752 Wietersheim, 1756 Rohr, 1758 Grabow, 1764 Nassau-Usingen, 1778 Lehwaldt.

Uniform   Blue coat, lemon yellow cuffs, lapels and collar, white waistcoat and breeches, fusilier cap with yellow top.

Record   Taken over from the Holstein service 1743. Heavy losses at Kunersdorf, and the survivors captured at Maxen.

Grenadier battalion   1745 with no 46. Seven Years War with Gar R no 7: 1756 Wangenheim, 1757 (December) Carlowitz, 1759 Buddenbrock, 1760 Bock zu Wülfingen. 1778 with no 30.
In heavy fighting at Kolin and Domstädtl. Highly esteemed by Frederick.

IR NO 48 (FUSILIER)

Station   Wesel. Recruited generally.

Designation   1756 Hessen-Cassel, 1757 Salmuth (also called 'Beringer'), 1763 Beckwith, 1766 Eichmann.

Uniform   Blue coat, red cuffs and lapels, straw waistcoat and breeches, fusilier cap with black top.

Record   Raised from a garrison battalion. Second battalion captured at Maxen.

Grenadier battalion   Seven Years War with no 45. 1778 with no 45.

IR NO 49 (FUSILIER) *

Station   Neisse (Silesia).

Designation   Originally the Pionier-Regiment Sers, 1758 Diericke, 1770 Schwartz.

Uniform   Plain blue coat, dark orange waistcoat and breeches, fusilier cap with top of blue above and dark orange below.

Record   Converted from the Pionier-Regiment 1758. In heavy fighting at Zorndorf, distinguished at Kunersdorf.

IR NO 50 (FUSILIER)

Station   Silberberg (Upper Silesia).

Designation   1773 Rossières, 1778 Troschke.

Uniform   Blue coat, light carmine red cuffs, lapels and collar, white waistcoat and breeches, fusilier cap.

Record   Raised 1773 by a former Swiss officer.

Grenadier companies   1778 remained in Silberberg.

IR NO 51 (FUSILIER)

Station   Marienburg (West Prussia).

Designation   1773 Laxdehnen, 1773 Krockow.

Uniform   Blue coat, lemon yellow cuffs, lapels and collar, fusilier cap with lemon yellow top.

Record   One of the new Polish regiments. Its experiences in 1778–9 are described by one of its first lieutenants (see Anon., 'Erinnerungen an die letzte Campagne').
Grenadier battalion   1778 Osorowsky, with no 52.

IR NO 52 (FUSILIER)

Station   Prussian Holland (East Prussia).
Designation   1772 Lengefeld, 1785 Schwerin.
Uniform   Blue coat, red cuffs, lapels and collar, white waistcoat and breeches, fusilier cap with light blue top.
Record   Distinguished at Zuckmantel 14 January 1779.
Grenadier battalion   1778 with no 51.

IR NO 53 (FUSILIER)

Station   Braunsberg (West Prussia).
Designation   1773 Luck, 1780 v. d. Goltz, 1784 Schwerin, 1785 Raumer, 1786 Favrat.
Uniform   Blue coat, red cuffs and collar, white waistcoat and breeches, fusilier cap with red top.
Record   A new Polish regiment.
Grenadier battalion   1778 with no 4.

IR NO 54 (FUSILIER)

Station   Graudenz (West Prussia).
Designation   1773 Rohr, 1784 Klitzing, 1786 Bonin.
Uniform   Blue coat, carmine red cuffs and collar, fusilier cap with carmine red top.
Record   A new Polish regiment.
Grenadier battalion   1778 Franckenberg, with no 55.

IR NO 55 (FUSILIER)

Station   Mewa (West Prussia).
Designation   1774 Hessen-Philippsthal, 1780 Blumenthal, 1784 Koschenbahr.
Uniform   Blue coat, rose-red collar and cuffs, straw waistcoat and breeches, fusilier cap with rose-red top.
Grenadier battalion   With no 54.

Former Saxon infantry regiments

Ten Saxon regiments of foot were forcibly enlisted in the Prussian service after the capitulation of Pirna in October 1756. Seven of these were disbanded within less than a year, on account of heavy desertion. The survivors were:

IR NO 54 (FUSILIER)

Designation   Saxon regiment Sachsen-Gotha, 1756 Saldern, 1758 Plotho.
Uniform   Blue coat, white cuffs, white waistcoat and breeches, fusilier cap.
Record   Broken up after the Seven Years War, and the troops sent to fill up IR no 33.

IR NO 55 (FUSILIER)

Designation   Saxon regiment Lubomirsky, 1756 Hauss, 1760 Roebel.
Uniform   Blue coat, white cuffs, white waistcoat and breeches, fusilier cap.
Record   Badly hit at Kunersdorf, where Major Ewald v. Kleist (the poet) was mortally wounded. The survivors captured at Maxen. The regiment was restored, but disbanded, after the peace, the men going to IR no 36.

IR NO 56 (FUSILIER)

Designation Saxon regiment Prinz August, 1756 Loen, 1758 Kalckreuth, December 1758 Wietersheim, December 1759 Horn.

Uniform Blue coat, yellow cuffs, yellow waistcoat and breeches, fusilier cap.

Record Restored after a mass desertion in March 1757. After the peace it took the place of the disbanded IR no 32.

Stehende grenadier-bataillone (*Standing grenadier battalions*)

Uniforms are as in the parent regiments.

ST G-B NO 1

Designation 1742 Byla, 1749 Kahlden, 1758 Wangenheim, December 1758 Buddenbrock.

Record Raised from Gar Bns nos 3 and 4 and the Charlottenburg Grenadiers. Fought hard and well in the Seven Years War.

ST G-B NO 2

Designation 1744 Gemmingen, 1746 Ingersleben, 1757–60 Unruh. 1763 new establishment, Ingersleben.

Record Raised from grenadiers of IR no 45 and Gar Bns nos 10 and 11. Captured at Glatz 1760 and not restored. Place taken 1763 by the G-B Ingersleben, no 16.

ST G-B NO 3

Designation 1744 Ingersleben, 1746 Gemmingen, 1757 Beneckendorff.

Record Raised from grenadiers of IRs nos 41 and 44. Captured at Maxen, but restored.

ST G-B NO 4 KÖNIGSBERGISCHES GRENADIER-BATAILLON

Designation As above. 1751 Trenck, 1751 Katt, 1753 Heyden, 1755 Lossow.

Record Raised from grenadiers of Gar Rs nos 1 and 13.

ST G-B NO 5

Designation 1753 Rath, 1760 Koschenbahr, 1761 Hachenberg.

Record Raised from grenadiers of Gar R no 5. Captured at Landeshut, but restored.

ST G-B NO 6

Designation 1753 Plötz, 1758 Rohr, 1759 Busche.

Record Raised from grenadiers of Gar Rs nos 6 and 8. Fled at Zorndorf.

Garnison regimenter und bataillone

GAR R NO 1

Designation 1740 L'Hôpital, 1755 Luck, 1757 Puttkamer, 1772 Hallmann, 1786 Bose.

Uniform Plain blue coat, white (later blue) waistcoat and breeches.

Record Based at Memel. Second battalion raised 1743.

Grenadier battalion 1744 with no 16. Seven Years War with Gar R no 11: 1756 Lossow. 1778 Hardt, with Gar R no 2.

At Gross-Jägersdorf and Kunersdorf.

GAR R NO 2

Designation   1740 Natalis, 1742 Schulenburg, 1743 Roeder, 1754 Sydow, 1759 Alt-Sydow, 1773 Tümpling, 1777 Pirsch.
Uniform   Blue coat, white cuffs, white (later blue) waistcoat and breeches.
Record   Based at Pillau. Second battalion raised 1743. Heavy losses at Gross-Jägersdorf. At Torgau and Freiberg.
Grenadier battalion   1744 Langenau, with Gar R no 11. 1778 with Gar R no 1.

GAR R NO 3

Designation   1740 Hellermann, 1756 Grolman, 1763 Marschall v. Biberstein, 1767 Heyden.
Uniform   Blue coat, red (later blue) cuffs, white (later blue) waistcoat and breeches.
Record   Based at Kolberg. Filled up with Saxons and deserters in the Seven Years War. Defended towns in Saxony 1759.
Grenadier battalion   Seven Years War and 1778 with Neues Gar R no 3 and Gar R no 4.

GAR R NO 4

Designation   1740 Weyher, 1746 Grape, 1759 Jungkenn, 1760 Lettow, 1763 Plotho, 1766 Groscreutz, 1769 Gohr, 1772 Puttkamer, 1775 Gotter, 1782 Rüchel, 1784 Hülsen.
Uniform   Plain blue coat, white (later blue) waistcoat and breeches.
Record   Based at Magdeburg. Defended Wittenberg 1759.
Grenadier battalion   Seven Years War with Gar R no 3.

GAR R NO 5

Designation   1741 Thümen, 1743 Mützschefahl, 1759 Jung-Sydow, 1763 Berner, 1770 Hasslocher, 1771 Arnstädt, 1778 Natalis.
Uniform   Blue coat, red (later black) cuffs, white (later blue) waistcoat and breeches.
Record   Based at Züllichau. Defended Schweidnitz 1757, fought at Kay and Kunersdorf.
Grenadier battalion   1744 with no 34. Seven Years War with Gar R no 10: 1756 Rath, 1760 Koschenbarh, 1761 Hachenberg. 1778 Lentzke, with Gar R no 10.
Heavy losses at Domstädtl, and almost destroyed at Landeshut.

GAR R NO 6

Designation   1741 Stechow, 1743 Saldern, 1745 Lehmann, 1750 Bosse, 1753 Lattorff, 1762 Sass.
Uniform   Blue coat, orange cuffs, white (later blue) waistcoat and breeches.
Record   Based at Brieg and Breslau. One battalion present at siege of Olmütz 1758.
Grenadier battalion   1744 with Gar R no 9. Seven Years War with Gar R no 8: 1756 Plötz, 1758 Rohr, 1759 Busche. 1778 Gillern, with Gar R no 8.
Heavy losses at Hochkirch and Kunersdorf.

GAR R NO 7

Designation   1741 Bredow, 1746 Jeetze, 1754 Lange, 1760 Itzenplitz, 1766 Rentzel, 1766 Puttkamer, 1771 Kowalsky.
Uniform   Blue coat, carmine red cuffs, white (later blue) waistcoat and breeches.
Record   Garrisoned Dresden in the Seven Years War.
Grenadier battalion   1744 with no 43. Seven Years War with no 47. 1778 with no 36.

GAR R NO 8

Designation   1741 Reck, 1745 Loeben, 1746 Knobelsdorff, 1748 Nettelhorst, 1757 Quadt v. Wickeradt, 1763 Le Noble, 1772 Bremer, 1778 Berrenhauer, 1782 Heuking.

Uniform   Blue coat, black cuffs, white (later blue) waistcoat and breeches.

Record   Stationed at Glatz and Neisse. In Seven Years War filled up with deserters and prisoners of war – especially Hungarians – and precipitated fall of Glatz 1760. Sixty men under Captain v. Capeller very distinguished in defence of blockhouse of Schwedelsdorf 17/18 January 1779.

Grenadier battalion   1744 with no 42. Seven Years War and 1778 with Gar R no 6.

GAR R NO 9

Designation   1743 Kroecher, 1748 La Motte, 1759 Bonin, 1763 Salenmon.
Uniform   Blue coat, black cuffs and collar, straw or white (later blue) waistcoat and breeches.
Record   Based at Geldern. Actually one battalion strong. Melted away from desertion August 1757, but restored at Magdeburg.
Grenadier battalion   1744 with Gar R no 6. Seven Years War with nos 45 and 46.

GAR R NO 10

Designation   1742 Puttkamer, 1744 Rettberg, 1747 Blanckensee, 1765 Mülbe, 1780 Könitz, 1786 Raumer.
Uniform   Blue coat, black cuffs, white (later blue) waistcoat and breeches.
Record   Based at Breslau and Neisse.
Grenadier battalion   Seven Years War and 1778 with Gar R no 5.

GAR R NO 11

Designation   1744 Puttkamer, 1748 Manteuffel, 1760 Mellin, 1769 Ingersleben, 1782 Berrenhauer.
Uniform   Blue coat, red cuffs, white (later blue) waistcoat and breeches.
Record   Heavy losses at Gross-Jägersdorf. The component battalions captured at Landeshut 1760 and Kolberg 1761.
Grenadier battalion   Seven Years War with Gar R no 1. 1778 formed an independent grenadier battalion, Bähr.

GAR R NO 12

Designation   1744 Kalckreuth, 1763 Courbière.
Uniform   Blue coat, light blue (?) cuffs, white waistcoat and breeches.
Record   Based in East Friesland. Captured 1757. Restored after the peace from the free battalion Courbière.

Neue garnisonregimenter (later Landregimenter)

N GAR R NO 1 (NEUES GARNISON BERLIN)

Uniform   Peasant clothing in 1740s. Seven Years War: blue coat, grey cuffs and lapels, blue waistcoat and breeches.
Record   Raised in 1740s, and again 1756.

N GAR R NO 2 (NEUES GARNISON KÖNIGSBERG)

Uniform   Blue coat, grey cuffs and lapels, blue waistcoat and breeches.
Record   Raised in 1740s, and again 1756. Disbanded 1757.

N GAR R NO 3 (NEUES GARNISON MAGDEBURG)

Uniform   Blue coat, grey cuffs and lapels, blue waistcoat and breeches.
Record   Raised in 1740s, and again in 1759.

N GAR R NO 4 (NEUES GARNISON STETTIN)

Uniform   Blue coat, grey cuffs and lapels, blue waistcoat and breeches.
Record   Raised in 1740s, and again 1756.

DAS NEUE GARNISONREGIMENT

Uniform   Blue coat, red (later blue) cuffs, straw waistcoat and breeches. The grenadiers (the 'Charlotten-burger Grenadiere') had blue coats with red cuffs.
Record   Based on the lower Oder fortresses. In 1744, the Seven Years War and 1778 the Charlottenburger Grenadiere formed a combined battalion with Gar Rs nos 3 and 4.

Freibataillone und freicorps

FB NO 1

Designation   1756 Le Noble.
Uniform   Blue coat, light blue cuffs, collar, lapels, waistcoat and breeches.
Record   Captured at Landeshut. Restored and a Second battalion raised. At Freiberg as a free regiment.

FB NO 2

Designation   1756 Mayr, 1759 Collignon, 1760 Courbière.
Uniform   Blue coat, light blue cuffs, collar, waistcoat and breeches.
Record   Original battalion captured at Landeshut, restored and captured again by Russians 1761. Second battalion raised 1760. At Freiberg as a free regiment.

FB NO 3

Designation   1756 Kalben, 1758 Salenmon.
Uniform   Plain blue coat, light blue waistcoat and breeches.
Record   Captured at Maxen, but restored and fought at Torgau. Second battalion raised 1761. At Freiberg as a free regiment.

FB NO 4

Designation   1756 Angelelli, 1760 Chossignon.
Uniform   Blue coat, light blue cuffs, light blue waistcoat and breeches.
Record   Distinguished at Breslau and Hochkirch. Captured at Landeshut, but restored and a Second battalion raised. Almost wiped out by French at Nordhausen 27 March 1761, but restored.

FB NO 5

Designation   1757 Chossignon, 1758 Monjou.
Uniform   Blue coat, light blue cuffs, collar, lapels, waistcoat and breeches.
Record   Captured at Bautzen 6 September 1757, but restored. 1759 incorporated with FB no 7.

FB NO 6

Designation   1757 Rapin, 1759 Lüderitz.
Uniform   Blue coat, light blue cuffs, waistcoat and breeches.
Record   Raised from French prisoners taken at Rossbach. Original battalion captured at Landeshut, restored, captured again at Berlin and restored once more. Second battalion raised 1760–1. At Freiberg as a free regiment.

FB NO 7

Designation   1758 Wunsch.

Uniform   Blue coat, light blue cuffs, collar, waistcoat and breeches.

Record   1759 became a free regiment with incorporation of FB no 5 as Second battalion. 1760 Second battalion captured by Russians at Charlottenburg, but restored.

FB NO 8

Designation   1758 Du Verger, 1759 Quintus Icilius.

Uniform   Blue coat, light blue cuffs, collar, lapels, waistcoat and breeches. The Jäger had green coats.

Record   At Hochkirch. Second battalion raised 1760/1, Third battalion 1761.

FB NO 9

Designation   1758 Hårdt.

Uniform   Blue coat, light blue cuffs, lapels, waistcoat and breeches.

FC NO 10

Designation   1758 Frei-Husaren Lubomirsky.

Uniform   Green dolman, red pelisse, fur hat.

Record   In existence only a few months.

FB NO 11

Designation   1758 Corps Franc des Volontaires de Prusse.

Uniform   Green coat, red cuffs and collar, green waistcoat.

Record   A Second battalion raised late 1762.

FC NO 12

Designation   1759 Kleist'sches Freicorps. Comprising (i) Volontair-Regiment Husaren 1759, (ii) Frei-Dragoner Regiment 1760, (iii) Kroaten 1761, (iv) Jäger 1761.

Uniforms   Hussars – red dolman, green pelisse, fur hat; dragoons – green coat, waistcoat and breeches, black fur hat; Croats – green coat, waistcoat and breeches, felt hat; Jäger – green coat, red cuffs, collar and lapels, green waistcoat.

Record   Hussars raided into Franconia and present at Kunersdorf; hussars and dragoons at Torgau; hussars, Croats and Jäger at Freiberg.

FC NO 13

Designation   1760 Freicorps Schony. Comprising (i) battalion of Ungarische Grenadiere, (ii) Frei-Husaren.

Uniforms   Grenadiers – blue coat with yellow decoration; hussars – light blue dolman, dark blue pelisse, fur hat.

FC NO 14

Designation   1760 Frei Dragoner-Regiment Glasenapp.

Uniform   Blue coat, light blue collar, lapels, waistcoat and breeches.

FB NO 15

Designation   1760 Freibataillon Jeney or Volontaires d'Ostfriese.

Uniform   Blue coat, light blue collar, lapels, waistcoat and breeches.

Record   At Freiberg.

FB NO 16

Designation   1760 Freibataillon Schack.
Uniform   Blue coat, light blue cuffs and collar, waistcoat and breeches.
Record   At Freiberg.

FB NO 17

Designation   1761 Freibataillon Heer or Schweizer-Bataillon.
Uniform   Blue coat, light blue cuffs, collar, lapels, waistcoat and breeches.
Record   At Freiberg.

FB NO 18

Designation   1761 Freibataillon Bequignolles.
Uniform   Blue coat, light blue cuffs, collar, lapels, waistcoat and breeches.

FB NO 19

Designation   1761 Freibataillon La Badie or Royal Etranger.
Uniform   Blue coat, light blue cuffs, collar, waistcoat and breeches.
Record   Disbanded within a few months on account of desertion.

FC NO 20

Designation   1761 Freicorps Gschray. Comprising (i) Freibataillon Gschray, (ii) Frei-Dragoner Gschray.
Uniform   Blue coat, black cuffs and lapels, straw waistcoat and breeches.
Record   Gschray and some of his band were captured at Nordhausen 27 March 1761.

FC NO 21

Designation   1761 Tartarisches Ulanencorps Krczowsky.
Uniform   Red dolman, brown pants, turban.
Record   Never at full strength.

FB NO 22

Designation   1761 Schwarze Brigade Favrat. Comprising (i) grenadiers, (ii) dragoons, (iii) Jäger, (iv) hussars.
Uniforms   Grenadiers – black coat, red cuffs and lapels, straw waistcoat and breeches; dragoons – black coat, red cuffs, straw waistcoat and breeches; Jäger – black coat, green cuffs, lapels, waistcoat and breeches; hussars – yellow dolman, black pelisse, felt hat.
Record   Never more than a single battalion raised.

FREIBATAILLON BELOW

This unit is not listed in the standard histories. It was a scratch force raised in May 1760 from several regiments, and was captured after a heroic fight at Landeshut.

Jäger-Corps zu Fuss

Uniform   Green coat, red cuffs and collar, green waistcoat, yellow leather breeches.
Record   Prague, Breslau, Leuthen and Hochkirch. Almost wiped out by the cossacks at Spandau 10 October 1760.

Regimenter zu Pferde (later Cürassier Regimenter)

Coats, waistcoats and breeches were straw-yellow in the great wars of the 1740s and 1750s, becoming gradually whiter towards the end of the reign. The distinctive regimental colours were to be found on such items as waistcoat, the turn-backs of the coat, the edges of the carbine belt, the sabretache and the saddle cloth.

CR NO 1

Station   Breslau.

Designation   1740 Buddenbrock, 1757 Krockow, 1759 Schlabrendorff, 1768 Roeder, 1781 Apenburg, 1784 Bohlen.

Distinctive colours   Red and white.

Record   One of the old 'Fehrbellin regiments'. At Chotusitz, Hohenfriedberg, Soor, Kesselsdorf, Prague, Kolin (distinguished), Leuthen, Hochkirch, Kay, Kunersdorf, Torgau and Freiberg.

CR NO 2

Station   Wusterhausen, Pritzwalk, etc.

Designation   1740 Prinz v. Preussen, 1758 Prinz Heinrich, 1767 Wirsbitzki, 1778 Weyher, 1782 Saher, 1783 Backhoff.

Distinctive colours   Dark carmine red. The regiment retained the original straw-coloured coat, waistcoat and breeches throughout the reign, hence the nickname of the 'Gelbe Reiter' (Yellow Troopers).

Record   Another of the 'Fehrbellin regiments'. In nearly all the major actions. Distinguished at Chotusitz, but fled at Kolin.

CR NO 3 LEIBREGIMENT ZU PFERDE

Station   Schönebeck, Wanzleben, etc.

Designation   As above. 1740 Wreech, 1746 Katzler, 1747 Katte, 1758 Lentulus, 1778 Merian, 1782 Kospoth.

Distinctive colours   Dark blue and white.

Record   A 'Fehrbellin regiment'. Distinguished at Rossbach and especially Liegnitz.

CR NO 4

Station   Zülz, Ober-Glogau, Krappitz, etc.

Designation   1740 Gessler, 1758 Schmettau, 1764 Woldeck v. Arneburg, 1769 Arnim, 1785 Mengden.

Distinctive colours   Dark blue and white.

Record   A 'Fehrbellin regiment'. Distinguished at Kesselsdorf.

CR NO 5

Station   Belgard, Arnswalde, etc.

Designation   1740 Prinz Friedrich (or Markgraf Friedrich), 1771 Lölhöffel v. Löwensprung, 1782 Mauschwitz, 1782 Württemberg.

Distinctive colours   Sky blue and white.

Record   Distinguished at Kunersdorf, Liegnitz and Torgau.

CR NO 6

Station   Aschersleben, Croppenstadt, etc.

Designation   1740 Prinz Eugen, 1744 Stille, 1753 Baron v. Schönaich, 1759 Vasold, 1769 Seelhorst, 1779 Hoverbeck, 1781 Rohr.

Distinctive colours   Light brick red and white.

Record   Distinguished at Hochkirch, but captured at Maxen. Stille was a mild and diminutive officer who was highly regarded by the king. Vasold, however, was banished from the royal company after the disgrace at Maxen.

CR NO 7

Station Salzwedel, Tangermünde, etc.
Designation 1740 Bredow, 1756 Driesen, 1758 Horn, 1762 Manstein, 1777 Marwitz, 1784 Kalckreuth.
Distinctive colours Yellow and white.
Record Distinguished at Rossbach, but captured at Maxen.

CR NO 8 **

Station Ohlau, Grottkau, etc.
Designation 1740 Jung-Waldow, 1742 Rochow, 1757 Seydlitz, 1774 Pannewitz.
Distinctive colours Dark blue and white.
Record For ever famous from its association with Seydlitz. Distinguished at Soor, Kolin, Rossbach, Zorndorf and Liegnitz.

CR NO 9

Station Oppeln, Löwen, etc.
Designation 1740 Katte, 1741 Wartensleben, 1741 Möllendorff, 1743 Bornstedt, 1751 Prinz v. Schönaich, 1758 Bredow, 1769 Podewils, 1784 Braunschweig.
Distinctive colours Dark blue and orange, later dark carmine red and white.
Record Distinguished at Soor and Hochkirch. Captured at Maxen.

CR NO 10 REGIMENT GENSD'ARMES **

Station Berlin.
Designation As above. 1740 Pannewitz, 1743 v. d. Goltz, 1747 Katzler, 1761 Schwerin, 1768 Krusemark, 1775 Prittwitz.
Distinctive colours Red and gold.
Record Distinguished at Soor, Rossbach, Zorndorf and Hochkirch. Colonel Albert v. Schwerin was 'like a chatty old woman' (Lehndorff) in his conduct and conversation, and one of the notable eccentrics of the army.

CR NO 11 LEIB-KARABINIERS

Station Rathenow, Burg, etc.
Designation As above. 1740 Wartensleben, 1741 Bredow, 1751 Penavaire, 1759 Bandemer, 1768 Hoverbeck, 1770 Kleist, 1775 Bohlen, 1784 Reppert.
Distinctive colours Sky blue and white.
Record Distinguished at Zorndorf.

CR NO 12 **

Station Ratibor, Leobschütz, etc.
Designation 1740 Alt-Waldow, 1743 Kyau, 1759 Spaen, 1762 Dalwig.
Distinctive colours Brick red and white.
Record Saw fighting in the major actions of the Seven Years War.

CR NO 13 GARDE DU CORPS

Station Charlottenburg.
Designation As above. 1740 Blumenthal, 1744 Jaschinski, 1747 Blumenthal, 1758 Wacknitz, 1760 Schätzel, 1773 Mengden, 1785 Byern.
Distinctive colours Red with silver braid.
Record Always brigaded with the Gensd'armes. Originally one squadron strong, but second and third squadrons raised 1756. Distinguished at Rossbach, Zorndorf and Hochkirch. A highly proficient unit, as well as being a socially prestigious one.

Dragoner Regimenter

DR NO 1 *

Station Wrietzen, Greifenhagen, etc.

Designation 1740 Platen, 1741 Posadowsky, 1747 Katte, 1751 Ahlemann, 1755 Normann, 1761 Zastrow, 1774 Wylich und Lottum.

Uniforms (i) until 1745 – white coat, black cuffs, collar and lapels, dark blue waistcoat, yellow leather breeches; (ii) from 1745 – light blue coat, black cuffs, collar and lapels, sulphur yellow waistcoat, yellow breeches.

Record Distinguished at Kolin, Leuthen and Liegnitz, and 'remarkable for its bravery in all the Prussian campaigns' (Archenholtz).

DR NO 2

Station Lüben, Bunzlau.

Designation 1740 Sonsfeld, 1742 Württemberg, 1749 Schwerin, 1754 Blanckensee, 1757 Krockow, 1778 Württemberg, 1781 Mahlen.

Uniforms (i) Until 1745 – white coat, sky blue or white cuffs, white lapels, straw breeches; (ii) from 1745 – light blue coat, rest as above.

Record Heavy casualties at Kunersdorf, repulsed at Liegnitz.

DR NO 3

Station Küstrin.

Designation 1740 Schulenburg, 1741 Rothenburg, 1752 Baron v. Schönaich, 1753 Truchsess, 1757 Meinicke, 1761 Flanss, 1763 Alvensleben, 1777 Thun.

Uniforms (i) Until 1745 – white coat, red cuffs and lapels; (ii) from 1745 – light blue coat, rose red cuffs, collar and lapels, straw waistcoat and breeches.

Record Disgraced at Baumgarten 27 February 1741 and lost the designation 'Grenadiere zu Pferde'. Distinguished at Chotusitz, Kolin and Rossbach. Fled under fire at Kunersdorf.

DR NO 4 **

Station Landsberg-am-Wartha, Woldenberg, etc.

Designation 1741 Bissing, 1742 Kannenberg, 1742 Spiegel, 1743 Bonin, 1752 Oertzen, 1756 Katte, 1757 Czettritz, 1772 Wulffen, 1782 Knobelsdorff, 1786 Goetzen.

Uniforms (i) Until 1745 – white coat, cornflower blue cuffs, collar and lapels; (ii) from 1745 – light blue coat, straw cuffs, collar and lapels, straw waistcoat and breeches.

Record Raised 1741 from five squadrons of DR no 3. Distinguished at Rossbach and especially Zorndorf.

DR NO 5 BAYREUTH DRAGONER (TEN SQUADRONS STRONG)

Station Pasewalk, Garz, etc.

Designation As above.

Uniforms (i) Until 1745 – white coat, red cuffs, lapels and collar, straw waistcoat and breeches; (ii) from 1745 – light blue coat, carmine red cuffs, lapels and collar, straw waistcoat and breeches.

Record One of the most celebrated regiments of Frederick's army. Highly distinguished at Hohenfriedberg, where its charge decided the battle. Distinguished at Leuthen and Torgau.

DR NO 6 (TEN SQUADRONS STRONG)

Station Insterburg, Darkehmen, etc.

Designation 1740 Alt-Möllendorff, 1747 Schorlemer, 1760 Meier, 1774 Posadowsky.

Uniforms (i) Until 1745 – white coat, light blue cuffs, lapels and collar; (ii) from 1745 – light blue coat, white cuffs, lapels and collar, lemon yellow waistcoat and breeches.

Record   The 'Porzellan-Regiment', taken from the Saxon service in 1717. Heavily engaged at Zorndorf and Kunersdorf.

DR NO 7

Station   Tilsit.

Designation   1740 Thümen, 1741 Werdeck, 1742 Roehl, 1745 Rüts, 1756 Plettenberg, 1763 Apenburg, 1781 Borck.

Uniforms   (i) Until 1745 – white coat, red cuffs and collar, white lapels; (ii) from 1745 – light blue coat, red collar and cuffs, straw waistcoat and breeches.

Record   Badly mauled at Chotusitz. Highly distinguished at Zorndorf.

DR NO 8

Station   Insterburg.

Designation   1744 Stosch, 1751 Langermann, 1757 Platen, 1758 Alt-Platen, 1770 Platen.

Uniforms   (i) Until 1745 – white coat, red cuffs, lapels and collar; (ii) after 1745 – light blue coat, red cuffs, lapels and collar, straw waistcoat and breeches.

Record   Distinguished at Gross-Jägersdorf and Zorndorf.

DR NO 9

Station   Marienwerder.

Designation   1741 Platen, 1743 Holstein-Gottorp, 1761 Pomeiske, 1785 Zitzwitz.

Uniforms   (i) Until 1745 – white coat, light blue collar and cuffs; (ii) from 1745 – light blue coat, light blue collar and cuffs, straw waistcoat and breeches.

Record   Raised 1741. Lightly engaged till 1761, when destroyed in the campaign around Kolberg.

DR NO 10

Station   Sagan.

Designation   1743 Jung-Möllendorff, 1754 Finck v. Finckenstein, 1785 Rosenbruch.

Uniforms   (i) Until 1745 – white coat, orange collar and cuffs; (ii) from 1745 – light blue coat, orange collar and cuffs.

Record   Formed 1743. An unspectacular regiment.

DR NO 11

Station   Sagan.

Designation   1741 Nassau, 1755 Stechow, 1758 Jung-Platen, 1770 Mitzlaff, 1778 Bosse.

Uniforms   (i) Until 1745 – white coat, orange (?) cuffs and collar; (ii) from 1745 – light blue coat, lemon yellow cuffs, lapels and collar, straw waistcoat and breeches.

Record   Distinguished at Prague and Leuthen, captured at Maxen after a hard fight.

DR NO 12

Station   Treptow, Wollin.

Designation   1742 Alt-Württemberg, 1749 Prinz Eugen v. Württemberg, 1769 Reitzenstein, 1780 Kalckreuth.

Uniform   It retained its light blue coat from the Württemberg service, possibly serving as the model for the light blue dragoon coat introduced generally in 1745. Black plush cuffs, lapels and collar.

Record   Taken from the Württemberg service 1742. Suffered from heavy desertion 1744. Badly mauled at Prague, fled and captured at Maxen.

Husaren Regimenter

HR NO 1 PREUSSISCHES HUSAREN-KORPS, OR GRÜNE HUSAREN

Station Goldap, Ragnit.
Designation As above. 1741 Bronikowsky, 1747 Dewitz, 1750 Székely, 1759 Kleist, 1770 Czettritz.
Uniform Light green dolman, dark green pelisse (hence the name 'Green Hussars'), fur hat.
Record Distinguished at Lobositz and Rossbach.

HR NO 2 LEIB-HUSAREN-REGIMENT, LEIBKORPS HUSAREN ZIETEN, OR ROTE HUSAREN **

Station Berlin.
Designation As above. 1741 Zieten, 1786 Brunner.
Uniform Red dolman (hence the name 'Red Hussars'), dark blue pelisse, fur hat.
Record Famous as Zieten's regiment. Distinguished at Hohenfriedberg, Prague, Zorndorf, Hochkirch and Torgau.

HR NO 3

Station Berlin.
Designation 1740 Bandemer, 1741 Malachowsky, 1745 Wartenberg, 1757 Warnery, 1758 Möhring, 1773 Somoggy, 1777 Rosenbusch, 1785 Keöszegy.
Uniform White dolman, dark blue pelisse, fur hat.
Record Distinguished at Ratibor 9 February 1745, distinguished at Prague, nine squadrons captured at Schweidnitz 1757, distinguished at Liegnitz. Wartenberg and Warnery were officers of high reputation.

HR NO 4 WEISSE HUSAREN

Station Wartenberg, Trebnitz.
Designation 1741 Natzmer, 1751 Vippach, 1755 Puttkamer, 1759 Dingelstadet, 1762 Bohlen, 1770 Podgurski, 1781 Württemberg.
Uniform Light blue dolman, white pelisse (hence the name 'White Hussars'), felt hat.
Record Raised as lancer regiment, converted to hussars 1742. Seydlitz entered as a Rittmeister 1743. Distinguished at Prague, repulsed at Kunersdorf.

HR NO 5 SCHWARZE HUSAREN **

Station Goldap, Lötzen.
Designation 1741 Mackerodt, 1744 Ruesch, 1762 Lossow, 1783 Hohenstock.
Uniform Black dolman and pelisse (hence the name 'Black Hussars'), felt hat with skull and crossbones badge of tin.
Record Renowned for the wealth of its officers and the ferocity of its hussars. Distinguished at Hennersdorf 1745, and three squadrons distinguished in western Germany in Seven Years War.

HR NO 6 BRAUNE HUSAREN

Station Pless, Schrau.
Designation 1741 Hoditz, 1743 Soldan, 1746 Wechmar, 1757 Werner, 1785 Gröling.
Uniform Brown dolman and pelisse (hence the name 'Brown Hussars'), felt hat.
Record Distinguished at Prague, but captured at Maxen.

HR NO 7 (FIRST)

Designation 1743 Hallasch, 1747 Seydlitz (Major Alexander v.), 1759 Gersdorff.
Uniform Red dolman, red pelisse.

Record Distinguished at Rossbach, but captured at Maxen. Disbanded after the peace, and place taken by the former HR no 8.

HR NO 7 (SECOND, FORMERLY HR NO 8) GELBE HUSAREN

Designation 1744 Dieuri, 1746 Billerbeck, 1753 Malachowsky, 1775 Usedom.
Uniform Lemon yellow dolman (hence the name 'Yellow Hussars'), light blue pelisse.
Record Distinguished at Zorndorf, lost six squadrons at Landeshut. After the peace took the number of the disbanded HR no 7. Frederick specifically exempted it from criticism 1778–9.

HR NO 8 (ORIGINALLY HR NO 9)

Designation 1758 Belling, 1779 Hohenstock, 1783 Schulenburg.
Uniform Black dolman, black pelisse, felt hat.
Record Raised 1758 at Halberstadt by Lieutenant-Colonel Wilhelm v. Belling in strength of five squadrons; ten more added 1760–1. Distinguished at Kunersdorf. On 29 August 1760 the regiment captured the Swedish hussar Gebhard v. Blücher in Mecklenburg. Blücher enlisted in the regiment, becoming its *Chef* in 1794, and ultimately the famous field-marshal.

HR NO 9 (SECOND) BOSNIAKEN–CORPS

Designation As above.
Uniform Red dolman, wide scarlet trousers, turban or fur hat.
Record Raised 1745 and attached to HR no 5. Became HR no 9 in 1771, but remained associated with HR no 5 until 1788.

HR NO 10

Designation Owstien.
Record Raised 1773.

Feldjäger-Corps zu Pferde

Raised 1740. Uniform as in the Feldjäger-Corps zu Fuss.

Artillerie

Plain blue coat, light blue waistcoat and breeches.

Ingenieur-Corps

Blue coat, dark red cuffs, lapels, waistcoat and breeches.

Bibliography

Biographies of Frederick and monographs on battles and campaigns have been omitted, except where they bear directly on matters mentioned in the text.

ANON. *Les Campagnes du Roi de Prusse en 1742 et 1745*, Amsterdam 1763. By a Prussian officer

ANON. 'Drei Jahre im Kadetten-Corps (1758–60)', *Jahrbücher für die deutsche Armee und Marine*, XXXIX, Berlin 1881

ANON. 'Erinnerungen an die letzte Campagne Friedrichs des Grossen', *Jahrbücher*, LIII, Berlin 1884. A subaltern's life in a West Prussian regiment (no 51) in the War of the Bavarian Succession

ANON. *Idée de la Personne, de la Manière de vivre, et de la Cour du Roi de Prusse*, British Museum, Stowe MSS 307, f60

ANON. 'Reflections on the general Principles of War; and on the Composition and Characters of the different Armies in Europe; by a General Officer who served several Campaigns in the Austrian Army', *Annual Register*, London 1766

ANON. 'Ueber das Verpflegungswesen im Siebenjährigen Krieges', *Jahrbücher*, XII, Berlin 1874

ARCHENHOLTZ, J. W. *Geschichte des Siebenjährigen Krieges in Deutschland* (1791), 5th ed, 2 vols, Berlin 1840. The author was a subaltern in the regiment of Forcade. His history is vivid and detailed.

BARSEWISCH, C. F. *Meine Kriegs-Erlebnisse während des Siebenjährigen Krieges 1757–1763*, Berlin 1863. He was a subaltern in the regiment of Wedell

Aus dem Nachlasse von Georg Heinrich v. Berenhorst, 2 vols, Dessau 1845–7

BERENHORST, G. H. *Betrachtungen über die Kriegskunst*, 3 pts, Leipzig 1798–9. Lively and disinterested, if not always reliable in detail

BERNHARDI, T. *Friedrich der Grosse als Feldherr*, 2 vols, Berlin 1881

BLECKWENN, H. *Das altpreussische Heer. Erscheinungsbild und Wesen 1713–1807*, Osnabrück 1969 and still in progress. A most important series of monographs and reprints. Hans Bleckwenn and his enlightened publishers (Biblio Verlag) are largely responsible for the present revival of interest in the Frederician period.

BLECKWENN, H. 'Zur Handhabung der Geschütze bei der friderizianischen Feldartillerie', *Zeitschrift für Heereskunde*, no 200, Berlin 1965

Boswell on the Grand Tour: Germany and Switzerland 1764, ed F. A. Pottle, London 1953

BOYSEN, F. E. *Eigene Lebensbeschreibung*, Quedlinburg 1795. Especially on conditions in Magdeburg in the Seven Years War.

BRÄKER, U. *Der arme Mann im Tockenburg*, Leipzig 1852. By an unwilling private in the regiment of Itzenplitz.

BRÜGGEMANN, F. *Der Siebenjährige Krieg im Spiegel der zeitgenossischen Literatur*, Leipzig 1935

BURCHARDI, H. 'Der kartographische Standpunkt beim Beginn des Siebenjährigen Krieges', *Beihefte zum Militär-Wochenblatt*, Berlin 1879

BURGOYNE, J. 'Observations upon the present military State of Prussia, Austria and France' (1767), in *Political and military Episodes . . . from the Life and Correspondence of the Right Hon. John Burgoyne*, ed E. B. Fonblanque, London 1876

BUSCH, A. *Militärsystem und Socialleben im Alten Preussen 1713–1807*, vol VII of *Vcröffentlichungen der Berliner Historischen Kommission*, Berlin 1962

BÜTTNER, G. A. *Denkwürdigkeiten aus dem Leben des Königl. Preuss. Generals von der Infanterie Freiherrn de la Motte Fouqué*, 2 pts, Berlin 1788

BUXBAUM, E. *Friedrich Wilhelm Freiherr von Seydlitz*, new ed, Rathenow 1890. Useful but uncritical

Unterhaltungen mit Friedrich dem Grossen. Memoiren und Tagebücher von H. de Catt, ed R. Koser, Leipzig 1884. By the king's reader.

COLIN, J. *L'Infanterie au XVIII Siècle: la Tactique*, Paris 1907. For the influence of Prussian tactics in France

Correspondence of Charles, First Marquis Cornwallis, ed C. Ross, 3 vols, London 1859

CRAIG, G. A. *The Politics of the Prussian Army 1640–1945*, Oxford 1955

CROUSAZ, A. 'Die Cavallerie Friedrichs des Grossen', *Jahrbücher*, XII, Berlin 1874

DECKER, C. *Die Schlachten und Hauptgefechte des Siebenjährigen Krieges . . . mit vorherrschender Bezugnahme auf den Gebrauch der Artillerie*, Berlin 1837. Old but good

DELBRÜCK, H. *Geschichte des Kriegskunst im Rahmen der politischen Geschichte*, 4 vols, Berlin 1900–20. A gifted scholar who was out of sympathy with the officially received views of Frederick. He had a private army which he drilled in the tactics of the Frederician period

DEMETER, K. *The German Officer Corps in Society and State 1650–1945*, London 1965

DETTE, E. *Friedrich der Grosse und sein Heer*, Göttingen 1914

DOYLE, J. B. *Frederick William von Steuben*, Steubenville 1913

DROYSEN, J. G. 'Die preussischen Kriegsberichte der beiden schlesischen Kriege', *Beihefte*, Berlin 1877

DUFFY, C. J. *The Wild Goose and the Eagle. A Life of Marshal von Browne 1705–1757*, London 1964. Augmented ed in German trans *Feldmarschall v. Browne*, Vienna 1966. For the strategic aims of contemporary commanders, and the events of the campaigns of 1740–1 and 1756

DUNDAS, D. D. *Remarks on the Prussian Troops and their Movements*, 1785, British Museum, King's MSS 241

DUPUY, E. R. and T. N. *The Compact History of the Revolutionary War*, New York 1963. For Steuben's influence

EASUM, C. V. *Prince Henry of Prussia. Brother of Frederick the Great*, Madison 1942

ECKARDT, W., and MORAWIETZ, O. *Die Handwaffen des brandenburgisch-deutschen Heeres*, Hamburg 1957

ERGANG, R. *The Potsdam Fuhrer. Frederick William I*, New York 1941

Erste Schlesische Krieg, see Grosser Generalstab

Frederick the Great. *Die Instruktion Friedrichs des Grossen für seine Generale von 1747*, ed W. Frank, Berlin 1936

——. *Oeuvres de Frédéric le Grand*, 30 vols, Berlin 1846–56, especially I–VII (historical) and XXVIII–XXX (military)

——. *Politische Correspondenz Friedrichs des Grossen*, 46 vols, Berlin 1879–1939. An indispensable source, after the destruction of the state archives by bombing on 14 April 1945

——. *Die Politischen Testamente Friedrichs des Grossen*, published as supplement to the *Politische Correspondenz* 1920

——. *Militärische Schriften*, vol VI of *Die Werke Friedrichs des Grossen*, Berlin 1913

Le Comte de Gisors 1732–1758, ed C. Rousset, Paris 1868. For a revealing conversation with Frederick in 1754

GOLTZ, C. V. D. *Von Rossbach bis Jena und Auerstedt*, 2nd ed, Berlin 1906. On the decay of the Frederician army

GÖRLITZ, W. *The German General Staff. Its History and Structure 1657–1945*, London 1953

GOTZKOWSKY, J. C. *Geschichte eines patriotischen Kaufmanns*, Augsburg 1768–9

GRAEWE, R. 'Die Feldprediger', pt X, 'Des Grossen Friedrich Feldprediger', *Zeitschrift für Heereskunde*, no 226, Berlin 1969

GRAEWE, R. 'Regimentstochter', *Zeitschrift für Heereskunde*, no 197, Berlin 1965

GROEHLER, O. *Die Kriege Friedrichs II*, East Berlin 1966. A good summary

GROSSER GENERALSTAB. 'Die taktische Schulung der preussischen Armee durch König Friedrich den Grossen während der Friedenzeit 1745 bis 1756', *Kriegsgeschichtliche Einzelschriften*, XVIII–XXX, Berlin 1900

——. 'Friedrich des Grossen Anschauung vom Kriege in ihrer Entwicklung von 1745 bis 1756', *Kriegsgeschichtliche Einzelschriften*, XXVII, Berlin 1899

——. *Die Kriege Friedrichs des Grossen*, 20 vols, Berlin 1890–1913, comprising *Der Erste Schlesische Krieg*, *Der Zweite Schlesische Krieg* and *Der Siebenjährige Krieg*. Very great expertise and resources were devoted to producing this, the most detailed account of Frederick's wars. *Der Siebenjährige Krieg* was completed only up to the end of 1759. In the 1930s E. Kessel set out to finish the work, but his papers were destroyed in World War II.

——. *Urkundliche Beiträge und Forschungen zur Geschichte des preussischen Heeres*. Includes 'Briefe preussischer Soldaten', II, Berlin 1901; Ferdinand of Brunswicks 'Réflexions . . . sur la Campagne de 1756',

II, Berlin 1901; C. Jany, 'Die Gefechtsausbildung der preussischen Infanterie von 1806', V, Berlin 1903; and 'Potsdamer Tagebücher 1740 bis 1756', X, Berlin 1906

GUIBERT, J. A. *Journal d'un Voyage en Allemagne, fait en 1773*, 2 vols, Paris 1803

GUIBERT, J. A. *Observations sur la Constitution militaire et politique des Armées de Sa Majesté Prussienne*, Amsterdam 1778

HAHN, W. *Hans Joachim v. Zieten*, 3rd ed, Berlin 1858

HANKE, M., and DEGNER, H. *Geschichte der amtlichen Kartographie Brandenburg-Preussens*, Stuttgart 1935

'Aus der Zeit des Siebenjährigen Krieges. Tagebuchblätter und Briefe der Prinzessin Heinrich und des Königlichen Hauses', ed E. Berner and G. Volz, *Quellen und Untersuchungen zur Geschichte des Hauses Hohenzollern*, IX, Berlin 1908

Militärischer Nachlass des königlich preussischen Generallieutenants . . . Henckel v. Donnersmarck, 2 vols, Leipzig 1858

HILDEBRANDT, C. *Anekdoten und Characterzüge aus dem Leben Friedrichs des Grossen*, 6 vols, Halberstadt 1829–55

HÜLSEN, C. W. *Unter Friedrich dem Grossen. Aus den Memoiren des Aeltervaters 1752–1773*, ed H. Hülsen, Berlin 1890. In the Seven Years War Hülsen was a subaltern in the regiment of Below

JÄHNS, M. *Geschichte der Kriegswissenschaften vornehmlich in Deutschland*, pt III, Munich and Leipzig 1891

JANSON, A. *Hans Karl v. Winterfeldt, des Grossen Königs Generalstabschef*, Berlin 1913

JANY, C. *Geschichte der Preussischen Armee vom 15. Jahrhundert bis 1914*, vols II and III, Berlin 1928–9. New Ed by E. Jany, Osnabrück 1967. Solidly patriotic in sentiment, but still the most detailed and reliable survey of the subject

JANY, C., and MENZEL, A. *Die Armee Friedrichs des Grossen in ihrer Uniformierung*, Berlin 1908

'Das Paroles-Buch des Feldmarschalls Kalckreuth', ed 'G.L.', *Jahrbücher*, LI, Berlin 1884

KALTENBORN, R. W. *Briefe eines alten preussischen Officiers verschiedene Characterzüge Friedrichs des Grossen betreffend*, 2 vols, Hohenzollern 1790

KALTENBORN, R. W. *Schreiben des alten preussischen Officiers an seinen Freund zur Erläuterung uber die Glaubwürdigkeit seiner Nachrichten von Friedrich II*, Hohenzollern 1792. The latter in answer to Feldprediger Ziesemer's *Briefe eines preussischen Feldpredigers verschiedene Characterzüge Friedrichs des einzigen betreffend*, Potsdam 1791. Major v. Kaltenborn was dismissed from the army in 1780, and he is heavily prejudiced against Frederick. All the same, if used with caution, his work yields much information on the period.

KLING, C. *Geschichte der Bekleidung, Bewaffnung und Ausrüstung des königlich preussischen Heeres*, 3 vols, Weimar 1902–12

KONIG, A. B. *Alte und neue Denkwürdigkeiten der königlich preussischen Armee*, Berlin 1787. A history of the regiment of Bornstedt

KOROBKOV, N. *Semiletnyaya Voina*, Moscow 1940

KOSER, R. 'Die preussischen Finanzen im Siebenjährigen Kriege', *Forschungen zur brandenburgischen und preussischen Geschichte*, XIII, Leipzig 1900

KOSER, R. 'Die preussische Kriegführung im Siebenjährigen Krieg', *Historische Zeitschrift*, new series LXXXXII, Berlin 1904

KRAUSE, G. *Altpreussische Uniformfertigung als Vorstufe der Bekleidungsindustrie*, Hamburg 1965

KROGH, G. K. 'Prag und Kolin . . . Nach dem Tagebuch eines norwegischen Offiziers', ed C. Aubert, *Beihefte*, Berlin 1913

KÜSTER, C. D. *Bruchstück seines Campagnelebens im Siebenjährigen Kriege*, Berlin 1791. The experiences of a Feldprediger, especially in the battle of Hochkirch

KÜSTER, C. D. *Characterzüge des preussischen General-Lieutenants v. Saldern*, Berlin 1793

'L.' 'Vor hundert Jahren. Skizzen aus dem Privatleben einiger Lieutenants in Potsdam,' *Jahrbücher*, XI, Berlin 1874

LANGE, E., and MENZEL, A. *Heerschau der Soldaten Friedrichs des Grossen*, Leipzig 1856, new ed (ed H. Bleckwenn), Krefeld 1970

Magister F. Ch. Laukhards Leben und Schicksale, 13th ed, 2 vols, Stuttgart 1930. Laukhard served for a time as a private in the regiment of Anhalt-Bernburg

LEHNDORFF, E. *Dreissig Jahre am Hofe Friedrichs des Grossen*, ed K. E. Schmidt-Lötzen, Gotha 1907; and *Nachträge*, 2 vols, Gotha 1910–13. Lehndorff was a member of the queen's household.

——. 'Kriegs und Friedenbilder aus den Jahren 1754–1759. Nach dem Tagebuch des Leutnants Jakob F. v. Lemcke 1738–1810', ed R. Walz, *Preussische Jahrbücher*, CXXXVIII, Berlin 1909. By a subaltern in the regiment of Anhalt. Especially on Prague and Kay

LIGNE, C. J. *Mélanges militaires, littéraires et sentimentaires*, vols I, II, IX, X, XIV–XVII, Dresden 1795–6

LIPPE-WEISSENFELD, E. *Militaria aus König Friedrichs des Grossen Zeit*, Berlin 1866

LIPPE-WEISSENFELD, E. *Hans Joachim v. Zieten*, Berlin 1885

LOSSOW, L. M. *Denkwürdigkeiten zur Charakteristik der preussischen Armee unter Friedrich dem Zweiten*, Glogau 1826. By a veteran. Pious but very informative

LUVAAS, J. *Frederick the Great on the Art of War*, New York 1966. A good collection of Frederick's military writings, in English translation

MALACHOWSKI, D. *Scharfe Taktik und Revuetaktik im 18. und 19. Jahrhundert*, Berlin 1892

MEYER, C. *Briefe aus der Zeit des ersten Schlesischen Krieges*, Leipzig 1902

MIRABEAU, H. G. *Système militaire de la Prusse*, London 1788

Memoirs and Papers of Sir Andrew Mitchell, K.B., ed A. Bisset, 2 vols, London 1850

MOORE, J. *A View of Society and Manners in France, Switzerland, and Germany*, 2 vols, London 1780

NATZMER, G. E. *George Christoph v. Natzmer, Chef der weissen Husaren*, Hanover 1870

Oeuvres, see Frederick the Great

ORTMANN, A. D. *Patriotische Briefe*, Berlin and Potsdam 1759. A mass of material on every aspect of the Seven Years War

OSTEN-SACKEN, O. *Preussens Heer von seinen Anfängen bis zur Gegenwart*, I, Berlin 1911. Shorter and more approachable than Jany

PACZYNSKI-TENCZYN. *Lebensbeschreibung des General Feldmarschalls Keith*, Berlin 1896

PALMER, J. M. *General von Steuben*, New Haven 1937

PALMER, R. R. 'Frederick the Great, Guibert, Bülow. From Dynastic to National War,' in *Makers of Modern Strategy*, ed E. M. Earle, Princeton 1943

PARET, P. *Yorck and the Era of Prussian Reform 1807–1815*, Princeton 1969. With a good chapter on the Frederician army

PAULI, C. F. *Denkmale berühmter Feld-Herren*, Halle 1768

PRIESDORFF, K. *Saldern*, Hamburg 1943

Unter der Fahne des Herzogs von Bevern. Jugenderinnerungen des Christian Wilhelm von Prittwitz und Gaffron, Berlin 1935. Prittwitz was a subaltern in the regiment of Bevern.

RETZOW, J. A. *Charakteristik der wichtigsten Ereignisse des Siebenjährigen Krieges*, 2 vols, Berlin 1802. Retzow was a subaltern in the Seven Years War, and the son of the unfortunate *Intendant*

RITTER, G. *Staatskunst und Kriegshandwerk*, pt I, *Die altpreussische Tradition (1740–1890)*, Munich 1954. English trans: *The Sword and the Scepter. The Problem of Militarism in Germany*, pt I, *The Prussian Tradition 1740–1890*, Coral Gables (Florida) 1969

ROSINSKI, H. *The German Army*, London 1966

SACK, F. S. *Briefe über den Krieg*, Berlin 1778

SCHARFENORT, L. A. *Kulturbilder aus der Vergangenheit des altpreussischen Heeres*, Berlin 1914

SCHARFENORT, L. A. *Die Pagen am brandenburg-preussische Hof 1415–1895*, Berlin 1895

SCHARNHORST, G. J. *Handbuch für Officiere*, 3 vols, Hanover 1790

SCHEFFNER, J G. *Mein Leben*, Leipzig 1823. This man of letters served as a subaltern in the regiment of Ramin in the Seven Years War

SCHLENKE, M. *England und das Friderizianische Preussen 1740–1763*, Freiburg 1963

SCHLÖZER, K. *General Graf Chasot*, Berlin 1878

SCHMETTAU, G. F. *Lebensgeschichte des Grafen v. Schmettau*, 2 vols, Berlin 1806. The life of a famous staff officer, by his son

SCHMETTAU, G. F. *Über den Feldzug der preussischen Armee in Böhmen im Jahre 1778*, Berlin 1789. Very revealing

SCHMITT, R. *Prinz Heinrich von Preussen als Feldherr im Siebenjährigen Kriege*, 2 vols, Greifswald 1885–97

SCHNACKENBURG, MAJOR V. 'Die Freikorps Friedrichs des Grossen', *Beihefte*, Berlin 1883

SCHNACKENBURG, MAJOR V. 'Heerwesen und Infanteriedienst vor 100 Jahren,' *Jahrbücher*, XLVI and XLVII, Berlin 1883

SCHWARZE, K. *Der Siebenjährige Krieg in der zeitgenossischen Literatur*, Berlin 1936

SCHWERIN, D. *Feldmarschall Schwerin*, Berlin 1928

Siebenjährige Krieg, see Grosser Generalstab

STEINBERGER, J. *Breslau vor hundert Jahren. Auszüge einer handschriftlichen Chronik*, ed A. Kahlert, Breslau 1840

STOLZ, G. 'Generalleutnant Daniel F. v. Lossow (1721–83)', *Zeitschrift für Heereskunde*, no 237, Berlin 1970

Testament Politique 1752 and 1768, *see* Frederick the Great

THIÉBAULT, D. *Mes Souvenirs de vingt Ans de Sejour à Berlin*, 3rd ed, 4 vols, Paris 1813

TOULONGEON and HULLIN, *Une Mission Militaire en Prusse, en 1786*, ed J. Finot and R. Galmiche-Bouvier, Paris 1881

Mémoires de Frédéric Baron de Trenck, 3 vols, Strasbourg and Paris 1789. Colourful but unreliable

UNGER, W. *Wie ritt Seydlitz?* Berlin 1906. An important study of cavalry and horsemanship in Frederick's time

VARNHAGEN V. ENSE, K. A. *Leben des Generals Freiherrn v. Seydlitz*, Berlin 1834. Very frank

VARNHAGEN V. ENSE, K. A. *Leben des Generals Hans Karl v. Winterfeldt*, Berlin 1836

WARNERY, GENERAL V. *Campagnes de Frédéric II Roi de Prusse, de 1756 à 1762*, Amsterdam 1788. Informative and dispassionate. Warnery was a colonel of hussars in the Seven Years War, and one of the closest friends of Seydlitz

WENGEN, F. *Karl Graf zu Wied*, Gotha 1890

WILTSCH, J. E. *Die Schlacht von nicht bei Rossbach oder die Schlacht auf den Feldern von und bei Reichardtswerben*, Reichardtswerben 1858

WITZLEBEN, A. *Aus alten Parolebüchern der Berliner Garnison zur Zeit Friedrichs des Grossen*, Berlin 1851

WOCHE, K. 'Christian Nikolaus v. Linger', *Zeitschrift für Heereskunde*, no 223–4, Berlin 1969

WRAXALL, N. W. *Memoirs of the Courts of Berlin, Dresden etc*, 2nd ed, 2 vols, London 1800

The Life and Correspondence of Philip Yorke, Earl of Hardwicke, ed P. C. Yorke, 3 vols, Cambridge 1913. General Yorke saw the Prussian army in the field in 1758

Zweite Schlesische Krieg, see Grosser Generalstab

Index

Page numbers in italic type indicate illustrations

41–2, prisoners, 41; promotion, 34–5, 169; punishments, 36–7; ranks, 30–4; recruitment and origins, 14, 27–8, 30, 34; religion, 47; uniforms and equipment, 39–40; wives, 46

orders and decorations, 35–6, 157, 202

pioneers, 125, 246

Pontonier-Corps, 125, 127

regiments (if cited in text): Anhalt IR No 3, 90, 163, 193–4, 236; Anhalt Bernburg, *see* Anhalt IR No 3; Bayreuth DR No 5, 36, 37, 42, 46, 47, 98, 104, 108, 141, 163–4, 178, 205, 256; Below IR No 11, 44, 182, 238; Bevern IR No 7, 59–60, 67, 237; Black Hussars HR No 5, 99, 102, 186, 204, 258; Blue Hussars HR No 3, 99, 258; Braun IR No 37, 191, 244; Jung-Braunschweig IR No 39, 199, 244; Bredow IR No 43, 90, 245; Chossignon FB No 5, 76, 251; Death's Head Hussars, *see* Black Hussars HR No 5; Etrangers Prusses, or Royal Etranger FB No 19, 76, 253; Prinz Ferdinand IR No 34, 35, 193–4, 243; Forcade IR No 23, 67, 241; Fouqué IR No 33, 80, 243; Garde IR No 15, 55, 62, 67, 70–2, 81, 78, 143; First Battalion of the Garde, 22, 32, 44, 56, 79, 172, 239; Garde du Corps CR No 13, 25, 37, 96, 108, 255; Gensd'armes CR No 10, 37, 44, 108, 169, 197, 255; Gersdorff HR No 7, 67, 258; Giant Grenadiers, 17, 72; Green Hussars HR No 1, 22, 99, 258; Hessen-Cassel IR No 45, 57, 245; Itzenplitz IR No 13, 56, 185, 239; Kalben FB No 3, 76, 251; Kalckstein IR No 25, 50, 141, 241; Kannacher IR No 30, 185, 243; Markgraf Karl IR No 19, 184–5, 240; Kleist IR No 27, 35, 242; Krockow IR No 51, 43, 246; Manteuffel IR No 17, 67, 176, 240; Meinicke DR No 3, 95, 256; Meyerinck IR No 26, 35, 139, 242; Normann DR No 1, 172, 256; Prinz v. Preussen IR No 18, 68, 185, 240; Quadt GAR R No 8, 67, 249; Ramin, *see* Kalckstein IR No 25; Rapin FB No 6, 76, 251; Red Hussars HR No 2, 27, 37, 98, 99, 102, 258; Rochow CR No 8, 108, 172, 173, 174, 255; Seydlitz, *see* Rochow CR No 8; Alt-Stutterheim IR No 30, 201, 243; Tresckow IR No 32, 176, 243; Wedell IR No 26, 138, 185, 242; White Hussars HR No 4, 50, 99, 173, 258; Württemberg DR No 12, 173, 257; Zieten Hussars, *see* Red Hussars HR No 2

size (1740), 157; (1756), 165; (1759), 186, 190; (1761), 196–7; (from 1763), 199

staff system, 37–8, 143–7; intelligence, 145–6; maps, 146–7; personnel, 143–4

supply system, 133–8; baking ovens, 135–6;

commissariat department, 136; contributions, 136–7; fodder, 134, 136–7; grain, 134–6; magazines, 134; rations, 58, 59, 134–8; sutlers, 59, 137; transport, 134–5, 137–8; uniforms and equipment, 133–4

transport system, 43, 127–8, 180

army, Russian, 121, 166, 180–1

army, Saxon, 166, 169, 240

Arnstedt, E. L., Colonel, 136

Baader, Major, 74

Balbi, G., Colonel, 123, 131, 180

Balke (preacher), 140

Barsewisch, C. F. (writer), 138, 242

Bastiani, Abbé, 56

Belle-Isle, Marshal, 161

Belling, family of, 199

Belling, W. S., General, 47

Berenhorst, G. H. (commentator), 38, 121

Berlin, 38, 44, 45, 55, 62, 116, 133, 134, 148; raided 1757, 175; raided 1760, 194

Bevern (Brunswick-Bevern), A. W., Duke, General, 34, 38, 43, 56, 128, 136, 159, 167–8, 174, 190, 237

Bevern, K., Prince, General, 177

Blücher, G. L., Field-Marshal, 211, 259

Bohemia, 159

Bornstedt, B. H., Colonel, 145

Boswell, James, 157, 200

Boysen, F. E. (preacher), 52

Bräker, U. (writer), 55, 56, 57, 65, 82, 239

Brandenburg, 13–14

Brandenburg, F. W., Margrave, General, 34

Brandenburg-Schwedt, K., Margrave, General, 184, 240

Breslau, 38, 134, 160; peace of (1742), 162; battle of (1757), 114, 128, 176, 181, 235; recapture of (1757), 179

Britain, Prussian influence in, 210

Broglie, V., Marshal, 209

Browne, M. U., Field-Marshal, 168

Brünn, 159; investment of (1742), 161

Brünning, W. M., General, 206

Brunswick-Bevern, *see* Bevern

Brunswick-Lüneburg, Ferdinand, Prince, Field-Marshal, 26, 36, 81, 159, 167, 186, 202, 203

Brunswick-Lüneburg, F. F., Prince, General, 34, 185

Brunswick-Lüneburg, K. W., Hereditary Prince, General, 203

Buddenbrock, J. J., General, 29

Bunzelwitz, camp of (1761), 127, 197

Burgoyne, J., General, 52, 149, 201, 209

Burkersdorf, action at (1762), 155, 198